FIELD EXCURSIONS
IN NORTH WEST
ENGLAND

ISBN 1-85284-063-3

FIELD EXCURSIONS IN NORTH WEST ENGLAND

Edited by Chris Park

Published by the University of Lancaster
and Cicerone Press

ACKNOWLEDGEMENTS

The book is published as a contribution to the University of Lancaster's Silver Jubilee (1964-89) celebrations. It reflects the commitment and interest of a great many individuals, to whom I am grateful.

The contributors (all lecturers at the University of Lancaster or its associated colleges) have written from personal experience, and their excursions bring different aspects of the geography of North West England alive in a vivid and inviting way. They cheerfully accepted fairly tight editorial control!

Elsa Drinkall oversaw the initial word-processing of the text by Siobhan, Hilary and Janet; Sandra Irish proof-read with meticulous attention to detail; Chris Dunne helped me to transfer files between computers (4 in all!). I have set up the book on an Apple Macintosh SE, with an Apple LaserWriter, on Aldus Pagemaker, in 12 point Palatino. Claire Jarvis turned doodles into fine maps and diagrams, with some help from Nick Adriano.

The Department of Geography at the University of Lancaster generously covered the cost of preparing the book for publication; I thank Colin Pooley, as Head of Department, for his commitment to the project.

Walt Unsworth and Brian Evans at Cicerone have provided much technical advice, as well as the photographs; I appreciate their interest in and commitment to this book.

Chris Park
University of Lancaster

CONTENTS

1 THE LAKE DISTRICT NATIONAL PARK : PROBLEMS OF PLANNING

Colin G Pooley
(University of Lancaster)

Outline: an introduction to the varied landscape of the National Park which highlights, through specific examples, some of the major planning problems experienced within the Lake District. The trip might be combined with some of the stops mentioned in Excursion 2, with a stop in Ambleside (Excursion 5) or possibly a walk in the Langdales (Excursion 3).

Start and finishing point: The route described starts and finishes at Windermere Railway Station (GR 414987) which is accessible from all parts of the region. However, it may be joined at any intermediate point and the sites visited in any order.

Distance: Around 100 km by road.

Route: Coach tour with five short walks.

Time needed: one full day. Waterproof clothing and reasonably stout footwear are advised.

Useful Maps: OS Tourist map of the Lake District (1:63,360); OS Outdoor Leisure maps (1:25,000), The English Lakes SE, NE, NW.

THE NATIONAL PARK - AN OVERVIEW

The Lake District National Park was established in 1951, and today the Lake District Special Planning Board is responsible for most planning decisions within the area. The Board consists of representatives from the County, the Districts, the local community and planning officers.

As in all the National Parks in England and Wales, the planners seek to fulfil three conflicting aims: the preservation and enhancement of natural beauty; the promotion of the Park for visitors; and the protection of the interests of locals with regard to employment, housing facilities etc. The sites visited on this excursion are chosen to demonstrate the ways in which these aims conflict in different settings. These conflicts are particularly difficult to reconcile in the Lake District because the National Park is relatively small (2,243 sq km), and it contains a substantial resident population (around 46,000). Moreover,

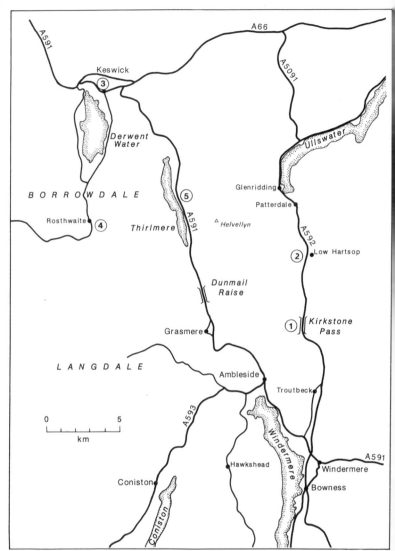

Figure 1a. The Lake District excursion route

land within the National Park is owned by many different private landowners, although the National Trust now owns some 25 per cent of the Park area. The Forestry Commission, North West Water Authority and Special Planning Board are also substantial institutional landowners. The small scale of the Lake District, and the variety of landscapes and landowners which exist within it, mean that even small changes can have very significant impacts. The planning authority must be sensitve to the conflicting needs of the environment, the local population and visitors.

The Lake District National Park Structure Plan (1980) identifies twelve different planning issues within the Park. More simply, these can be reduced to three crucial areas on which this excursion will focus. First, there is the need to promote economic development within the National Park. For at least a century, and certainly since long before the creation of the National Park, agriculture and forestry, quarrying and mining, small-scale manufacturing, the provision of local services and tourism have been the main sources of local employment and income. However, in recent years the promotion of tourism has taken precedence over the other four areas. It is important to consider the extent to which a more balanced economic base is desirable, and the degree to which the economy of an area like the Lake District should become dependent on tourism.

Second, there is the need to protect and enhance the environment of the National Park. However, it is important to realise that the landscape that we seek to protect today is a relatively recent creation which has been moulded by the hands of men and women over previous centuries. It is also important to note that the value we place upon this landscape is a subjective product of the imagination of a relatively affluent and leisured population. We should not necessarily assume that landscape change is bad, or that any particular landscape is the most appropriate. Moreover, all the aspects of economic change outlined above will themselves have a different impact on the landscape, and there is the possibility that economic expansion of one activity may cause financial ruin for another through the impact which it has on the landscape.

Third, there are acute social problems within the National Park which have to be tackled. Decades of population change have led to outmigration of the young and active population and their replacement by older families, retired people and those who use the Lake

District as a second home. This has led to the inflation of house prices, providing a further stimulus to outmigration for the young and less affluent, pressures for new building, and the situation where in some villages a third of all properties are second homes or holiday homes. This decline in the permanently resident population in many villages has prompted a further reduction of services in these areas. Affluent retired residents are more likely to travel to towns to buy food and other goods, and thus village shops have closed, bus services have been withdrawn, the availability of health care has diminished and village schools have closed. Shops and bus services that remain cater mainly for tourists, and service provision in the summer is far superior to that provided for residents in the winter months. We should question whether the financial profits which occur from tourism are being sufficiently ploughed back into the local environment and communities which attract visitors in the first place.

EXCURSION

The coach route (Figure 1a) is built around five stopping points where a short walk is advised. The walks are not essential (and could be abandoned in bad weather), but they do ensure that the party remains awake!

STOP 1 KIRKSTONE PASS (GR 401081)

From Windermere travel along the A592 past Troutbeck to the summit of Kirkstone Pass. Park in the car park opposite the Kirkstone Inn (Figure 1b).

The suggested walk is to St Raven's Edge (GR 405083), about 1.6 km return. Walk ENE along the path that starts behind the Kirkstone Inn towards the stone wall which climbs onto St Raven's Edge. A convenient vantage point can be found as the ground levels out. Return by the same route. A number of themes can be discussed from this point including:

(a) Problems of traffic management

What is the impact of tourist traffic on small high-level roads like Kirkstone Pass? What level of use is acceptable? Should certain categories of vehicle be banned? Should roads like this be improved and widened to provide better access for tourists and commercial/industrial vehicles? What is the attitude of local residents to the high volume of tourist traffic in summer?

As the County (Cumbria) is the highway authority the Special Planning Board can only make recommendations to the Highway Department. In general the Board take the view that major road improvements would be environmentally damaging and that self-regulation is more effective (ie if a road becomes very congested tourists will avoid it and go elsewhere). The major congestion is caused by vehicles

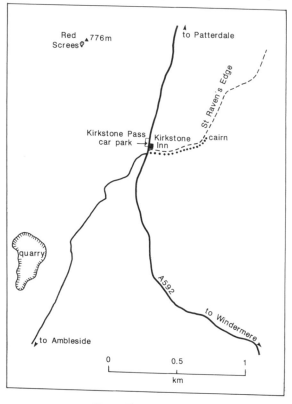

Figure 1b. Kirkstone Pass

stopping for short periods for passengers to admire the view. Few vehicles stay long at a site like Kirkstone Pass. The Planning Board recognise this requirement through the provision of more off-road parking places which they do have control over.

(b) The impact of quarrying

Substantial quarry works are clearly visible in the middle distance (GR 393072). These are typical of the slate and other quarries found in the National Park. Quarrying is a traditional source of employment in the area and their impact on the landscape is of long standing. However, the environmental impact of large quarries is considerable and the amount of employment generated in a mechanised modern industry is relatively small. Are the visual scars, the pollution, noise and traffic a price worth paying for local employment?

The attitude of the Planning Board has been to allow existing quarries to continue, but to examine carefully any demands to significantly extend workings, and to encourage the visual screening of quarry sites where possible. In reality, the main factors governing the expansion and contraction of quarry workings are economic, particularly fluctuations in the demand for slate. Lake District quarries can open and close over short periods of time, particularly as the ownership of companies changes. As in other areas, the factors influencing landscape change are often beyond the direct control of the planning authority.

STOP 2 HARTSOP (GR 408132)

From Kirkstone Pass continue north along the A592. A coach can be parked at Cow Bridge (GR 403134). Hartsop village is a short walk back along the main road and then down a minor road. Walk through the village to a small car park (GR 410130) where a number of themes can be discussed, total return walk about 1.5 km (Figure 1c). A car or minibus could be brought into the village and parked there. This stop might focus on two main themes:

(a) Origins of the settlement pattern

Villages like Hartsop originated in the sixteenth and seventeenth centuries following the dissolution of the monasteries in 1536. Originally the Yeomen farmers were tenants to a Lord, but their tenancy had

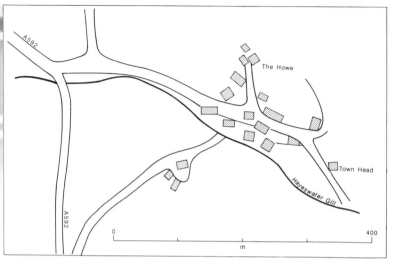

Figure 1c. Hartsop Village

the right to succession and by the seventeenth century many held their property in freehold. They farmed sheep and cattle, traded in wool and timber, mined lead in the Hartsop valley and became a powerful middle class in Lakeland. Hartsop still contains several fine examples of Statesmen's farms including the traditional long house design with an exterior spinning gallery. By the late-eighteenth century hamlets like Hartsop were already in relative decline. Farm amalgamation and enclosure of common land led to the exclusion of smaller farmers, many of whom left for the towns, and the dual economy of farming/spinning/mining began to disintegrate. Relatively little new building has taken place since the early-nineteenth century, and the settlement pattern and architecture of Hartsop are reminiscent of a bygone era.

Try to imagine what it would have been like to live in this village in the eighteenth century, and how the experience of the rich Statesman farmer would have been different from that of the poor farm servant.

(b) Modern economy and social structure

As you walk through the village try to work out the economic and social characteristics of Hartsop today. How many farms are still active? How many farms have been turned into holiday or retirement homes? How many residents in the village are economically active? What services are available to present-day residents of the village? Typically an area like this contains a small economically active population (around one third of the total), with around 30 per cent of the population of retirement age. The three active farms in the village employ little labour beyond the family (although seasonal help is taken on at busy times) and most farms gain extra income from bed and breakfast and tourist-related activities.

It is estimated that the Hartsop area can accommodate four times its resident population in the summer. Approximately one third of properties in Patterdale Parish (including Hartsop) are second homes, and Hartsop village contains ten listed buildings (Rural Planning Services, 1976). There is little opportunity for those on low incomes to obtain housing in the area, and the preponderance of holiday and second-home accommodation makes it difficult to develop an economically thriving and socially active village community.

What do you consider to be the benefits and the disadvantages of living in Hartsop today? Are there any ways in which you would seek to alter recent developments in the village's economy and social structure?

STOP 3 KESWICK (GR 265235)

From Hartsop drive north along the A592 to the southern end of Ullswater. About 4 km after Glenridding turn left onto the A5091 to Dockray and proceed to the junction with the A66. Turn left for Keswick which is a convenient lunch stop. Coaches can usually be parked by the bus station. There are large car parks for cars/minibuses by the lake or in the town centre.

If time allows, Keswick provides opportunities to study many aspects of urban geography. The town is a service centre for the northern Lake District, and a tourist honeypot which has recently seen significant new developments including Keswick Spa (on the site of the old railway station) and time-share properties.

Consider how these developments are affecting the town and evaluate their impact on the local economy. You could also consider the range of retail provision in Keswick. Does it cater adequately for local needs or is it geared mainly to the demands of tourists? What further developments in housing, industry and service provision would you consider appropriate to Keswick and what impact might these have on the local environment?

STOP 4 ROSTHWAITE, BORROWDALE (GR 258148)

From Keswick drive down Borrowdale (B5289) to Rosthwaite. There is a small car park on the right suitable for cars and minibuses. Coaches can usually pull in on the left just before the shop to drop passengers; they will have to go on to Seatoller car park to turn round (at the pull-in used by service buses). It is probably easier for a coach to wait down the valley and return to pick up passengers after about 45 minutes.

The suggested walk is to Resting Stone (GR 264156), about 2 km return (Figure 1d). Take the well-defined path that climbs NE towards Watendlath. After about 1 km or so it is possible to find a convenient vantage point which offers excellent views of Borrowdale. Return by the same route. A number of themes can be discussed here including:

(a) Settlement patterns and land use change in Borrowdale

Place-name evidence suggests a Scandinavian (10th century) origin for many of the settlements in this part of Borrowdale. 'Thwaite' means clearing and Rosthwaite is probably 'the clearing by the cairn'. Scandinavian settlement established a series of nucleated hamlets in Borrowdale, possibly replacing previously scattered Celtic farms. Consider the precise site of Rosthwaite: well-sheltered and situated on raised ground to protect it from flood water.

In 1209 most of Borrowdale came under the control of Furness Abbey. During this time woodland was cleared, enclosures were pushed up the valley sides and new settlements (such as Grange) were established. The area was used for grazing sheep and cattle, and wool was exported over long distances, initially being carried by packhorse over the mountain passes. As at Hartsop, the seventeenth century saw the establishment of Statesmen's farms with further woodland clearance and enclosure. There were also extensive mining and quarrying operations in the area. Today only small areas of woodland remain, and stonewalls mark the limits of previous colonization.

From the nineteenth century Borrowdale experienced outmigration and rural depopulation, enclosure walls and farm buildings fell

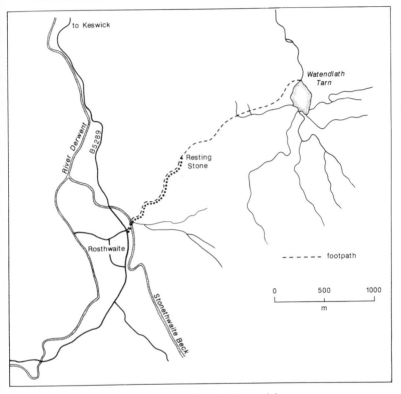

Figure 1d. Rosthwaite, Borrowdale

into disuse, and lack of economic opportunity forced much of the population to move to the towns.

From this vantage point, consider the interaction of agricultural and tourist-related land uses in Borrowdale today. Many farmers are tenants of the National Trust and an extensive subsidy system is necessary to maintain agriculture which typically consists of cattle rearing on valley bottoms and extensive sheep grazing on the fells. A typical upland farm might have 100-200 acres of good quality 'in-bye' land for hay and grazing and 'intake' land on the lower enclosed slopes, plus the rights to fell grazing. This might support some 600 ewes, 12 rams (mostly Herdwick and Swaledale), and a small herd of cattle. Farming interacts with tourism through the provision of holiday accommodation, camp sites, farm open days and an extensive network of valley-floor footpaths. The separation of tourists and walkers from valuable valley-bottom farm land is an important aspect of land management and planning in the Lake District. One effect of depopulation and dependence on tourism is the lack of services in Borrowdale. There are no primary schools in the valley, few shops and a limited bus service. Try to imagine what it would be like to live in Rosthwaite today in both summer and winter.

(b) Upland footpath management

The footpath from Rosthwaite to Watendlath is well-used by walkers and it illustrates many of the problems caused by upland recreation. A combination of heavy use, steep slopes and high rainfall has caused footpath erosion and deep gullying in places. Throughout the central Lake District organisations like the National Trust and the Planning Board are engaged in a constant battle to prevent further unsightly erosion.

What intervention measures would you consider acceptable in an area like this? Should the footpath be given a hard, artificial surface? Should it be paved with local stone? Should it be graded and realigned? Should it be fenced to prevent walkers damaging land on either side? Should footpaths be clearly signed with way-marked trails? The Planning Board is constantly having to achieve a balance between intervention to protect the environment and allowing walkers the freedom to wander at will over the fells.

STOP 5 HELVELLYN GILL, THIRLMERE (GR 315170)

Drive north up Borrowdale back to Keswick, then take the A591 towards Ambleside. There is a large pull-in (suitable for coaches) on the NE shore of Thirlmere and a car park and picnic area opposite this point. If a short walk is required there is a clear path which begins to climb up Helvellyn Gill. Good views of Thirlmere are afforded from above the treeline (less than 1 km). Alternatively, relevant themes can be discussed by the roadside.

(a) Reservoirs and forestry in the central Lake District

In addition to agriculture, quarrying and tourism, significant employment in the Lake District is generated by the Water Authority and by forestry. This is particularly true around Thirlmere (also discussed in Excursion 2, stop 4) where most of the people who live in the hamlets of Wythburn and Legburthwaite work for the Water Authority. Until recently the Water Authority has also owned much of the housing in the area, and the creation of Thirlmere reservoir has had a massive impact on society and economy in this part of the Lake District over the past century.

From the 1870s Manchester experienced water shortages, and Manchester Corporation sought to secure the city's water supply by using Cumbrian water. At Thirlmere there was a natural lake 5 km long, and it was thought to provide excellent potential for water supply. Despite considerable opposition, in 1890 work on a dam was begun, and the level of the lake was raised by 17 m, drowning several farms and hamlets. At the same time the surrounding fell-sides were planted with conifers by the Water Authority and much of the area was closed to public access. During the construction phase a massive gang of workmen lived in the valley. Try to imagine the impact which this had on local communities.

The main objections to reservoirs and afforestation are aesthetic. Artificial fluctuations in water level can cause ugly scarring along the banks and the harsh lines of coniferous plantations are unsightly. Recently there have been some changes in the area. As with Forestry Commission plantations elsewhere in the Lake District, a selective felling and replanting policy has begun to relax the hard edges of plantations and has introduced more varied species.

The area has also been opened up to public access with picnic areas and way-marked trails through the woods by the lakeside. The local employment generated by the Water Authority has also prevented outmigration and second-home colonization on the scale experienced elsewhere in the Lake District. Water supply for large urban areas is obviously essential. Do you consider that the creation of Thirlmere reservoir damages or enhances the Lakeland landscape? What impact will the privatization of the water supply industry have on this area?

To complete this excursion around the Lake District continue south along the A591 to Windermere. The National Park Visitor

Centre is situated at Brockhole south of Ambleside (GR 390010). On a wet day the walks described in this guide could be curtailed and a visit to Brockhole included instead.

Selected References

Baldwin, J R and I D Whyte (editors) (1985) *The Scandinavians in Cumbria.* Scottish Society for Northern Studies

Brunskill, R W (1974) *Vernacular Architecture of the Lake Counties.* Faber

Capstick, G M (1987) *Housing dilemmas in the Lake District.* University of Lancaster, Centre for NW Regional Studies Resource Paper

Lake District Special Planning Board (1977) *Draft National Park Plan.* LDSPB, Kendal

Lake District Special Planning Board/Cumbria County Council (1980) *Cumbria and Lake District Joint Structure Plan.* LDSP/CCC, Kendal

Lake District Special Planning Board/Cumbria County Council (1986) *Cumbria and Lake District Joint Structure Plan : First alterations and roll forward to 1986 ; proposals report.* LDSP/CCC

Marshall, J D and J K Walton (1981) *The Lake Counties.* Manchester University Press

Millward, R and A Robinson (1974) *The Lake District.* Methuen

Rollinson, W (1974) *Life and Tradition in the Lake District.* Dent

Rural Planning Services (1976) *A Study of the Hartsop Valley.* Countryside Commission

2 LANDFORM DEVELOPMENT IN THE EASTERN AND CENTRAL LAKE DISTRICT

Ada W Pringle (nee Phillips)
(University of Lancaster)

Outline: a broad introduction to the physical geography of the eastern and central Lake District, considering both the core area formed on Lower Palaeozoic rocks (Skiddaw Slates, Borrowdale Volcanic Group and Silurian Series) and the peripheral area formed on Upper Palaeozic rocks (mainly Carboniferous Limestone). Key themes are the links between geology and landform development; the evidence for the existence of pre -glacial Tertiary landforms; the erosional and depositional effects of glaciation; and water resources development.

Starting and finishing point: Junction 36 on the M6.

Distance: 150 km round trip.

Route: Travel by coach, minibus or car between sites: opportunities for walking on some sites (waterproofs and sensible footwear required).

Time needed: One whole day.

Maps needed: OS Tourist Map, Lake District (1:63,360); Landranger Series Sheets 91, Appleby-in-Westmorland Area, and 97, Kendal to Morecambe (1:50,000); British Geological Survey Sheet 54N 04W Lake District, Solid Edition (1:250,000). A geological map postcard of the Lake District (from Moseley 1978) is available from the Yorkshire Geological Society (details in Appendix).

EXCURSION

This circular route is described with the start and finish in the south-east of the Lake District, but other entry and exit points can be used as desired (Figure 2a). From the starting point at Junction 36, take the M6 north to Junction 37, and then take the minor road east of (and parallel to) the M6 to Beck Foot. Continue north along the B6257 to its junction with the A685, then drive north through the Lune Gorge to Tebay. Rejoin the M6 at Junction 38, and drive north to Junction 40. Then go west along the A66 to Keswick, with a diversion along the minor road to the south to reach Castlerigg Stone Circle (at GR 294236). From

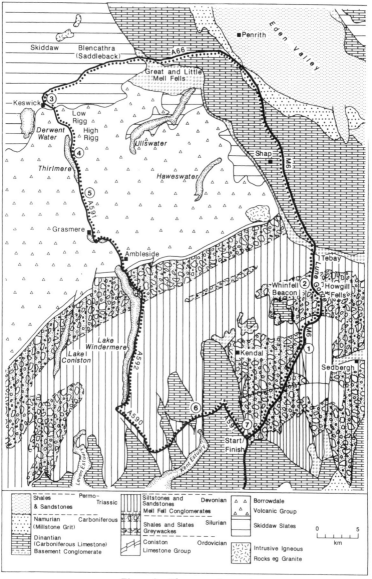

Figure 2a. The excursion route

Keswick drive south along the A591 to Ambleside and continue to the junction with the A592 north-west of Windermere. Drive south along the east shore of Lake Windermere to Newby Bridge, then east along the A590 to the Kendal Bypass section of the A591. This takes you east to Junction 36 on the M6.

STOP 1 HOWGILL FELLS VIEWPOINT

There is a pull-in suitable for coaches at the off-set cross roads on the west side of the road (GR 601954).

(a) Geology

The Howgill Fells are the eastward extension of the southern part of the Lower Palaeozoic core area of the Lake District (Figure 2a). During the Silurian Period sediments were deposited in a narrow geosynclinal trough which was the final diminishing form of Iapetus, the Proto-Atlantic Ocean. During the Caledonian orogeny the fine sediments were metamorphosed into slates, but the coarser grits were only gently folded. (Examples of this folding can be seen later beside the A685 between Stop 2 and Tebay). The area was uplifted during both the Caledonian and Hercynian orogenies, and subsequent uplift during the Tertiary Era produced a monoclinal block, with an east-west axis, and steep southerly and gentle northerly dips. Sediments of Carboniferous age lie unconformably on the Silurian rocks along the northern margin of the Howgills and are faulted against them in the east along the Dent Fault.

(b) Topography

On the broad scale, the Silurian rocks produce long smooth slopes in the Howgills. The greywackes of the Coniston Grits form the higher parts of both the Howgills and the Whinfell Beacon area west of the M6, whereas the mudstones and siltstones of the Bannisdale Slates form lower ground to north and south. Investigations of summit areas and slopes in the Lake District and Howgill Fells have yielded evidence of erosion surfaces, some of which are believed to be of Tertiary age. These features are especially clearly seen in the Howgills, where McConnell (1940) has identified six erosion surfaces of sub-aerial origin, with the higher ones of Tertiary age:

Erosion Surface	Altitude (m OD)
I	610
II	520-560
III	460-490
IV	380-430
V	300-350
VI	210-270

(c) Glaciation

The Howgill Fells have undergone a relatively small amount of glacial modification in comparison with the Lake District for two reasons. Firstly, because of their lower altitude and the rain shadow effect of the higher Lake District mountains, the mean annual precipitation (about 1800 mm per year) was comparatively low. Consequently the ice cap in the Howgill Fells was relatively thin. Secondly, the Howgill Fells ice moved fairly slowly because it was impeded by more vigorous ice streams from the Lake District and Northern Pennines which flowed along its margins.

The only conspicuous glacial erosion forms are the poorly developed eastward-facing corries of Cautley Crags and the Whinfell Beacon area.

STOP 2 LUNE GORGE VIEWPOINT

There is a parking area for cars and coaches (GR 607006).

(a) Drainage Pattern Evolution

The evolution of the drainage pattern in the Howgill Fells area has been summarised by King (1976). Drainage was established on the Tertiary upwarp with its major east-west watershed continuous with that of the Lake District. Northward flowing streams drained the gentle slope towards the downwarp of the Eden Valley; former stream courses are indicated by notches at about 300m in the Carboniferous Limestone scarp north of the Howgills (Figure 2b). Southward flowing streams on the steeper south limb of the upwarp had higher velocities and one such stream south of Tebay, guided by faults west of Sedbergh, cut headwards to breach the main watershed probably in the early Pleistocene. Glacial diffluence (divergent flow) during an early glaciation may have helped to complete the breaching. Carlin Gill and Borrow

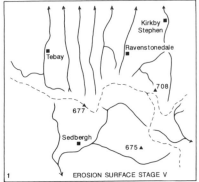

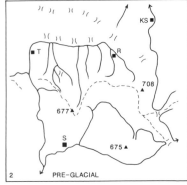

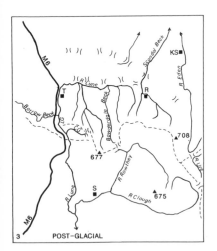

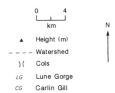

Figure 2b. Evolution of the drainage pattern of the Lune Gorge area (after King 1970).

Beck were diverted to the south-flowing Lune drainage because of this.

When the Carboniferous basal conglomerate was exposed near Tebay, rapid subsequent drainage development occurred eastwards along this outcrop. The upper River Lune thus extended eastwards to Ravenstonedale, finally capturing Scandal Beck from the upper River Eden drainage (although this was subsequently restored by glacial diversion).

This explains the strange course of the River Lune which flows northwards in the Howgill Fells as Bowderdale Beck, then westwards along the northern edge of the Howgills and finally turns southwards near Tebay to flow through the Lune Gorge.

(b) Glaciation

The Lune Gorge was overdeepened by ice flowing through it from the north, this direction of movement being confirmed by the presence in the gorge of Shap granite erratics derived from the outcrop north of Tebay. Note that the Civic Trust Award plaque beside the parking area is mounted on quarried Shap granite, with its distinctive characteristics.

ROUTE NORTH BETWEEN M6 JUNCTIONS 38 (TEBAY) AND 40 (KESWICK)

The M6 Service Station, northbound only, provides a convenient refreshment stop if required.

This section of the M6 in the Lake District periphery lies diagonally across rocks of Carboniferous age (Figure 2a), with the earliest basement conglomerates outcropping near Tebay and the youngest Namurian (Millstone Grit) rocks outcropping south-west of Penrith. Note the varying character of the rocks as you drive along the motorway.

West of the M6, south of Shap village, is the Shap granite outcrop which is quarried (GR 56084). The granite was intruded into Borrowdale Volcanic and adjacent Lower Paleozoic rocks early in the Devonian Period. Note the cement works based on the Dinantian (Carboniferous Limestone) quarries near Junction 39 (Shap).

ROUTE WEST ALONG A66 FROM M6 JUNCTION 40 (KESWICK), WITH DIVERSION TO CASTLERIGG STONE CIRCLE

This section of the route passes back down the Carboniferous rock succession through the Dinantian (Carboniferous Limestone) to the Basement conglomerates (Figure 2a). Note the character of the dry stone walls. South of the road an extensive area of Devonian/Carboniferous Basement conglomerates, laid down on the flank of the Caledonian mountains under hot arid climatic conditions, has been eroded

Stratigraphical divisions		Principal lithological groups and formations	
QUATERNARY Devensian			glacial deposits
JURASSIC Liassic			calcareous shales
TRIASSIC		MERCIA MUDSTONE GROUP	Stanwix Shales
		SHERWOOD SANDSTONE GROUP	Kirklinton Sandstone, St Bees Sandstone
PERMIAN	upper		Eden Shale, St Bees Shale with evaporites
	lower		Penrith Sandstone, Brockram
CARBONIFEROUS	Westphalian	COAL MEASURES	upper (barren, red beds), middle, lower
	Namurian	MILLSTONE GRIT	Roosecote Mudstone, Hensingham Grit, First Limestone
	Dinantian	CARBONIFEROUS LIMESTONE	Gleaston Formation 2nd Limestone, Urswick Limestone 3rd Limestone, Park Limestone 4th Limestone, Dalton Beds 5th Limestone, Red Hill Oolite 6th Limestone, Martin Limestone 7th Limestone, Basement Beds Cockermouth Lavas, Basement Beds
DEVONIAN			Mell Fell Conglomerate
SILURIAN	Downtonian		Scout Hill Flags
	Ludlow		Kirkby Moor Flags, Bannisdale Slates, Coniston Grits, Coldwell Beds
	Wenlock		Brathay Flags
	Llandovery		Stockdale Shales — Browgill Beds, Skelgill Beds
ORDOVICIAN	Ashgill–Caradoc	CONISTON LIMESTONE GROUP	Ashgill Shales, Applethwaite Beds, Stockdale Rhyolite, Stile End Beds, Drygill Shales
	Caradoc–Llandeilo	BORROWDALE VOLCANIC GROUP	Yewdale Breccia, Wrengill Andesites, Lincomb Tarns Ignimbrites, Lickle Rhyolite, Dunnerdale Tuffs, Airy's Bridge and Birk Fell ignimbrites and rhyolites, Ullswater and Honister Andesites
	Llanvirn	EYCOTT GROUP	Tarn Moor Mudstones, High Ireby Formation, Binsey Formation
	Arenig	SKIDDAW GROUP	Latterbarrow Sandstone, Kirk Stile Slates, Loweswater Flags, Hope Beck Slates

Igneous intrusive rocks, mainly associated with the Caledonian orogeny

granites	Skiddaw, Shap, Eskdale	diorite, microgranite	occurring as sills, dykes and volcanic necks
granophyres	Buttermere and Ennerdale, Carrock Fell	dolerite, picrite, minette	
microgranite	Threlkeld		
gabbro	Carrock Fell		

26   Table 2.1 Geological succession in the Lake District (Cumberland Geological Society 1982)

into the distinctive shapes of Great and Little Mell Fells. East of the junction with the A5091 lies the Carboniferous junction with the Ordovician age Skiddaw Slates; the latter are exposed on the south side of the A66 west of this road junction. Westwards only hedges and fences border the road. A brief stop may be made in a roadside layby here, if desired.

STOP 3 CASTLERIGG STONE CIRCLE

Coaches and cars may be parked beside the minor road opposite the gate into the field containing the Stone Circle (GR 294236).

As well as having historic interest, Castlerigg provides a good location from which to compare the landforms developed on the Ordovician age Skiddaw Slates to the north and the Borrowdale Volcanic rocks to the south, within the Lake District core area.

(a) Skiddaw Slates
The Skiddaw Slates of Lower Ordovician age (Table 2.1) consist of about 3,000 m of fine mudstone and coarser greywacke sediments deposited in Iapetus (the Proto-Atlantic Ocean) close to the continental margin with ancient Europe. The sediments subsequently suffered complex deformation and metamorphism during the Caledonian orogeny. The resulting rocks weather readily into small sliver-shaped fragments which produce long screes to give the northern fells, such as Skiddaw and Blencathra (Saddleback), their characteristically long, even slopes.

(b) Borrowdale Volcanic Group
The Borrowdale Volcanic Group of rocks formed in the Upper Ordovician Period from a string of volcanoes at about latitude 20°S. Moseley (1978) suggests that they were a cross between an island arc and continental margin situation, similar to the present North American Cascade Mountains. About 5,000 m of basalt, andesite and dacite lavas and tuffs, with acid ignimbrite tuffs were erupted partly subaqueously and partly sub-aerially. The eruptions occurred along a south-eastward dipping subduction zone associated with the gradual closure of Iapetus. The frequent lithological changes, both vertical and lateral, within the Borrowdale Volcanic Group, lead to different weathering responses; differential erosion has produced the craggy

topography typical of the high fells of the central Lake District.

(c) Low Rigg-High Rigg Ridge

Low Rigg (north) contains outcrops of Skiddaw Slates and the intruded St John's microgranite. The east-west faulted junction with the Borrowdale Volcanic Group lies near St John's Church. High Rigg (south) reveals a Borrowdale Volcanic sucession with a conglomerate of Skiddaw Slates and lavas at the base and alternating lavas and tuffs above, all dipping south to give a distinctive ribbed topography (Moseley, 1981). (This can be viewed also from the A591 south of Keswick).

Keswick provides a useful refreshment stop with plentiful car and coach parking facilities near the Bus Station (see Excursion 1, stop 3).

STOP 4 THIRLMERE

There is a roadside car and coach park at 315169. This area can be viewed from the track leading westwards towards the lake shore. Alternatively, follow the forest trail from the east side of the road, up the valley side to a high vantage point. A range of educational and information leaflets about Thirlmere are available from North West Water (details in Appendix). This area is also described briefly in Excursion 1, stop 5.

(a) Water Resources

The glacially overdeepened valleys of the Lake District provide considerable water storage potential in raised lakes and valley reservoirs. This is one of the wettest parts of Britain (mean annual precipitation 2360 mm), and the remoteness of the area reduces the risk of serious pollution. The Lake District provides about 30 per cent of the piped water used in north-west England, much being piped considerable distances to the main population centres.

Thirlmere and Haweswater are greatly enlarged natural lakes, whereas Windermere and Ullswater are natural lakes from which water is abstracted. The Lake District water sources were first developed in the nineteenth century to meet Manchester's needs; now many other parts of north-west England are supplied also.

(b) Thirlmere

The Thirlmere Bill (1879) enabled Manchester to develop Thirlmere as a major reservoir, despite considerable opposition in the Lake District.

Enlargement of Thirlmere began in 1890. A solid dam 17.7 m high and 361 m long was constructed at the north end of two natural lakes. The water level was raised to 16.5 m, giving a total storage capacity of 40,900 Ml. The construction of the dam and a 155 km long aqueduct was an advanced engineering feat for the Victorians, with flow in the aqueduct being entirely by gravity through tunnels, buried channels and pipelines. The water supply scheme was officially opened in 1894 at Thirlmere and Manchester.

Thirlmere provides up to 227 Ml of water per day. It is now linked with the newer Haweswater aqueduct on a ring main to allow greater flexibility of water use from the different sources.

The 4856 ha catchment is used for sheep farming and forestry. Trees were planted on the steep valley slopes formed in Borrowdale Volcanic rocks and partly covered by scree, to help to stabilize them and anchor the thin soils which are liable to leaching and erosion. This minimises the amounts of sediment carried into the reservoir. Public access to the catchment was prohibited until the early 1960s, when two forest trails were opened. Improved water treatment and greater demand for recreational facilities have led to steadily increasing access to the catchment and to the lake shore itself since then.

STOP 5 DUNMAIL RAISE

There is a roadside layby for car and coach parking (GR 327117).

A short stop will allow you to see the nearby glacial features and consider the impact of the last major glaciation of the area. Its effects can be considered subsequently as the excursion continues southwards in Borrowdale Volcanics terrain past Grasmere and Rydal Water to Ambleside, and then across the lower, more subdued topograpy of Silurian rocks south of Ambleside around Lake Windermere.

(a) Glacial Transfluence

During the Main Lake District Glaciation (in the Devensian), active glaciers from a Lake District ice cap flowed down the valleys which in pre-glacial times had formed a radial pattern on the structural dome.

Ice flowing northwards down such valleys as those now containing Thirlmere, Ullswater and Haweswater met ice moving southwards from the Scottish Southern Uplands ice cap, probably in the Solway Lowlands. The Lake District ice backed up in these northern valleys and some reversal of flow up-valley caused erosion and lowering of cols on the main east-west watershed. Dunmail Raise, with its clearly defined 'U' shaped cross-profile, is a good example of such glacial transfluence.

The glacial deposits on the floor of the col at Dunmail Raise include hummocky kame and kettle moraine, which resulted from downwasting of ice stranded here as the climate warmed towards the end of the glaciation.

(b) Glacial Confluence and Diffluence

During the maximum phase of glaciation, transfluent ice would have been joined by ice originating at the head of the Far Easedale and Easedale valleys, especially in the corrie glaciers of the Codale and Easedale Tarn basins (Figure 2c). The confluent ice caused over-deepening in the Grasmere basin.

Gresswell (1952) suggested that ice was not able to escape sufficiently rapidly along the pre-glacial valley, now containing Rydal Water, to prevent the ice level in the Grasmere Basin rising to allow glacial diffluence over the Red Bank col. Consequently Grasmere ice joined ice originating in the Great and Little Langdale valleys at this point. The main confluence of Grasmere and Langdale ice was in the northern basin of Lake Windermere which reaches a depth of -21 m OD (Howell, 1971). Some ice from the Windermere basin probably escaped eastwards along the Gowan and Winster Valleys, leaving a pronounced rock bar which separates the northern from the southern Lake Windermere basins. At various glacial stages ice appears to have escaped from the southern basin southwards along the pre-glacial valley through Cartmel (which is now blocked by glacial deposits), and south westwards through Backbarrow along the present route of the River Leven which drains Windermere.

STOP 6 LYTH VALLEY NEAR SAMPOOL BRIDGE

Park on the old loop of the A590, leading off the present dual carriageway (GR 471854).

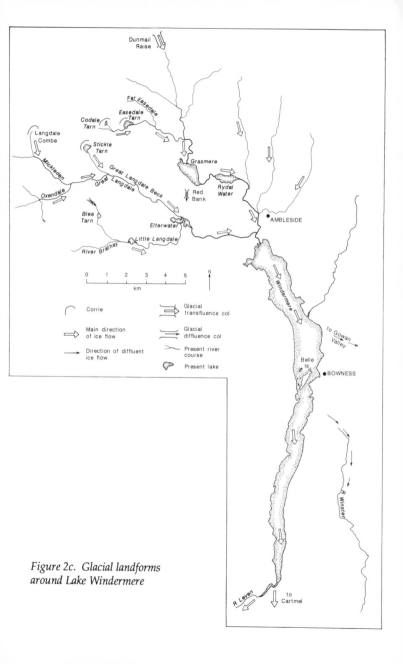

Figure 2c. Glacial landforms around Lake Windermere

(a) Escarpment Development

The broken ring of Dinantian (Carboniferous Limestone) rocks surrounding the central Lake District is here interspersed with outcrops of Silurian rocks, as a result of a series of north-west to south-east faults. In cross-section (Figure 2d) Newton Fell, (north of Lindale) is cut in eastward dipping Silurian Bannisdale Slates, which are overlain by Dinantian limestone, in which the escarpment of Yewbarrow has formed. A fault on its east side, with downthrow to the west, brings the Silurian Bannisdale Slates to the ground surface again and this forms lower ground. The pronounced Whitbarrow escarpment is formed in the overlying Dinantian limestone outcropping to the east. A similar fault along its eastern flank again brings up relatively easily eroded Silurian Bannisdale Slates to form the bedrock of the Lyth Valley which was overdeepened by glacial erosion. On its eastern side the overlying Dinantian limestone forms the prominent escarpment of Scout Scar, west of Kendal.

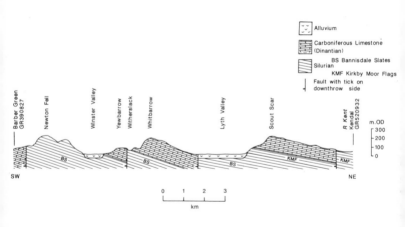

*Figure 2d. Geological cross-section between Newton Fell
and Scout Scar*

Wythburn, Thirlmere (Exc 1 & 2) - reservoirs and forestry in Central Lakeland. Photo: R.B.Evans.

A spinning gallery at Hartsop (Exc 1).　Photo: Walt Unsworth.

Thirlmere (Exc 2), a good example of a glacial 'U' shaped valley.
Photo: R.B.Evans.

Blea Tarn sits between Great and Little Langdale. A fine example of a glacially breached col (Exc 3). Photo: R.B.Evans.

STOP 7 KENDAL BYPASS

Park in one of the laybys between the B6385 and M6 Junction 36.

The final stop is on the low ground close to the finishing point of the excursion. On many parts of the lower ground surrounding the Lake District glacial deposition is in the form of drumlins. Here part of the Kendal-Lancaster drumlin field is seen with drumlins aligned between north-south and north-east to south-west. (This area is also described in Excursion 11).

Selected References

Cumberland Geological Society (1982) *The Lake District*. Unwin

Gresswell, R K (1952) The glacial geomorphology of the south-eastern part of the Lake District. *Liverpool and Manchester Geological Journal* 1; 57-70

Howell, F T (1971) A continuous seismic profile survey of Windermere.*Geological Journal* 7; 329-334

King, C A M (1976) *Northern England*. Methuen

McConnell, R B (1940) Relic Surfaces of the Howgill Fells. *Proceedings of the Yorkshire Geological Society* 24; 152-164

Moseley, F (Editor) (1978) *The Geology of the Lake District*. Yorkshire Geological Society

Moseley, F (1981) Northern Lake District 18-19 May 1979, in Field Meetings 1979. *Proceedings of the Yorkshire Geological Society* 43; 395-399

Appendix

Information on Thirlmere can be obtained from: Public Relations Office, North West Water, Dawson House, Great Sankey, Warrington WA5 3LW (Tel. 092 5724321).

Geological map postcards of the Lake District in colour are obtainable, price 12p each, from the Yorkshire Geological Society through: Mr Murray Mitchell, 11 Ryder Gardens, Leeds LS8 1JS.

Acknowledgement

We acknowledge, with thanks, permission from the Cumberland Geological Society to use Table 2.1, which is taken from their 1982 book *The Lake District*.

3   THE LANGDALES: LANDSCAPE AND LAND USE

Doreen Harrison
(Charlotte Mason College of Education)

Outline: an opportunity to study the glacial features, village structures, land-use and farming landscape in the Langdales, a pair of typical Lake District valleys.
Starting and finishing point: Ambleside.
Distance: around 20 km.
Route: a walk for which stout footwear and outdoor clothing are essential.
Time needed: one whole day.
Maps needed: OS 1:50,000 scale, sheet 90 Landranger Series; OS 1:25,000 scale (Outdoor Leisure Series) English Lakes SE and SW sheets.

INTRODUCTION

The Langdales represent typical Lake District valleys, and they offer many opportunities for studies in both human and physical geography. Suitable physical themes include the study of glacial landforms (including till fabric analysis), slopes, soils, vegetation, rivers and lakes. Human themes include farming, settlements, land use and historical geography. The evolution of the human landscape also provides a setting in which to consider how planning issues of today may affect life in this beautiful corner of England.

Before we describe the excursion route (Figure 3) it is useful to outline the general character of the Langdales.

(a) Geology
The southern portion of the Lake District consists of lavas, ashes, slates and agglomerates of the Borrowdale Volcanic Group which form the core of the whole district (see Excursion 2). To the north are the Skiddaw Slates, whilst beyond the narrow band of Coniston limestone lie the Silurian series of rocks which form the tame scenery of Windermere shores and the undulating country of Furness (these Silurian

rocks form a series of mudstones, slates, flagstones and shale).

The volcanic country produces the dramatic central fells and peaks such as the Langdale Pikes (GR 277074), Bowfell (GR 246065), Crinkle Crags (GR 250053) and the little fell of Loughrigg (GR 347052). These extend north and east to the Helvellyn range (GR 341151) and westward to include the Scafells (GR 215072).

The whole central area has undergone major vertical movements, including changes in land/sea relationships, crustal contortions and complex faulting and folding which have brought the volcanics up against the Skiddavian massif, and produced the faulting between Shap and Broughton in Furness. The Langdale area was subject to Caledonian and later earth movements which raised the Lakeland 'dome' over a granite intrusion. Its drainage has been strongly influenced by faulting and glaciation.

(b) Landforms

The most striking feature of the landscape is the array of textbook glacial landforms. During maximum glaciation, ice blocked the main valleys, glacier streams were directed across the watersheds where cols permitted. Such glacially breached cols (known locally as 'raises') occur between Little Langdale and the Duddon valley (Wrynose Pass; GR 280029) and between Great and Little Langdale (the Blea Tarn area; GR 293044). Later glaciations may have left the 'tops' exposed to intensive frost action as nunataks, whilst the lower slopes were ice-covered. Corries were extensively deepened during maximum glaciation; a good example of a corrie with tarn (freshwater lake) is Stickle Tarn (GR 287077) below Pavey Ark, and above a fine hanging valley with waterfall. There are numerous truncated and over-ridden spurs within both Great and Little Langdale.

Glacial depositional features occur in both valleys. Moraines in Little Langdale block the outlet to the tarn, and in the main valley there are many types of morainic material (lateral and stadial).

Along the valley floors there are several steeper sections separating the lacustrine or glacio-fluvial flats. These are usually related to resistant rock bars, glacial over-deepening at constricted sites and coalescence of tributary glaciers. There are also roches moutonnees and striae, especially around Chapel Stile (GR 320054).

Great Langdale was the site of a proglacial lake which probably extended from above Chapel Stile to Mickleden (GR 270065). Borings have revealed a considerable depth of alluvium together with varying amounts of (possibly re-deposited) glacial clays. The lacustrine flat has flooded periodically in the past and the beck is now channelised between embankments (levees). Elterwater (GR 335042) also shows evidence of post-glacial infilling from a much more extensive mere, and Skelwith Pool in the lower Brathay valley (GR 352035) is probably another remnant of a larger proglacial lake.

(c) Vegetation

The natural vegetation was mixed woodland (oak, ash, beech, birch and sycamore) with rowan (mountain ash) and juniper on the higher fells, but most of it has been cleared. Much of the valley floors were cleared for Norse farms and the Elizabethans sought timber for smelt mills and ships' timbers in this and neighbouring dales. Many of the fells have been seriously overgrazed and eroded, bracken has replaced much of the heather in the last 150 years.

Cotton grass (*Eriophorum vaginatum*) occurs in the wetter areas, and dry heather heath (ling) and *Nardus stricta* occur on better drained soils. Even on the rocky tops there is mat grass, and the ghylls house some interesting periglacial and postglacial survivals. The lower scree slopes, which have a skeletal soil cover, are often colonized by bracken which extends down to the intakes (the boundary of cultivation). Inaccessible crags which are safe from sheep grazing have heather (*Calluna vulgaris*) and bilberry (*Vaccinium myrtillus*). Bog moss, sedge and bent fescue grassland grow where springs emerge at joints or breaks of slope. Moor rush (*Juncus squarossus*) is found in the wetlands.

Above the tarn in Little Langdale there is heather-covered raised peat and bog myrtle (*Myrica gale*) with purple moor grass beyond (*Molinia caerulea*). Sphagnum bog is found locally throughout the dales; in severe winters it is grazed by sheep (together with juniper, holly and even lichen). The acid soils in the valley floors have been improved by liming, and drained.

(d) Farming

Land use in the dales reflects a simple zonation:-

　　　i)　　the inbye land (or inlands) around the farmsteads
　　　ii)　　the intakes on the lower slopes

iii)　the tops or high fells which form rough grazings.

Only 2 per cent of Lakeland's fell country is arable, the main crop being grass for hay and silage. Wool is the main produce of Langdale, with hill farmers engaged in a relentless struggle against marginal land and never ending bleak conditions on the tops.

There are about 14 farm holdings in the two dales, most of which can be traced back through the Coucher Book of Furness Abbey to the early medieval and probably Norse period. The site of most farmsteads conforms to a Norse pattern and the early clearances for agriculture were the characteristic 'thwaites' in the woodlands of the tenth century. Much of the farmland today is leased by the National Trust which tries to preserve the customs of the area. The sheep flock is included in the tenancy and the farmer must leave the same number of animals on the holding when he gives up his tenancy. He is entitled to the 'increase' (ie the wool and lambs) from which he makes his living. The flock is usually Herdwick (an indigenous type of sheep well suited to conditions on the fells), which may be crossed with Suffolk or Leicester tups (rams).

Since the 1950s more attention has been paid to cattle, especially dairying. The black cattle (Angus and Galloway) for beef have now been joined by Ayrshires and Friesians for milk and some farmers have local milk rounds. The Charolais is also appearing in the area.

The farmhouses are usually of Lakeland vernacular style, with a slated porch with stone seats. Inside, the 'hallan' (hall) runs the width of the house. To one side is a back hall (the 'mell') which brings you into the 'house' (or firehouse), the main living room. Beyond the 'house' on the ground floor was the chamber (or 'best' bedroom). Children, servants and elderly relatives slept upstairs in the long loft, divided by lath and plaster partitions and open to the rafters and slates. On the other side of the 'hallan' was the 'downhouse' where baking, brewing, and household chores were done. Next to that was the barn ('shippon'), where animals were wintered. The farmhouse sometimes has a long sloping roof at the back over a kitchen/wash-house (the 'outshut'). On a sheltered wall outside there would be a stone shelf and 'roof' for the beehouse.

(e) Settlement

The relief and drainage of the Langdales have had a profound effect on the distribution and form of settlement patterns and the siting of individual dwellings. Farmsteads occur mainly on the better drained, sheltered valley slopes with the added bonus of maximum light and warmth above the winter hill shadow on the northern (ie south-facing) slopes.

Nucleated settlement consists of hamlets and the small villages of Little Langdale and Elterwater, together with the larger focus of the valleys at Chapel Stile. The traditional ways of life of these places were farming and slate quarries respectively; the growth of tourism in the present century has gradually overtaken both settlement and economy.

Demand for second homes and holiday lets has forced up the price of housing in the whole parish, and younger local people have had to seek affordable accommodation elsewhere. Older properties of character have been renovated and converted to desirable residences by their 'offcomer' owners or by speculative (and sometimes absentee) owners who then develop them as holiday lets. The in-coming retired population have in some cases contributed to the life of their communities, but it is less easy to gauge the contribution of the weekenders and holiday visitors. Barns have been converted, some new town houses have been built in Chapel Stile, and the old gunpowder works (a traditional industy associated with the quarries) became a caravan site (GR 327050) and more recently has been developed as an exclusive timeshare estate of chalets and cabins. Another former caravan site (GR 343038) has become almost a new 'village' with chalets (officially caravans) being offered freehold. Perhaps the most promising development has been the building of terraced houses for letting to local people, on the glebe land at Chapel Stile (GR 321054), by the Diocese of Carlisle.

The few local service shops include the Post Office in Little Langdale, the shop in Elterwater and the Post Office and Co-op store in Chapel Stile. Bus services are minimal, but supplemented during the tourist season. The nearest shopping centre is Ambleside (see Excursion 5).

EXCURSION

The route is shown in Figure 3. It can be followed in either direction. It is described here in a clockwise direction, starting at Ambleside.

Leave Ambleside by the Kelsick and Rothay roads, crossing

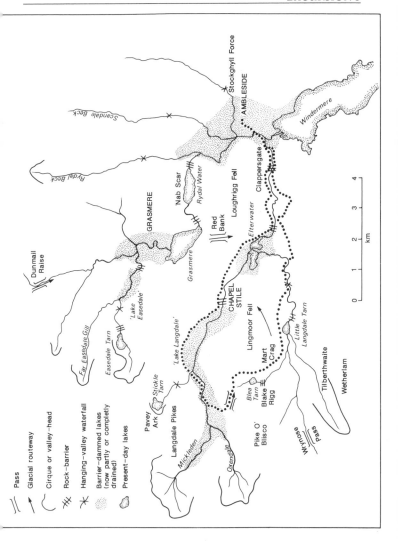

Figure 3. The excursion route

Rothay Bridge above the delta of the Rothay/Brathay system at the head of Windermere. The delta itself is of interest as are the remains of the Roman fort (Galava) in Borrans Field (GR 373034).

Ambleside to Skelwith

The route follows the Coniston Road and the hamlet of Clappersgate has a former hotel (the Croft) now converted to flats. Turn left at the road fork (GR 366035) on the Hawkshead Road and cross Brathay bridge (into the former county of Lancashire). The River Brathay offers opportunities for studies of physical geography; here it is accessible and has rapids, pools and transported boulders and it flows through a resistant rock barrier within a wooded gorge.

Keep to the minor road along the south bank of the river, noting the rocky gorge at Brathay Church. At Spy Hill note the conversion of farm buildings to holiday flats. The road to the right here, which leads to Skelwith Bridge, offers varied views of the Langdale valleys and fells.

As the valley opens out you can clearly see the glacial deposits, drumlin and moraines; land use may be related to relief and drainage. The main road on the north side of the valley keeps to the better drained land and some of it has been excavated through solid rock.

Skelwith Bridge and Little Langdale

At Skelwith Bridge (GR 344034) there is a slate processing yard which uses diamond encrusted saw blades to cut the slate and carborundum to polish it. Parties are not allowed access to the works, but you can visit the showrooms. The sawmill on the Coniston Road used to produce chocks (pit prop supports) for coal mines.

A brief detour may be made to visit Skelwith Force (GR 341035); a footpath on the right of the Coniston Road gives access. The cascade is located at another rock barrier, and the slate works used water extracted from the northern bank of the river for power and to cool the saw blades. Floodwater channels and potholing action are visible in the river. Return to the Coniston road and take the next footpath on the right signposted 'To Colwith'.

This footpath leads through farmland and some mixed woodland. The hanging valley section of Little Langdale can be seen where the view opens out. The path then leads down a steep bluff to rejoin the road to Colwith.

At the T junction beyond the bridge turn left up the steep road to Little Langdale. (There is a track on the south side of Colwith Bridge which gives access to the stream and falls and rejoins the road at several points between here and Little Langdale. It passes close to the Tilberthwaite slate quarries which are dangerous and MUST NOT be explored without an experienced guide.

The main route leads directly into Little Langdale (GR 315035), a sprawling settlement of farmsteads and cottages. The old school is presently a field centre for a Cumbrian secondary school, the church occupies the upper floor of cottages, and the shop/Post Office is in the same block of buildings. The Three Shires Inn has been modernised and its facilities extended recently.

The road continues beyond the village towards Little Langdale Tarn, where you can see active infilling and the moraine dam at its lowest outlet. The slate quarries of Tilberthwaite and on the slopes of Wetherlam can be seen from several points along the whole of this road.

Blea Tarn and Watershed

Beyond Busk Farm, within 0.5 km, is the junction between the road over Wrynose Pass and the Blea Tarn road to Great Langdale (GR 302033). If you intend to explore the Wrynose area, note that at Fell Foot farm there is the site of a Norse 'Thing-mount' (a terraced hill which was probably a meeting place like the Tynwald Hill in the Isle of Man). The remains are indistinct and not readily accessible, but the presence of this monument indicates the importance of the Wrynose road throughout history. At the top of the pass is the Three Shires Stone which marked the meeting point of the boundaries of Westmorland, Cumberland and Lancashire prior to 1974.

The route to Great Langdale follows the Blea Tarn Road. Between Blake Rigg and Mart Crag you can see the morainic deposits and solid rock which blocks the valley and beyond which lies Blea Tarn. It is interesting to study the vegetation of this, in relation to the glacial features, altitude, aspect, and soils.

Great Langdale

Cross the watershed and there is scope for simple but rewarding exercises in map-setting; for example locate Crinkle Crags, the Band, Bowfell, the Pikes, Oxendale, Rossett Gill and Mickleden. Estimate angles of slope and note the associated land-use. You can also make field sketches of glacial features from here. The track follows Red Acre Gill to Wall End. Continue on to Middlefell Place and the Old Dungeon Ghyll Hotel, near the terminus for the bus service.

If you plan to continue the walk down Great Langdale, the first section (along the main road) gives good opportunities for land use studies, showing the contrasts between the three types of farmland (inbye, intake and fell tops) as well as small scale adaptations to drainage, stone wall systems, and the siting of farmsteads.

Chapel Stile

At Chapel Stile (GR 321054) consider the problems of living in the Langdales parish; isolation, yet with pressure from tourism and commercial interests (from beyond the region) and the varying demands of and for slate quarrying. As its name suggests, Chapel Stile is the centre of the parish with the main church. The present building replaces a 'mountain chapel' typical in these dales during the late medieval and Tudor periods. The Church of England primary school is a small two-teacher establishment for all the children of the two valleys between the ages of 5 and 11; for secondary education they must travel to Coniston (11 km) or Windermere(15 km).

From Chapel Stile you can cross the footbridge (at GR 323053) and walk through the slate workings to Elterwater (GR 327047). The present quarry is dangerous and still working (do NOT enter it). From here you can see the spoil heaps and remains of the old adits, and glimpses of the timeshare estate across the river.

Elterwater

At Elterwater you can examine the effects of tourism on a small village. The path along the north bank of the river leads to the marshy lake margins (note that this path may be waterlogged after heavy rain). It continues through the Skelwith Force gorge (GR 341035) to the slate treating yard and the hamlet of Skelwith Bridge.

Return to Ambleside

From here follow the A593 to Ambleside. This busy narrow, winding road offers the opportunity to consider the effects of tourist traffic. Note the variety of properties which show the impact of holiday visitors and the retired population of the dale.

Between the rock barriers of Skelwith and Brathay/Clappersgate is the wide valley floor in which Skelwith Pool lies among glacial mounds and water meadows.

Selected References

Harvey, G A K and J A G Barnes (1970) *Natural History of the Lake District.* Warne

Marshall, J D and J K Walton (1981) *Lake Counties: 1830 to mid-twentieth century.* Manchester University Press

Millward, R and A Robinson (1974) *The Lake District.* Eyre and Spottiswood

Pearsall, W H and W Pennington (1977) *Lake District: a landscape history.* Collins

Rollinson, W (1981) *Life and Tradition in the Lake District.* Dalesman

Shaw, W T (1983) *Mining in the Lake Counties.* Dalesman

Smith, A H (1967) *Placenames of Westmorland.* English Placename Society

4 INDUSTRY IN THE UPLANDS: THE CONISTON COPPER MINES

Ian Whyte
(University of Lancaster)

Outline: a study of the remains of past mining activity in part of the Coniston fells, which considers how the copper mining industry was influenced by problems of power supply, drainage and transport in an upland environment.

Starting and finishing point: car park in Coniston Village.

Distance: about 5 km.

Route: walking, involving 400 m of ascent on footpaths which are sometimes rough or wet. You will need stout footwear and waterproofs.

Time needed: about 4 hours.

Maps needed: OS 1:25,000 English Lakes, SW sheet; 1:10,000, sheet SD 29 NE

INTRODUCTION

The Lake District is not generally thought of as an industrial area. Today quarrying is the most important extractive industry but in the past the mining and smelting of iron and non-ferrous metals, charcoal burning, wood turnery and gunpowder manufacture were also significant. Remains of all these activities can still be seen in the landscape but mostly as isolated features.

Because of their remoteness the Coniston copper mines have not been greatly affected by later development. Although some structures associated with mining there have been demolished and others have decayed, the remains still form one of the most interesting early mining landscapes in Britain. In this area one can study how the ore was mined, treated and transported. The remains range from the simple mining operations of the seventeenth century to the larger-scale and more sophisticated activity of the mid-nineteenth century.

Many of the old levels and shafts are still open. NONE OF THESE WORKINGS SHOULD BE ENTERED AS THEY ARE HIGHLY DANGEROUS! Apparently safe and solid horizontal passages may have unexpected shafts in their floors. In other cases, levels have been built across deeper workings using earth and timber floors which are rotten and may easily collapse.

A BRIEF HISTORY OF MINING AT CONISTON

It has been suggested that the Romans may have worked minerals here but there is no evidence of this. The mining of non-ferrous ores, principally copper and lead, was widespread in the Lake District between the sixteenth and later nineteenth centuries. Some 75 per cent of the Lake District's copper came from the Coniston massif. The first recorded phase of mining at Coniston began in 1599 when the Company of Mines Royal, which had been mining around Keswick since 1564, began operations.

Mining continued through the seventeenth and eighteenth centuries. Operations were small-scale before the later eighteenth century when the use of gunpowder and better pumping equipment became widespread and allowed deeper working. Production reached its peak during the 1850's when up to 600 men were employed in the mines and adjacent processing plants. The maximum annual output was over 3,000 tons of ore but the heavy cost of pumping water from the deeper workings reduced profits. By 1875 production was under 1,400 tons a year.

The expansion of the Rio Tinto mines in Chile lowered world copper prices and made the Coniston mines uneconomic. The mines were closed for all but small-scale production in 1884 and operations ceased entirely in 1891. As the mines were progressively abandoned, supporting rock pillars were removed to extract the remaining ore and many of the deeper workings collapsed. Efforts to reopen the mines or to find new, profitable veins have been made at various times since then but to no effect. There is still copper to be extracted but it is too deep and expensive to be worth mining.

EXCURSION

Coniston Village
Walk into the centre of the village and take the minor road which leads off at the west side of the bridge over Church Beck.

Today Coniston is oriented largely towards tourism, but you can

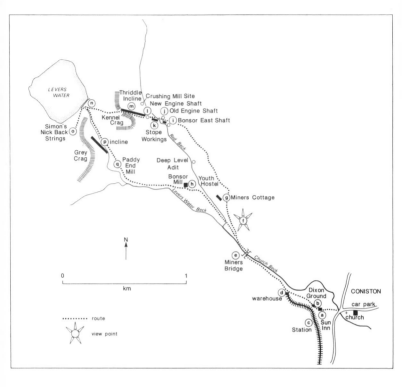

Figure 4. The excursion route

still see traces of its earlier agricultural and industrial past. Hotels such as the Crown and the Black Bull were once more simple inns and before that farmsteads.

Follow the minor road westwards from the village centre which passes the Sun Hotel (a on Figure 4), a sixteenth-century inn that has later been extended. Just beyond is Dixon Ground (b), a seventeenth-century Lakeland farmstead of traditional design. Mining also provided a good deal of employment in Coniston and in the mid-nineteenth century the company had a number of terraces of cottages built for its workers in the village. In 1851 43 per cent of heads of household in Coniston worked in the mining industry.

Transporting the ore

A short way uphill from the Sun is a level area below a substantial cliff. This was the terminus (c) of a branch railway, partly owned by the mining company, which opened in 1859 to transport ore from the mines and slate from the Coniston quarries. It was closed in 1958. Transporting the ore from mines in such rugged country was always a problem. In the seventeenth century, when the veins at Coniston were worked by the Company of Mines Royal, ore was carried by pack horse to Keswick to be smelted. In the eighteenth and early nineteenth centuries the ore was taken by cart to a lakeside wharf near Coniston Hall and was carried down the lake by boat to Nibthwaite. From there it was carted to the coast at Greenodd and, at a later date, to the canal at Ulverston for export by sea.

Follow the footpath which runs up-valley from Dixon Ground. On your left is a bridge over a tributary stream and beside it some buildings, now a small slate-carving workshop (d). These were originally sheds in which ore which had been brought down from the mines by cart was stored. It was taken over the bridge to the railway terminus on a tramway. A short distance further up the valley is the Miner's Bridge (e) spanning the stream above a waterfall. The bridge was built after the coming of the railway to allow carts laden with ore to cross the stream and reach the terminus. Prior to this the ore had been brought down the northern side of the valley into Coniston.

The Coppermines Valley

Cross the bridge (e) and follow the track up the north side of the stream. On the way note the glacially scoured rock surfaces with prominent striae (glacial scratches) on rock beside the track. Soon you come over a crest and the wider upper part of the valley comes into view. A short way beyond this point take the track which climbs gently up the northern side of the valley and, having gained a little height, stop to study the view (f).

In the centre of the valley ahead you can see the large dumps of spoil which surround the site of the main nineteenth-century ore-dressing plant. The stream, choked with debris, follows a braided course over the valley floor. The whitewashed cottage in the centre of the valley amid the ruins of other buildings is now a Youth Hostel (h) and was originally the mine-manager's house. The row of nineteenth-century cottages immediately in front of you (g) housed some of the workers at the mines.

Above the workings on the valley floor you can see two tributary valleys separated by a steep rocky spur. Mining activity was concentrated in these two valleys. The one on your right is the Red Dell valley (Red Beck). In it you can see a stone pillar which formed part of the housing for one of the waterwheels which drained the mines in the eighteenth and nineteenth centuries. The left-hand valley leads to Levers Water, a tarn under the crags of Coniston Old Man. The prominent cleft in the face of Grey Crag above the western side of this valley is Simon's Nick, part of the seventeenth-century workings.

Immediately uphill from where you are standing you can see the first of a line of quarries which runs up the side of the valley following a particular band of slate. Quarries above Low Water Beck at the head of the main valley are still being worked.

The Red Dell Valley working: problems of power supply in the uplands

From the distribution of mining remains you get a good impression of the trend of the main mineral veins. These ran roughly north-west to south-east. The two main veins were the Paddy End Vein which outcropped in the crags to the west of Levers Water and in Grey Crag to the south of the tarn, and the Bonsor Vein which outcropped in the Red Dell valley. There were many other smaller, less productive veins though. The veins contain few minerals other than those of copper: chalcopyrite, malachite, azurite, and chrysocolla though some magnetite iron ore was found at depth. The best ore contains from 5 per cent to 13 per cent copper in veins which are only up to 20 cm thick.

Follow the track until you are above the row of miners' cottages (g). A short way above this turn left on to the footpath which heads along the valley side towards the prominent stone pillar. Above this path there are some classic roches moutonnees (glacially scoured rock outcrops). One, immediately beside the track, has numerous sets of initials carved in it, some cut by nineteenth-century miners. When you get to the pillar you will see a deep stone-lined trench below it (i). This is a waterwheel pit. The bottom half of the wheel sat in the pit and water dropped on to the top of the wheel from a wooden flume, fed from the stream by means of a lade, which ran along the top of the pillars. The wheel was used for pumping water and raising ore from the Old Engine Shaft (j) which is located a short way inside the open level close to the pit (DO NOT ENTER IT). The mid nineteenth-century wheel had a diameter of thirteen metres and a width of nearly three metres.·

Providing power at upland mining sites was always a problem. Power was needed to pump water from the mines, raise the ore, and to work the machinery for treating the ore. In the seventeenth century, when the scale of working was small, human effort was the main power source. By the mid-seventeenth century, however, workings had reached a depth of over sixty metres on the Bonsor vein and operations became more sophisticated: manpower gave way to the use of horse gins and then water wheels.

It is sometimes believed that the advent of the improved steam engine in the later eighteenth century led to the immediate demise of water power. In remote mining areas like Coniston this was far from true. To have brought coal by sea to Greenodd or Ulverston, then by track and lake to Coniston, and finally up the steep climb to the mines, would have been prohibitively expensive. Because of this water provided the main source of power even at the peak of production in the nineteenth century, at which time there were thirteen large water wheels in operation. Fortunately in an area with high precipitation and impervious rocks there was a good water supply but the quantity of water available was not limitless. Water resources were carefully husbanded so that water passed from one water wheel to another down the valley, and even from one valley to another, by a series of sluices.

Various techniques were used to locate and extract the ore. The simplest and earliest workings were where the veins outcropped at the surface. In valley sides the veins were followed into the rock by cutting vertical clefts. On valley floors, as here at Red Dell, the workings resembled irregular trenches or 'stopes' (k) whose line on the surface followed the outcrop of the vein. These stopes were cut deeper and deeper as rock-cutting and drainage technology improved.

You can see a collapsed stope on the Bonsor Vein as a trench below the path a short way downstream of the waterwheel pit. These workings were started by the Company for Mines Royal in the early seventeenth century. Even more spectacular are the open stopes in the fenced off area immediately across the stream. These workings are extremely deep; THE FENCED OFF AREA SHOULD NOT BE ENTERED.

At a later date veins which were located deep within a hillside were worked by means of horizontal levels or adits which were driven into the rock until the vein was reached. The vein was then worked above and below the adit by stopes. Levels were used for bringing out the ore using tramways and trucks and for draining the mine.

Drainage was always a problem in any kind of mining. The stopes downstream from the Old Engine Shaft (j) must have been especially difficult to keep dry in wet weather due to water cascading from the crags above and you can see traces of attempts to divert the small tributary streams. The normal way of draining workings in hilly country like this was to drive a deep level from the lowest possible point on the valley floor back into the workings in the hillsides. Water drained down inside the mine from workings above this level and along it to the surface.

Here the Deep Level reaches the surface lower down on the east side of the Red Dell Beck. It was used for removing the ore and was eventually extended back to connect with the Paddy End workings. Over a million tons of ore and rock came out of here during the nineteenth century. Any excavations on the veins which were carried below this level had to be pumped out constantly. At Coniston the Deep Level lies over 80 m below the outcrop of the Bonsor Vein in the bottom of the Red Dell Valley but during the nineteenth century workings were driven to a maximum depth of 375 m below the level. It would have been technically feasible to have driven a longer level starting from a lower point - say by the Miner's Bridge (e) - in order to provide natural drainage for workings at a greater depth. However, because the rock in this area was so hard it was very slow and expensive to tunnel through and this was not economically viable. When the mines were finally abandoned and pumping operations ceased the lowest workings began to fill with water which gradually rose until it reached the main drainage level. Today all workings below the Deep Level are flooded.

Across the stream from the Old Engine Shaft water wheel is an even larger waterwheel pit. This served the New Engine Shaft (l) which drops down at the west end of the fenced-off area and was merely a cleared space running down through the open stopes. Above the waterwheel pit you can see a ramp of stone, the Thriddle Incline (m), down which ore was carried from mines in the slopes of Kennel Crag above. If you walk up the incline you get a good view of a disturbed area on the valley floor a short way upstream. This is the site of a seventeenth-century mill where the ore was crushed and treated. Water for the New Engine Shaft wheel was collected in a small reservoir just above this site. Water was fed into the reservoir from the Red Dell Beck but also from the neighbouring valley via a canal which you can see running round the hillside a short way above the water-wheel pit.

At the top of the incline skirt the crags and follow the faint path towards Levers Water (n).

Levers Water, a natural tarn, has been dammed to provide a greater reserve for the water-powered machinery. Mineral veins outcrop on the gentle slopes immediately south-west of the tarn, above Grey Crag. These veins have been worked by open stopes which form a complex pattern of clefts and trenches. The deepest chasm is Simon's Nick (o), the one which is prominent on the skyline when seen from below. Although some of these clefts seem fairly shallow YOU SHOULD NOT CLIMB DOWN INTO THEM UNDER ANY CIRCUM-STANCES. Their floors are often artificial, made from earth laid upon timbers. Workings on the vein extend below them for hundreds of feet and if you descend into them you may cause the floors to collapse. Most of these stopes date from the seventeenth century though many were deepened in later times. Between the workings you can see the foundations of crude huts and piles of waste. The huts were occupied by ore dressers, probably in the seventeenth century. They broke the ore into small pieces by hand using hammers and separated out the dross which was left behind in these spoil heaps.

The Paddy End workings
Follow the track down from Levers Water to the main valley and walk to the footbridge over the Levers Water Beck.

Above you on the left hand side of the beck you can see the remains of another inclined plane (p) down which ore was brought from the workings in Grey Crag. Loaded wagons were lowered on a winch and as they ran down they pulled empty wagons up. On either side of the beck further up, you can see two stone pillars. These were the bases for pylons carrying a winding rope over 660 m long, from the New Engine Shaft water wheel. The rope was used to hoist ore from the Paddy End mines and this cumbersome expedient was considered cheaper than erecting a new winch closer to the mine. Lower down on the flat ground to the east of the beck is the site of the former Paddy End ore-processing mill (q). The ruins of the smithy and office can be seen on the hillside above.

Water power and water resources

Follow the track down the valley towards the Youth Hostel (h).

Providing power to drive all the machinery required that none of the available water should be wasted. On the walk down the valley you can see part of the complex system of water races by which this was achieved. We have seen that water was drawn from below Levers Water and taken round the slopes of Kennel Crag to help drive the wheel at the New Engine Shaft (l). From here water was channelled to the wheel at the Old Engine Shaft (j) and then back round the spur to the mill at Paddy End (q). You can see the channel on your left as you leave Paddy End. From here the water went back round the spur at a lower level to the Bonsor dressing floors (h) further down the valley via a channel which crosses the track halfway between Paddy End and the hostel.

The Bonsor Mill site: treating the ore

The ore which was mined at Coniston was not smelted on site. To reduce transport costs it was essential to refine it by extracting a high proportion of the dross. This was done in dressing mills which became more sophisticated from the seventeenth to the nineteenth century. Even in the nineteenth century the ore was initially broken by hand with sledgehammers and hand sorted by women and children to separate out the purest ore. It was the lumps with mixed ore and rock which were a problem. An early form of treatment was in a stamping mill where the ore was crushed by water-driven hammers. A more sophisticated system used crushing rollers to reduce the ore and rock to the consistency of a fine sand. This was then transferred to washing and settling tanks where flotation was used to separate the heavier ore from the lighter rock.

Many of the buildings which made up the Bonsor Dressing Floors have been removed but enough remains to get an impression of how the site functioned. Remains of the settling tanks can be seen behind the youth hostel. Because of the remoteness of the mines the works formed almost a self-sufficient community with its own smithy and sawmill - the building above the Youth Hostel (h) which has been restored.

PERSERVING AN INDUSTRIAL SITE

The remains of mining at Coniston have been scheduled as an industrial monument. Ownership of the land on the site of the Bonsor Mills has passed to a company which has been making efforts to turn the old sawmill into a hotel and conference centre. Restoration work on the sawmill has begun, the area adjoining the youth hostel has been landscaped, and an information board erected. There has been considerable local opposition to these changes.

Is this capital-intensive commercial approach the right way to preserve sites of this kind and to inform people of their history? Do the newly-planted trees around the youth hostel and the ornamental gateway clash with the character of the site and the rest of the landscape as some people have suggested? Should the track up from Coniston be improved to allow easy access by car or should access be restricted to walkers?

Selected References

Holland, E G (1981) *Coniston Copper Mines: a field guide.* Cicerone Press, Milnthorpe

Holland, E G (1982) *Coniston Copper.* Cicerone Press, Milnthorpe

Marshal, J D and M Davies-Shiel (1974) *Industrial archaeology of the Lake Counties.* David and Charles

5   AMBLESIDE: HISTORICAL GEOGRAPHY AND RECENT CHANGES

Doreen Harrison
(Charlotte Mason College of Education)

Outline: a walk around Ambleside to look at evidence of its evolution and past. The route will also allow study of recent changes and current trends within this Lake District tourist town.
Starting point: Market Place in Ambleside.
Finishing point: Waterhead.
Distance: 3 to 4 km.
Time needed: half a day, or longer.
Maps needed: the largest scale obtainable, such as the OS 1:25,000 or the local street map produced by the Ambleside Publicity Association.

INTRODUCTION

Ambleside is located on the east side of the Vale of Rothay, 1.5 km above the waterhead of Windermere. Its nucleus is where Stock Beck emerges from the ghyll (hanging valley) on to the flat floored vale below, from which rise rocky outcrops (the former islands in Windermere when the lake extended to Rydal after glaciation).

The main valley is part of the structural trough through which passes the north-south route through the Lake District (the A591). This location gives Ambleside its importance as the most central town of the Lakes. Within a few km of the town are the majority of the classical Lakeland beauty spots, yet Ambleside remains "stubbornly local" (Nicholson, 1969). Local writer, Hunter Davies (1984) admits "it is very busy in summer, yet unlike some places it does not die in winter".

The original settlement may have been the vicus at the gate of the Roman Fort at Waterhead. Then in the tenth century the Norse-Irish shielings were located on the sunny southwest-facing slope of Chapel Hill above the vale. Its name became, appropriately, A melr saetr (literally, "the shielings above the sandy river bank") and then Amelsate, and finally Ambleside. Old Norse placenames, like rigg, fell, dale, how (hill), thwaite (clearing), beck, mere or water (lake), still abound in the district.

Like most Lakeland towns, the early economy of Ambleside relied on wool, the chief harvest of the fells. Mills grew on the River Stock, and pack ponies carried wool and cloth along the narrow fellside routes above the marshy dales. The market charter was granted in the mid-seventeenth century, and this indicates the growing importance and size of the town as it began to spread along the morainic ridges towards Waterhead.

Traditional buildings show the vernacular styles, with dripmoulds above small deeply set windows, timber lintels and mullions, porches with stone seats, cylindrical chimneys capped by slates or stone slabs, "wrestler" slates along ridges (their sides indented to interlock in the style of Westmorland wrestlers!) and deep overhanging eaves to shed the rain! The early thatched roofs have given way now to the stone flags or slates from local quarries.

The turnpike road brought improved coach services, and soon after the rebuilding of the church in 1812 the town was already outgrowing its capacity and had begun to spread on to the flatlands towards the new church which was built in 1854. Later Victorian boarding houses and hotels illustrate the use of neatly dressed slates, which contrast with the primitive beck boulders and random ragstone walling used earlier. Twentieth century development has been confined mainly to the infilling of old gardens and building of modest council estates on the margins of the town, together with some private housing.

Tourism dominates the economy today, though the market has been revived and there are small industrial enterprises (eg sheepskins and woollens). The Victorians came by rail, but today's visitors come by way of the M6 motorway. There is a plan for a 'relief road', though this has caused some controversy.

The population shows a mix of both income and age groups, though there is inevitably an influx of retired people. Changing habits in tourism have led to an increase in self-catering and, more recently, the appearance of timeshare units.

Ambleside presents a fascinating complex of social geography, a rich resource for the historical geographer, and a lively community with much to offer to resident and visitor alike.

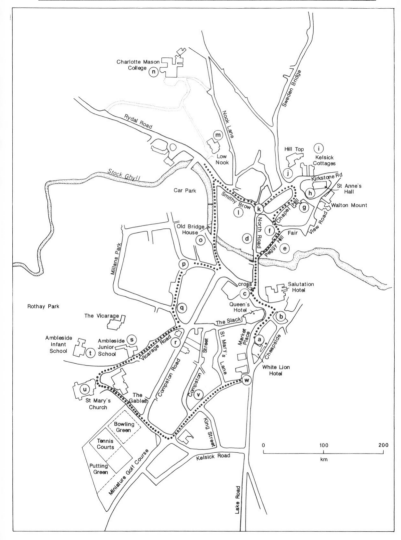

Figure 5. The excursion route.

EXCURSION

Market Place

Start in the Market Place (a in Figure 5) where it is clear that the central area has been infilled with administrative buildings in the past. The Town Hall and Mechanics Institute building was rebuilt in 1858 and its main doorway (now blocked) is still visible on the north side. The main window facing the Market Place had beneath it the magistrates' bench when local ore smugglers were tried there; the shops still have storerooms below which there were once cells! The Market Hall, built in 1863, replaced the earlier Cross House on this site, whilst Barclays Bank (b) occupies the site of the poorhouse known as Bedlam (Bethlehem).

The original market cross has been removed to a site near the modern bus station because of the traffic; its original site was revealed in recent excavations to renew public service pipes and cables between the Queen's Hotel and the old Town Hall.

Behind the Market Place on the east side is the narrow street called Cheapside, a reminder of its former commercial importance as part of the original open market place. Modern garages have replaced former stables.

The west side of the Market Place once held low thatched buildings and the half-timbered building forming the archway to The Slack (a narrow lane) which is still flanked by a shop called the Archway. Here also is Brown's Coaches office and dwelling, once the post office. The new Post Office has returned to this central area (after several moves!) and occupies the site of a gracious Georgian house where William Green the artist lived (more recently it has been a doctors' surgery). Old prints show the name of The Queen's Hotel as The Cock.

The southern end of the Market Place has two inns of contrasting style and origin. The White Lion is a tourist hotel and the Royal Oak was previously a typical farmstead. At the head of the Market Place stands the Salutation Inn. Its pre-Reformation designation indicates its age as a hostelry, the core of the building shows signs of its original function as a coaching inn. All of these inns were on the main road and coaching routes through the town.

North Road

Leave the Market Place at this northern end and walk to the Market

Cross (c), opposite the bus station. This cross was provided (possibly in the late seventeenth century) by the Braithwaite family. The cross head was removed and later found in the grounds of their Calgarth (Windermere) property - it was being used as a sundial!

Walk along North Road, the original main road to Keswick, and you can still visualise the coaches which congested this narrow way and used the Unicorn Inn (d) as yet another establishment for changing horses. To the left is Bridge Street (formerly Rattle Gill) which once held weavers' houses (hence the rattle!). It has in recent years been restored by the local civic society. From here you can also see the structure of the bridge over the Stock Beck, and the Old Mill with the former mill wheel being replaced by a working replica in the 1970s. The footpath along the mill wall follows the route of the mill race along which water was drawn for the overshot wheel.

Cross the road and take the narrow path up Peggy Hill (e). You pass the printing works and stationers on the right, a former wash house half way up the hill, and at the top arrive at the oldest part of the town - the location of the Norse shielings around the sunny south-west facing Chapel Hill area. The former tiny plots were gradually built upon by cottagers and tradesmen, giving the present complex of 'islands' with narrow trackways between. Here are some of Amblesides best vernacular buildings.

At the top of Peggy Hill, on the left hand side (f) is a former farmhouse with porches, dripstones over its windows, flagstone roof and walls of beck boulders (rendered or 'roughcast') and with a crowstepped (or corbie-stepped) chimney stack.

Chapel Hill and St. Anne's Church

Emerge from this area at the top of Chapel Hill, and you will see the old residence of How Head (g) opposite the former church of St. Anne. How Head has been divided into several units, but it has been carefully restored and exhibits several local features; oak lintels, oak mullions, construction of beck boulders and random ragstone walling (very little visible mortar) cylindrical 'roofed' chimney stacks, and wrestler slates along the roof ridge.

The ancient 'mountain chapel' of pre-Tudor times was replaced in 1812 by the present structure of St. Anne's church (h) which - in its turn - was superseded by the 'new' church of 1854 in the valley. It has been converted to residential units in recent years. The whole of this

Chapel Hill area forms the core of historic Ambleside and of the recently-designated Conservation area. There is evidence of restoration work to individual properties and to the general milieu.

On the side of Kirkstone Road opposite St. Anne's Church (h) is the old grammar school (now Kelsick Cottages, i) and Hill Top (j) a former girls' academy, later the Hill Top Hotel and now a part of Charlotte Mason College complex.

Smithy Brow and Rydal Road

Walk down the hill again and reach the junction with North Road. The electrical contractor's shop here (k) is a former butcher's premises (and may have once been a smithy); you are at the top of Smithy Brow. The stage coaches had to turn sharply here to negotiate the steep brow on their way to Keswick.

On the left is the Golden Rule Inn (l), another example of a connection with things ecclesiastical; at one time the Church ran inns for travellers and brewed ale! On the same side and further down the brow is the Old House, the former home of the Braithwaite family. Another smithy occupied the next group of cottages. To the right Nook Lane leads to the Pinfold and Green, this was the original track to Rydal.

Emerge on to Rydal Road, near a Victorian postbox on your left. From here you can view the northern end of the town. On the corner is the six acre main campus of Charlotte Mason College, centred on Scale How (n), a gracious residence (heavily restored by the Victorians). At the gate is Low Nook (m) formerly Compstone Lodge, which shows local architectural features of a somewhat more affluent style than those of Chapel Hill.

You can take a detour to the north along Rydal Road to see the Police and Fire stations of the 1960s, modern bungalows and houses along Stony Lane. College residences and the Health Centre fill in former green areas, whilst the prize-winning Council estate of Greenbank (and its extension Castlefield) cluster round a small beck. The remainder of the town in this direction is a mixture of Victorian and more modern houses of varied character.

Turn left from the foot of Smithy Brow towards Ambleside and cross the road. From here see Stock Beck (Stock Ghyll or River Stock) as it begins to cross the vale towards its confluence with the River Rothay. Rydal Road was built in 1833. The Friends' Meeting House on the east side is a former Police Station. Visitors are intrigued with the Bridge House (o), the original summer house and apple store of the Braithwaites at Ambleside Hall (the Old House). Note the wrestler slate roof ridge and the oak lintels and exterior stairway. The bridge beneath it is of the 'packhorse' type, with no keystone, and originally no parapets.

Millans Park and St. Mary's Church
Beyond the lower end of Bridge Street and Dodd's corner, turn right into Millans Park (p). This area was built towards the end of the nineteenth century (its buildings show the square cut stones of modern technology); it is a Victorian residential square. Many of the houses have converted attic rooms with new dormer windows. They were built without garages, and parking for residents and visitors is a chronic problem. Recent developments have included extensions for holiday units, a major new complex of flats for the elderly and Ambleside's new vicarage.

The southern end of Millans Park leads back into Compston Road, with shops to the left and mixed shops and housing to the right. At this corner are the Cinema (q) (former Assembly Rooms) and an arcade of shops, the Gospel Hall (r) and the Walnut fish shop (both this and the arcade were former Post Offices!) Turn right into Vicarage Road, which brings you to the schools and church. The school buildings include the former Wordsworth Library, the remaining section of the junior school now occupied by the Association Football Club and the new junior school (s). Beyond this is the infants' school (t) and the entrance to Rothay Park. At the far end of the path through the park, over the River Rothay, is Miller Bridge (a good example of the packhorse bridge design).

The church of St. Mary the Virgin (u) stands on one of the knolls which rise from the vale. They are rocky sites and several of these roches moutonees are to be found in the park (at the end of the last glacial period they would form islands within the lake which then extended to Rydal). Some of these rocks bear glacial striae.

We can learn much of the development and character of the town from the church and churchyard. Here is a record in stone, slate, carved oak, and printed and handwritten archives of the community over the last 150 years and more. The church building is unusual in several respects. It was built by a London architect, Sir George Gilbert

Scott, whose perfect rendering of the Early English style looks incongruously modern for the town, and its spire is out of keeping in a region of sturdy towers. The use of freestone and elaborate carving and tracery seems an urban anachronism in a rural area.

Church Street and Lake Road

Return to the town through the south east gate near White Platts recreation area. Cross Compston Road, and proceed into Church Street. This street was formerly called Ratten (or Rotten) Row, the new name was a result of the 'new' church having been built among what were then open fields at its southern end.

In Church Street, the Information Offices on the right occupy yet another former Police Station (there are barred windows on the opposite (King Street) side of the building!). Further up on the left (v) are some of the eighteenth-century cottages with signs of timber crucks in the lower walls, and footings of considerable width.

At the top of Church Street, on the left, is the former grocers' shop, which was the home and shop of John Kelsick the young grocer who left his fortune in 1723 to endow the grammar school which bore his name. His Educational Trust has survived, though the school (rebuilt on the slope of Wansfell in 1907) was closed in 1965 with the opening of the comprehensive school at Troutbeck Bridge. Across the road the old Stamp House was the office of Wordsworth when he was Distributor of Stamps.

Turn right at the top of Church Street, along Lake Road (w). You can make a diversion up Old Lake Road to the Blue Hill and Fisherbeck area. Or walk along Lake Road past the top of Kelsick Road (note the new Library building) past the hotels and boarding houses and Hayes Garden Centre to Waterhead, Ambleside's port. The Roman Fort of Galava stands in the field beyond Borrans Park and is freely accessible. At Waterhead you can see examples of Victorian hotels with modern adaptations, a new timeshare development, the British Rail steamer pier, and the lake shore area of Waterhead Green.

Selected References

Brunskill, R W (1974) *Vernacular Architecture of the Lake Counties*. Faber
Davies, H (1984) *The Good Guide to the Lakes*. Foster Davies
Lake District Special Planning Board / Cumbria County Council (1978)

Joint Structure Plan. LDSPB/CCC

Marshall, J D and J K Walton (1981) *The Lake Counties from 1830 to the mid-twentieth century.* Manchester University Press

Nicholson, N (1969) *Greater Lakeland.* Hale

Rollinson, W (1978) *History of Cumberland and Westmorland.* Phillimore

6   KENDAL: THE MORPHOLOGY OF A PRE-INDUSTRIAL TOWN

Ian Whyte
(University of Lancaster)

Outline: a study of the origins and development of a planned medieval town and the evidence in the modern townscape for its former functions and activities.
Starting point: Parish Church in Kendal (GR 516972).
Finishing point: Castle Park (GR 522930).
Distance: 3.5 km.
Route: walking through the town.
Time needed: about 3 hours.
Maps needed: OS 1:2,500 plan SD 5092/5102 covers most of the town centre.

INTRODUCTION

North-western England was not highly urbanised before the Industrial Revolution. Towns were small and widely scattered with trading and market functions often being performed by centres which were scarcely urban. However, Kendal was one of the earliest boroughs in this area, its origin as a centre going back to pre-medieval times. Unlike many medieval boroughs, Kendal weathered successfully the period of urban decline in the later fourteenth and fifteenth centuries. The manufacture of cloth, particularly coarse woollens brought prosperity, as indicated by the motto *"Pannus mihi panis"* (Cloth is my bread) on the town's coat of arms. By the sixteenth century Kendal was the largest and most important town in Cumbria after Carlisle.

Although it has continued to be an important regional market town and minor industrial centre, Kendal has remained comparatively small. It was too far from the heartland of the Industrial Revolution in south Lancashire to grow rapidly in the nineteenth century. Consequently a good deal of its past can be deciphered in the layout and fabric of the modern town.

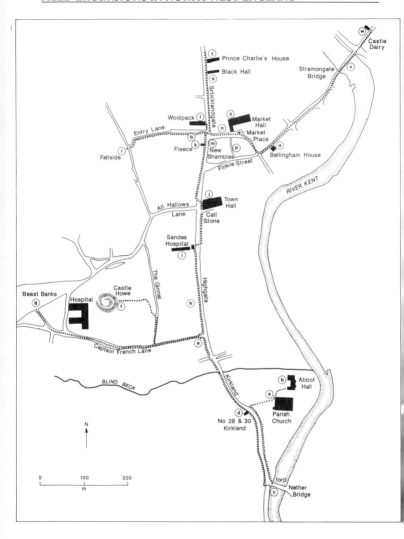

Figure 6. The excursion route.

The Coppermines Valley, Coniston, from Red Dell (Exc 4).
Photo: R.B.Evans.

Old Shambles Yard, Kendal (Exc 6).   Photo: Walt Unsworth
On Farleton Knott (Exc 8). Photo: Walt Unsworth

Ingleborough (Exc 9). Photo: Walt Unsworth

Settle-Carlisle Railway through Mallerstang (Exc 10).
Photo: W.Unsworth

EXCURSION

The excursion involves a walk through the town centre, starting from the southern end and working northwards, examining the evidence for Kendal's development and functions from medieval times until the nineteenth century.

This guide begins at the Parish Church (a on Figure 6), although the places mentioned can be visited in any order.

KIRKLAND

Kendal was just far enough south to be within the Norman England of 1086 and thus to be included in Domesday Book. There it is described as "Cherchebi", or "Kirkby", a prefix derived from the Old Norse words for "church" and "settlement". This indicates that there was a church here at the time of the Scandinavian settlement in the tenth century, and probably earlier. The survival of part of a ninth-century cross shaft, which is preserved inside the church, indicates the existence of an Anglian ecclesiastical foundation, possibly monastic in character. There is no evidence to show what the first church was like or where it was located but the probability is that it was on or close to the site of the present one (a).

Parish Church

The present parish church (a) is not nearly as old as the ninth century. The earliest masonry dates from the thirteenth century and most of the fabric is from late-medieval times onwards. The most notable features of the church are the wide double aisles and side chapels on either side of the nave and choir. These make the church unusually wide with a square rather than a rectangular plan. Inside the effect is of a single huge open space broken up by pillars. The great size of the church, one of the largest parish churches in England and almost as wide as York Minster, relects the prosperity which Kendal enjoyed during the fifteenth and sixteenth centuries as a result of the cloth trade. Some of the wealth of the merchant clothiers was channelled into extending and embellishing the church.

Abbot Hall

Immediately north of the church is the mansion of Abbot Hall (b). It

65

stands on the site of a hall which was, as the name suggests, associated with the church. It may have been connected with the abbey of St. Mary's in York to which the parish church of Kendal was granted in the eleventh century. The hall passed into lay hands after the Reformation and in 1759 was rebuilt as a classical-style town house for a local landowning family with the spacious layout of a country mansion. It now houses a museum and exhibition centre.

Nether Bridge

A short way downstream of the church is the Nether Bridge (c), on the main road south from the town. There was a bridge here from the fourteenth century. In the seventeenth century the bridge was still narrow, designed for pack horses rather than wheeled vehicles. Heavy wagons crossed the river by a ford just upstream where you can see a low weir today. The bridge was rebuilt in 1772 and 1908 to accommodate a growing volume of traffic. As was the case with the bridge at the foot of Stramongate (v), this was accomplished by adding new masonry to the existing structure. If you look under the arch of the Nether Bridge you can see the three phases of construction with the seventeenth-century bridge at the core.

Kirkland, the section of the main street from the Nether Bridge to just beyond the church, is the pre-medieval focus of Kendal. It is divided from the planned medieval borough by a small stream, Blind Beck, which is barely visible today. Kirkland remained quite separate from the borough, with its own manorial court, until 1905. As it lay outside Kendal's jurisdiction it was popular with poor tradesmen who could set up here without paying the £10 entry fee which was required for anyone carrying on a trade in the borough. The irregular, curving layout of the main street of Kirkland contrasts with the more regular plan of the medieval borough.

Timber frame housing

The houses on the west side of Kirkland (d), some of them dating from the seventeenth century though partly remodelled in later times, are interesting because some are of timber-frame construction. No 30 has a projecting first floor supported on pillars while its neighbour, No 28, has a jettied upper floor from which wooden beams can be seen protruding.

Situated close to outcrops of carboniferous limestone, Kendal has acquired the nickname 'the old grey town' from the widespread use of this building material. However, down to the eighteenth century there was still plenty of timber in the area. Timber-frame construction, in which the weight of the roof was transmitted to ground level not by solid walls but by a wooden skeleton infilled with lightweight wattle and daub panelling, remained common for houses in the Cumbrian lowlands. Projecting upper storeys are a feature of such construction and can be seen elsewhere in Kendal, the timbers often being totally masked by rough-casting and plaster.

CASTLE HOWE

From Kirkland walk north into Highgate and turn left up Captain French Lane (e). Then turn up a narrow lane, the Ginnel, to reach the open ground above (f).

Motte and bailey
This was Kendal's first medieval fortress, a motte and bailey castle of earth and timber constuction. The motte, shaped like an inverted pudding basin, still stands over 10 m above the level bailey which is surrounded by a ditch and covers an area of about 1 ha. Little is known about the date of the castle; it is presumed to have been built in the late eleventh or twelfth century. It probably pre-dates the planned borough and may have been located with a view to protecting the older settlement of Kirkland.

From here you have a good view of the town and can look across to the drumlin on which stands the ruins of the later stone castle. The castle replaced the motte on a position which, although across the river from the town, was better for defence. It is thought to date from the later twelfth century but none of the badly ruined stonework is earlier than the thirteenth century.

Medieval borough
You can also see the layout of the planned medieval borough of Kendal which extends on either side of Highgate and Stricklandgate, the main street. Kendal received its first market charter in 1189 but this was probably attached to the existing settlement in Kirkland. The actual markets may have been held in the churchyard (a) which would at that time have been an open green space uncluttered with tombstones or

grave markers.

At some time in the thirteenth century it was decided to lay out a new borough on the gently rising slope north of Kirkland. The plan was a conventional one which is found in many other medieval British towns. There is a single straight main street from which the burgages (building plots with a standard width of about 12 m) ran back at right angles in a herringbone pattern. To the east the plots extend to the River Kent and are about 150 m long. To the west, running upslope, they are shorter; just over 100 m, ending against the Ginnel (the lane below you).

The principal feature which distinguishes the plan of medieval Kendal is that instead of the main street widening in the centre to form a market place, the market place is offset to the east and from it another street, Stramongate, on the line of the old road to Scotland, leads off at right angles. This layout was to condition the development of Kendal through succeeding centuries.

Return to Captain French Lane and continue uphill until it opens out at the top beside the hospital.

Beast Banks

This triangular open space, known as Beast Banks (g) is an interesting feature. It has been interpreted as the green of a former village which was separate from the borough and which may have grown up in the shelter of the castle. This is possible but no distinctive early place name seems to be attached to this area and early maps do not show it as being built up. A more likely explanation is that this triangular area is the apex of an old driftway, a wedge of open pasture funnelling out from the town, over which livestock were driven to pastures on the limestone scarp of Scout Scar two km to the west. This helps to emphasise that despite its trade and industry the medieval town was still partly agrarian in character.

Return down Captain French Lane to Highgate.

HIGHGATE-STRICKLAND

In medieval times most of the houses and workshops in the town would have lined the frontages of the burgage plots which ran back on either side of the main street. The rear of these plots would have been open, occupied by gardens, orchards and smallholdings. Through time, as pressure for space increased with a growing population, infilling of the open spaces occurred as the burgages became increasingly built up behind the street frontages. This infilling often consisted of small workshops and cottages but also sometimes other functions, like the shambles and stabling for the town's many inns. These buildings and functions required access to the main street. Sometimes this was provided by lanes opened along the lines of the plot boundaries but more often it was by means of openings through the street frontages into long courtyards flanked by buildings.

Yards

This was the origin of the famous Kendal "yards", a variant of the kind of burgage infilling found elsewhere. There were at one time around 150 yards in Kendal, most of them named after the families who owned the buildings fronting on to the main street. During the late eighteenth and nineteenth centuries, when the woollen textile trade was booming, large numbers of weavers' cottages were crammed into vacant spaces in the yards. Similar dense infilling, on a far larger scale, with the attendant problems of water supply and waste disposal, created the worst slum conditions in mid-nineteenth century cities like Liverpool and Manchester.

Many yards have been modernised and the most densely set buildings demolished. However, many still retain something of their traditional character (h) and almost all are worth exploring. Many traces of old crafts and industries, including workshops and warehouses, can be found in them. In recent years the trend has been towards renovating and modernising the older buildings rather than demolishing them. New Inn Yard, between the Brewery Arts Centre and Sandes Hospital has some good examples. Next to it is Webster's Yard, named after a local firm of architects who had their premises here. A display board in the entry to the yard shows how this one firm influenced the look of Kendal between the later eighteenth and later nineteenth century.

SANDES HOSPITAL

Before the Reformation much of the care of the urban poor was undertaken by the church. After the Reformation poor relief became a matter of civic care and personal charity. Many private individuals left funds for the maintenance of the poor of their parish and richer people might establish hospitals, schools for the education of poor children, and almshouses providing accommodation for the needy. Sandes Hospital (i), founded in 1670 by Thomas Sandes, a wealthy Kendal clothier, is a good example of this.

The building fronting the street dates from 1659, as indicated by the plaque which also displays the initials of Thomas and his wife Katherine. It contains the original school and schoolmaster's house. Under the archway you can see an old alms box for donations urging you to "Remember the Poor". Inside the yard are a row of almshouses with small gardens and a chapel in the centre. These only date from 1852 when the original cottages were rebuilt to provide more spacious accommodation. They were established to house eight poor widows of Kendal clothiers.

Another private foundation in the town was Dowker's Hospital, a set of almshouses for six poor spinsters, at the south end of the borough. It was demolished in the 1960s but the charity still functions. The area to the south of Sandes Hospital is being redeveloped, part of which involves the construction of a group of luxury retirement homes, a function which is in keeping with the adjacent almshouses.

TOWN HALL

The present Town Hall (j) was built in 1897 on the site of a previous one. This had in turn replaced the earlier Moot Hall, the meeting place and courtroom of the burgh from the sixteenth century. The Moot Hall, the most important civic building in the town, stood at the corner of Stricklandgate and the Market Place. The original hall, dating from 1591, was destroyed by fire in 1969 and the building which occupies the site today is a modern replica of how the Moot Hall would have looked in the eighteenth century.

Call Stone

In front of the Town Hall is the Cold or Call Stone. This is the base of Kendal's medieval market cross, the symbol in stone of the town's status as a borough and of its right to hold markets and fairs. The cross originally stood in Stricklandgate, opposite the Market Place and adjoining the Market Hall. It was removed in 1765 but the base was left on its original site. Eventually the base was moved into the Market

Place, to allow a freer flow of traffic in the main street, and then to its present location. The stone, and the cross before it, was the site from which proclamations were read (hence 'Call Stone') and business transacted. It was at the cross that the Jacobites proclaimed James III as king during the rebellions of 1715 and 1745.

KENDAL INNS

As an important market and industrial centre Kendal had a large number of inns. Walking up Highgate you will already have noticed a number of them including the Kendal Bowman, the Highgate Hotel dated 1769 and the New Inn dated 1654. These and many others provided more than food, drink and accommodation; they also functioned as places where business was transacted and transport organised. From the mid-eigthteenth century stage wagons, and later stagecoaches left from these inns.

The Fleece Inn (k) and the Woolpack (l), on the west side of the main street near the Market Place, are typical examples of traditional inns. Their names emphasise the importance of the wool trade in the past. The Fleece is particularly interesting as it preserves one of the traditional timber-framed arcaded fronts which were once common in the town. The jettied first floor is supported on pillars forming an arcade under which, in the past, people could walk in shelter.

In later times these arcades were sometimes filled in and the ground floor frontage of the building extended forward to the line of the pillars. This was a crafty way of extending one's property further into the street. Titus Wilson's shop, adjacent to the Fleece, is an example. The present shop front dates from the early nineteenth century, replacing an earlier arcaded front. The Woolpack (l) was rebuilt in 1791. The high arch leading to the rear of the inn was designed to admit laden wagons.

Old Shambles Yard next to the Fleece was the yard in which butchers operated into the early nineteenth century. The bottom part of the yard is one of the least altered and most attractive in Kendal with two lines of limestone-built cottages and a view of the houses of Fellside above. The attractive Georgian-fronted building at the top of the yard was originally an inn, appropriately named the Butcher's Arms.

In the main street between Finkle Street and the Market Place is

Farrer's tea and coffee shop (m). It is a good example of a late eighteenth/nineteenth-century shopfront with Georgian bow windows. The building itself dates from the mid- seventeenth century and you can see many of the old beams exposed inside. It was originally yet another inn but was converted to a shop and coffee house in 1819 and has retained this function ever since.

THE MARKET PLACE

Kendal's Market Place (n) is rather small and on market days in the past trading would have spilled out into the main street to north and south. The Globe Hotel is another of Kendal's traditional inns. The facade, with its jettied first floor, is fairly modern but has been built in a similar style to the original one. Adjoining it is the Market Hall (o), built in 1887. It replaced an earlier one which stood in the middle of the Market Place at the Stricklandgate end and had a chapel above with a corn and butter market below.

New Shambles
Adjoining the Market Place on the south side is the New Shambles (p), dating from the early nineteenth century and well preserved. Two rows of single-storey shops with overhanging roofs (one of them still a butchers) are separated by a narrow cobbled lane. The neat shops which occupy the site today give a poor impression of the smell and mess that were a feature of it in earlier times: the New Shambles was deliberately laid out on a slope to allow the blood and offal to drain away.

Return to the Market Place and the main street: cross to Entry Lane (q) on the opposite side of the main street.

FELLSIDE

Entry Lane (q) is an old access way through the medieval burgage plots to the open fell above. It leads to the district of Kendal known, appropriately, as Fellside. From the sixteenth century onwards Fellside (r) developed as a suburb of the town, becoming the artisan's and workman's quarter, a separate and distinctive tight-knit community. It was built up in an irregular, unplanned way among a maze of lanes, steps and alleys. Many of the textile workers who lived here were nonconformists and there were a number of chapels in this district as well as a great many pubs. Because of poor housing, intense overcrowding, bad sanitation and a limited water supply the area was a health hazard in the nineteenth century and a breeding ground for diseases such as cholera. Many of the poorer buildings were cleared out in the early 1960s. The area has been opened out and much new housing inserted, but in places it still retains a good deal of its original character.

Return to the main street and continue north along Stricklandgate.

STRICKLANDGATE

Black Hall (s) is an imposing building, built in the sixteenth century as a town house. In the early nineteenth century the massive round chimney stacks, in traditional Westmorland style, were added. The building then became a brush factory, using local pigs' bristles. The sign above the building recalls this.

The whitewashed house a few doors down (t) which today functions as a YWCA centre is dated 1724 and is a good example of an early Georgian town house. Known as Prince Charlie's House, it was occupied briefly by the Young Pretender during the rebellion of 1745.

Return to the Market Place and walk through it into Stramongate.

STRAMONGATE

The far end of the Market Place drops steeply down Branthwaite Brow to the top of Stramongate. A short way down is Henry Roberts' bookshop. It occupies a sixteenth-century house which was formerly used by the Bellingham family, notable Westmorland landowners, as a town house (u). It is one of the oldest buildings in Kendal which is still in use and emphasises the importance of the town as a social centre for local landed gentry in the days when travel from Cumbria to larger provincial centres or London was still slow and difficult.

Walk down Stramongate and across the river (v) to Wildman Street.

The Castle Dairy on the left hand side of the street (w) is the oldest house in Kendal. It was built in the fourteenth century as a hall-house, open to the rafters with a central fireplace and a smoke hole. At each end of the hall was a wing, one to provide private apartments for the occupants, the other housing the kitchen and storage facilities. The hall

73

was rebuilt in 1564 and a fireplace with a massive chimney stack was inserted. The exterior of the house has not been greatly altered since this time.

Selected References

Curwen, J (1900) *Kirkbie Kendal*. Titus Wilson, Kendal
Nicholls, A R (1986) *Kendal town trail*. Westmorland Gazette, Kendal
Nicholson,T (1861) *The annals of Kendal*. Titus Wilson, Kendal

7 RAVENSTONEDALE AND CROSBY GARRETT FELL: SETTLEMENT AND AGRICULTURE IN A MARGINAL UPLAND AREA

Ian Whyte
(University of Lancaster)

Outline: a study of the evidence for changes in settlement patterns and land-use in a marginal upland area from later prehistoric times until the nineteenth century.

Starting and finishing point: car park beside the school in Ravenstonedale (GR 722042).

Distance: about 5 km.

Route: walking, sometimes over rough or wet ground. You will need stout footwear and waterproofs.

Time needed: 2 to 3 hours.

Maps needed: OS 1:25,000 sheet NY 70; 1:50,000 sheet 91.

INTRODUCTION

In the core areas of rural settlement and agriculture, such as the lowlands of the Eden Valley, traces of early human occupation are largely obliterated by later activity although features like settlements and field systems may show up on aerial photographs as crop marks. In more marginal areas, such as the limestone plateaus which lie between the Eden Valley and the Howgill Fells, human occupation in recent centuries has been less intensive and more intermittent.

As a result it is in such areas that traces of activity from earlier times are most likely to survive on a large scale. The plateau between Shap and Kirkby Stephen, much of which lies at altitudes of between 300 and 350 m, has always been marginal but at certain periods, when climatic conditions were more favourable or population pressure more intense, settlement and agriculture have expanded on to its thin, fragile limestone soils.

There is evidence of human activity in early prehistoric times in the form of a Neolithic long cairn at Rayseat (GR 684073) and Bronze Age cairns (eg at GR 692085). These remains are sporadic but an entire landscape survives from late prehistoric times, with settlements, arable fields, enclosures for livestock, boundary dykes and access ways, covering an area of several square km. There are also many traces of settlement and human activity from medieval and later times.

EXCURSION

RAVENSTONEDALE

To start with the more recent and more familiar aspects of the landscape, the walk begins in Ravenstonedale village. Park in the car park beside the school (a on Figure 7).

The parishes in this area tend to focus on nucleated villages, like Ravenstonedale, situated adjacent to a nucleus of good agricultural land. Further away from the villages are larger areas of good quality pasture and, above about 300 m, extensive areas of rough pasture. Like most of the medieval and post-medieval settlements in the area, the village of Ravenstonedale is sited in a relatively sheltered location - in this case strung out across a low ridge between the Scandal and Lockholme Becks. It is likely that there has been a settlement here from at least the eleventh century and possibly for some centuries before this.

Church

The church (b) is largely Georgian, having been rebuilt in 1744. The internal fittings, - with the fine three-decker pulpit, the carved pews facing inwards, and the gallery for the more notable parishioners - is all pure eighteenth century but there are indications that the basic fabric of the building is much older. The south porch appears to date from around 1200 and the chancel arch from around the same time. On the north side of the church you can see a series of excavated foundations which may have been the accommodation for a small cell of Gilbertine monks; Watton Priory on Humberside was granted the valley in 1336. Adjoining the church is the school, again possibly on the site of an earlier building. The present one was built in 1873 by a local landowner.

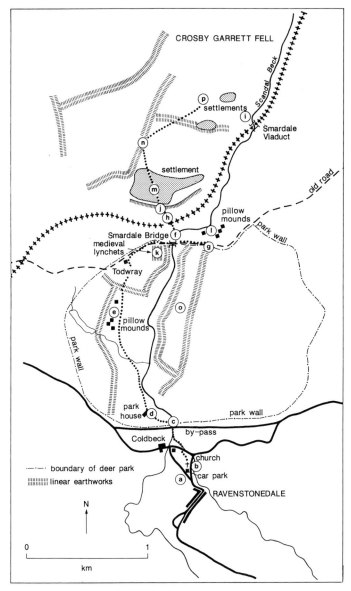

CROSBY GARRETT FELL

settlements

Smardale Viaduct

old road

settlement

park wall

pillow mounds

Smardale Bridge
medieval lynchets

Todwray

pillow mounds

park wall

o

park house

park wall

by-pass

Coldbeck

church

car park

RAVENSTONEDALE

—·—·— boundary of deer park
⫴⫴⫴⫴⫴ linear earthworks

N

0   1
km

Figure 7. The excursion route

The Village

The church stands between the main village and the outlying hamlets of Coldbeck and Garshill. In the village one of the oldest buildings is the seventeenth-century house beside the Black Swan Hotel. It preserves a fine spinning gallery, which provided a well-lit but sheltered place for women to spin woollen yarn, indicating the pastoral orientation of the economy before the era of agricultural improvement. The other houses and cottages range from eighteenth century to modern in date but the almost universal use of the grey local limestone gives the main street great homogeneity despite the differences in architectural style.

In the eighteenth and nineteenth century the inhabitants of remote valleys like Ravenstonedale were often very independent in their religious beliefs. You can see two non-conformist chapels in the village, one a Wesleyan chapel dating from 1839, the other belonging to the United Reformed Church.

Note that many garden walls are decorated with fretted blocks removed from limestone pavements. Although greater efforts are now being made to preserve some of the best limestone pavements in the North West many have been destroyed by this fashion (see Excursion 8).

THE VALLEY OF THE SCANDAL BECK

From the village walk north to the King's Head inn and take the track which continues north, under the modern by-pass, along the west side of Scandal Beck.

Deer Park

The bridge carrying the by-pass interrupts a stone wall which is marked as "Park Wall" on the 1:25,000 scale OS map (c). Note also the names Park House for the farm ahead of you (d) and Park Hill to the east of the beck.

This wall is the boundary of Ravenstonedale deer park; you will see a better-preserved section of it further on. Deer parks were common in late-medieval and early-modern England. As the open areas of royal hunting forests and private chases were gradually encroached upon and colonised during the medieval population expansion, deer were increasingly confined to these custom-built parks. Most of them were enclosed by a ditch and outer bank surmounted with a palisade. These earthworks are rarely very obvious features in the landscape today although the boundaries of deer parks are often identifyable among later field patterns.

The deer park here, however, was enclosed by a substantial stone wall which is still a prominent feature up to 3 m high in places. It was enclosed for the first Lord Wharton in 1560 and covered an area of over 200 ha. It can be traced on the ground as a circular enclosure whose wall is more crudely built than the later enclosure walls dating from the nineteenth century. Its stones also have a more varied range of lichen and moss species than the surrounding later walls. Because it was a deer preserve no cultivation was allowed inside the park and as a result many earlier features were preserved which have probably been obliterated in the surrounding fields by prolonged ploughing.

The right of way continues along the west side of the Scandal Beck below Park House (d), on a faint and in places muddy path. An easier way is to go through the farmyard at Park House (with permission). Follow the track beyond as it crosses a tributary stream and climbs up the slope beyond.

Pillow Mounds
As you come towards the gate at the top of the hill look to your left. On the hillside between the track and the plantation of trees around the small reservoir you should be able to see two low rectangular mounds (e). There is another closer to the track a little further on. These features are known as 'pillow mounds'; they are rectangular earthen mounds up to 25 m long, 5 m wide, over 1 m high, and surrounded by a shallow ditch. They are marked on the O.S. map, rather picturesquely, as "giants' graves".

The function and date of pillow mounds have been debated and they are often confused with prehistoric burial mounds. However, they are generally found in association with medieval and later deer parks and are thought to be the remains of rabbit warrens. This is only a theory though and they form a class of landscape feature which is particularly puzzling.

Follow the track through fields over the top of the hill, past the building in the small plantation of conifers. Go through the gate in the wall immediately beyond and follow the track which runs parallel to the far side of the wall eastwards down to Smardale Bridge (f).

Smardale Bridge

The bridge is more substantially built than you might expect for such a minor field track, but if you look more closely you can see indications that this route has once been more important than it is today. The track down which you have come, westward of Smardale Bridge, is deeply hollowed by the passage of traffic. To the east the track climbs up the hillside between two stone walls and you can see evidence of use in the rutted ground between the walls. If you follow the route on the 1:25,000 OS map, you will see that the line of this track continues eastwards across Smardale Fell to join the modern road near Kirkby Stephen.

Until well into the nineteenth century this was the main route from Kendal to Barnard Castle in Teesdale by the pass of Stainmore. Much of the traffic took the form of strings of pack horses which were better able to negotiate the steep gradients than carts. You will see that although Smardale Bridge is quite substantial it is only just wide enough for a cart. In the late eighteenth and early nineteenth century coal from the thin seams that outcrop around Stainmore was brought in by packhorse over this road to allow the burning of lime for use as an agricultural fertilizer. Some of the lime was used locally but much of it was sent down into the Eden Valley to areas which did not have any local limestone.

To the east of Smardale Bridge the dyke which forms the southern edge of the road is the boundary wall of Ravenstonedale deer park (g). Although it is no higher than other walls, if you look closely you will see that it is more massive and more roughly constructed than the later enclosure dykes in this area.

Railway

From the west end of the bridge follow the path that climbs up towards the disused railway track (h). This thinly populated area is crossed by two railway lines. The Lancaster to Carlisle railway via Tebay was opened as early as 1846 but the South Durham and Lancashire Union Railway, the branch line from Tebay over Stainmore into Yorkshire, a less significant route, was not opened until 1861. The difficulties of building a railway through this hilly terrain were considerable and if you follow the line for a short way northwards you will have a good view of the Smardale viaduct (i), one of the most impressive pieces of railway engineering in the North.

The Settle to Carlisle railway (see Excursion 10), which was opened in 1875, runs just over 1.5 km to the north-east, past Crosby Garrett village. This line, which is still in use in 1989 but under threat of closure partly because of high maintenance costs, involved even greater engineering problems - the Scandal Beck is crossed by another impressive viaduct which requred over 60,000 tons of stone to construct, with a long tunnel through the hillside immediately beyond.

Viewpoint
Cross the railway by the bridge (GR 723062) and climb up to the thin limestone scar (j) that forms the skyline. You now have a good view of the valley below. On the east side of the valley, a short distance above the stream, you should be able to see a turf-covered bank running along the hillside. Two similar earthworks run parallel with it, one on the opposite side of the beck at the same level, the other higher up the hill on the same side. These form part of a prehistoric dyke system which may have been related to the settlement on Crosby Garrett Fell above you. The dykes are better preserved and more clearly defined within the deer park than outside it because cultivation within the park was restricted. Their significance and function will be discussed below.

Strip Lynchets
To the west of Smardale Bridge, on the slope rising to the south of the old road, you should be able to see a set of faint parallel terraces (k) running across the hillside with a boundary running parallel to them further upslope and another one at right angles running downslope through the set of features. The horizontal features are cultivation terraces or "strip lynchets". They probably date from medieval times, representing cultivation which occurred before the deer park was constructed. You can also see two prominent pillow mounds to the east of Smardale Bridge below the line of the old road (l).

CROSBY GARRETT FELL: A PREHISTORIC LANDSCAPE

On the plateau between the limestone scar overlooking the railway and a high limestone wall to the north are the remains of an extensive settlement (m) and field system. The boundaries of the fields and settlement sites take the form of low grassy banks, sometimes with traces of stone foundation showing through.

Do not be disappointed if you cannot make very much out at first - a good deal depends on the quality of the lighting at the time of your visit and even in good conditions it may take you some time to accustom your eyes to identifying the small-scale contrasts in relief and vegetation which distinguish the settlement sites and fields. The site is much clearer from the air. It is one of a large number of similar settlements and dyke systems on these fells.

Prehistoric Settlement

The prehistoric settlement sites in this area have been known since the nineteenth century and excavations during the 1930s showed that they related to the Romano-British period. It was originally thought that this had been the main focus of settlement in the late Iron Age. It was believed that late prehistoric communities did not have the technology to clear the dense woodlands of the Eden Valley or cultivate the heavy clay soils and were confined, as a result, to the higher ground on thin, easily-worked limestone soils.

Aerial survey during the 1970s has shown, however, that the Eden lowlands were in fact densely colonised and that they were the main area of late prehistoric settlement. Expansion on to the marginal land of the limestone fells was late and relatively short-lived, occurring during the Roman occupation. Climatic conditions seem to have been favourable, encouraging both the build-up of population and the colonisation of marginal land. Peaceful conditions under the Roman occupation may have led to population growth and the needs of the garrisons of the Roman forts in the Eden Valley for grain may have encouraged an expansion of cultivation.

The limestone plateau was densely settled by a series of communities occupying small nucleated settlements or "villages". The one on Crosby Garrett Fell is one of the largest. The economy was mainly a pastoral one but some settlements had small areas of arable fields close to them. The rest of the land below about 300 m was parcelled out into larger enclosures for regulating livestock.

Boundary Dykes

A major boundary dyke divided off the better-quality enclosed pasture below 300 m from the open rough pasture above. This dyke (n) can be traced running north eastwards to the west of the settlement, as shown on the map. Linear earthworks were sometimes built to divide off the areas beside the streams, which may still have been thickly wooded, from the blocks of enclosed pasture on the hillside above. The two lower dykes (o) which face each other across the Scandal Beck to the south of Smardale Bridge are an example. At around 275-300 m a boundary dyke divided the enclosed pasture from the rough moorland above. In this case the boundary runs along the low crest to the west of the settlement.

The remains of the field boundaries continue to the north beyond the high limestone wall (which should be climbed only with the greatest of care). Further smaller settlement sites (p) are located at GR 723069, on the crestline of a low spur running eastward towards the viaduct, and at GR 725072.

Later Cultivation

If you examine the ground closely you should be able to find some natural sink holes in the limestone and also a number of small workings where stone has been quarried for dyke-making. Under certain light conditions you may be able to see that much of the moorland vegetation has a faint ribbed effect. Again this shows up more clearly on aerial photographs.

These are the remains of cultivation from the late eighteenth and early nineteenth century. During the Napoleonic Wars, when grain prices were high, a lot of marginal land was taken into cultivation on a temporary basis and sown with wheat, oats, turnips and sown grasses. The new turnpike roads made it easier to transport grain out of the area to lowland market centres. During the Crimean War corn growers in this area also did well but competition from cheap grain from the American prairies in the 1870s caused large-scale cultivation to be abandoned in favour of livestock rearing. This emphasises the problems of landscape interpretation in an area like this; features from widely differing periods may be juxtaposed.

Abandonment

Settlement in this area survived the withdrawal of the Roman legions in the early fifth century. Society reverted to its pre-Roman tribal organisation but population levels continued to remain high. However, there are signs that the limestone plateaus were beginning to be abandoned, perhaps as a result of progressive deterioration of the land

and soil erosion. There was a progressive concentration of settlement in the valleys at sites like Crosby Garrett village to the north.

The name "Crosby" (the settlement with the cross) was given by Norse settlers, probably during the tenth century, but it suggests that there was already a settlement here with a religious focus. The modern parish church at Crosby Garrett has traces of masonry going back to Anglo-Saxon times.

Some of the dyke systems on the fellsides show signs of later re-organisation to enclose smaller perimeters. Abandonment may have begun before the collapse of Roman rule but it was only in the late sixth century that the area was fully deserted - perhaps as the result of major epidemics which reduced population and allowed the survivors to concentrate lower in the valleys.

The existence of foundations of a number of isolated rectangular buildings overlying the Romano-British hut foundations has caused speculation. An example can be seen to the north at GR 724080. Some people have suggested that these are farmsteads relating to the Scandinavian settlement when the uplands were re-occupied by pastoral farmers. It is possible, however, that these structures are shieling huts or shepherds' shelters from medieval times or later.

RETURN TO RAVENSTONEDALE

Return to Smardale Bridge and follow the east side of the stream back towards Ravenstonedale. The footpath runs along the top of one of the linear earthworks for much of the way back to Park House and you can see how it has been eroded in some places by small tributaries but is well preserved in others.

Selected References

Higham, N (1986) *The Northern Counties to AD 1000*. Longman

Whyte, I (1989) The Dark Ages. In W Rollinson (editor) *The Lake District*. David and Charles

8   LIMESTONE PAVEMENTS IN THE MORECAMBE BAY AREA

Greg Lewis
(University of Lancaster)

Outline: a study of the diversity of vegetation , form, structure and morphology of three limestone pavements to the east of Morecambe Bay - Gait Barrows, Farleton Knott and Hutton Roof Crags.

Starting point: the sites can be visited in any order; it may be convenient to start at Gait Barrows (GR 483774).

Distance: the distance by road around all three sites is 12 km.

Route: drive between sites, and walk within them. The pavements are all easily accessible by minibus.

Caution: field-work on these limestone pavements must be properly planned. When wet, the pavements are very slippy and they should be approached with due care. Also it is easy to become disorientated, especially if visibility is poor; a map and compass are essential.

Time needed: ideally a whole day to visit Gait Barrows and one other site.

Maps needed: OS 1:50,000 Kendal and Morecambe Landranger Map 97.

INTRODUCTION

The limestone scenery to the east of Morecambe Bay contains some fine and morphologically diverse pavements. They were exposed when Lake District ice swept across the limestone outcrops removing the soil cover. The consequent differential plucking and abrasion of these outcrops produced a characteristic stepped landscape of limestone pavements separated by cliffs. Good examples of this topography occur at Farleton Knott and Hutton Roof Crags (Figure 8a).

Compared with their counterparts in the Craven area (40 km to the east; see Excursion 9) these pavements are relatively unvisited by field excursions. They provide an interesting contrast in that they are at a relatively low altitude. This makes them usable for a variety of

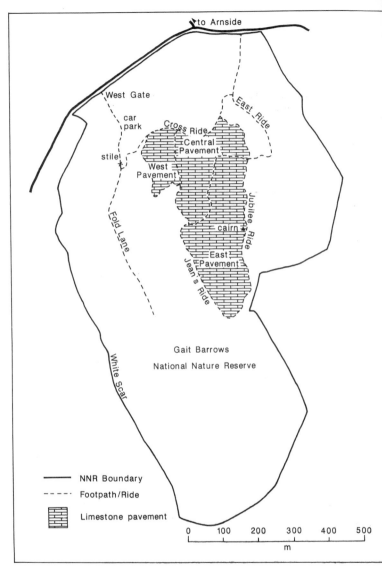

Figure 8a. Gait Barrows National Nature Reserve

fieldwork themes, principally studies of pavement morphology and vegetation. The features of interest at three specific sites are described here: Gait Barrows, Farleton Knott and Hutton Roof Crags (Figure 8b).

They are relatively close together, so an excursion based on a visit to Gait Barrows and one of the other two sites would provide an ideal introduction to the diversity of form, structure and morphology of pavements in this area. The journey between the two areas also allows a visual study of human use of limestone through quarrying, dry stone walling and house decoration.

EXCURSION

SITE 1 GAIT BARROWS

Gait Barrows is a National Nature Reserve administered by the Nature Conservancy Council (NCC). The site (Figure 8a) has its own car park but you need a permit to visit this Nature Reserve (see Appendix for details). The entrance to the Reserve is on the road from Waterslack (GR 473763). Drive about 2 km northwards, then turn right into a concealed entrance (with a gate), marked "NCC property". (If you have reached the junction for Arnside (B5282) then you have overshot the entrance by 200 m!) Go through the gate and the car-park is on your left about 100 m down the track.

The flora and geomorphology of this site are of great interest. Ratcliffe (1977) describes it as "the most important single example of limestone pavement in Great Britain".

The reserve covers about 70 ha, of which about 5 ha is intact pavement, surrounded by coppiced woodland. To the south of the pavement lies wet and dry meadowland.

The morphology of the pavement itself is very interesting, and you can see a variety of surface solution features (karren) on a series of blocks and fissures (clints and grikes).

To reach the pavement from the car park follow Fold Lane away from the West Gate until you reach a stone stile. Immediately after the stile turn left up a track marked 'No Entry without a Permit'; continue for about 100 m until you can see the pavement on your right. Find an appropriate break in the trees and move onto the pavement - be careful because many grikes are concealed by grasses so walk on the bare clint tops. You are now on the west pavement which shows extensive damage by man as you walk eastwards across it.

Limestone Removal

Goldie (1986) lists five geomorphological changes caused by clint removal, and evidence of each can be found in this area of Gait Barrows. First, there is a lowering of the pavement level, and a morphological change to longer, wider clints and shallower grikes. Secondly, the rock surface is rougher than surrounding unaffected pavement areas. Thirdly, there is the residue of removal, small debris on the surface and infilling of the grikes. The fourth change is the isolated and disorientated clints that have not been removed from the site after excavation. Finally, there is the reduction of lichen growth on freshly damaged pavements. A study of this growth can be used to date the damaged areas.

Pavement Morphology

Moving due east onto the central pavement you come to a magnificent area of massively bedded pavement, which is characterized by a sequence of huge, horizontally bedded clints. Spend some time here to examine the clint-grike relationship and its associated surface drainage features and extensive solution hollows (kamenitzas). This area may also be contrasted to the subsequent east pavement which varies both in surface morphology and structure. To reach the east pavement walk south-east; the eastern edge is bounded by a grassy path, Jubilee Ride. A sensible place to stop is the cairn - an easily identifiable feature mid-way along the pavement.

From here you can see the structural change to a sloping pavement, more obvious to the south. Immediately to the east is a horizontal exposure of limestone bedding planes; here you can examine the lithology and structure, (eg bed thickness) of the rock.

This is perhaps the easiest and best section of the pavement for group fieldwork exercises. A number of groups can be spread out along the whole section from the near horizontal northern end to the more steeply sloping southern fringes. This provides contrasting surface morphology along a change in slope. A well defined clint-grike system is present throughout this section, with an intricate surface drainage system of rounded runnels (rundkarren) comprehensively covering the clint surfaces. Sharp edged runnels (rillenkarren) and glacial erratics can also be found locally.

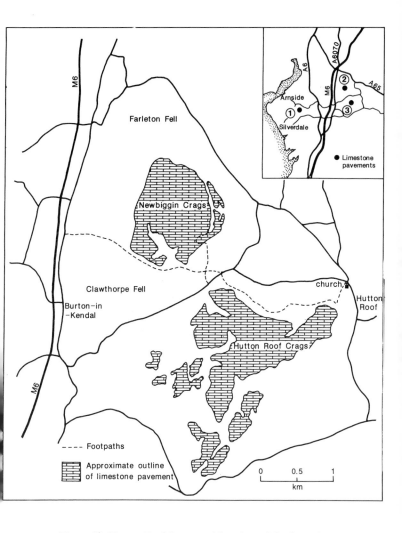

Figure 8b. Hutton Roof Crags, and locations of the three sites.

SITE 2 FARLETON KNOTT

Farleton Knott is approached from Clawthorpe (GR 532775) along a narrow unclassified road. Park on the grassy verge at the brow of the hill (GR 552788), and follow the footpath on to the pavement.

The site lies about 8 km north-east of Gait Barrows (Figure 8b) It is more exposed, rising to about 240m OD (Gait Barrows is only 20m OD). Fieldwork can be concentrated at three particular areas at this site.

At the northern end is an area known as Farleton Fell (GR 542802). Here is an expanse of horizontal pavement, which in parts has been weathered out into a honeycomb pattern giving a lumpy appearance to the clints. Also there is an area of sloping pavement where smooth surfaces with small steps (trittkarren) can be identified.

To the south-west is Holme Park Fell (GR 542792). This is an easily accessible area of relatively undissected pavement with wide clints and narrow grikes. This accessibility has encouraged much removal of limestone in the past, which is clearly evident here.

On the eastern edge of the limestone exposure is Newbiggin Crags (GR 549795). This is an area of massive clints with a similar honeycombing to that at Farleton Fell. The "textbook" geometric patterns of limestone pavements are well illustrated here. Again there is much evidence of clint top removal by man in the recent past.

SITE 3 HUTTON ROOF

Park in the lay-by opposite the church (GR 568787), 0.5 km to the north of the village. Follow the footpath, starting at the corner of the road junction, up on to the pavement area.

Hutton Roof (GR 560780) lies about 4 km to the south-east of Farleton Knott (Figure 8b). Both sites have a similar altitude and exposure. Hutton Roof also has distinctly different areas of pavement in close proximity to one another. These include steeply sloping pavement, areas of gently dipping limestone with well developed runnel systems, and almost horizontal areas characterized by massive clints. This area is extensively covered by bracken and shrub and it provides a contrast to Farleton Knott and indeed Gait Barrows.

CONCLUSION

The Morecambe Bay area is rich in limestone scenery and it contains some particularly noteworthy pavements. The contrasts between the low-level Gait Barrows, and Farleton Knot and Hutton Roof at higher elevations provide a wide variety of pavement structure and morphological variations. Any one site may provide a full days fieldwork but an ideal introductory visit would include a visit to Gait Barrows and one of the other two sites.

Apart from morphological studies, process studies could be attempted (see Paterson and Chambers 1982). The site also provides ample scope for a calcareous vegetation study (see Ward and Evans 1976) possibly linked to the altitudinal change between sites.

Selected References

Goldie, H S (1981) Morphometry of the limestone pavements of Farleton Knott (Cumbria, England). *Transactions of the British Cve Research Association* 8; (4) 207-224

Goldie, H S (1986) Human influence on landforms: the case of lime stone pavements. 515 - 540 in Paterson and Sweeting

Johnson, R H (Editor) (1985) *The geomorphology of north-west England*. Manchester University Press

Paterson, K and W Chambers (1982) Techniques for the study of limestone pavements. *Teaching Geography* 8; 3-9

Paterson, K and M M Sweeting (Editors) (1986) *New directions in Karst*. Geo Books

Ratcliffe, D A (1977) *A nature conservation review, Volume 2*. Cambridge University Press

Rose, L and P Vincent (1986) The Kamenitzas of Gait Barrows National Nature Reserve, North Lancashire, England. 473 - 496 in Paterson and Sweeting

Trudgill, S T (1985) *Limestone geomorphology*. Longman

Trudgill, S T, R W Crabtree and PJC Walker (1979) The age of exposure of limestone pavements - a pilot lichenometric study in Co Clare, Eire. *Transactions of the British Cave Research Association* 6; 10-14

Vincent, P (1985) Quaternary geomorphology of the southern Lake District and Morecambe Bay area. 159-177 in Johnson

Ward, S D and D F Evans (1976) Conservation assessment of British

Limestone pavements based on floristic criteria. *Biological Conservation* 9, 217-233

Ward, S D and D F Evans (1976) *Limestone pavements: A botanical survey and conservation assessment based on botanical criteria.* Institute of Terrestrial Ecology

Appendix

Permission to visit Gait Barrows NNR can be arranged through the Regional Office (NCC - North West Region), Blackwell, Bowness, Bowness-on-Windermere, Cumbria, LA23 3JR.

9 GEOLOGY AND LANDFORMS IN THE INGLEBOROUGH AREA

Frank H Nicholson
(Liverpol Polytechnic)

Outline: description of a series of locations or routes in the Ingleborough area which are useful in the study of karst (limestone) and glacial geomorphology. Some sites can be used to study soil and vegetation in this upland area within the Yorkshire Dales National Park.

Starting point: Helwith Bridge (GR 814697).

Finishing point: White Scar Cave (GR 713745).

Distance: 21 km by road, and a further 8.5 km walking.

Route: travel by car, transit or coach between sites: on foot within sites. Stout footwear and waterproof clothing are essential.

Time needed: 5 to 6 hours.

Maps needed: OS 1:25,000 Outdoor Leisure, Sheet 2 Yorkshire Dales, Western Area.

Permission: permission in advance is needed to visit the two nature reserves described here (details in Appendix).

INTRODUCTION TO THE INGLEBOROUGH AREA

Geology

Much of Ingleborough is Carboniferous rock, with the Great Scar Limestone (a typical Carboniferous Limestone) overlain by the Yoredale Series (Figure 9b). Pre-Carboniferous rocks are exposed in the valleys, especially Greta Dale and Ribblesdale. They include the probably Pre-Cambrian Ingletonian and also Ordovician and Silurian slates and coarse sandstones. A bed of coarse arkose (feldspathic gritstone) is quarried and sold as Ingleton Granite - a good example of how "trade" descriptions of rocks are much broader than strict geological definitions. The Pre-Carboniferous rocks were strongly folded and then eroded so that there is an obvious angular unconformity between them and the overlying Carboniferous.

The Carboniferous Limestone varies between 100 and 200 m in thickness on Ingleborough. As is usual with Carboniferous Limestone

93

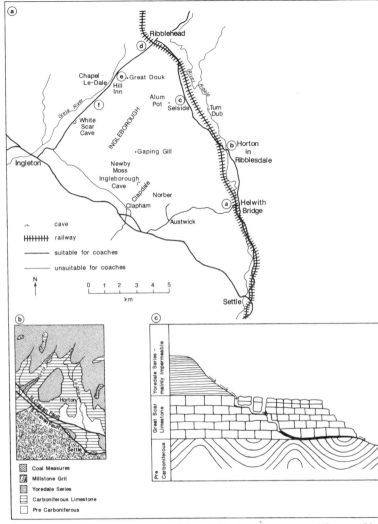

Figure 9. The excursion route (a) with details of the geology of the area (b) and a typical geological cross-section (c)

the porous permeability is negligible whereas fissure permeability is very important. Initial movement of water through the limestone is via bedding planes, joints and faults, and the subsequent development of cave systems and limestone pavement is strongly influenced by them.

The Yoredale Series overlying the Great Scar Limestone (Figure 9c) consists of repeated rhythms or cycles of limestone, shale and sandstone. They were deposited in a subsiding deltaic area in which sediments were accumulating; the associated variations of water depth were the main control on type of sediment deposited. Up to nine cycles of sedimentation have been recognised in this area. Millstone grit overlies the Yoredale Series on nearby Penyghent and Whernside, but not on Ingleborough.

The Quaternary deposits, which complete the succession, are mainly till, with some fluvioglacial deposits, alluvium and colluvium (slope deposits, including scree).

Glacial Features
The whole area has been glaciated and even the summit of Ingleborough was beneath the ice in the last (Devensian) glaciation. However, in the retreat stages Ingleborough and other nearby higher hills would have been nunataks (peaks rising above the surrounding ice). The ice has left obvious evidence of its presence including extensive till deposits, drumlins, glacial trough form to the dales, erratics and fluvioglacial deposits. No 'exotic' erratics are found in the glacial deposits, which suggests that it formed relatively locally. The local centre of ice dispersion is thought to be about 20 km north of Ingleborough summit.

Obvious evidence of the direction of ice movement is seen in the drumlin field at Ribblehead (stop 4 on Figure 9a). Here the drumlins align north-east to south-west, indicating ice flow south-westwards down the Greta Valley towards Chapel-le-Dale. A little to the south, in the Upper Ribble Valley, the drumlins are aligned north-south, indicating ice flow down Ribblesdale. The deepest moraine deposits are on the south-west side of Ingleborough in the Newby Moss area, again indicating a southerly or southwesterly ice movement.

Karst Features
Karst features in the area are abundant: sinking streams, resurgences (risings), caves, closed surface depressions, limestone pavements and

so on. Most of the caves form where streams collect on the impermeable Yoredale beds and then disappear underground soon after reaching the limestone (Figure 9c). Most commonly the water resurges at the base of the Great Scar Limestone where the impermeable Pre-Carboniferous rocks force the water back to the surface. A series of major sinkpoints some distance out from the current shale edge may indicate the position of the shale edge before the last glaciation. The caves of the area show forms indicating cave development both above (vadose) and below (phreatic) the water table (Figure 9c).

Examples of various types of closed surface depression can also be seen: solution, collapse and stream sink depressions. Closed depressions are not as numerous as in some unglaciated areas of karst in the UK, but there is a range to be seen, including some spectacular large depressions.

Limestone Pavements are exceptionally well developed in this area. It should be remembered that strong pavement development in the UK is normally a glacio-karst feature, a vital factor being the action of ice in stripping soil and weathered rock leaving a relatively clean bedding surface (see Excursion 8).

A wide range of pavement types can be seen. Clints and grykes are present in a range of sizes and with a range of forms on the clints. Common forms include: flat bottomed, steep sided kamenitzas or solution pans; shallow true runnels (often dendritic and normally deepening progressively down channel or thalweg) and undercut runnels (with baglike cross-sections and usually not a progressively deepening thalweg). The true runnels are typical of bare rock pavement development. The bag shaped runnels are characteristic of partly covered pavement, with plants growing in the runnels and encouraging more solution. Organic activity also plays its role in runnel development.

The range of forms on what is clearly the same bed is also striking, including the presence of some flat almost featureless pavement. We should not ignore "shillow" (a Yorkshire term for pavement broken into irregular fragments), where solution and frost action are probably working in cooperation. The influence of changes of vegetation has been debated, although there is little doubt that the soil cover has been reduced in parts of this area and some of the more generally rounded pavement forms were almost certainly developed under soil which has now been eroded.

EXCURSION

STOP 1 UPPER RIBBLESDALE

The excursion starts 6 km north of Settle (at GR 814697), near Helwith Bridge (Figure 9a). From here the angular unconformity between Carboniferous rocks (almost horizontal near the top of the slope) and Pre-Carboniferous rocks can be clearly seen to the west. Note that the unconformity is higher here than elsewhere on Ingleborough.

STOP 2 HORTON

Driving northwards from stop 1, you will get a good view of quarrying on the west side of Ribblesdale. The compatibility of quarrying with the aims of a National Park can be considered, though where else is this rock to be obtained when the National Park is so large? Are these quarries and associated buildings well designed, and if not how might they be improved? Are these fresh rock faces really out of place in a rocky valley? The car park in Horton (GR 808726) is a good place to briefly consider such issues; it also provides a toilet stop.

Continue northwards and note that the valley bottom and lower sides are still in Pre-Carboniferous rocks and the upper slopes are Carboniferous. Some drumlins can be seen aligned parallel to the valley.

STOP 3 ALUM POT AREA (Walk A)

A major stop for about two hours is suggested immediately north of Selside (GR 783757) (stop 3 on Figure 9a), where a walled track leads west-south-west on the first bend north of the large group of farm buildings. The track is heavily used by vehicles for potholing and outdoor education; it is suitable for parking minibuses but not a coach. The track is rough, so park near the main road. Access to the Alum Pot area is allowed on payment of a small fee (around 10p per head - telephone Horton in Ribblesdale 07296 367 to check).

The visit to this site allows study of a range of karst features and hydrological relationships. The regolith can also be studied here.

Walk up the walled track to the stile and gate (point a on Figure 9d). Note that all caves are dangerous: do NOT enter any caves without proper equipment and an appropriate number of experienced

97

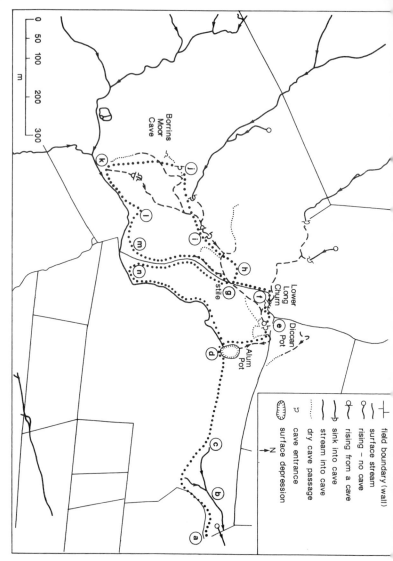

Figure 9d. Features of the walk around Alum Pot.

leaders with knowledge of the area.

Walk up the valley to point b, on the bend in the track overlooking the small main valley running up the hill and a minor side valley with the track being round it. This is a good place to examine the terrain. The exact position and amount of water flow varies with recent weather but the streams and springs are never as shown on the Ordinance Survey maps! Also look at the low bank left (SE) of the track where 0.3 m of till is exposed. Note the wide range of particle sizes, almost all local Carboniferous Limestone fragments with occasional striated fragments.

Continue walking up the slope past the spring (c), to Alum Pot (d). This is a very spectacular open pothole, about 50 m deep, which can be safely viewed from the wire fence at the south (lowest) end. Do not go inside the boundary wall (the stile is for properly equipped cavers only). Do not throw stones into the pothole - cavers have been killed here due to careless visitors throwing in stones, and there are frequently cavers below. The resurgence of water from Alum Pot is at Turn Dub (GR 797748), 2.5 km away (Figure 9a), having crossed under the River Ribble.

Proceed from Alum Pot to Diccan Pot (e). Note the depressions along the way, which are most frequent when near the cave passage below. At Diccan Pot the cave roof has broken down, exposing a short section of cave stream and a cave entrance up and downstream. Continue walking up slope to point f (in a small fenced enclosure), where there is another cave roof breakthrough. This occurred at a stream junction, though the modern cave stream has found a new route a few metres to the south (the main stream can usually be heard but not seen). This is the 'Lower Long Churn' cave entrance - the upper entrance to Long Churn Cave will be seen later.

Walk along to the stile (g) then turn right to point h on the limestone pavement. Cross the pavement (with care) to point i, where there are a few trees growing in the depression. There is a short section of unroofed cave passage, with Long Churn Cave downstream and the lower entrance to Borrins Moor Cave upstream (yes, cavers do go in here!). Note that although this has a new cave name it is obviously still the same original cave 'accidentally' exposed to daylight. From here walk to the main (and more comfortable) entrance to Borrins Moor Cave (j). This is in a small hollow at the downslope end of a small dry ravine. Note that to the south you can see a line of depressions. There is a section of cave below that is related to these depressions and it is possible for persons in these depressions to speak to someone in the cave passage below. From here walk due south to Alum Pot Beck (k), across the limestone pavement (in which there are several small cave entrances).

Stop to consider the apparently peculiar behaviour of the stream at this site (k). On the pavement just south of here, micro erosion measurements by the author over a period of three years show an erosion rate of 0.33 m per 1,000 years. This agrees remarkably well with a rate of 0.40 m per 1,000 years as an average since deglaciation, estimated by Sweeting (1965) by measuring the height of pedestals under erratics left upstanding (at Norber, a few km to the south).

Walk down Alum Pot Beck, noting the behaviour of the water. Alluvium is obvious on the valley floor. Regolith can be examined at point l, where there are exposures on steep slopes facing the Beck. Continue down the Beck to where the stone wall crosses it (m) then return to the stile (g) and walk back along the eastern side of the wall to the stream (n). Do NOT climb on or damage the wall. It is worth going to point n and following Alum Pot Beck down to Alum Pot (d). Then retrace your steps down valley to your transport.

STOP 4 UPPER RIBBLESDALE - RIBBLEHEAD

Drive northwards towards Ribblehead (Figure 9a). You pass more drumlins, especially after crossing east of the railway line. Turn left (west) onto the B6255; at GR 76077885 there is a layby on the left which is large enough for two coaches. To the north (right) of the road there are drumlins aligned NE-SW (down Greta Dale). A series of surface depressions ring these drumlins. It seems that where the till is thick little water penetrates to the limestone. However, where the till thins near the edge of a drumlin the water draining off the drumlin is able to penetrate in quantity, dissolving the limestone below and producing depressions.

STOP 5 GREAT DOUK - SOUTHERSCALES AREA (Walk 2)

Drive south-westwards along the B6255 (towards Ingleton) (Figure 9a). At GR 74487774 there is a larger layby on the right to park for

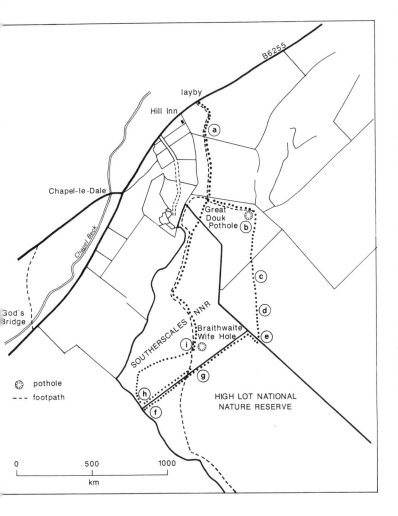

*Figure 9e. Features of the walk around Great Douk Pothole
and Braithwaite Wife Hole.*

another extended visit. If you need toilets and/or a lunch spot at this stage, you can go to the Hill Inn (200 m down the road - some bar meals at 'cavers' prices). The alternatives are White Scar Cave (and Cafe - see below) 4.5 km down valley, or Ingleton 7 km away.

From the layby walk to the well signposted footpath 50 m downvalley. At GR 74477760 (point a on Figure 9e) note the low pedestal erratic opposite the old lime kiln. Follow the footpath to Great Douk Pothole (b, at GR 74707702) - another spectacular deep open hole the bottom of which can be safely reached from the north-west end. Great Douk cave stream enters at the south-east, flows across the hole and sinks into the floor. Many attempts at excavation have so far failed to find the cave passage that must lead downstream out of the depression. Climb back up to ground level and note the area of limestone pavement to the north where grazing has been prevented for some time. This is Scar Close Nature Reserve to which no access is allowed. But even from the edge of Great Douk Pot it is obvious that when grazing is prevented trees and shrubs can colonise and produce a very different landscape.

At the south-east end of the Pot Hole there is a path leading southwards. Just 60 m along this path there is a small but deep pothole with Great Douk Cave stream at the bottom. Walk along the path to c (GR 747765) where there is footpath erosion on peat. Further along (d, at GR 74737642) there is a small area of limestone pavement upslope of the path. A stream sinks into the upslope edge of the pavement - this is the stream that emerges in Great Douk Pot Hole. Note that the underground route follows the same route as the footpath and that it has ignored the small ridge you cross en route, underlining the fact that underground drainage catchments may be very different from surface catchments.

Continue along the footpath to the stile (e, at GR 74647618). The stile takes you into High Lot National Nature Reserve, which is signed. You will need a permit (obtainable in advance from the address in the Appendix) if not following the footpaths. Follow the wall along the downslope edge of the Reserve. Note that in the first 200 m there are a series of sinking streams. The nature of the soils and regolith can be observed in small sections of the stream banks. Continue along the wall past the pair of stiles to point f (GR 73987583), where naturally exposed peat sections up to 0.5 m deep can be seen over leached till. The vegetation is an acid cottongrass bog association with common

Sphagnum moss and some heaths on slightly drier areas. At least the upper part of the peat is formed from a very similar vegetation to that now seen on the surface. Deeper in the peat note the birch wood which shows some marked vegetation changes in the past. This may have been caused by climatic factors, but is more likely to be due to changed land use (grazing eliminating tree species).

Return to the pair of stiles on the main footpath (g, at GR 74297607) and enter Southerscales National Nature Reserve (run by the Yorkshire Wildlife Trust; see Appendix for details of permission required). DO NOT use the gate near point f. Walk south-westwards along the wall to its western end (h, at GR 73877586). At point h there is notable gradation of vegetation and soils within a very short distance. Note the soil profile in the scar where a small stream sinks in wet weather. The soil is developed on till and is a peaty podsol. The profile consists of peat, a bleached layer below and then an iron pan. On the raised areas of till there is an acid cottongrass bog association with relatively few species. Only a few metres away, on lower ground where plant roots reach the limestone, there are rendzina soils with a much richer flora.

The extensive limestone pavement here is also worth examining. North-westwards towards the valley there is a broad stretch of pavement. Near point h, where there is till on the limestone (and it is likely the pavement had a soil cover relatively recently), the runnels in the pavement are notably deeper. Going further towards the valley (where the pavement has probably not had a soil cover recently), the runnels are much shallower and the pavement is almost featureless in places.

Return to your transport via Braithwaite Wife Hole (i, at GR 7437621) another large pot hole comparable in size to Great Douk and Alum Pot.

STOP 6 CHAPEL-LE-DALE-GREAT DALE-TWISTLETON DALE

Drive down the B6255 (Figure 9a) to God's Bridge (GR 733764), where the main river rises at the Pre-Carboniferous/Carboniferous unconformity in normal water conditions. In wet weather the river may rise considerably further upstream.

A good end to your day is to drive another 4 km south-west to visit White Scar Caverns (phone Ingleton 05242 41244 for prices and booking). This is a rising cave at the Carboniferous/Pre-Carboniferous unconformity; you can see the unconformity and classic vadose passage at close quarters.

OTHER SUGGESTIONS

There are many other possible excursions, and sites in this area. Information on other sites is available from the Yorkshire Dales National Park Committee, Yorebridge House, Bainbridge, Leyburn, N Yorks (phone 0969 50456) or (simpler) call at the Clapham National Park Centre (GR 745692). For geological interest you might consider the Ingleton Waterfalls Trail (GR 693734) in combination with part of this excursion.

For a fit group in good weather (have an alternative plan to avoid high ground in bad weather) you could try going from Clapham (GR 745692) up Clapdale to Ingleborough Show Cave (GR 695711) a classic phreatic cave (phone 04685 242), to Trow Gill (GR 695717) and Gaping Gill (GR 691727) over the top of Ingleborough (GR 741746) and then descending to the Great Douk-Southerscales area described above.

Waltham and Davies (1987 p.15-18) give a geomorphological excursion guide from Clapham to Gaping Gill; the 'Reginald Farrer Trail' National Park Guide covers the vegetation. Another interesting site (minibus access only, plus 1 km walk) is to the Norber Erratics - park at GR 77226965, go via public footpath to GR 76956975 (Pre-Carboniferous/Carboniferous unconformity exposed alongside the path in a small cliff) to GR 760701, where the erratics are widespread. Please do NOT cross the wall where the footpath ends.

Finally it is worth noting that the Remote Sensing Society (c/o the Remote Sensing Unit, University of Nottingham, Nottingham NG7 2RD) have recently made available sets of satellite images at about £4 for 10 copies, and the coverage of Image A includes Ingleborough. Land use, the extent of limestone pavement and the Ribblehead drumlin field are all clearly seen, as well as many other features.

Selected References

Jennings, J N (1985) *Karst Geomorphology*. Blackwell

Sweeting, M M (1966) The weathering of limestones with particular reference to Carboniferous Limestones in Northern England.

177-210 In G H Dury (editor) *Essays in Geomorphology*. Heineman

Sweeting, M M (1974) Karst Geomorphology in North-West England. 45-75 in Waltham

Trudgill, S (1985) *Limestone Geomorphology*. Longmans

Waltham, A C (1974) *The Limestones and Caves of North-west England*. David and Charles

Waltham, A (1987) *Karst and Caves*. Yorkshire Dales National Park Committee

Waltham, A and M Davies (1987) *Caves and Karst of the Yorkshire Dales*. British Cave Research Associaton and Yorkshire Dales National Park Committee

Appendix

You will need a permit to walk along the wall on the downslope edge of High Lot National Nature Reserve. Write in advance to Nature Conservancy Council office, Archbold House, Archbold Terrace, Newcastle upon Tyne NE2 1EG (Tel. 0632 816316).

You will also need permission to enter the Southerscales Nature Reserve, although educational parties are welcomed. Permission should be sought from the Chairman of the Nature Reserve Mr Neale (Tel. 0468 4115 outside office hours).

10   THE SETTLE-CARLISLE RAILWAY

David Halsall
(Edge Hill College of Higher Education)

Outline: a trip along the route of the Settle-Carlisle railway with
      opportunities to study route selection, engineering features,
      stations, buildings for the railway employees and navvy
      settlements.
Starting point: Settle Junction (GR 814604).
Finishing point: Ais Gill (GR 778963).
Distance: a total drive of 56 km.
Time needed: one whole day.
Maps needed: OS 1:50,000 Land Ranger series, sheets 98 and 103; OS
      1:25,000 Outdoor Leisure Map "The Three Peaks"; OS 1:25,000
      sheets SD86, 87, 77, 78 and 79.

INTRODUCTION

Historical Background

Since its conception in the 1860s, the Settle and Carlisle railway has
been controversial. Ironically, it was unwanted by both its first (the
Midland Railway Company) and its present (British Rail) owners. The
Midland, beset by competitive rivals, was forced by its allies (the
Lancashire and Yorkshire and North British Railway Companies) and
the government to build the 116 km line at high cost, when it preferred
to use the neighbouring route (to the west) controlled by the intractable
London and North Western Railway (LNWR) for its Scottish traffic.
British Rail (BR) considered the railway a financial liability, and
rerouted many through trains onto the former LNWR route.

      The decision by the Secretary of State for Transport to reprieve
the line on 11 April 1989 curtailed the eight year long attempt to close
it and relieved considerable public concern.

      The Settle and Carlisle (S & C) line was opened on 1 May 1876. It
was the third main Anglo-Scottish rail route, built for fast, high quality

express trains but also catering for some local traffic to provide railway service to remote agricultural communities. It was the last major construction work completed mainly by traditional methods, using gangs of navvies.

Threat of closure
By 1988 it appeared that without private investment the line would cease to operate in 1989. To many people, both local and non-local, closure would have been a tragedy. Despite local high car ownership rates, the meagre train services are used by local people, especially those without access to cars - children, the elderly, those unable to afford a vehicle, and often women. Local roads are poor, existing bus services sparse and the railway is better able to cope with harsh winter weather conditions. Moreover, recent research (eg by Whitelegg 1984,1987) demonstrates the often unappreciated social and economic effects of rail closures.

Despite its inclusion in Beeching rationalisation proposals in the 1960s, the line escaped closure though intermediate stations were lost. It links West Yorkshire with Carlisle and Scotland, is designated by BR as a "Scenic Railway" and is a crucial diversion route for BR's West Coast Main Line (WCML) services affected by adverse weather or engineering work. Without it, BR could face operational difficulties in maintaining WCML services without undue increases in journey time.

Tourist clientele has increased markedly through more vigorous marketing since 1983. Withdrawal of local passenger services in 1970 (reinstated 1986) led to the development of the Yorkshire Dales National Park Committee's "Dales Rail" services from 1975, which take ramblers into the country, and local people to shop in urban areas. The line also attracts crowds of enthusiasts to ride on and photograph diesel and steam hauled special trains.

The determined campaign by the Friends of the Settle-Carlisle Line Association, Transport 2000 and the Railway Development Society through their Joint Action Committee since 1983, together with active support of the involved local authorities of all political parties, provided an unprecedented organisation of opposition to BR's closure proposals. The number of individual protesters has also been unequalled. Thus, the government's role as final decision-maker was particularly sensitive. The situation should be viewed in a much broader context than a narrow local focus allows.

MAJOR THEMES

This excursion (Figures 10a and 10b) demonstrates the relationships of the line with the land surface (through its engineering), and with the local population (through its service function). It also illustrates railway route development and contraction related to transport policy-making. The following key themes are considered:

(i) Engineering features and route selection from Settle Junction to Ais Gill

This section is arguably the most dramatic part of the line. It is dominated by the need to raise the railway from 134 m (Settle Junction) to 356 m (Ais Gill Summit) over a distance of 40 km. Local engineering works should thus be viewed within this context, as well as the requirements of smaller scale landforms. From Settle to Carlisle there are 14 tunnels, 21 viaducts and 325 bridges.

(ii) Stations

The Midland Railway (MR) provided standard architectural designs for passenger and goods facilities, graded according to traffic potential. The large station buildings at Settle, Kirkby Stephen and Appleby have three gables whilst intermediate stations (all north of Ais Gill) and small stations (including Settle Junction, Horton-in-Ribblesdale, Ribblehead, Dent) have two gables. These are complemented by standard designs of waiting shelter (at all stations) and goods shed. None of the latter remain in the study section. Building materials are stone - millstone grit, limestone or sandstone according to location. The overall railway landscape is the poorer after the disappearance of detail features such as signalling.

(iii) Houses and cottages for Midland Railway employees

These include standard MR gabled designs for station masters' houses and two-storey and bungalow cottages for workers at Settle, Horton, Selside, Garsdale and Ais Gill. The MR initially planned 149 houses for S & C workers; they remain a visible suggestion of social and economic impact locally.

(iv) Navvy settlements and life

The rigours of railway construction are related to specific sites for which there is documentary or very little field evidence. No navvy settlements survive today, but an examination of their sites and the lives of their inhabitants adds much to understanding the difficulties of construction.

EXCURSION

Views from the railway give impressions of the line's engineering structures, station facilities and contemporary operations. The civil engineering works and the place of the railway in the landscape are often better appreciated from adjacent roads. It is possible to make the return journey between Leeds and Carlisle within a day. Whilst no public bus services cover the entire recommended route, much of the line can be followed by road (see Figures 10a and 10b).

RIBBLESDALE (SETTLE JUNCTION TO RIBBLEHEAD)

Settle Junction

At Settle Junction (GR 814604) (a on Figure 10a) adjacent to the A65, the railway from Leeds splits into two. One line goes to Carnforth and Morecambe. The main Settle-Carlisle line continues northwards and allows the fast running of expresses through the junction, commencing the "Long Drag", named by steam era railwaymen because of the almost continuous 1 per cent adverse northbound gradient for the 24 km to Blea Moor.

The wide north-south glaciated Ribble valley offered an ideal routeway. Only the narrow gorge between Stainforth and Helwith Bridge (caused by rejuvenation of the river) appeared a problem. Fortunately for John Crossley, the MR civil engineer, older structural elements were of less importance in route selection. The Ribble cuts through the South Craven Fault near Settle; to the West the fault forms the major limestone barrier of Giggleswick Scar which is clearly visible from Settle Junction (and is described in Excursion 9). South of the Junction are the remains of Settle Junction station platform adjacent a gateway from the A65. Here the MR signal box, built in 1913, remains operational.

To the north, the line uses cuttings and embankments to maintain the 1 per cent gradient throughout the study section. The skew bridges crossing the A65 at Anley (GR 814617) and Settle (GR 815628) have

109

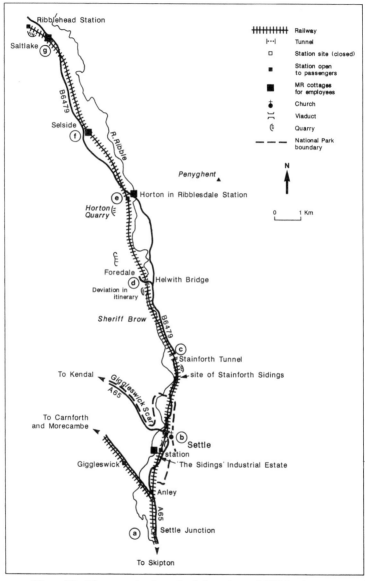

Figure 10a. The excursion from Settle Junction to Ribblehead Station.

wing walls with relieving arches and abutments, typical of the bridges along this line. The railway structures reflect local building materials of West Yorkshire - millstone grit and limestone in this southern section - and they match the local landscape.

Settle

The railway forms an important element of the urban fabric of Settle (b) even though much of its economic impact has now gone. The former goods yard south of the station is now the appropriately named "The Sidings" industrial estate.

The wooden signal box, out of use since 1984, survives by the goods shed site. The goods yard east of the station remains undeveloped; the impressive MR water tank house (GR 817635), an iron tank surmounting a millstone grit base, survives, together with the weigh office. The station approach has been extended over former sidings and cattle docks to allow further car parking provision. The main station building (southbound platform) is one of the larger MR designs, built of millstone grit like the adjacent station master's house. Opposite is a standard millstone grit waiting shelter. The station continues to maintain its former pride; it won third prize in the 1987 "Best Kept Station" competition and it retains gardens. The ornate sign including a coat of arms has disappeared from the southbound platform although the distances to Carlisle (71 miles, 114 km) and London (237 miles, 379 km) are still discernible.

The two most important S & C passenger stations were Settle and Appleby: they accounted for about 38 per cent of the total receipts for the line's 20 stations between 1916 and 1922. The situation was similar for livestock although for coal and mineral traffic Settle's returns were almost ten times as high as Appleby's. Only Horton-in-Ribblesdale (below) had mineral returns of high magnitude.

The railway crosses Settle on an embankment with massive walls supporting the northbound station platform and two viaducts - Marshside (GR 818637) and Church (GR 818638) - which dominate the town and mark its approximate western edge in the nineteenth century. Apart from a small alteration of Bond Lane the street pattern was unaltered; Station Road was built in 1849 as a link with the original Settle station (now Giggleswick, GR 802629) on the "little" North Western Railway. Six distinctive terraced and gabled MR cottages (Midland Terrace) were built west of the railway (GR 816633).

In the porch of the parish church (GR 820639) a memorial tablet erected by the MR and its workforce commemorates those killed by accidents during construction of the line between Settle and Dent Head between 1869 and 1876. There is an identical tablet at Chapel-le-Dale (below). In Settle churchyard is one of the few marked graves for a Settle and Carlisle navvy - John G Owen of Holyhead who died in 1873 aged nineteen after a crane leg fell on him at Langcliffe.

Stainforth

North of Settle the line follows the Ribble climbing almost continuously at 1 percent, steeper than and gaining height over the river's long profile. Stainforth (Taitlands) Tunnel (GR 822668) (c) is approached by rock cuttings. Little remains of Stainforth Sidings which served the Craven Lime Company's limestone quarry (GR 823662) east of the line. This traffic was so important that the rail link opened in 1873 ahead of the main line itself. The quarry is now being infilled.

North of Stainforth the line crosses the North Craven Fault onto pre-Carboniferous rocks for the short distance to Horton, with no surface change in relief. However the narrow Stainforth gorge (resulting from considerable rejuvenation of the river) caused considerable engineering problems. In the event, the line followed the river, which was suitably diverted, crossing it twice at Sheriff Brow on skew bridges (GR 815682, 813685). The river level falls 9 m between them. Maintenance of the 1 per cent gradient to the south placed the railway at a viable level to allow it to traverse the gorge.

The line crosses the river again at Helwith Bridge (GR 811698) and thereafter remains on the easier western side of the valley above the drumlins.

To view the bridge against a background panorama of Penyghent, deviate left from the B6479 at GR 813695 and then turn right into the quarry roadway (GR 811695). Sidings on the west side of the line serving the Ribblesdale Lime Company (d on Figure 10a) (Foredale Quarry) and Helwith Bridge Granite Company have been lifted (GR 809702)

Horton-in-Ribblesdale

The station (e) was formerly busy, especially for minerals - annual tonnages handled 1896-1915 and 1954-63 exceeded all other individual station returns. Lifted sidings, the derelict cattle dock and the weigh office indicate past activity and subsequent decline. The constant flow of lorries serving the nearby (formerly rail-linked) Horton Quarry of Tarmac Ltd (GR 803722) are in stark contrast. The main station building (southbound platform) is a MR standard small design with a standard waiting shelter opposite. The wooden signal box south of the station survives, closed since 1984. The station master's house and six cottages (standard MR terrace) are located on the approach road.

Horton is interesting too for evidence of the temporary navvy population during construction of the line. Census data shows a marked anomalous peak in the village's population. This rose from around 400 in 1861 to nearly 900 in 1871, then fell again to around 500 in 1881.

Good views of the valley, its glacial features, and the railway maintaining its 1 percent gradient are obtained from the B6479. Selside signal box (formerly at GR 785758), closed in 1975, is now in use at Steamtown Museum, Carnforth. Two terraces of four MR gabled cottages each (GR 788752, 789751) lie south of the hamlet (f). A similar set of four cottages, associated with the Craven Lime Company's quarry siding opened 1877, are on the reputed site of the navvy shanty town of Saltlake (GR 774785) (g).

Ribblehead - Blea Moor

This area is a microcosm of the Settle-Carlisle railway. The MR standard small station at Ribblehead (GR 766784, h on Figure 10b) had, like other isolated rural stations, little passenger potential. Note the tiling to protect exposed northern facing walls. Only southbound trains can call since the northbound platform was removed after closure to provide space for an extra quarry siding. Other goods services have ceased; the cattle dock, for example, is derelict (southbound side). The station master's house is located north of the main building. An unusual duty of the staff was to compile weather reports for the Meteorological Office. The station offers magnificent views west, north and east to Ingleborough, Whernside, Penyghent and Batty Moss (Ribblehead) viaduct.

Ribblehead Viaduct

The condition of this impressive but deteriorating viaduct (i) and the cost of repairing it - estimated in 1988 at about £2.7 million - are often quoted as major factors in closure proposals. The limestone viaduct

113

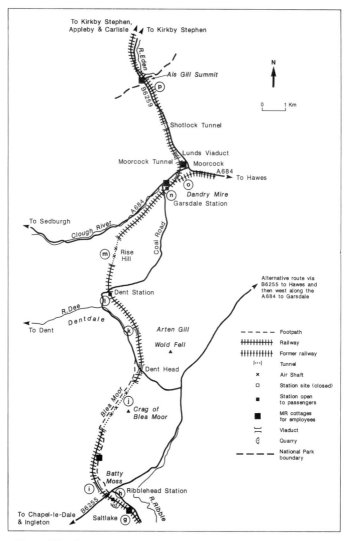

Figure 10b. The excursion from Ribblehead Station to Ais Gill Summit

(single track since 1985) crosses the windgap left by the probable capture of the Ribble headwaters (source at GR 776796) by headwaters of the Greta at Batty Moss (i). It took five years to build and required deep foundations through the glacial deposits.

The area is the site of navvy settlements - Batty Green (which included a hospital, shops, schools, post office, public library, mission and public houses), Inkerman, Sebastopol, Belgravia, Jericho, Jerusalem and Tunnel Huts on Blea Moor. The walk suggested by Swallow and Mitchell (1987, 20-23), which starts by the cave used by navvies as a cold store (GR 765791) includes a loop of the tram way (GR 762794 to 758798) built to link navvy settlements and constructional works. It is a useful route to Blea Moor Sidings to view the site of demolished MR cottages and a later railway house, the site of watering facilites and the signal box (GR 758807). There are good views south to the viaduct and Ingleborough (see Excursion 9).

The approach cutting (GR 762819) to Blea Moor tunnel is crossed and then followed by the footpath. Above the tunnel, it follows the line of the three ventilation shafts (j) (three of the original seven construction shafts) to the north portal (GR 775835). Waste from construction of the tunnel 152.5 m below and remains of winding houses built for this work are clearly visible.

Chapel-le-Dale

Turn left at GR 765792 onto the B6255, to visit the church at Chapel-le-Dale (GR 738772). Here, over 100 navvies and their families are buried in unmarked graves, killed either by accidents or by disease, especially the smallpox outbreak at Batty Green in 1871. The memorial in the church is identical to that at Settle.

THE MOUNTAIN SECTION (BLEA MOOR TO AIS GILL)

The walk suggested by Swallow and Mitchell (1987) provides a panoramic view north of the line curving along Upper Dentdale and the hillside of Woldfell to Dent station using two high viaducts - Dent Head and Arten Gill (GR 777843, 776859) - to cross deep tributory valleys. The unclassified road provides clear views of the railway and the viaduct. Spoil from excavating approach cuttings is clearly visible at Arten Gill (GR 776857) (k).

Dent station

Dent's isolated station, 7.25 km away from the town (l), is perched on the hillside, accessible only by the twisting, 17 per cent graded "Coal Road" which is frequently closed in winter. Snow fences above the station cutting indicate the problems of severe winters. The station master's house (GR 763876) is prominent by the station. Views from the four arch brick overbridge (GR 764896) south along Upper Dentdale again demonstrate the railway route and its engineering. To the north the railway follows Cowgill with a cutting and embankment to Rise Hill tunnel (m) to emerge on the south side of the Clough Valley, where the railway remains near the 350 m contour before falling to Garsdale Station (n).

Garsdale

Garsdale (n) was an isolated small railway community based upon the junction between the Settle-Carlisle line and the Hawes branch. The panorama from the "Coal Road" (GR 788916) shows the station area and sixteen MR houses, eight less than was originally intended. South of the station is the site of the MR water tank (GR 787917), similar to that at Settle and formerly used as a village hall. The station is non-standard with waiting room blocks on each platform (the northbound building formerly used as a chapel) and a signal box, now unused, on the northbound platform. To the north-west is the site of the locomotive turntable formerly protected from winds by a stockade of old sleepers.

Dandry Mire

Like Batty Moss this wide windgap (o) results from river capture - the Clough and Eden have truncated the Ure headwaters. The infilling of glacial deposits would not support the planned embankment, replaced by Moorcock viaduct (GR 792922). The skew bridge crosses the A684 (GR 794926) alongside another terrace of six MR cottages. Note the slate protection on the end walls.

Lunds and Ais Gill

The close relationship between topography and railway engineering work is again demonstrated in the short distance (5 km) between Moorcock and Ais Gill. Closely paralleled by the B6259, the railway utilizes cuttings, embankments, two tunnels - Moorcock (GR 794929) and Shotlock (GR 788943) - and Lunds viaduct (GR 792932) to maintain the final climb of about 15 m through the Upper Ure valley to Ais Gill summit (356 m) (p), the watershed between the Ure (to the south) and the Eden (to the north) (GR 780962). Ais Gill signal box is now preserved at Buttlerley and the sidings for holding freight trains are also gone, but two MR cottages survive (GR 778963). The line continues north on down gradients via Mallarstang and the Eden valley.

CONCLUSION

Closure of England's highest main line railway would have benefited no one, neither the developing clientele nor BR who would have lost an important diversionary route and continued to incur maintenance costs. Surviving local traffic and growing tourist traffic are increasing patronage, and the heritage elements of the line - its history and transport archaeology - together with the scenic quality of its route, show considerable potential. Heritage and tourism are emphasised by the government in advocating the operation of the line by BR, but with stronger links with central and local government, the private sector and tourist interests.

Tourist development will, however, require careful regulation. Limited road access and a general absence of the more obvious elements of commercial development help the area to retain its landscape and cultural values, of which the railway forms an important part. The Ribblehead area is already suffering from over use.

New developments will therefore require a sensitive approach or may endanger the very character that strengthens the appeal of the railway and its routeway. The needs of the local community should not be overlooked. Better marketing, new 'Sprinter' diesel trains, and other improvements are to be considered in a major review of the line. It is hoped that BR can consolidate upon the recent increases in passenger receipts (40 per cent increase in 1988-89 over 1987-88), and the continuing goodwill of interested public and private bodies and potential customers.

Selected References

Abbott, S (1986) *To Kill a Railway*. Leading Edge Press, Hawes
Anderson, V R and G K Fox (1986) *Stations and Structures of the Settle and Carlisle Railway*. Oxford Publishing Company, Poole

Edwards, W and F M Trotter (1954) *British Regional Geology. The Pennines and Adjacent Areas*. HMSO

Halsall, D A (1982) Policies and practice of steam train operation on British Rail Scenic Routes, 1981. 145-173 in D A Halsall (editor) *Transport for Recreation*. Institute of British Geographers Transport Geography Study Group, Lancaster

Hillman, M and A Whalley (1980) *The social consequences of rail closures*. Policy Studies Institute no.587.

Jenkinson, D (1980) *Rails in the fells*. Peco Publications, Beer

Mitchell, W R (1988) *Shanty Life on the Settle-Carlisle Railway*. Mitchell, Settle

Mitchell, W R and D Joy (1982) *Settle to Carlisle. A Railway over the Pennines*. Dalesman, Clapham

Settle-Carlisle Line Supplement (1989). *Rail* 94; ii-vii

Speakman, C (1982) "Dales Rail" and "Park Link": recreational transport packages in the Yorkshire Dales. 63-73 in D A Halsall (editor) *Transport for Recreation*. Institute of British Geographers Transport Geography Study Group, Lancaster

Swallow, R W and W R Mitchell (1987) *Walks from the Settle - Carlisle Railway*. Dalesman, Clapham

Whitelegg, J (1984) Closure of the Settle-Carlisle railway line. The case for a social cost-benefit analysis. *Land Use Policy* (Oct); 283-298

Whitelegg, J (1987) Rural Railways and Disinvestment in Rural Areas. *Regional Studies* 21; 55-63

Yorkshire Dales National Park (1976) *Dales Rail Settle and Carlisle Railway*. YDNP Committee, Leyburn

Acknowledgement

I am most grateful to Edge Hill College for financial assistance in the preparation of this article.

11   FEATURES OF THE GLACIAL LANDSCAPE AROUND LANCASTER

Hugh Cutler and Arton Medd
(St Martin's College)

Outline: a study of the variety of glacial features in the area around Lancaster, including drumlins, morainic material associated with drainage diversion and a complex suite of channel features associated with marginal and sub-marginal fluvio-glacial action

Starting and finishing points: Lancaster.

Distance: a drive of about 40 km in total. It is assumed that small groups will be taken in a minibus; narrow roads on some sections make access difficult, and alternative routes are given for parties using a coach. Two circular walks are included that allow for closer inspection of fluvio-glacial features.

Time needed: 3 to 4 hours excluding walks; 6 to 8 hours including walks.

Maps needed: OS 1:25,000 Pathfinder sheets 637 (SD56/57) and 648 (SD36/46).

INTRODUCTION

Lancaster is situated where the lowland, representing the northward extension of the Fylde, is confined to a narrow strip 10 km wide between the Forest of Bowland in the east and Morecambe Bay in the west.

During the Quaternary, the area was extensively glaciated by ice deriving both from the Lake District to the north-west and from the Pennines to the north-east. Because of the position of the Forest of Bowland, particularly its westward extension Clougha Pike, ice from these two directions coverged in the vicinity of Lancaster. This pattern of ice activity has lead to the development of drumlins, morainic material associated with drainage diversion and a complex suite of channel features associated with marginal and sub-marginal fluvio-glacial action.

119

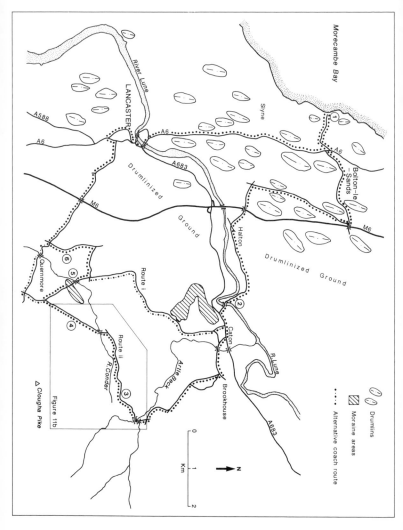

Figure 11a. The excursion route.

EXCURSION

Leave Lancaster northwards across the Lune on the A6, heading towards Carnforth (Figure 11a). After the built-up area of the city the road traverses the drumlin field which covers much of the lower ground in the area. After passing through the village of Slyne, you will see a large example drumlin, called Inglebrick, on the right. This feature is some 800 m long, 300 m wide and 35 m high. As you approach Bolton-le-Sands from the south there is a set of traffic lights. Turn left here (signposted Morecambe) and then take the first lane on the right (signposted to the shore). This lane crosses the railway and ends on the shore by Morecambe Lodge. A cattle grid marks the access to a large area of beach parking.

The route is shown in Figure 11a.

SITE 1 RED BANK DRUMLIN (GR 471679)

As you walk a short distance north from the car park, you approach the tail (down-ice end) of a small drumlin. On its seaward side are extensive exposures of the till from which it and other drumlins in the area have been formed. The till is very stony, with large boulders of limestone and smaller clasts of limestone, gritstone, sandstone and shales set in a sandy-clay matrix. Striations (scratch-marks) can be identified on some particles and igneous erratics (crystalline stones) can be found at times. Many of the large limestone boulders on the foreshore are almost certainly derived from the till.

The location also gives you good views across Morecambe Bay north-west to the Lake District (the source of the igneous erratics) and immediately northwards to the Arnside/Silverdale area and Kendal beyond (source area of much of the limestone). Other particles in the till are either from the local Carboniferous shales and grits or from the Silurian of the southern Lake District. A study of the till fabric will allow for inferences about ice direction. If such a study is intended then parties are encouraged to move northwards along the west flank of the drumlin, where there are lengthy exposures (to avoid over-use of the initial section).

The salt marsh that fringes the bay here is being eroded at its seaward edge. Its history of development is linked to variations in postglacial sea-level, tide patterns and movement of main channels in

Morecambe Bay.

Retrace the route back to the traffic lights and turn right, heading back to Lancaster. Almost immediately, on crossing the canal, turn left into the centre of Bolton-le-Sands. At the crossroads in the middle of the village turn right (signposted Nether Kellett) and follow this road across the drumlin swarm. The road essentially follows the hollows and bends left round the tail of one drumlin to bear right round the stoss (up-ice end) of an adjacent drumlin.

Immediately before the road passes over the M6 Motorway (GR 501681) turn right (signposted Lancaster) and follow this road to Four Lane Ends (GR 490654). The road follows a ridge of higher ground that has been 'drumlinized' by ice; there are good views to the west and south of the drumlin field. You are travelling in roughly the direction of ice movement.

Turn left at Four Lane Ends, signposted Halton. Take the opportunity to look southwards to the city of Lancaster; note the drumlins to the south-west and identify the high point of Clougha Pike (see Excursion 17) to the south-east. Ice moving from the north and north-east down the Lune valley was controlled by the high ground of Clougha Pike before it moved further south into the area of the Fylde beyond.

The road drops down into the Lune valley, crossing the M6 to enter Halton at an oblique crossroads. Go straight ahead, signposted Caton, and follow the Lune valley eastwards, noting the steep northern slopes. The road turns south along a spur across the valley. After a short distance enter the signed car park (at GR 522648); there are toilet facilities here.

SITE 2 CROOK OF LUNE (GR 522646)

Walk from the southern end of the car park, where there is a map of the locality, and drop down onto the disused railway line that forms the main path along the Lune valley. Turn left and move onto the bridge over the Lune. First, look north-east up the Lune valley. It is flat floored and has steep northern slopes. With good visibility, Ingleborough (see Excursion 9) stands out clearly in the background. Now, turn to look southwards, down-valley. The Lune, which is some 60 m wide at this point, appears to be flowing into a dead end!

The floodplain has narrowed rapidly and the ground beyond

rises as a wall some 40m above the river. The river, in fact, turns back north-west in a sharp meander that cuts through the spur in a deep gorge. The spur is made up of the local Carboniferous grits and shales in the form of a steep anticline. The western arm of the meander can be viewed by retracing the path back past the car park and under the road for a short distance onto another bridge.

Why does the river make this abrupt change in direction? Ice moving down the Lune valley originally continued to the south along the Quernmore valley (viewed later in the excursion). During deglaciation a mixture of ice and debris blocked the Quernmore route and the spur at the Crook of Lune was breached. The river subsequently adopted this path and incised (cut down) as it adjusted to its short westward route to the sea through Lancaster.

Return to the car park, and drive along the road in the direction of Caton (GR 532647). Turn left on joining the A683 and follow either (i) or (ii) below.

(i) If you are in a coach, take the first turning right, signposted Quernmore. On leaving Caton the road bends sharply right and climbs upwards past Collier Gate Farm (GR 526633). This rise in the ground marks the line of morainic material that has been dumped across the northern end of the Quernmore valley, possibly contributing to the diversion of the Lune. The road gradually crosses the valley; the steep tree-covered eastern slopes are spectacular. As the road begins to climb the western slopes, fork left (signposted Quernmore) to remain in the valley. After about 1 km stop a little way before the bridge over the Conder that leads past the church. Turn to Site 5.

(ii) Otherwise take the second turning on the right, signposted Brookhouse and Littledale, which is in the centre of the village opposite the Post Office.

This route through Caton and on to Brookhouse crosses some of the morainic material that blocks the southern side of the Lune Valley. Approaching Brookhouse (GR 542646), turn right immediately before the Black Bull pub (signposted Littledale). You are now climbing steadily up the northern flanks of Clougha. After 2 km or so the road takes a sharp right followed by a left that brings you alongside the gorge of Artle Beck (GR 550627). The incision of the beck into the general slope of the area is linked to the post-glacial adjustments of the Lune, of which it is a tributary. Take the next turning right (signposted Quernmore), dropping into the valley and crossing Artle Beck and

Udale Beck in quick succession. The road then climbs steeply from here in a winding route up to Cragg House (GR 549618). Cross the cattle grid at the top of the climb and park in the car park beyond.

SITE 3 LITTLE CRAG CAR PARK (GR 547617)

Turn to Walk 11a below. If you do not intend to take the walk, refer to Point (a) of the walk only and then continue the excursion route.

Continue past Baines Crag in the direction of Quernmore. As the road drops down the Conder and associated melt-water channels are on your left. Take the first turning left and follow this narrow lane for about 1 km to enter the car park on your left.

SITE 4 RIGG LANE CAR PARK (GR 526604)

Turn to Walk 11b below. If you are not intending to take the walk, refer to Points (a) and (b) of the walk only and then continue the excursion route.

Turn left out of the car park and at the end of the lane turn right. Go past Quernmore school and church and stop at the edge of the road a little beyond the bridge over the Conder.

SITE 5 CHURCH BRIDGE (GR 517605)

First, look northwards up-valley. The steep valley sides are marked and similar to those looking up stream from the Crook of Lune. The valley floor in the foreground is particularly flat but it becomes more hummocky in the distance. These hummocks mark morainic material that divides the Quernmore valley from the Lune valley; it was probably contributory to the Lune diversion. The flat floor of the valley is underlain by a sequence of clay, mud, sand and peat resting on till (Moseley & Walker 1952), indicating the former presence of a lake, probably of immediate post-glacial origin.

Next, turn to look south and east. Here you can identify the feature that was responsible for ponding up the lake. Greenlot farm (GR 519606) to the east and Quernmore church (GR 518603) to the south stand on top of a marked ridge with a steep northern slope. The Conder cuts through this ridge in a narrow valley to the west of the church. This ridge marks a moraine deposited during deglaciation that blocked the valley and allowed for the development of the lake. Continue the excursion following either (i) or (ii) below.

(i) If you use a coach, continue southwards past the church and stop at the side of the road in a safe position near the next turning left (GR 522597). Walk up the lane to the car park. Turn to Site 4.

Returning from Site 4, continue the excursion by driving to the crossroads at Quernmore Post Office (GR 520591). Turn right (signposted Lancaster) and cross the valley. As you climb out of the valley take the opportunity to view up the valley towards Caton and across to the western slopes of Clougha. Continue over the ridge that separates the Quernmore valley from Lancaster, under the M6 and past Lancaster Leisure Park. Turn right at the end of the road to return to the centre of Lancaster.

(ii) Otherwise continue northwards and at the crossroads immediately ahead turn left (signposted Lancaster). The road climbs steeply out of the valley and at the end of the lane turn left. On the initial straighter section, stop at the edge of the road.

SITE 6 LITTLE FELL ROAD (GR 508602)

This vantage point overlooks the Quernmore valley. Look northwards to Caton and the Lune valley, which appears to link directly into the Quernmore valley. Eastwards, some of the channels that have been visited can be seen on the western and northern slopes of Clougha. Southwards you can see the continuation of the valley out onto the northern part of the Fylde area.

At the crossroads ahead turn right (signposted Lancaster). Continue over the ridge that separates the Quernmore valley from Lancaster, under the M6 and past Lancaster Leisure Park. Turn right at the end of the road to return to the centre of Lancaster.

WALK 11A   CONDER HEAD MELTWATER CHANNELS

Most of this excursion (see Figure 11b) is on access land which is closed for a few days a year in the autumn. Dogs are not permitted at any time, even on a lead.

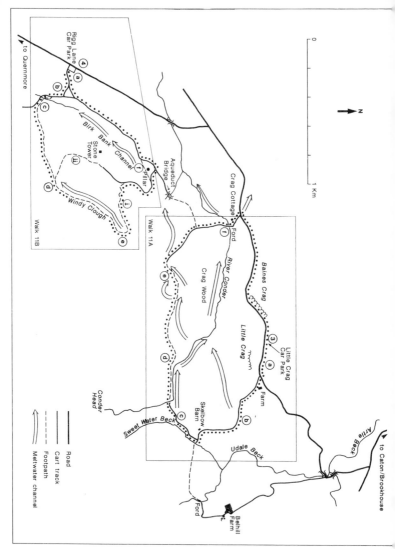

Figure 11b. Details of the two walks around meltwater channels

(a) Little Crag Car Park (GR 547617, 205m OD)

A grassy summit just before the cattle grid at the top of the hill is a useful vantage point for an overview of the whole area included in this chapter. The coastline of Morecambe Bay is clearly visible extending southwards to Fleetwood and Blackpool. The drumlin at Red Bank is approximately in line with the TV transmitting mast. To the north the immediate foreground slopes down to the valley of the deeply incised Artle Beck, beyond which is the valley of the River Lune. Across to the north-east is Caton Moor and other fells which form the northern part of the Forest of Bowland.

At a passing place on the left just beyond the car park is a notice-board with a map of the Clougha Access Area; this clearly shows access points, footpaths, and stiles and the valleys (which were the meltwater channels) now occupied by small becks. To the west is Baines Crag; this gritstone rock also outcrops in Little Crag about 80 m south of the noticeboard.

Walk across the *Juncus* covered ground (or go round via the wall if it is too wet!) and stand above Little Crag. The backdrop extending to the horizon southwards is the gritstone moorland of the top of the Clougha escarpment dip slope. In the foreground a steep slope drops down to the wooded valley bottom then the ground rises to a grassy knoll. The valley beyond this knoll is the former meltwater channel which forms part of this walk. These landforms are repeated in Crag Wood to the west. To the south-east is the solitary stone building of Skelbow Barn and beyond it are the valleys of the headwater streams of Artle Beck. Eastwards, to the right of the farm and trees, a dip in the skyline marks the area of the through valley between Closegill and Bladder Stone Becks (GR 588622). This valley is also part of the meltwater channel series.

If you are not intending to complete the walk, continue on the excursion route at this point.

Walk eastwards along the top of the crag towards a stile/gate to the right of the cattle grid. The route from here to Skelbow Barn is marked by yellow arrows. It leads down the cart track to the right of a stone building, following a wall to the corner; it then turns left.

(b) The cart track below the farm opposite the end of the wood (GR 550615, 185m OD)

The small valley to the right of the track is the head of the steep Crag

Wood Valley. There is *Juncus* in the valley bottom but no running water; this poses questions as to the possibility of its being the sole source of water to erode such a large valley below. Tractor tyres have exposed the weathered shale bedrock to the left of the track here.

Continue along the track across a small col with a valley head on the left, through a gate, and then turn right up the edge of the field to Skelbow Barn. Pass in front of the barn, through a gateway between a wall and hawthorn trees. Then follow the wall to the right over a stile and along a track parallel to the small but steep sided valley of Sweet Beck. A stile/gate is at the next corner, but keep straight on to the stile over the boundary of the access area.

(c) The watershed stile (GR 550601, 215m OD)

You are standing on the only firm ground on the floor of a valley which is fed by streams, springs and seepage from the steep slope opposite. To the left Sweet Beck runs towards Artle Beck which joins the River Lune near Caton (GR 5364). To the right the wet boggy Conder Head valley drains westwards to reach the Lune estuary near Glasson (GR 4556).

Can the water courses now apparent in the valley bottom have eroded this valley form? The answer is almost certainly no; a much greater volume of water is needed and meltwater is the most likely source. From about the position of the stile, the gradient falls to both east and west. For this through valley to have been formed, there must have been an ice cover to enable the up gradient flow of water under pressure from the east.

Pick a route above the marshland westwards, aiming for a marked stony path at the end of the valley (NOT the nearby grassy track) up to the break of the slope.

The glacial drift exposures can be studied when crossing the streams. From a point on the path where you can see down valley between the trees, look back the way you have come to appreciate the form of the valley - particularly the convex slope on the north side.

(d) Top of stony path at junction of tracks (GR 547611, 220m OD)

A well marked path continues straight ahead, but take a less determinate sheeptrack which stays close to the top of the valley side. Note its steepness and the existence of other small in-out and reverse gradient channels by Crag Wood en route.

The Water Witch pub on the Lancaster Canal was formerly stabling for canal horses (Exc 12). Photo: R.B.Evans

Derelict Central Pier at Morecambe on a winter afternoon. The Lakeland
fells lie across Morecambe Bay (Exc 15). Photo: R.B.Evans

The Langden Valley in the Forest of Bowland (Exc 18).
Photo: Walt Unsworth

**The Receptacle, old almshouses - at Haigh, in the
Douglas Valley (Exc 19). Photo: W.Unsworth**

(e) Path junction near end of higher channel (GR 541611, 200m OD)
When a point is reached almost opposite the end of the wood, the track meets a wider path. Some 15 m before this, notice a high level dry channel incised some 20 m into solid rock on the left. If time allows divert left up the path to about 50 m beyond a shooting butt to see the curvature of this channel. Return by the same route, then follow the path down to a stile over the quality dry stone wall. Is the stile on a natural or man-made reverse gradient?

Follow the path round the spur to another stile. An interesting detour for the energetic is to turn south-eastwards along a faintly marked car track which curves round to a bridge with railings (Haweswater Aqueduct) and continues to the head of the Birk Bank Channel. This is marked by a stone pillar of distinctive stepped form (see point f of walk 11b). Alternatively, climb over wall and follow the track leading down to a stone house by the River Conder.

(f) Crag Cottage (GR 537615, 125m OD)
The Conder flows over a concrete flume here (an estimate of its discharge can easily be made). Downstream from this point the river meanders within a steep-sided flat bottomed valley, again very much a 'misfit'. Cross the fence/stile and walk up to the road on the far side of which begins another valley heading north-west without any surface watercourse. It seems likely that this formed an alternative outlet at some stage for meltwater from the present Conder valley channel, either with a reversed gradient or at an earlier stage of downcutting.

Either return up the hill to the car park or send a driver to collect the vehicle while stream measurements or field sketches are made.

WALK 11B : BIRK BANK AND WINDY CLOUGH CHANNELS

This excursion (Figure 11b) is on access land which is closed for a few days a year in the autumn. Dogs are not permitted at any time even on a lead. The car park will take minibuses but not coaches (7 ft (2.1 m) bar).

(a) Rigg Lane Car Park (GR 526603, 110m OD)
There is a map of the Clougha Access Area at the entrance to the car park. Climb over the fence-stile at the southern corner of the car park and follow the track up the slope to a junction near the crest of the hill,

where it veers to the left. Take the right fork which leads down a slope; stop when you reach the next junction. (If you are linking these two excursions, and approaching from the head of Birk Bank channel (point (f)), fork left to point (b) before the path turns down right).

(b) Birk Bank Channel (GR 528603, 125m OD)

From here you can clearly see the line of the Birk Bank channel, an asymmetrical valley running NNE/SSW. The opposite slope of the valley is steep and boulder covered northwards, and it becomes more vegetated and less steep to the south. The side on which you are standing is low and more gently sloping. The floor is flat and there is a noticeable vegetation change along its length, indicative of changes in soil depth, composition and moisture content. The upper part of this valley floor can be seen later, but the route to be followed now crosses the wet peaty section.

If you are not intending to complete the walk, return to the car park at this point.

Turn right on the track to a gate, cross the stile on its left, then follow a wooden causeway along the edge of the wall. The water table level is obvious and may be over some of the boards! If you have a ranging pole, soil auger or even a garden cane test the depth of the peat at various points along the causeway. This marshy area appears to be an infilled hollow along the length of a marginal channel, cut when ice formed the western boundary. It is a tributary to the major higher channel but their relative ages are indeterminate.

(c) The stile beyond the peat infill (GR 528601, 120m OD)

Over the wall alongside the path is a gentle slope on which there has been some land drainage to give reasonable pasture. At the far end of the field is a small man-made lake on the line of the channel. The slopes above are irregular and show signs of slumping of glacial till over the shale bedrock.

From here the path leads up a steep valley, taking diverse routes in parts to avoid waterlogged sections. To its left the vegetation covers boulder strewn slopes while to the right is more slumping (as noted earlier).

(d) Bottom of Windy Clough (GR 534603, 205m OD)

Stop at the two stiles at the top of the path. This is at the summit of the up gradient section of the valley - in both directions!

Beyond the wall is the boulder strewn valley of Windy Clough, with a scramble down to a hollow beneath the oak trees and a second water sink some 30 m further on. This reverse gradient is sufficient for a closed contour to be shown on the 1:25,000 map. The valley is at right angles to the general dip of the Clougha slope, and it cuts a huge notch in the skyline. (Best seen from a distance, such as M6 Exit 33 looking north-east). The trickle of water in the valley bottom moves some fine sediment, but again the meltwater hypothesis is needed to explain the landform. This feature, and also Little Windy Clough to the south (GR 538603), require an ice cover and a sub-marginal channel carrying powerful meltwater discharge to carve such a chasm through hard gritstone.

From this point a choice of routes is available, depending on time available.

(i) The longest, but most complete, route is to cross the left hand stile into the Windy Clough valley and, via the water sinks, follow the watercourse to its head returning via Birk Bank channel (2 km). Follow the route to point (e) below.

(ii) The second is not to cross the style but to turn left on the path climbing up across the slope and follow it round the spur to above the stone tower. It then leads past a solitary tree gradually downslope northwards to the head of the Birk Bank channel near a 1.8 m high stone pillar. When you reach the flat valley floor before it, turn left (1.2 km). Continue the description from point (f) below.

(iii) The shortest is to simply retrace your steps back to the car park (1 km).

(e) Route to Head of Windy Clough (GR 537607, 235m OD)

Cross the left hand stile into the Windy CLough valley and - via the water sinks - follow the watercourse to its head. The boulder filled valley has obviously been altered by periglacial activity and most of the boulders have just fallen under gravity; but the uneven valley floor remains. Beyond the boulder field there is a stile over a wall and beyond this a fairly level boggy section. Boulders reappear with bilberry cover. Don't lose heart! Stay in the valley bottom, duck under the oak trees and scramble up a boulder clog into a shallow valley which veers left. As soon as the ground levels out and a view across to Baines Crag opens up, there is a narrow path some 0.3 m wide running east-west.

Turn round and look at the characteristic head of the valley from which you have just emerged. It lacks any present water course and cuts across the general slope of the land. A sub-glacial origin for the channel seems likely. Follow the path eastwards along the crest of the slope and over a stile. Beyond this turn half right down a narrow path, aiming approximately towards a stone tower. The path leads downslope and when you reach a junction with another path double back right. This descends and eventually curves round towards the 1.8 m high stone pillar near the head of the Birk Bank channel.

(f) Head of Birk Bank Channel (GR 531608, 145m OD)

This site shows a marked contrast to the lower end of the channel at the start of the walk. Here it is quite wide and shallow and can be wet underfoot; but any attempt to sink an auger will not be easy beyond a few cms. The channel then narrows into a wooded gorge which is not followed by the path! Stay on the path eastwards beyond the wood after which can be seen some partly submerged boulders and a few trees on the valley floor. This is where the lower section of the meltwater channel has begun to be infilled and the gradual disappearance of the boulders and increase in vegetation density along it show a successively deeper incision and subsequent infill.

Continue along the track until you reach the car park.

Selected References

Gresswell, R K (1952) The glacial geomorphology of the south-eastern part of the Lake District. *Liverpool and Manchester Geographical Journal* 1; 57-70

Johnson, RH (1985) *The geomorphology of North West England.* Manchester University Press.

King, C A M (1976) *Northern England.* Methuen

Leedal, M (1988) *An investigation of the glacial meltwater channels of Clougha, north-west Bowland, Lancashire.* Unpublished BA thesis, S. Martin's College, Lancaster

Moseley, F (1954) The Namurian of the Lancaster Fells. *Quarterly Journal of the Geological Society* 109; 423-454

Moseley, F (1961) Erosion surfaces in the Forest of Bowland.
  Proceedings of the Yorkshire Geological Society 32; 173-96
Moseley F & D Walker (1952) Some aspects of the Quaternary period
  in North Lancashire. *Naturalist* (Apr/Jun); 41-54
Oldfield, F (1960) Late Quaternary changes in climate, vegetation and
  sea-level in lowland Lonsdale. *Transactions of the Institute of
  British Geographers* 28; 99-117

12 THE INDUSTRIAL ARCHAEOLOGY OF THE TEXTILE INDUSTRY IN THE LANCASTER AREA

James Price
(St Martin's College)

Outline: an introduction to the historical geography of the textile industry of North Lancashire through the study of the physical remains it has left, specifically in and around Lancaster.
Starting point: Lancaster.
Finishing point: Garstang.
Distance: 80 km round trip.
Route: by vehicle between sites, walking within sites.
Time needed: one full day.
Maps needed: OS 1:50,000 sheets 102 (Preston and Blackpool) and 97 (Kendal and Morecambe).

INTRODUCTION

Industrial Archaeology can be defined as "the study of the early days of industrialisation in terms of the housing of the workers, the buildings, sources of power and transport". Thus Industrial Archaeologists survey, study and interpret the remains of past industry and use a wide range of documentary materials to create a picture of the social and economic environment in which industries operated.

There have been two types of industrial organisation in the manufacture of textiles since medieval times - the domestic system and the factory system.

(a) Domestic textile industry

The Domestic or Cottage based system existed up to the eighteenth century, was rurally based and could take one of two forms. In the first, capitalist clothiers bought wool and "put it out" to hand spinners and hand weavers to convert into cloth. They then collected it and processed it further before selling it. This was the pattern of the Kendal industry from the sixteenth century with fulling and dyeing being done in the town (see Excursion 6).

A second form, found in the West Riding of Yorkshire, involved independent small clothiers who purchased wool and yarn and produced cloth which they took weekly to the Cloth Hall. In neither case were there large mechanised factories; most processing took place in and around the home, with women and girls carding and spinning the wool and the men weaving. There are some examples of "embryo" factories with a dozen or so looms but this was not the norm, and only in fulling was use made of water power.

(b) Factory-based textile industry

The second major organisational change came with the Industrial Revolution, in the second half of the eighteenth century, when a factory-based industry was created. At first it was still rurally based, using water power, but after 1783 - with the introduction of steam - it developed in towns on the coalfields.

In North Lancashire there are few obvious remains of the domestic phase, but there are records of wool and flax being processed in the seventeenth and eighteenth centuries. In the Warton-Yealand area there was a linen industry using local flax and later Irish flax imported through Lancaster. Woollen hats and gloves were made by Quaker groups in the Quernmore and Wyre valleys. These had no specialist factories, though several small barn-like buildings were called Hat factories. With the development of the Kendal woollen industry producing "Kendal Green", it may be that the Lune Valley was one area where the clothiers "put-out" work. If this was so, there is no physical evidence except that some houses had their window space enlarged or added to, to give increased light.

After 1750 a number of inventions transformed textiles, especially cotton manufacture. Kay's Flying Shuttle (1733) speeded up weaving and led to a search for methods of increasing the output of spun yarn. This resulted first in Hargreaves' Spinning Jenny (1769) and then the Water Frame of Richard Arkwright (1769). The "Frame" operated by water power was installed by Arkwright into a factory or Mill at Cromford in 1771 which developed into the world's first mechanised factory-based textile community.

The concept of a factory powered by an inanimate force soon spread to other areas including North Lancashire. Between 1780 and 1835 a number of water powered mills were erected on the Lune and Wyre systems (Figure 12a) processing cotton, wool, flax and silk. This

135

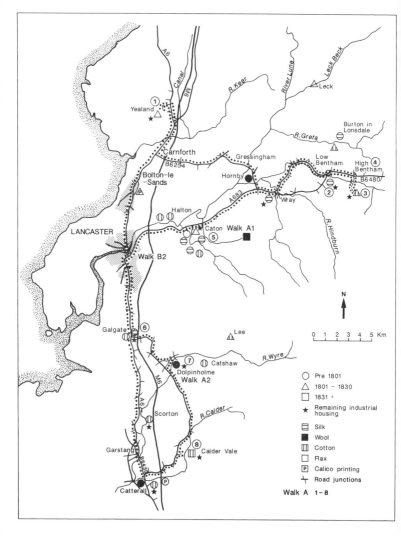

Figure 12a. The excursion route.

era was unfortunately short lived, but it left the area with a fine set of industrial remains.

With the introduction of steam power after 1783, when the first Boulton and Watt engine was installed into a Manchester cotton mill, the centre of gravity of the cotton industry moved. By 1800 there were 42 engines in Lancashire alone, and these were in large mills in towns on the Lancashire coalfield. Many of the small rural mills closed. The area lacked coal in any real quantity and had to import it by sea from Cumberland and Wigan. Transport inland was facilitated by the Lancaster canal (opened 1797) and steam powered mills were erected alongside it in Lancaster after 1802. These brought the steam era to North Lancashire, though many larger rural mills augmented their water wheel with a steam engine.

EXCURSION A

Leave Lancaster northwards across the Lune on the A6 towards Carnforth (Figure 12a). About 4 km beyond Carnforth turn left to Yealand Conyers, then turn left at the T junction for 400 m.

Site 1 Flax Mill and Weavers Cottages (GR 503742)

Just before the corner is a row of two storey stone cottages facing the road. These were handloom weavers cottages for linen weavers. The barn-like building at the end was the heckling and spinning mill for processing the flax into yarn. This was built in 1825 and was steam powered. It closed in 1851 when the operations were transfered to Home Mill. Across the road is Waithman House where the owner lived.

Drive back to Carnforth and turn left at the traffic lights onto the B6254. Continue through Over Kellet to Gressingham, then over the River Lune to Hornby. Follow signs for Wray on the B6480, then straight on to Low Bentham (5.5 km). Turn right after the Punchbowl Inn under the railway bridge to the mill (Figure 12a).

Site 2 Low Bentham Silk Mill (GR 649693)

The mill was built initially in 1785 to spin and weave flax, and it was rebuilt after a fire in 1852. From 1877 to its closure in 1970 it spun silk.

Behind the 1928 addition is the "Ridge and Furrow" roof of the weaving sheds. Evidence of water power includes a weir on the River Wenning, and a mill race which crosses the river on a metal bridge (launder). Steam was added later and the engine house and lower part of the chimney remain. Today the mill is mainly used as a Trout farm.

Adjacent to the mill are several cottages, including Rose Cottage. In the village itself there are a number of terraces of small stone cottages built for the workforce in the late eighteenth-early nineteenth century. One is dated 1786.

Continue up the main road to High Bentham (Figure 12a). Turn right at the Black Bull, cross the railway line and turn first right along a lane to the site of the former mill on the left.

Site 3 High Bentham Mill (GR 665688)

A large flax spinning mill was built here using water power before 1800. A steam engine was added later and the mill produced a variety of products - hemp twine, artificial silk, real silk. Further along the lane at Wenning Avenue is an L-shaped development of two and three-storey stone workers cottages. Probably built around 1800, they still have their original privvies at the rear (which have long been converted into water closets).

Retrace your steps to the Black Bull and turn right. About 400 m up on the left is Lairgill.

Site 4 Lairgill (GR 671693)

This is a terrace of seventeen stone cottages with cellars. It was built by Roughsedge, Hornby and Co of Kirkham who were flax spinners and linen weavers in 1816. The cellars were used for weaving sailcloth. It is a rare survival of a loomshop.

Turn around and follow the main road back to Hornby. Then drive south along the A683 to Caton.

Site 5 Caton (GR 5364)

Park at the bottom of Quernmore Road (Figure 12b). If you do not intend to do the whole of Walk A1 (below), then refer only to points a and b and then continue on the excursion route.

Drive south into Lancaster and follow the one-way system southwards to the A6. You will reach Galgate in 6.5 kms. At the Police Station (on your left) turn left onto Chapel Lane and follow it round to the mill. Park in front of the mill or on the car park at the north (distant) end.

Site 6 Thompson Mill Galgate (4GR 83554)

This mill opened in 1792 and was the oldest mechanised silk spinning mill in England when it closed in 1971. There is a weir on the River Conder (at GR 485562) and the mill race which runs across the fields originally filled two millponds (the one on the site of the car park is now infilled). The mill buildings are of three periods. The original (converted from a corn mill) is a narrow three-storey building west of the road; in the 1830s a three-storey extension of irregular shape was added; finally in 1852 the large five-storey brick mill was built. At the north end is the former beam engine house (with an arched entrance and square brick chimney).

There are a number of workers houses in Galgate. Walk back down Chapel Lane past the Methodist chapel and note the small terraced properties on Chapel Street including Makinsons Row (which was built before 1845). On the A6 below the Catholic Chapel are some later two and three-storey houses.

Rejoin the A6 and drive south (left) to the traffic lights. Turn left onto Stoney Lane and carry straight on for 3 km to a crossroads (GR 509532). Turn left by the Fleece Hotel and follow the sign to Dolphinholme.

Site 7 Dolphinholme (GR 5153)

Park opposite the school (GR 518537) and if you do not intend to do the full walk (A2, described below and shown on Figure 12c) refer only to point k and then continue on the excursion route.

Return to the Fleece Hotel and turn left. Follow the signs to Chipping and Oakenclough. At the crossroads at GR 536475 (5.5 km) take the right hand road to Garstang. After 2.5 km turn left, past the garage, to Calder Vale. Go down the hill and park in front of the Methodist Chapel.

Site 8 Calder Vale (GR 5346)

Hidden in a steep sided valley, this is the best surviving example of a factory village in North Lancashire. The mill and the first workers housing were built by the Jackson brothers in 1835. There is a chapel, school, shop (Co-op) and housing, but in common with many similar villages there is no public house. Think why?

Long Row is a terrace of nineteen stone cottages built at the same time as the mill. Beyond them is the Millpond fed by the River Calder, with a sluice controlling the water to the head race behind the cottages. The Lappet Mill is a large four-storey building with a warehouse at the north end. To the south-west is the site of the former waterwheel and a boiler house and chimney for the later engine. Weaving sheds were added after 1880 and the factory is still working (no visits) weaving high quality cotton goods. Across the river are three terraces of stone houses - including Victoria and Albert Rows.

Turn left at Albert Row and walk to the millpond for a weaving shed (around 1848) and the "Holme" a small square of houses, six unusually in brick. Follow the millrace running alongside the path and you come to the site of the weaving shed (now demolished) and a terrace of nine houses.

Return to the main road and follow the signs to Garstang to end the excursion.

WALK A1 CATON (Figure 12b)

Park at the bottom of Quernmore Road, cross the main road and turn left. Go down the narrow lane to Low Mill (a). This is a very fine cotton mill and warehouse built by Thomas Hodgson in 1784. It passed into the hands of the Gregs of Styal in 1817 who rebuilt it after a fire in 1838; it was spinning cotton until it closed in 1970. It was initially water-powered, and it has a large pond on the river terrace behind it; it later had a steam engine and the chimney remains. Both Hodgson and Greg used apprentice labour to ensure a continuity of supply - in 1808 around half of the 150 workers were apprentices. They were orphan children, mainly from Liverpool, and they were housed in the adjacent apprentice house now converted to housing. Bank House was the Manager's House.

At the top of the lane turn left, walk 150 m and turn left after the

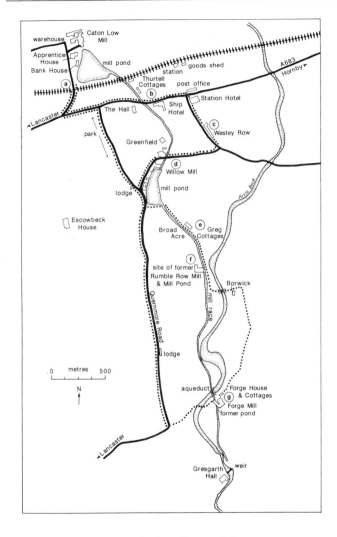

Figure 12b. The walk around Caton.

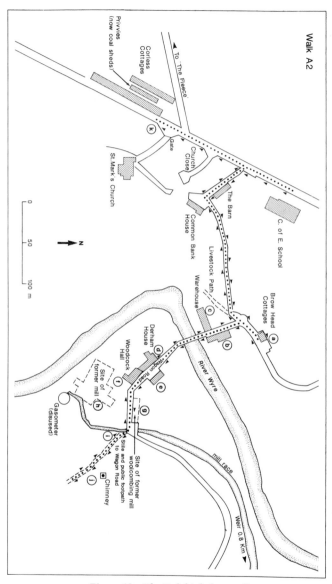

Figure 12c. The Dolphinholme walk.

cafe (b). Here is the millrace which fed Low Mill pond and powered three other mills. It starts at a weir on the Artle Beck behind Gresgarth Hall. Thurtle Cottages at the bottom of the lane were built by the Gregs as workers' homes. Unlike Dolphinhome, Caton was already a village, so only a limited amount of housing was built by manufacturers.

Continue up the A683 and cross the road at the Station Hotel. Along Brookhouse Road is Wesley Row cottages (c) built by William Stubbs of Willow Mill in 1838 for his silkworkers. At the junction with Copy Lane turn right to Willow Mill (d). This four-storey mill was built 1790-5 as a cotton mill. It was water-powered though a steam engine was added later. It was in the silk trade for nearly 50 years, and the silk warehouse is now a youth club. Across the road is the former Apprentice House. Further along are the Rock m'Jock cottages which were rebuilt in the 1890s by Albert Greg.

Turn left up Quernmore road past the wall of the Escowbeck estate (formerly owned by the Gregs) and into Broadacre. On the left is the former millpond for Willow Mill and the line of the millrace. Further along on the left (e) are Croft Cottages built by Samuel Greg in 1831. At the top of Broadacre is the site of the former Rumble Row Mill, which is now occupied by a primary school (f). The mill race can still be seen on its way from Forge Mill.

Go down the path to the Artle Beck, cross on the footbridge, over a stile and across a field to join the path at Borwick to Forge Mill (g). Forge Mill is 300 m further on. It is an example of a mill with the site of the water wheel marked by a round arched window. Beyond is the line of the mill race and a drained pond. The race crosses the stream on a metal trough (or launder), and at the rear of the mill is the later engine house. The owner's house and a set of former cottages also still survive.

Continue up the lane, over the bridge and come out in front of the Gresgarth Estate (private). Walk down Quernmore Road to where you parked.

WALK A2 DOLPHINHOLME (Figure 12c)

In 1771 Richard Arkwright created his factory village at Cromford on the River Derwent. By providing housing he ensured a reliable and permanent labour force for his mills in a sparsely populated area. The concept of a mill village was soon taken up by other industrialists who found that many suitable water power sites lacked an adequate local labour supply. Mill work was not very popular anyway and the draw of a house to go with the job made it more attractive.

Dolphinholme, located on a superb water power site on the Wyre, is such a village. The first mill of 1784 which spun woollen yarn was not a success but in 1795 Thomas Hinde of Lancaster built a new mill away from the river fed by a long millrace off the Wyre. This had a 30 foot (9m) water wheel and spun worsted yarn brought from Bradford and East Anglia. The mill rapidly became very successful; by 1798 it had 2 shifts and in 1809 there were 1,000 workers with 200 outworkers carding wool. It was one of the first mills to be lit by gas (1811) and in 1822 a Boulton and Watt engine was installed. In 1839 the firm of Hinde and Derham closed but the mill remained in wool to 1851. From 1852 to 1867 it was a cotton mill but it then closed largely due to its remoteness. Other than the demolition of the mill, Dolphinholme remains very much as it was in its heyday.

Park by the school and walk back to the unnamed lane leading to Common Bank House (Figure 12c). Turn left opposite this house and follow the Livestock path to Dolphinholme Bottoms. Ahead of you are Brow Head Cottages (a), the remains of a bigger terrace which had balconies originally suggesting that each house was in shared occupation. On the corner is a row of cottages (b) several of which are painted white, something noted by the Factory Inspector in 1838. Across the road is the former warehouse (c). Underneath were cellar dwellings occupied by workers families, while the top floor could have been used for weaving at some time. This building has been converted into seven terraced houses.

Over the bridge on the right is Derham House(d), the manager's house. On the corner is the last gas lamp of those installed by Mr Hinde to light the street at the same time as he lit his mill. The two houses opposite (e) were recently converted from what were in 1845 a coach house, stables and piggery for the mill owner. Woodcock Hall, the owner's house (f) formerly faced the mill (h) which stood in what is now the large walled garden. Opposite the high wall was a woolcombing mill (g) now demolished. A little further up the Wagon Road (i) is where the race crossed under the road. On the left the former race is almost dry, on the right it has been infilled. Beyond this point (on private property) is the site of the Gasometer. Climb up the public footpath from the stile and on the hill top are the remains of a double chimney - for the gas works and the steam engine (j).

Retrace your steps, go back up the hill and walk to the Corless Cottages (k). These were built around 1796 to house some of the workers, probably by Mr Hinde. The nearest row are two-storey; those at the rear are three-storey and they may have been shared by several families. Between the two rows are the former privvies, now converted to coal houses.

EXCURSION B LANCASTER

Parts of this excursion (Figure 12d) may be combined with the Lancaster Historic Town Trail (Excursion I3) and/or parts of Excursion 14.

The building of the canal to the east of Lancaster stimulated both new industrial development and later house building. Eight steam powered mills were erected here between 1802 and 1864. The canal was used to bring in coal and other raw materials and export the manufactured goods. All of the mills were initially independent but after 1850 most came into the hands of two firms - James Williamson and Storeys - who used their cotton as the backing for oilcloth.

CANALSIDE

Park at Aldcliffe Basin (a on Figure 12d), cross the Roving Bridge (b) and walk towards Aldcliffe Basin (c) with the remains of its coalyards. The site of Queens Mill (d), a cotton mill built in 1840 and now demolished, is occupied by a DIY store. The Water Witch (e), now a pub, provided stables for canal horses.

Under Penny Bridge you come to White Cross Mill (f) built in 1802 but added to by Storeys up to around 1900. Their former offices were converted from a Militia barracks. The whole site is now an industrial estate. The canal was used until the 1940s to bring in coal (see the mooring rings on the towpath). On the other side of the canal is the former Power Station (1893 and 1904) which also used the canal for transporting coal.

Beyond White Cross is the Primrose Estate of small stone terraced houses erected in the 1880s and 1890s. Behind the Cathedral is a similar housing area (Moorlands) built around 1900. Both areas provided housing for workers in the canalside mills.

Cross back to the other side of the canal at Quarry Road and notice the former coal and timber yards along the canal (the one to your

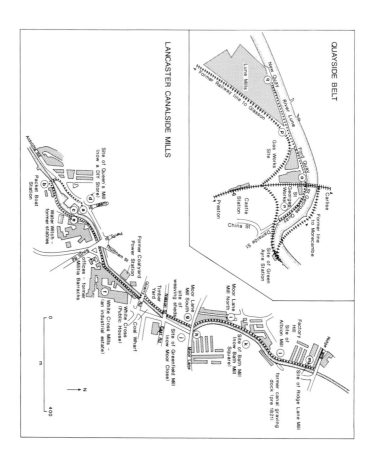

Figure 12d. The Lancaster canalside and quayside walk.

left now built on) and the one in front of the Cathedral. Continue past Moor Lane Mill South (g), which was built by Samuel Greg 1825-31 as a cotton mill. Recently the weaving sheds have been demolished to make way for an industrial innovation centre. Note the round topped window, the site of the engine house. Moor Lane Mill North (i) built in 1819 as a woollen mill, has been converted into a Hall of Residence for St Martins College.

If you stood on the canal bridge over Moor Lane (h) in the 1970s, you would have seen four mills. As well as the Moor Lane mills there was Greenfield Mill (j) (1864 to 1975), its site now built on. Further along was Bath Mill (k) (1837 to 1974) of which the only remains are a row of cottages and a stable block. Continue walking by the canal until you reach the embanked section (l), which offers a good view of Lancaster. On the other side of the canal is the Freehold Estate begun by an ancestor of the Building Society Movement in the 1850s. Some remains still exist of the Albion Mill (l), which was built between 1821 and 1825 as a cotton mill, though the rest was demolished around 1960. On this site William Jackson (the owner) built a set of back-to-back houses at the top of Factory Hill. Finally at Ridge Lane there is the remaining part of the silk mill (m) built in 1837. The rest was demolished in 1888 and houses built on the site.

Retrace your steps to Aldcliffe. Drive around the one-way system down King Street and China Street; turn sharp left at Damside Street into St George's Quay.

QUAYSIDE

St. George's Quay was the eighteenth century port (n) and this river-side location is also the site of the factories of James Williamson and Sons. Williamson, a local man, began to make oilcloth in a small factory on Duke Street before 1844. In 1854 he moved to a large factory (o), the St. Georges Works. In 1870 he purchased the site of the ill-fated shipyard and built Lune Mills there (p). By 1895 this site covered 8.5 ha and the firm had over 2,500 workers making oilcloth and linoleum. Both of these were popular Victorian requirements - oilcloth was used for clothing, furniture, table cloths and lino was an ubiquitous hard wearing floor covering.

The siting of both mills by the river was the result of several factors. First, the land was relatively cheap and there were large areas available - unlike along the congested canal-side. Secondly, the river provided large amounts of water for processing. Thirdly, river transport could be used to bring in raw materials.

The New Quay (q) was used to import linseed oil, china clay and so on to Lune Mills. On it are the remains of a horse-drawn narrow gauge railway to take goods into the factory. The mill works also benefitted from the fact that the railways were on this side of the town on the flatter land by the river. In 1883 the line to Glasson (see Excursion 16) actually passed the rear of Lune Mills after leaving the main line at Castle Station, and a spur line went into the factory. The railway gave access to markets all over the country and abroad. The line was closed to passengers in 1930 and to freight in 1964.

Selected References

Ashmore, O (1969) *Industrial Archaeology of Lancashire*. David and Charles

Marshall, J D and M Davies-Shiel (1969) *Industrial Archaeology of the Lake Counties*. David and Charles

Price, J W A (1983) *The Industrial Archaeology of the Lune Valley*. University of Lancaster, Centre for N W Regional Studies

Price, J W A (1989) *The Industrial Archaeology of Lancaster*. Lancaster Museum

Schofield, M M (1946) Outline of an Economic History of Lancaster from 1680-1860. 2 vols *Transactions of the Lancaster Branch of the Historical Association*.

13 HISTORIC LANCASTER: BACKGROUND AND EIGHTEENTH CENTURY TOWN TRAIL

Geoff Boulton
(St Martin's College)

Outline: a walk through parts of eighteenth century Lancaster which looks at surviving buildings and the early urban fabric of the city, and offers suggestions for individual work based on a seven teenth century source. This excursion could be combined with Excursion 14, which explores the planning implications of recent pressures to develop the city centre.

Starting point: Customs House, Maritime Museum (GR 474624).

Finishing point: Castle Hill (GR 475618) - then return to start.

Distance: a walk of 1.5 km.

Route: footpath walking in urban setting.

Time needed: about 1.5 hours for the basic walk; allow up to half a day to include visits to named buildings.

Maps needed: Lancaster and Morecambe Town Map. OS special sheet, 1:10,000 with City Centre insert at 1:7,000.

INTRODUCTION

Lancaster is one of England's old-established towns with a continuous urban history stretching back to the Middle Ages, or possibly to Roman times. Throughout, it has been the main market and commercial centre for north Lancashire and has had important administrative and legal functions. In the eighteenth century its port expanded its trade world wide, notably to the West Indies. In the nineteenth century, following improvements in inland communications, a group of distinctive industries were located here. In the twentieth century the provison of medical services and higher education together with tourism have assumed greater importance in the local economy. The effects of these activities can be readily observed in the city today.

The industrial and retail structure of the city is undergoing considerable change at present. Large parts of the central area are likely to be rebuilt (see Excursion 14). This excursion passes through the parts of the eighteenth century city unlikely to be affected by redevelopment.

Physical setting

Lancaster stands on the northern extension of the Lancashire Plain where the lowland is constricted by the western edges of the Forest of Bowland (see Excursions 17 and 18) and by the eastward sweep of Morecambe Bay (see Excursion 19). Castle Hill (40 m OD) consists of gritstone beneath a thin glacial capping. Westwards and northwards the landscape consists of drumlins (30 to 50 m OD) aligned roughly north-south (see Excursion 11). Southwards and eastwards structural elements give the relief a distinctive NNE-SSW "grain" with the 100 m high Bowerham ridge falling steadily to the tidal river in less than 1.5 km.

Just upstream from Lancaster the River Lune has a braided channel with small islands which have only recently been stabilised. Downstream the estuary opens out and is bounded by extensive tidal salt marshes. However, between Skerton Bridge and Carlisle Bridge the river flows in a more confined bed in solid rock, which made it easy for the Romans to ford the river here and facilitated the construction of medieval and later bridges.

These physical features have all affected the growth of the town. The prominent Castle Hill overlooking the best river crossings was the obvious site for the Roman Camp and the later Norman Castle. Early route ways avoided badly drained areas such as the cut-off river meander at Green Ayre, which is now the site of the bus station.

John Rennie in the eighteenth century planned the Lancaster Canal as a contour canal at 68 feet (20 m) above sea-level. It snaked round the edge of the existing town to cross the river on a high aqueduct about 1.5 km upstream. In the nineteenth century John Locke took the Lancaster-Preston and Lancaster-Carlisle Railways to the west of the town where it was easier to excavate cuttings in the glacial material of the drumlins and to cross the river with a high level bridge. At various times local variations of relief and aspect have made some sites more desirable for residential development than others.

Approaching the city there are good vantage points on each side to get an overview of its setting and in suitable weather conditions to record it by photography or field sketching.

Vantage Points

GR		
489650	Kellet Lane	South-west (distant)
484639	Lune Aqueduct towpath	South-west
471624	Carlisle Bridge foot way	South, south-east
473619	Priory Church yard	North, west
474606	Haverbreaks	North

(path from Aldcliffe Road canal footbridge 472608 to Ashton Road Railway Bridge 476605)

486608	St. Martins College field	North west

(consult porter in lodge for permission which will normally be given)

488614	Ashton Memorial,	West, north-west

Williamson Park. (Small charge. When closed use old bandstand alongside)

Orientation Marks

Castle	(Castle Hill)	474618
Priory Church	(Castle Hill)	474619
College of Further Education (7 storey block		
	Torrisholme)	459633
Castle School	(Bowerham Ridge)	488623
Ashton Memorial	(Bowerham Ridge)	488614
St. Martins College	(8 storey block,	
	(Bowerham Ridge)	485607
Town Hall	(Baroque Tower,	
	centre)	479615
St. Peters Cathedral	(Slender Spire,	
	centre)	481615

Relict geography in an historic city

One approach in historical geography is to look for relict features of past geographies in the modern landscape.

In Lancaster there is a unique source for such work in the Townley Hall Map of 1684. This map by an unknown surveyor was discovered at Townley Hall in 1952, together with the surveyor's measurements and notes. A local historian, Kenneth Docton, drew a tidy version of the map and compiled a directory from the notes (Docton 1952, 1954). The originals are in the County Record Office at Preston, but copies are available in Lancaster Library, and in the Geography Department of St. Martin's College. A simplified version appears in Stephen Penney's (1981) book *Lancaster : the evolution of its townscape.*

The basic street pattern of the present city centre had been fixed by 1684. The two settlements recorded in Domesday Book (1086) - 'Lancaster' centred on Stonewell, and 'Church-Lancaster' on Castle Hill near the existing church - were linked by Church Street which essentially follows the line of the Roman civil settlement (see Figure 13). Market Street and St. Nicholas Street formed a later east-west route, possibly leading from the main gate of the Castle started in the early 12th century. There were two north-south routes. Penny Street is considered by some authorities to be Roman while King Street - China Lane - Bridge Lane led down to the medieval bridge. With the exception of Bridge Lane (which was removed in 1930s slum clearance) and St. Nicholas Street (demolished to build the new shopping centre in the 1970s), all these streets are still in use today. Stephen Penney gives a concise description of the growth of the town (Penney 1981).

As in other towns property boundaries of burgage plots along main streets or between fields have affected subsequent development. A local historian describes how this can happen. "In 1756 Thomas Mackerell, a maltster, by his last will directed the street called Mackerell Lane, or Spring Garden Street to be constructed through his garden from Penny Street to Back Lane (now King Street)" (Chippindall 1926). This field can be identified on the 1684 map. The narrow burgage plots on the east side of Penny Street can be clearly observed from Mary Street which was laid out along the edge of the Friarage land in the eighteenth century as part of the Dalton Estate. Many similar examples can be found.

The second half of the eighteenth century was a period of prosperity for Lancaster arising from its involvement in the West Indies trade. This resulted in the construction of many new public and private buildings, of St. Georges' Quay (1764) and the Lancaster Canal (1797) and of a new river bridge (1788) and several new streets. Most of these have survived.

In recent years a number of examples of eighteenth century life have been recreated to give a fuller picture of the social and economic structures which would have affected peoples' decision-making. Stephen Makreth's large scale map of 1778 gives a good cartographic picture of the town. Copies are available in local libraries and reproductions can be purchased cheaply from the City Museum.

EXCURSION

It is logical to start the excursion at the source of the town's wealth, the Quayside (a on Figure 13) (GR 474624) (see Excursion 12b and Figure 12d). Parking for cars and mini-buses is available behind the Customs House and for buses further west along the Quay.

St George's Quay

Morecambe Bay has a large tidal range and boats engaged in the coastal trade would have come up river at high tide, beached on the tidal edge and been unloaded into carts at low tide. One of the first actions of the Port Commissioners appointed by Act of Parliament in 1749 was to construct a stone faced quay at which boats could be moored at all stages of the tide. Warehouses and three and four storey dwellings were built facing onto this with poorer cottages behind in River Street. The Customs House was built in 1764, thus confirming Lancaster's position as the main port in the region.

Although many have changed their function most of the eighteenth century buildings on St. Georges' Quay are still present (the trees and grass verges were planted this century after the quay had ceased to be used commercially). The Customs House together with the neighbouring warehouse are now the home of the Lancaster Maritime Museum. The Customs Receiver's Office on the ground floor has been restored to its eighteenth century form together with samples of goods such as bales of cotton and large conical blocks of sugar. (This is just one part of the Museum for which there is an entrance charge).

Priory Church

Walk south-east along the Quay to Vicarage Walk (signposted to Castle and Priory) and follow this up the hill to the Priory Churchyard (b). Looking north from the churchyard down onto the Quayside it is easy to imagine the river filled with ships, as shown in the prints on display in the Maritime Museum.

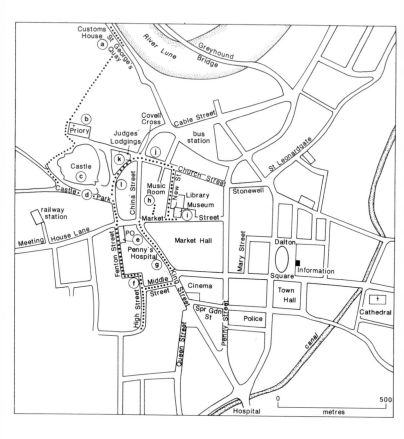

Figure 13. The Lancaster eighteenth century town trail.

The Priory Church of the Blessed Mary of Lancaster is mainly fifteenth century but the tower was built in the eighteenth century. Many of the memorial statues and tablets in the church date from this period, and indicate the wealth of the town during this period of prosperity.

154

Castle
Lancaster Castle (c) has been in continuous use since the Middle Ages, mainly as a prison and as an Assize and County Court. In 1788 major works were begun to build new outer walls and a new Shire Hall to plans by William Harrison, the local architect who had designed the new Skerton Bridge in 1783. The Shire Hall is an early example of Gothic Revival and contains much expensive carving. (Parts of the Castle, including the Shire Hall, are open to visitors when courts are not sitting).

Continue along the western edge of the Castle to Castle Park (d). The south side is lined with the type of elegant town houses built by rich merchants and local gentry in the eighteenth century.

Eighteenth Century developments
The area west of King Street, just outside the medieval core of the town, was developed at this time. Enter the area by going down Castle Park, crossing Meeting House Lane and proceeding down Fenton Street, alongside the modern Head Post Office (e). In Fenton Street, except for the house that is now the Trades Hall, most of the eighteenth century property has been demolished by the GPO (now Royal Mail and British Telecom).

Immediately south in High Street there is a quite different situation. The first terrace (on the left) has recently been restored. The Girls' Blue Coat School (1772) opposite (f), now a furniture store, is substantially unchanged with its suitably uplifting inscription on the gable end. There are two fine gentlemen's houses on the west side. High Street House, built for a local landowner Thomas Saul in 1773, now houses the District Education Offices. The Independent Chapel with its small graveyard was completed in 1774 (it is now the United Reformed Church).

Turn east down Middle Street with its former Girls' Charity School to King Street still lined on its west side by mainly eighteenth century property. Continue north to Penny's Almshouses or Hospital which can be seen through the arched gateway (g). Alderman William Penny founded a charity which built the almshouses for "twelve poor men" together with a small chapel in the 1720s. The Trustees built the Assembly Rooms alongside in 1759 as an investment. Social events such as balls and concerts were held here particularly during the period of the Assizes which was the town's social season.

The Music Room

At the traffic lights cross the road and walk east into Market Street. From the north side of Market Street, just before Barclay's Bank, go up the alleyway on the left into Sun Street Passage (signposted "Music Room"). This opens into what remains of Dr Marton's garden shown on Mackreth's map. Rev Dr Marton was vicar of Lancaster from 1767 to 1794 and he lived in one of the largest houses on Church Street as befitted his position as one of the leaders of local society. In one corner of the garden stood the Music Room (h), which was built around 1730. Inside it is embellished with lavish Italian plasterwork. It may have been used for recitals or for entertaining people using the private garden. (The building was restored by the Landmark Trust in 1978 and is open most summer afternoons). Sun Street was constructed later within the confines of the garden.

City Museum

Return to Market Street and visit the City Museum (i), which was built as the Town Hall in 1783. Originally the ground floor was left open for market stalls while the large room on the first floor hosted the town council. There are portraits of eighteenth century citizens and paintings of contemporary views. Mackreth's map has been used as the basis for a scale model and there are photographs of buildings now demolished. Artefacts include examples of Gillow furniture and other humbler manufacturers, shop signs and military exhibits. (Admission to the Museum, which is open daily except Sundays, is free. The Museum has a collection of monographs and maps on sale).

Behind the Museum is New Street, which was laid out in 1747 "through the garden of Joshua Whalley", along one of the Church Street burgage plots. Most of the west of the street is still original above the modern ground floor shop fronts. Follow New Street to Church Street and turn left. Most of the gentlemen's houses on upper Church Street have survived, albeit in commercial use. One of the finest of these is the Conservative Club (j) with its wrought iron railings, lantern frame and torch snuffer. This belonged to the Marton family and is supposed to have housed Bonnie Prince Charlie when he passed through Lancaster twice in 1745.

Church Street and Judge's Lodgings

Just beyond the crossing over China Lane is Covell Cross (an Edwardian replica of an earlier market cross) and The Judges' Lodgings (k). This is Lancaster's oldest surviving house. The main part is seventeenth century (using earlier materials) but it was extensively improved in the eighteenth before being bought by the County justices for the visiting Assize Judges in 1826. It is now a museum administered by the County Council and part of the original Judges' quarters have been restored. The dining room with its Gillow furniture is laid out with silver as if the Judge was about to entertain some of the local establishment. (The Museum also houses a Museum of Childhood. There is a small charge).

Castle Hill

Walk up Castle Hill to the south of the Judges' Lodgings to No. 15, a cottage built in 1739 (l). With many alterations this remained in use until 1961 when it was condemned as unfit for human habitation. It has since been restored by the City Council and furnished to illustrate the way of life of a respectable, though not affluent, working-class household of about 1830. Its confined spaces, steep stairways and poor illumination and ventilation is in marked contrast to the upper class eighteenth century buildings which have more usually survived.

A few metres further on stands a symmetrical two storey building. The panel above the door formerly housed a plaque of the Good Samaritan which is now over the main door of the Lancaster Royal Infirmary. Between 1785 and 1832 this was the town's Dispensary supported by public subscription to give medical help to the poor.

This forms a convenient end to an eighteenth century excursion. If you have time, you may like to explore comparable areas to the east of the town, perhaps following the walk suggested by John Champness (1986).

CONCLUSION

This excursion has linked together external observation of surviving features of the eighteenth century landscape with visits to reconstructions of contemporary conditions. Together these show the activities of a confident class of merchants and gentry who were aware of their social and economic position. They were able to build sound properties, both public and private, which have survived, and to raise capital for such ventures as the Lancaster Canal. There was an increasing social conscience with the construction of schools, almshouses and a dispensary but there were obviously wide social disparities. The 'respectable' working-class cottage on Castle Hill is almost a lone survivor of poorer property and the overcrowded, insanitary houses in which the majority of the urban poor lived have long since disappeared. Thus, this examination illustrates the underlying social structures, an understanding of which is essential in the historical geography of north-west England in the eighteenth century.

Selected References

Boulton, A G (1976) *Lancaster 1801-1881.* Unpublished MA, University of Liverpool

Champness, J (1986) *A new walk around Historic Lancaster.* Lancaster

Chippindall, W H (1926) *Chapters in the History of Lancaster in the 18th and 19th centuries.* Lancaster

Docton, K H (1952) Lancaster in 1684. *Transactions of the Historical Society of Lancashire and Cheshire* 109

Docton, K H (1954) *A Directory of Lancaster.* Lancaster

Penney, S H (1981) *Lancaster: The evolution of its Townscape to 1800.* University of Lancaster Centre for North-West Regional Studies Occasional Paper No. 9

Published guides to Lancaster Castle, Lancaster Priory, the Maritime Museum, the Judges' Lodging and No. 15 Castle Hill

14 HISTORIC LANCASTER: PROBLEMS OF PLANNING

Colin G Pooley
(University of Lancaster)

Outline: a walk around the historic city of Lancaster highlighting some of the major current planning problems created by retail expansion, tourist development, conservation and transport planning. This excursion could be combined with Excursion 13 (which explores the historic connections) and parts of Excursion 12 (which deals with industrial archaeology).

Starting and finishing points: Lancaster Castle (GR 473619).
Distance: 1.5 km.
Route: walking mainly along footpaths.
Time needed: about 2.5 hours.
Maps needed: OS Landranger (1:50,000) sheet 97; OS Lancaster and Morecambe Town Map (1:10,000).

PLANNING ISSUES IN LANCASTER

Much of the urban fabric of Lancaster dates from the late-eighteenth and early-nineteenth centuries, although a few buildings together with the street plan have a much earlier origin (see Excursion 13). In the eighteenth century the town was a busy port and wealth generated through coastal and Atlantic trade helped to create the rich Georgian townscape which has been carried through to the twentieth century. Although textile and linoleum, iron, furniture and railway waggon industries were developed in the nineteenth century, Lancaster never became a large manufacturing centre. Twentieth century redevelopment has progressed relatively slowly.

In the late 1980s Lancaster thus presents particular problems when the desire to stimulate economic development is combined with the need to conserve and enhance the historic townscape of the city.

The city of Lancaster forms part of the much larger administrative unit of Lancaster District which had a population of 118,589 in 1981, and is projected to rise to 131,400 by 1996. The economic, social

159

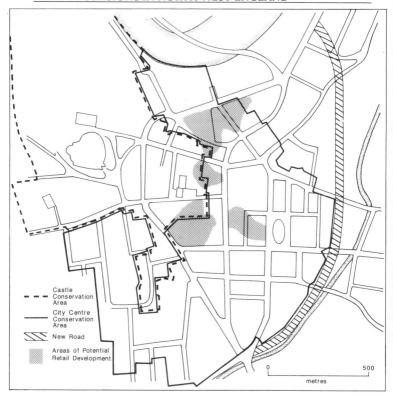

Figure 14a. Details of the Lancaster Local Plan (1980)

and administrative needs of this population are largely served by the city of Lancaster (together with the town of Morecambe, see Excursion 15), although only about 40 per cent of the population actually live within the city.

The Lancaster Local Plan (1987) highlights five major areas where large scale change is planned into the 1990s. Of these, the most significant for the historic centre of Lancaster are the need to generate economic development through retail expansion and the promotion of tourism, the desire to conserve the historic townscape, and the need to

Thurstaston, Wirral (Exc 21). Photo: Merseyside Tourism Board

Port Sunlight, a model factory village (Exc 24)
Photo: Merseyside Tourism Board

Albert Dock, Liverpool (Exc 25). Photo: Merseyside Tourism Board

An artist's impression of Edge Hill (Exc 26).
Photo: Merseyside Tourism Board

ease traffic congestion. Other themes such as the promotion of industry and new housing developments are concentrated on the urban fringe; they are beyond the scope of this excursion.

Conservation

Like other towns, Lancaster has used Conservation Areas (Kain, 1981) to protect buildings of historic value and townscape significance over the last 12 years. The Local Plan proposes the creation of two new Conservation Areas which encompass most of central Lancaster (Figure 14a). However, the protection to buildings afforded by Conservation Area status is limited, and the Lancaster Local Plan offers a higher level of protection to buildings in the Castle Conservation Area than to those in the city centre. This is justified on the grounds that there has already been more change in the city centre area and, although there are "many fine individual buildings" (Lancaster Local Plan, 1987 p.37) there is also considerable scope for redevelopment.

Critics of this proposal argue that the creation of a hierarchy of conservation areas is unacceptable, that the overall context of large and small buildings in the city centre is as important as in the Castle area, and that significant redevelopment of the City Centre Conservation Area will destroy one of Lancaster's most attractive features.

Redevelopment of Retailing

The major threat to Lancaster City Centre, and one reason why the protection afforded to buildings in this area is limited, is the planned redevelopment of the city's retail centre. It is argued that if Lancaster is to compete as a major service and retail centre in North Lancashire, and if it is to attract tourists and economic investment, then it must provide a shopping centre which is comparable with those found in other towns in the region.

A consultant's report on retail development in the City (BDP/ Donaldsons, 1986) forecast increased market penetration of the city's secondary hinterland for durable goods spending and forecast a high demand from traders for new stores in Lancaster. On this basis it was proposed that new retail developments amounting to some 200,000 square feet (18,580 square metres) of additional retail space should be planned. These proposals were incorporated into the Lancaster Local Plan and four major redevelopment areas were proposed, all of which fall within the City Centre Conservation Area (Figure 14a).

The major features of the planned redevelopment include:

(i) the removal of the Victorian Market from its present site to allow the expansion of multiple stores and the creation of a new shopping precinct,

(ii) the redevelopment of the present bus station to include a new bus station, a multi-storey car park, large retail store and a repositioned market, and

(iii) the redevelopment of two further sites with smaller shop units.

Critics of the scheme claim that it will inflict irrevocable damage on the historic townscape of Lancaster, that the scale of the development is far too massive, that the demand for new retail sites in Lancaster has been overestimated and many empty units will be created, that the new market site will be inconvenient for shoppers, and that the scheme will destroy those features which could make Lancaster attractive to tourists.

City Centre Access Road

As well as improvements to Lancaster's retail sector, the Local Plan also proposes a major new road scheme (Figure 14a) which is designed to ease traffic congestion around the city's present ring road. This is also seen as a major element in plans to make Lancaster more attractive for tourism and economic investment. Until the early 1970s most traffic passed through the centre of Lancaster, but following pedestrianisation of the shopping centre a one-way inner ring road carries all traffic. At peak times this is congested, leading to delays and the diffusion of traffic into residential side streets.

New road proposals have been under consideration in Lancaster for some 15 years, and the Local Plan (1987) proposes a 'City Centre Access Road' which would follow a line close to the canal on the east side of the town (Figure 14a). This, together with other more minor changes, is expected to relieve congestion and increase the pedestrianised shopping area.

Critics of these proposals have argued that the road will both damage Lancaster's environment and townscape and fail to provide an adequate solution to the city's traffic problems. Whilst one solution is a larger (more environmentally damaging) road, an alternative is the development of policies which concentrate on the management and limitation of traffic. New roads frequently generate additional traffic and themselves become saturated in a short period of time. It can be argued that new road building is not an appropriate solution to the traffic problems of historic towns.

By August 1988 the major proposals outlined in the Local Plan (1987) had been adopted (but not implemented) by the City Council. A protracted Local Plan Public Enquiry during the summer of 1987 generated much criticism of the plan but achieved only minor changes. Redevelopment of retail sites in the City Centre looked imminent in early 1989, but major road developments are likely to be delayed both by lack of finance and further planning enquiries. Assuming the plans go ahead in something like their proposed form, visitors to Lancaster during the 1990s are likely to see a historic townscape undergoing significant and irrevocable change.

EXCURSION

The proposed route (Figure 14b) provides an interesting walk which gives the opportunity to discuss all the planning issues outlined above. The route may easily be varied to suit individual requirements, and can be altered to accommodate some or all of the stops outlined in Excursion 13 and Excursion 12b.

(a) Lancaster Castle
Castle Park is the centre of the well-protected Castle Conservation Area. Consider the problems of conserving these seventeenth- and eighteenth-century buildings, their future uses and the ways in which tourism might be stimulated. It is likely that the Castle will cease to be used as a prison during the 1990s. How might this building then be used?

(b) Judges Lodgings and Covell Cross
Walk a short distance down Castle Hill and stop at Covell Cross (by China Street). Consider the problems of conservation and redevelopment here. The seventeenth-century cottages and the fine Judges Lodgings are well preserved, but some of the warehouses are in less good condition. Do you consider the multi-storey car park and DHSS office (Mitre House) blend in well with their surroundings? They won a Civic Trust Award when they were built.

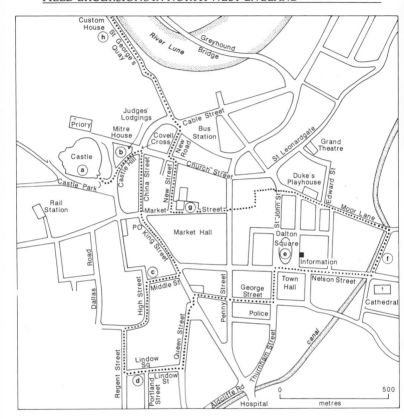

Figure 14b. The excursion route.

(c) High Street/Middle Street

Walk south down China Street and King Street (the ring road) and turn right up Middle Street. Discuss the problems of conservation and redevelopment in an area of town which is less fashionable and impressive than Castle Park (but still in the Castle Conservation Area). Is the new in-fill successful, and what effect does the ring road have on properties on this side of town?

(d) Lindow Square

Walk south along High Street, Regent Street and into Lindow Square. What problems face this quiet residential district close to the City Centre and the ring road? This is in the City Centre Conservation Area: can you justify and explain the distinction between the two areas?

(e) Dalton Square

Walk along Lindow Street and Queen Street to Queen Square, then cross King Street and proceed along Spring Garden Street and George Street to the Town Hall. Consider problems of landuse planning and the effects of new retail developments on this southern periphery of the town centre as you go. Cross Thurnham Street and walk north to Dalton Square. Stop here to consider the impact of traffic on Lancaster's urban fabric. The proposed new road (Figure 14a) passes just to the east of Dalton Square (by the canal). What impact is a new road likely to have on this part of town?

(f) St Peter's Road

Walk east along Nelson Street crossing the line of the proposed City Centre Access Road, turn left into St Peter's Road, overlooking Lancaster Canal. Several cotton mills clustered by Lancaster Canal in the nineteenth century (see Excursion 12). Some remain and have been converted into new uses, others have been demolished and the sites redeveloped for housing. How successful has this redevelopment been? What do you consider to be the most appropriate uses for old textile mills? How would you plan to improve the environment of the canal corridor and what impact will the proposed road have on this area?

(g) Market Square

Walk west down Moor Lane to Stonewell. The proposed new road crosses Moor Lane by the junction with Edward Street. How has this area been affected by planning blight in the period preceeding road construction? Cross St. John Street and walk through the pedestrian precinct to Market Street and Market Square. What are the essential features of Lancaster's historic townscape in this area and how would you formulate a policy to conserve them? How successful have past conservation and redevelopment schemes been and what is the likely impact of the changes that are currently taking place? Is there any evidence that new retail development is having an impact (positive or negative) on existing shops in the town centre?

(h) St George's Quay

Walk down New Street and New Road to Damside Street. How is (or will) the retail development affecting this area? Cross Cable Street and walk along to St George's Quay. The eighteenth century warehouses (see Excursion 12b) along the Quay have gradually been renovated and put to new uses, some industrial and some residential. How successful do you consider conservation and redevelopment to have been in this area? How would you further enhance this area as a tourist attraction for Lancaster and can you think of ways in which commercial development along the quay might aid Lancaster's economic development?

If you have time a visit to Lancaster's Maritime Museum situated in the old Customs House is worthwhile. Then walk up the hill to Priory Church and the Castle via Vicarage Walk.

Selected References

Building Design Partnership and Donaldsons (1986) *Lancaster City Centre Retail Development: A Report for public consultation.*

Kain, R (editor) (1981) *Planning for conservation.* Mansell

Lancaster City Council (1987) *Lancaster Local Plan.* Lancaster CC

Lancaster City Council (1988) *Report on objections to the Local Plan.* Lancaster CC

Lancaster Plan Action Group (1986) *A better future for Lancaster: Responses to the Draft Local Plan.* Lancaster Plan Action Group

Maguire, D J *et al* (1983) *Lancaster District: A computer-drawn census atlas 1981.* University of Lancaster Department of Geography

Schofield, M M (1946, 1951) *Outlines of an economic history of Lancaster.* Historical Association (2 volumes)

15 MORECAMBE: FISHING AND TOURISM

Gordon Clark
(University of Lancaster)

Outline: a walk mostly along the seafront at Morecambe which examines evidence for the town's maritime connections particularly in terms of fishing, tourism and migration.

Starting point: the Battery (west end of promenade) (GR 421636).

Finishing point: Morecambe Town Hall (GR 439649).

Distance: about 3 km.

Route: walking along footpaths.

Time needed: about 1.5 hours.

Maps needed: OS 1:50,000 Sheet 97 (Kendal and Morecambe); OS 1:10,000 Town Map of Lancaster and Morecambe.

Warning: you may be tempted to explore the Bay itself beyond the 50 m zone nearest to the Promenade. Be warned that it is exceedingly dangerous to attempt this; from time to time people are drowned walking in the Bay. There are three dangers: first, quicksands; second, the fast incoming tide which can easily cut you off from land and trap you; third, the channels of the major rivers which can sweep you away as you try to ford them. NEVER venture into the Bay without an experienced local guide.

EXCURSION

The Battery and Promenade

The walk starts at the Battery, a small promontory into Morecambe Bay at the town's "West End" (a on Figure 15). The name "Battery" survives in the hotel and derives from the former use of the site for artillery practice across the Bay. To the south stretches Sandylands Promenade, built in stages in the early 1930s after serious flooding in 1927. The most southerly of Morecambe's hotels and guest houses line the Promenade which eventually reaches the sandy Half Moon Bay and Heysham Head, an outcrop of Millstone Grit.

Heysham

On most days you should be able to make out the breakwaters of

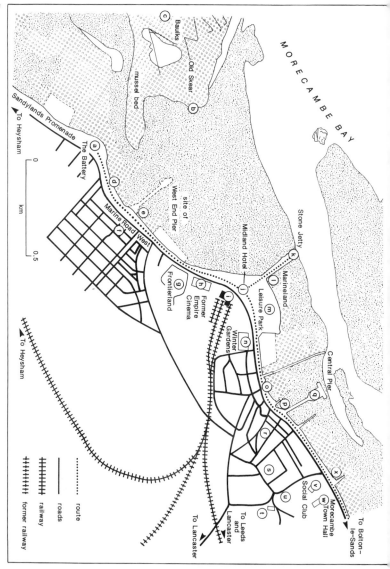

Figure 15. The excursion route.

Heysham Harbour which was opened by the Midland Railway Company in 1904 as the port for their fast London-Belfast boat-trains. Today the port handles ferries to the Isle of Man, containers to Ireland and general cargo (particularly timber and fruit). There are berths for supply boats to the offshore Morecambe Bay gasfield.

Next to the harbour at Heysham are the two nuclear power stations whose construction throughout the 1970s and 1980s attracted over 4,000 workers to the area. Tours of the power stations can be booked (see Appendix for details).

Barrow-in-Furness and Lake District
Now look out across Morecambe Bay and you may be able to see the T-shaped cranes of the Vickers shipyard at Barrow-in-Furness, 24 km to the west-north-west. To the north, the wide sweep of Morecambe Bay - one of the largest inter-tidal areas in Great Britain - is backed to the north by low wooded hills with higher ones behind. The low hills are blocks of Carboniferous Limestone, faulted and tilted.

Grange-over-Sands is located on the side of one of these blocks due north of where you now stand. Then the higher mountains of the central Lake District provide the final back-drop to the scene. Turn east (to your right) and you will see Morecambe's seafront which we shall explore later.

Morecambe Bay
Before we move off, it is worth looking at the Bay itself. It is the most easterly extension of the Irish Sea, shallow and mostly exposed at low tide. The tidal range in the Bay can be huge (up to 10.5 m).

The Bay is fed by three main rivers - the Leven which drains Windermere, the Kent which flows through Kendal and the small River Keer which enters the Bay near Carnforth. The Bay itself may look flat and featureless at first glance, but its topography is important for the use made of the area. The three rivers flow across the Bay in incised sinuous channels which regularly shift their position from the east side of the bay to the west and back. Their courses affect how much sand is on the beaches: for many years the sand has been in the middle of the Bay rather than on the foreshore where the holiday-makers would like it to be!

Fishing

Notice the stonier ridges (locally called "skears") about 0.5 to 1 km west and north-west of the Battery (b). These were ideal sites for fishing. The oldest settlements in this area - the villages of Heysham, Poulton-le-Sands and Bare - were all fishing villages specialising in mussels, cockles, shrimps, prawns and flat fish particularly plaice, flounder (locally called "flukes") and dabs. The catch used to be sorted on the seafront. The arrival of the railway in 1848 opened up a much wider market for the fish in Yorkshire and south Lancashire.

Fishing here has always been a local family business using modest technology. Wood and brushwood structures (called "baulks"(c)) were built on the skears to trap fish including eels at low tide. In other areas broad hand-held nets called "haafs" were used for catching fish including salmon. Another traditional method, now the usual one, is dragging nets ("trawls") along the sea-bed using a horse, tractor or, for deeper water, a small boat ("trawler"). Even in water only 1.5 m deep this method can effectively catch shrimps. Health worries stopped the catching of mussels for human consumption in the 1930s but the market for shrimps is strong.

Before refrigeration became widely available, a serious problem for the local fishermen was how to keep the catch in good condition for their more distant markets. The Morecambe potted shrimp - a mixture of seasoned shrimps and butter was the solution and a co-operative society (Morecambe Trawlers Ltd) was set up in 1921 to market this local delicacy. The industry displays a mixture of the individualism of the lone fisherman and the co-operative spirit which can so help small-scale businessmen.

Provision for the Retired

The Battery itself has an interesting history with a small theatre having been demolished in the mid-1980s. The area now has several blocks of retirement flats with fine views over the Bay. Morecambe has established a reputation as a low-cost retirement area and purpose-built flats have been built in several parts of the town. Morecambe has about one-third of the total population of Lancaster District, but 42 per cent of the retired population and 50 per cent of those over 75 years old. This obviously affects the kind of social-service and hospital provision that is necessary. The conversion of hotels and guest houses to retirement or nursing homes is a trend which has gathered momentum recently.

Sea wall and Flooding

Walk north-eastwards along the Promenade and notice the three-foot-high curved concrete wall on your right (d), separating the Promenade from the gardens and Marine Road West. This is part of a scheme developed in stages in the 1980s to protect the seafront from storms. A particularly severe flood in 1976 demonstrated how vulnerable the town was to a combination of storm-force south-westerly winds, low air pressure and a high spring tide. On that occasion water was funnelled up the Bay, the interwar sea wall was breached in several places and flooding extended inland for several streets.

The new sea wall will be supplemented by an offshore barrier which is planned to reduce further the height and force of waves before they reach the shore. Such engineering is expensive, of course, but the insurance premiums on seafront properties were becoming so high that the viability of many businesses was threatened. There are few visible remains of the former West End Pier (e) which was washed away in the 1976 storm, except that the Promenade is much broader where the Pier used to be.

Tourism

As you walk along the Promenade towards the railway station you will see many small hotels and guest houses on the other side of the road (f). A few streets inland, similar property is sub-divided into flatlets for holiday use between June and October; out of season they provide accommodation for second-year students at Lancaster University. As the traditional seaside holiday trade has declined, so the student market has become more important in streets such as Balmoral Road, Chatsworth Road and Westminster Road.

On your right, 700 m from the Battery, you will pass Frontierland (g), Morecambe's theme park, and then (by the traffic lights) the former Empire cinema (h), the town's last and now closed.

Station

Further along is the railway station (i). The railway first reached Morecambe in 1848 (though the station then was further inland) and a line to Yorkshire was opened in 1850. The current station building dates from 1907 and is far bigger than a town of 41,000 people would require. The size of the station recalls the days when special trains would bring in large numbers of holiday-makers and trippers for the day, week or fortnight. Wakes weeks in the mill towns of Lancashire and Yorkshire and the Fair Holiday in Glasgow were all hectic times at the station. Today, through trains go only to Lancaster and Leeds. There have been recent proposals to redevelop the station site.

Stone Jetty

Opposite the station is the Midland Hotel (j) once run by the railway company of that name. The hotel's current building is a superb example of 1930s architecture.

The Stone Jetty which protrudes into the Bay at this point (k) was built in 1850 and now contains Marineland (l) which was Europe's first dolphinarium when it opened in 1964. The Jetty used to be an industrial area since it was a shipbreaker's yard from 1905 to 1933 and before that it was the base for ferries to Ireland (until Heysham Harbour opened).

Leisure Park and Winter Gardens

Next door is the Bubbles Leisure Park (m) with its swimming pools and children's play area and the Superdome hall for shows. The resort of Morecambe has been slower than, say, Blackpool to develop modern indoor facilities for sport and entertainment, although the need for these has been recognised for over a century. A new indoor leisure pool was opened in 1989.

Just beyond the Leisure Park and on the other side of the street you will see the impressive red-brick frontage of the Winter Gardens (n) - once Morecambe's major answer to what to do on a wet day. Opened in 1878 as the People's Palace, the current building dates from 1896. It used to provide dancing and live entertainment. The Winter Gardens have been closed for many years due to lack of trade; considerable uncertainty exists over the building's future role, although there have been moves in recent years to re-open it as a theatre or conference centre.

Central Promenade

Cross Marine Road Central by the traffic lights at Woolworths and carry on walking along the built-up side of the road (o). You will pass a familiar pattern of gift shops, cafes, pubs, fortune tellers, restaurants and amusement arcades. They could be found in almost any British seaside resort which has not had the capital to move up-market. Some of the shops are seasonal, closed in winter. You will soon be opposite the Clock Tower (p) a landmark built in 1905 for which most Morecambe people have some affection. Next to this is the entrance to Central Pier (q) which in its heyday featured dancing and music-hall stars. The structure is currently in an unsafe condition and is no longer open to the public. In 1989 plans were announced for a large marina and associated development filling eight hectares of reclaimed seabed between the Stone Jetty (k), the Central Pier (q) and beyond.

Poulton-le-Sands (Old Morecambe)

Turn right into Clarence Street which runs inland from Central Pier. Along Clarence Street (r) you will cross Back Morecambe Street and Morecambe Street which contain older houses pre-dating the expansion of the town for tourism after 1850. At this time the settlement was still known as Poulton-le-Sands: it was re-named Morecambe, after the Bay, in 1889 to help the town's tourist promotion.

At the end of Clarence Street turn left at the junction and you will enter the open-air market (s) which is active on Tuesdays and Thursdays. Bear left along Poulton Road past the market and in 100 m you will come to Poulton Square. This is the core of the old Poulton-le-Sands whose street layout lacks the rectangular pattern of post-1850 Morecambe. It still has a village atmosphere to it (if you ignore the block-like Police Station (t)); here we find the largest collection of buildings in central Morecambe which substantially pre-date the tourist trade. This small section bounded by Clarence Street, Poulton Road and Lord Street roughly delimits the extent of the old Poulton-le-Sands. Leave the square by Lord Street (u) which runs down to the Promenade again. This old street was the home of many of the traditional fishing families in Morecambe.

Town Hall

At the end of Lord Street, where it joins the Promenade, there is a large site on your right now occupied by the Granada Social Club (v) and Morecambe Town Hall (w). It was here that the Morecambe Tower Company (founded in 1898) started constructing a tower to rival the one at Blackpool. A framework rose nearly 30 m before the money ran out. The structure was demolished during the First World War after being struck by lightning. The Town Hall, another typically 1930s building, lost its status in 1974 when Morecambe and Heysham were linked with Lancaster to form a single local government district. The building is still used as offices for some of the departments of Lancaster City Council.

Morecambe Bay Barrage

When you reach the Promenade, cross to the seaward side of the road (x) and you should be able to see at anchor some of Morecambe's remaining fleet of shrimp trawlers. The view across the Bay is worth admiring if only because it could have been very different. Over the last 200 years numerous schemes have been proposed to construct barrages, roads and railways across the Bay. Many of the proposals were simply aimed at shortening the journey to Ulverston and Barrow-in-Furness.

The most recent scheme, proposed in 1972 by the (then) Water Resources Board, sought to combine a fast road link with the storage of fresh water in reservoirs on the landward side of the barrage. Opposition to the numerous versions of this scheme focused on the ecological and environmental effects of the work on the Bay. When the recession of the later 1970s cut the industrial demand for water in South Lancashire, the idea was shelved.

Travel across the Bay, rather than round it, is not a new idea, of course. In the eighteenth century regular horse-drawn coach services plied across the sands from Ulverston. Some of the coaches never made it to the other side, trapped by quicksands or the fast incoming tide, or swept away when fording the channel of the River Kent.

CONCLUSION

We have now reached the end of our excursion through Morecambe. We have had time to look at only a part of the town. We have referred only briefly to Heysham with its rapid industrial regeneration. Nor have we ventured inland to the shopping centre, to White Lund Industrial Estate or to Bare, another of the old fishing villages now incorporated into northern Morecambe.

We have concentrated on central Morecambe and particularly its maritime connections; the fishing, shipping and tourism in their various forms. The shipping has been transferred to Heysham Harbour. The fishing continues but only by a handful of boats. Tourism is still a major part of the local economy but it is having to adjust to a world where foreign package holidays to sunny areas with modern hotels have been experienced by many people. Can guest houses and hotels find the capital to upgrade their standards (eg en suite private facilities)? Some of the larger and better hotels have managed this but the smaller establishments experience more difficulty in attracting a clientele willing to pay the higher accommodation costs needed to recoup the investment. How is the town to make better use of its under-used assets such as the Winter Gardens? Can sufficient wet-weather indoor entertainment be provided? Which segments of the tourism and leisure markets should Morecambe aim for? The answers to these questions will determine the shape of the town's tourist industry into the next century.

Selected References

Potter, T F (1976) *The growth of Morecambe.* Morecambe Visitor

Robinson, N A and A W Pringle (editors) (1987) *Morecambe Bay: an assessment of present ecological knowledge.* University of Lancaster Centre for North-West Regional Studies and Morecambe Bay Study Group

Robinson C and W R Mitchell (1980) *Life around Morecambe Bay.* Dalesman

Stocker, D (1988) *Potted tales; recollections and views of Morecambe Bay fishermen.* Lancaster City Museums, Local Studies No 8

Appendix

Free tours of the Nuclear Power Stations at Heysham can be booked through: Station Manager (Guided Tours), CEGB, Heysham 1 Power Station, PO Box 4, Heysham, Morecambe, Lancs. LA3 2XQ.

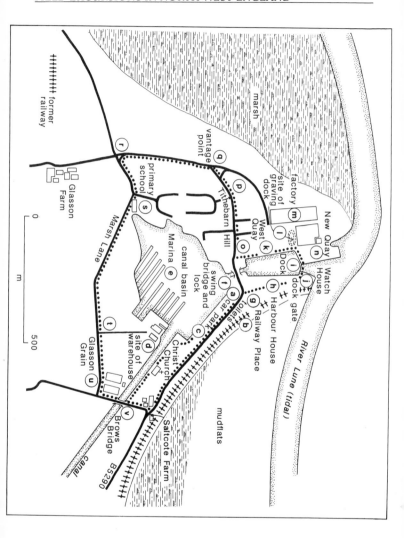

Figure 16. The excursion route.

16 GLASSON: THE VILLAGE AND THE DOCK

Gordon Clark
(University of Lancaster)

Outline: a walk around Glasson, a small settlement and port at the mouth of the River Lune near Lancaster, which highlights evidence for the port's history and its current uses.

Starting and finishing points: Glasson car park on the B5290 (GR 445560).

Distance: either 2.3 km or 3.7 km (depending on route).

Route: walking on paved surfaces.

Time needed: either 1 hour or 1 hour 45 minutes.

Maps needed: O.S. 1:50,000 Sheet 102 (Preston and Blackpool); 1:25,000 Sheet SD45/55 (Pathfinder map number 659) (Galgate and Dolphinholme).

INTRODUCTION

Glasson is a village and port on the southern bank of the River Lune before it enters Morecambe Bay. It is reached from the A588 Lancaster to Blackpool road and lies on the B5290 (formerly the B5270) about 7 km south-west of Lancaster. It is best to start the tour at the large car park on the left as you enter the village (a on Figure 16). Coaches may be parked here and there are public toilets opposite.

Foundation of Glasson Dock

Glasson is a new settlement. Before 1779 there were only a few farms here, one called Glasson farm and another was Saltcote farm which you passed on your right as you entered the village. The village of Glasson was conceived in 1779 by the Lancaster Port Commissioners who wanted an outport for Lancaster. In the early and mid-eighteenth century Lancaster was the fourth busiest port in Britain (see Excursions 12 and 13), trading extensively with the West Indies. Yet an outport was needed because of difficulties upstream. A rock bar below St. George's Quay in Lancaster limited the size of ship entering the town, the shallowness of the River Lune was a similar restriction and the high

177

tidal range of the river meant the expensive use of lighters to transfer goods from ships in mid-river to the quay.

The Port Commissioners' first attempt at a solution was to establish an outport at Sunderland Point on the right bank of the River Lune near its mouth. This scheme failed because the only road access across the marshes to Sunderland Point was tidal and the site was badly exposed to southwesterly gales. Although there had been mooring facilities off Glasson since 1751, development onshore began in 1780 when the Port Commissioners bought the site at Glasson from the Dalton family who lived just inland at Thurnham Hall (Glasson is in Thurnham parish). The dock opened to traffic in 1787 when a Lancaster captain brought in a Lancaster-built ship.

EXCURSION

Leave the car park, cross the B5290 and walk the short way to the line of the Glasson branch railway which opened in 1883 (b). It closed to passengers in 1930 and to freight in the 1950s. A final journey took place in 1964 and by 1969 demolition of the line was complete. The 1:25,000 OS map shows the route of the line along the riverside from Lancaster's Castle Station to its terminus at Glasson dock. The station was near to Christ Church (500 m on your right); little remains of its very modest wooden buildings. The 8 km route of the former railway now forms a pleasant riverside walk to Lancaster. The late arrival of a railway connection to the dock both reflected and perpetuated the port's modest development.

Standing by the River Lune at this point, you can also see the tall pylons crossing the river and carrying the electricity from the two nuclear power stations at Heysham. The wooded area on the eastern side of the river (now a country club and golf course) was formerly the country seat of Lord Ashton (James Williamson) whose linoleum works at Lune Mills in Lancaster (see Excursion 12b) were a prime destination for the freight traffic on the railway. On a clear day the red-brick chimney of the mills is visible straight ahead of you. The River Lune is strongly tidal here: at low tide extensive mud flats are exposed.

The Canal and Canal Basin
Returning to the main road, cross the car park and stand facing the seven-hectare canal basin (c). Water enters the basin from the Glasson

branch of the Lancaster Canal (d) on your left and leaves the basin by the lock into the dock on your right. The Glasson branch canal was opened in 1826, twenty-nine years after the Preston-Tewitfield section of the Lancaster Canal was built. Six locks lower the water from the level of the Lancaster Canal to that of the basin.

The canal was designed to increase Glasson's hinterland and encourage more trade. To an extent it did succeed because canal traffic to Kendal and Preston was common in the 1820s and 1830s. However the canal's effect was limited by the fact that the Lancaster Canal is an isolated route: it is not connected to any other canals. For a brief period in the 1840s the Lancaster Canal Company owned and ran (indeed, ran down, it was alleged) the Lancaster-Preston railway, but after 1849 a larger railway company took over the canal company and traffic on the canal was largely restricted to the local area. The canal is now run by the British Waterways Board.

The canal basin in front of you is notable for the large number of pleasure craft berthed at the Marina (e) on the opposite (southern) side. Motor boats from the canal and sea-going yachts mix in this bustling dock, one of the few in Britain where a canal reaches the sea. The increase in the number of yachts has been steady for over twenty years and chandlery, berthing and repair of these vessels provides employment. A five storey warehouse was built (at d) in 1825 to store goods being trans-shipped between the canal and the sea. It was demolished to make way for the marina buildings where the canal enters the basin to your left.

The Dock and Sea Traffic
Turn right and walk along the main road into the village. On your left are the lock and swing-bridge road crossing (f) which separate the basin from the dock. On your right are two hotels (the Victoria and Caribou) and other buildings including the Harbour House (h). Continue along the eastern quay of the dock as far as you can, past the dock gates (i) and up to the red and white Watch House (j). Since Glasson is a working port, look out for dock traffic while walking along the quays.

The dock was opened to traffic in 1787 and, until the western quay (k, opposite) was built in 1958, there was only a single quay which was widened in 1883 to allow railway lines to run alongside the ships. The row of houses called Railway Place (g) pre-dates the railway and

179

was bought by the London and North Western Railway Company for its staff. The outlines of the capstan which operated the dock gates (i) are visible near the Watch House.

Glasson can be judged to have been either a success or a failure as a port. It clearly failed to stem the erosion of trade from the Lune. Liverpool moved ahead of Lancaster throughout the nineteenth century to become our principal west-coast port whereas Lancaster languished. On the other hand the port has usually been busy for its size. At the start it captured trade from Preston whose docks were well inland up the hazardous River Ribble. The type of traffic has varied over the years. Cargoes of stone, salt, agricultural lime and coal were recorded in the late eighteenth century. In the 1870s and 1880s coal was both exported to Ireland and imported for the Lancaster gasworks (closed in 1960) and for Williamson's Lune Mills (Excursion 12b). Opened in 1870 and covering 8.5 ha, the site was claimed to be the "largest manufactory of its class in the world" and traffic to the mills was brisk in coal for fuel, and cork for the linoleum which was made there. Spanish iron ore was also imported for Carnforth iron works.

The opening of Heysham Harbour by the Midland Railway in 1904 was a serious blow to Glasson. Although intended for the Company's boat trains to Belfast, Heysham soon captured a lot of Glasson's coastal and Irish trade. As a harbour it offered 24-hour traffic whereas Glasson dock was open for only an hour or so at each high tide. Depending on the state of the tide, the difference in water level between the river and lock can be up to 6 m.

The depression during the 1930s saw trade at a very low ebb whereas during the Second World War there was hectic activity. Up to 1907 Nicholson's shipyard on the west side of the dock built small vessels, thereafter the graving dock (l) was the focus for ship repairing until 1969. The graving dock was then filled in (although the entrance to it can be seen in the stonework opposite you. The site now has no connection with the port, being a factory (m).

Glasson's commercial traffic has recently been helped by the New Quay (n) built in the Lune outside the dock gates. The port is also re-capturing trade by being cheaper than rivals since it uses non-unionised labour and is more efficient at cargo handling. Traffic today is varied and includes coal, timber, fertilizers, building materials, scrap metal and animal feedingstuffs. There are usually a few fishing boats to be seen.

The Village

Cross by the dock gates (i) to the west quay (or if the dock gates are open, retrace your steps to the road crossing between the dock and canal basin). Walk along the west quay (k) and turn right up Tithebarn Hill (o). Notice how few shops there are in this small village: most people shop in Lancaster or Garstang although the bus services to these towns are limited. The attraction of Glasson for day-trippers has encouraged a few cafes to be set up. Continue walking up to the top of Tithebarn Hill. The last house on your right is Norfolk House (p), built around 1850 as the home of a Lancaster merchant who wanted to keep an eye on his ships.

Follow the road as it curves left and at the junction there is a splendid vantage point (q) to see the whole of the village and its setting. A small private housing estate of bungalows for Lancaster commuters nearly reaches the top of the hill. As in so many villages, further housing is strictly limited by the capacity of the sewage system. The layout of the village, the estuary of the River Lune and parts of Lancaster can be clearly seen. The white roofs of the University of Lancaster stand out to the north-east and the massive shapes of the power stations at Heysham are obvious to the north-west. Sunderland Point is due west.

Alternative route

If your time is limited, retrace your steps down Tithebarn Hill (o), cross the lock gates (f) and turn right to the car park (a) where the walk ends.

However, if you have another three-quarters of an hour, carry on walking southwards away from Glasson until you come to a cross-roads (r). Turn left and follow the main road into Marsh Lane; you will pass the village primary school (s). As in so many villages proposals to close the school are made from time to time. A little further on is the entrance to the marina (t); this is well worth a visit if time permits. Carrying on along Marsh Lane you then pass the sheds of the Glasson Grain Company (u) which imports animal feedingstuffs through the dock. It supplies local dairy, pig and poultry farmers.

Turn left at the road junction and cross the canal by Brows Bridge (v); take care as there is no pavement along this section of the road. Return to the car park either by walking along the canal towpath (which takes you past Christ Church) or follow the B5290.

CONCLUSION

Glasson is a small community with only just over 200 years of history, yet its development has been varied and its current economy is mixed. It is partly a commuting village, a recreational centre, a manufacturing base and a focus for day-trippers - and all surrounded by good quality pastureland and dairy farming. As with so many villages it helps greatly to have a car if you live in Glasson: local services are modest and public transport limited. With no new housing being built until there is a bigger sewage system, property for purchase is limited and quite expensive.

Glasson as a port shows two important features clearly. First, any port will reflect the economic activity in its hinterland: as particular industries grow or decline or change their needs (eg coal or oil for fuel) so the dock's traffic will alter. There is much that a small port can do to survive. It can invest in new quays or specialise in particular cargoes; it can capitalise on its smallness to react more quickly than larger more bureaucratic ports to new trends in shipping; finally, it can try to survive by keeping its costs low and undercutting rival ports' prices.

So far, the lively commercial traffic in the dock has managed to co-exist with the steady growth in pleasure craft in the canal basin. Yet like all small settlements Glasson remains vulnerable to outside forces substantially beyond the control of local people. Decisions made elsewhere on whether the bus service and primary school will continue, whether a new sewage works is built or whether the engineering factory stays open will have major impacts on the future development of Glasson.

Selected References

Hayhurst, J D (1987) *Glasson Dock: a walk around the village*. Thurnham Parish Council

Jenkins, S C (1987) The Glasson Dock branch. *British Railway Journal* 16; 267-274

17   THE BOWLAND FELLS: CLOUGHA PIKE

Colin G Pooley
(University of Lancaster)

Outline: a short high-level walk up Clougha Pike (413 m OD) which provides an opportunity to introduce some major features of the human and physical geography of the region. This might be combined with the drive through Forest of Bowland described in Excursion 18, or with the walk to see glacial meltwater features described in Excursion 11.

Starting and finishing points: Birks Bank Car Park, near Quernmore (GR 527604).

Distance: about 5 km.

Time needed: about 2.5 hours. Stout footwear and waterproof clothing are required. The excursion is not recommended in misty conditions.

Maps needed: OS 1:50,000 Landranger Sheets 97 & 102, and OS 1:25,000 sheet SD 55, SD56

INTRODUCTION

The Forest of Bowland forms an upland area of millstone grit, rising to a series of summits between about 400 and 560 m OD. It was affected by ice during the last glaciation (although the summit plateau was probably not ice covered) and there is extensive evidence of the impact of glacial meltwater in the area (see Excursion 11). The fells are now covered by extensive layers of blanket peat with significant outcrops of gritstone. Vegetation consists mainly of heather and bilberry at upper levels, with rough grazing and light woodland cover at lower levels.   Most of the upland in the Forest of Bowland is in private ownership and is managed by large landowners for grouse shooting and sheep grazing. In recent years, landowners have taken advantage of European Community grants to improve drainage and enclose many of the lower pastures. Even so, it is an area which has only limited economic potential and it does not lend itself to easy afforestation. There is no Ministry of Defence activity in the area and only one

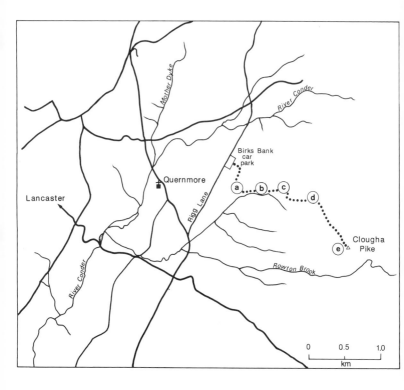

Figure 17. The excursion route.

large reservoir (Stocks Reservoir; see Excursion 18). In comparison with many other upland areas, the landuse conflicts experienced here are relatively limited.

The Forest of Bowland is designated as an Area of Outstanding Natural Beauty (AONB) and as such it enjoys limited protection from development. Facilities for recreation and tourism are restricted to small car parks and roadside picnic spots and the intensity of recreational use is low. Situated in close proximity to much better known

184

recreation areas in the Lake District and the Yorkshire Dales, the Forest of Bowland is used by locals, but is relatively unknown to visitors from further afield. Because the upland is in private ownership, access for fell-walking is limited. In the Lancaster area the County Council has negotiated a public access area on Clougha Pike and a footpath to Ward's Stone and Tarnbrook, but much of this upland area remains an infrequently visited wilderness

Human settlement is confined to the valley bottoms, with substantial villages on the northern fringe along the Lune Valley, to the west where the Bowland Fells join the Lancashire coastal plain and in the valleys of the Hodder and Ribble to the east and south. Elsewhere small hamlets and isolated farms extend up to about 250 m, but increasingly these are being purchased as holiday homes or by people who commute daily to towns such as Lancaster and Preston. The population of towns such as Clitheroe, Blackburn, Preston and Lancaster have relatively easy access to the Forest of Bowland, but roads remain mostly small and only one high-level route crosses the area from Lancaster to Clitheroe through the Trough of Bowland. Many of these themes are illustrated in Excursion 18.

EXCURSION

This route (Figure 17) provides an interesting walk over rough and often wet terrain, through the Clougha Access Area to the summit of Clougha Pike. The access area may be closed to the public on certain days during the grouse shooting season.

Leave Birks Bank car park (Figure 17) by the fence/stile in the south-east corner and follow the obvious path which bears right after a few hundred metres and descends slightly to a ladder stile on your left. Climb this stile onto a wooden walkway which crosses a marshy area.

(a) Marshland ecosystem (GR 529603)

Pause on the wooden walkway to discuss the elements of a marshland ecosystem. Most stages in the development of a hydrosere (freshwater succession) can be seen. Woodland - mainly Oak (*Quercus*), Alder (*Ulnus*), Birch (*Betula*) and Willow (*Salix*) - can be seen around the edge of the marsh, with bilberry (*Vaccinium myrtilis*) and heathers (*Culluna vulgaris* and *Erica tetralix*) on the drier margins. Within the wetland

185

vegetation ranges from substantial rushes (*Juncus*) and grasses, cotton-grass (*Eriophorum*) and purple moor-grass (*Molinea*) to sedges (*Carex*) and mosses (*Sphagnum, Polytrichum*). Consider the association between soil, vegetation and drainage in this area, and suggest how this area may have changed during the recent past.

(b) Oak and Birch woodland (GR 532602)

Follow the path over a ladder-stile and climb gently through gorse bushes with the stream on your right. After a few hundred metres the path passes through an area of upland woodland consisting mainly of sessile oak and birch. This is near the present treeline; it is typical of the sort of vegetation which would have reached a much higher level two thousand years ago. Consider reasons why the treeline has changed, including the impact of changing climate, the effects of grazing and the impact of man. Suggest why woodland survives at this point today.

(c) Glacial overflow channel (GR 535603)

Negotiate a boggy area, and follow the path uphill until you reach two stiles by a wall junction. Take the right hand stile and pause by the rocky outcrop on your right. A deeply incised valley is clearly visible to the east, although today there is little water flowing through it. This is one of several distinctive overflow channels cut through the northern ridge of Clougha by glacial meltwater (described in Excursion 11). Try to trace the line of the meltwater channel by eye, and discuss how vegetation in the valley would have changed since the end of the last ice age.

(d) Small rocky valley (GR 539601)

With the wall on your left, walk up a steep bank, then (approximately following the line of the wall) follow the path across a wet area to the fell gate. Once through the gate follow the path across open moorland towards the small rocky valley which cuts through the ridge ahead. This is another glacial meltwater channel and evidence of a relict over-deepened pool below a rock step can be seen on your right. Discuss how the vegetation has changed as you have climbed onto the open moorland of heather and bilberry and consider the possible economic uses of this area. Improved pasture and the effects of drainage can clearly be seen on the lower slopes, but at this level management of the heather for grouse shooting is the main use.

(e) Clougha Pike Summit (544594)

Follow the path across open moorland until you reach a clear ridge and stone wall. Turn right and follow the line of the wall up the ridge, over a small rock step and then over open moorland to the summit cairn. The summit offers a fine view from which many features of the human and physical geography of the region can be discussed.

A relatively flat gritstone plateau covered with blanket peat extends to the east, rising to 561 m at Ward's Stone, the highest point on the Bowland Fells. Discuss the conditions under which gritstone plateaus like this were created and the subsequent climatic changes that have created the present-day landscape.

To the west there are excellent views across the Conder Valley (the course of the pre-glacial Lune) and across Morecambe Bay to the Lakeland hills. Consider the settlement pattern in the Conder Valley and the main characteristics of agriculture on the lower slopes. Can you suggest any ways in which this area could be made more economically productive without damaging the environment?

Even on this climb, in an area which is relatively little used for recreation, you will have seen evidence of footpath erosion and the impact of walkers through litter and possibly damage to walls and stiles. How do you consider that recreation in an area like this should be managed? Should the area be opened up for tourism and actively promoted with the provision of more car parks and other facilities, or should it be left to the small number of people who currently use the fell? Consider how a desire to protect the environment conflicts with the different landuses that are found in this area, and examine the impact of landownership on management of the uplands.

After a suitable rest, return to Birks Bank car park via the same route used on the ascent. Take care not to miss the point where the path turns left off the ridge if conditions turn misty.

Selected References

Johnson, R H (editor) (1985) *The Geomorphology of N W England*. Manchester University Press

King, C A M (1976) *Northern England*. Methuen

Lancashire County Council (1967) *Forest of Bowland Recreational Study*. LCC

Lancashire County Council (1986) *Lancashire Structure Plan*. LCC

18 LANDSCAPE AND LAND USE CONFLICT IN THE FOREST OF BOWLAND AONB

Ian O Brodie
(University of Lancaster)

Outline: a series of locations through the Forest of Bowland which are useful for examining the effects of differing land use claims and their consequences for the landscape. Landownership, game shooting, water gathering, informal recreation and conservation can be considered as conflicting claims within this nationally designated Area of Outstanding Natural Beauty.

Starting and finishing points: a circular route which can be joined at any point. It is described as starting and finishing at Garstang (GR 4845) on the A6 between M6 junctions 32 & 33.

Distance: 87 km.

Route: travel by car or minibus between sites; coaches are banned on many of the roads used. Walking on public rights of way needs stout footwear and waterproof clothing.

Time needed: one full day.

Maps needed: O.S. 1:50 000 sheets 102 (Preston) and 103 (Blackburn); or 1:25 000 sheets SD 44/45, 45/55, 63/73, 64/74 and 65/75.

Permission: permission will be required to wander off public rights of way.

INTRODUCTION

The purpose of an Area of Outstanding Natural Beauty (AONB) designation is to preserve and enhance the quality of the landscape. The designation is equivalent to that of National Parks but does not carry the recreational duties under the 1949 National Parks and Access to the Countryside Act, nor do they have the same administrative machinery. There are nearly 40 such designations covering over one eighth of the land area of England and Wales. The landscape should thus be of the highest quality in a national sense.

The Forest of Bowland AONB encompasses some Medieval Royal Hunting Forests and was designated in 1964. It is a large area,

803 sq.kms of uplands that form an offshoot from the Pennines. The scenery is a mixture of moorlands, field patterns, stone villages, wooded cloughs and commercial afforestation. The area drains into the River Lune and River Ribble and is underlain by rocks of the Pennine Millstone Grit series.

The sites chosen reflect the main issues arising in a designated area of countryside - changes in agricultural practice, increasing pressure for afforestation and, in some areas, the demands for rural housing. The area is made more interesting by huge landholdings of a limited number of owners and the lack of public access to the upland areas largely through the interests of game bird shoots. All along the route there is evidence of these issues to a differing degree. However, the sites recommended bring together several factors in competing land uses and the effect they can have on a designated landscape.

EXCURSION

The route is shown in Figure 18. From Garstang drive north on the A6 then turn east to Scorton (502488) (4 km; W C: cafe). Continue, following signs to the Trough of Bowland (16 km past Scorton).

STOP 1 THE TROUGH OF BOWLAND (623531)

Park near the cattle grid. The Grey Stone of the Trough, an ancient Lancashire - Yorkshire boundary stone, is a Grade II Listed Building. The fence which runs up the moorland on each side was the subject of a dispute between the estates and conservationists. A short walk along the east side of the fence will show more of the line.

The fence marks the boundary between land owned by North West Water (east) and the Abbeystead Estate (owned by the Duke of Westminster, to the west). It was erected to help keep sheep from wandering over the grouse moors from the tenant of North West Water onto land owned by the Duke. Too many sheep can spoil the heather needed for grouse and too few can also have adverse effects. The conservationists argued that several km of this fence stretching over the watershed of the moors would spoil the natural beauty.

There are several issues for discussion here: i) Should anyone be allowed to change the open nature of a nationally designated landscape by erecting such a fence without first seeking public approval

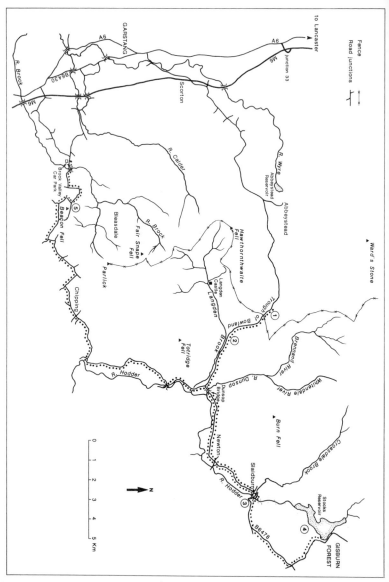

Figure 18. The excursion route.

through the planning system? ii) Should there be public grants to maintain other methods of sheep farming that would not result in the erection of a fence? Would the expenditure of such money be right to ensure the private pleasures of a major landowner?

Drive down the far side of the pass to reach the entrance to the Langden Intake (GR 633512) (2 km). Park by the roadside.

STOP 2 THE LANGDEN VALLEY

Walk along the access track and continue past the water intake to follow the track alongside Langden Beck. Go as far as suitable for the party but preferably to Langden Castle, which was built as a shooters refreshment hut. Return by the same path.

The area is owned by North West Water and used as gathering grounds for water which was extracted at the intake along the way - originally for Preston. It is stored and treated near Longridge before reaching Preston. At one time all public access was barred from this catchment; now there are a few public paths, some permissive footpaths and a reasonable right to wander over the catchment.

The right of access to open fells is an issue in itself. As in many similar areas there are other factors coming into play. North West Water obtain water from the area; and receive rent from the tenant farmer and from the shooting tenancy. The shooting tenants in turn employ a gamekeeper to maintain heather (a major contributor to the landscape of the AONB), keep down 'vermin' and ensure that the grouse are not disturbed. North West Water, or their predecessors, have in such areas bulldozed roads across the open fellsides - such as the one you have been walking on - so that the shooters can drive to their butts to have the game driven towards their guns. The roads have been bulldozed without the planning permission that is needed for such roads by stating they are also for the tenant farmer to use and such agricultural roads do not need planning permission. The same situation occurs in National Parks.

The area you are in is part of the Bowland Fells Site of Special Scientific Interest (SSSI). It has been designated by the Nature Conservancy Council because "These extensive upland fells support the largest expanse of blanket bog and heather moorland in Lancashire and provide suitable habitat for a diverse upland breeding bird community which includes three species (hen harrier, merlin and peregrine) ... Additional interest is provided by locally uncommon plant species and a variety of upland habitats and their associated avifauna" (NCC designation statement, March 1988).

There are several issues to discuss, including i) Who should have prior claims in a competing land use - landowner, farming tenant, shooting tenant, rambler, nature conservationist? What is the relevance of the AONB or SSSI designation in making such a decision? What ways are open to managing real and potential conflicts between the various demands? ii) Do the shooters' roads have any impact upon the landscape? Should such agricultural development be brought under planning control in an AONB? iii) What would be the effect on this landscape if grouse shooting was banned by future governments? iv) What would be the effect and newly competing demands on the landscape if North West Water (or its successors) wanted to build a storage reservoir in this section of the Langden Valley?

Go back to the road. On a Sunday and some other days there are several vans selling ice cream, tea and coffee or barbequed meat by the roadside here. Such commercial activities attract many cars to the site and over a day there are several hundred people visiting the area. Issues to discuss include: i) What visible effect do these people have on the landscape? ii) Accepting that people should enjoy the country-side, are these the sorts of activities that should take place in an upland AONB or any other remote rural location - or should they be directed to less sensitive areas? iii) Some of the area is invaded by bracken. The plant looks attractive in autumn colours but is poisonous to sheep and harbours sheep ticks. What would be the advantages and disadvantages of wholescale bracken clearance by herbicide?

This location and Dunsop Bridge (GR 660501) and Slaidburn (GR 713525) would provide good opportunities for visitor surveys. This would also be possible at the last two sites on the itinery but local authority permission is required.

Drive down to Dunsop Bridge (3 km; WC). Turn left at the junction and pass through Newton (5 km; WC) to Slaidburn (another 2 km; WC; refreshments). There is a car park near the river.

STOP 3 SLAIDBURN (GR 713525)

The 1981 census showed that over 90 per cent of all the houses in the village were tenanted. Most were owned by one person. Such high rates of house tenancy is not unusual in some villages and rural parishes of Bowland. In some cases estates have been broken up over a period of time; in others they have become even more monolithic in ownership. In such areas the villages and parishes retain their unspoilt appearances and, like Slaidburn, form attractive tourist centres. However such areas have suffered greatly from rural depopulation this century and show a higher than UK average for numbers of retired people resident. Landowners will only consider building houses or selling property from their stock for estate management reasons - usually economic. They act as their own "planning authority" in not permitting new development and largely to protect their own interests.

Consider the need to strike a balance between preserving rural areas and considering the needs of local communities. Should landowners be answerable to society wider than their personal interests? Landowners in this sense include individuals, private estates in the legal title of trusts and Water Authorities.

From Slaidburn drive over the River Hodder and east along the B6478. Take the first left turn at the crossroads to arrive at Stocks Reservoir.

STOP 4 STOCKS RESERVOIR AND GISBURN FOREST (GR 772566)

The reservoir can be best seen from the approach road and from near the car park. There are three circular waymarked walks from the car park and public rights of way go through the forest.

The reservoir was orginally constructed to supply water to Blackpool and the Fylde Coast. Other water supplies from the area were gained by taking the water directly from the watercourses. It is now owned by North West Water (NWW) as is the surrounding catchment land. The forest was planted by the Forestry Commission, on land leased to them, during 1949-1965.

The reservoir is an important site for wintering birds and the island is used as a nesting site. NWW, like all the Water Authorities at the onset of privatisation, are becoming more commercially active and have granted a concession for the hire of boats (with small engines) to anglers. Bank fishing also takes place. In the first few years of operations the commercial activities have increased the number of boats and the length of the fishing season in order to increase profitability. Naturalists believe that the bird life of the reservoir has suffered. In an earlier report NWW considered stocking and managing the reservoir as a trout fishery, providing hotel and 'log cabin' accommodation, establishing a small picnic site and allocating a small part of the reservoir as a nature reserve.

Issues for consideration include i) Is the reservoir a suitable site for increased commercialisation? ii) What would be the environmental costs? iii) What would be the gains and losses for the local people?

Three thousand acres of the catchment area is leased by the Forestry Commission and the largest planting is Gisburn Forest adjacent to the reservoir. NWW was reluctant to lease futher land because of the impact of forests in reducing the water yields and reservoir silting problems. However following privatisation NWW will be under pressure to maximise its turnover and conservationists believe that such catchment areas could be sold and that forestry groups are the most likely buyers. The altitude, soil type and rainfall suggest that conifers would be the most likely trees to be planted.

Further blanket forestry would be a major land change in the AONB and the landscape would alter from open moorland to conifer forest. There would be considerable changes in wildlife, shooting and recreation.

Consider for example; i) Should an area designated as an AONB because of its open moorland be allowed to change its character significantly or to any degree by large scale afforestation? ii) Is it relevant that commercial afforestation does not need planning permission? iii) Will the imposition of a sheep meat regime by the European Community make afforestation of bare uplands inevitable?

Drive back to Dunsop bridge, turn left towards Whitewell and turn right by Burholme Bridge (GR 658479). Follow the road past the limestone reef knolls, the Carboniferous Limestone normally underlies the Millstone Grit, and follow the signs for Chipping (GR 6243) (11 km after Dunsop Bridge; WC; cafe). From Chipping follow signs initially for Garstang but use signs and your map to navigate to Beacon Fell (7 km further). There are several car parks off the road which encircles the fell.

STOP 5 BEACON FELL COUNTRY PARK (GR 5642)

The fell was owned by a small water undertaking as a catchment and the trees were planted partially to keep people off. Before then it was farmed. The 1968 Countryside Act, in response to the growing number of people visiting the countryside, allowed local authorities to set up Country Parks as 'honeypots' in the countryside - providing people with somewhere to go but relieving the pressure on the remaining countryside. Lancashire County Council (LCC) acquired the fell and it became one of the first Country Parks in Britain. LCC produce leaflets about the fell. It is easy to walk up from the roadside car parks to the fell summit.

Look north from the summit and you will see the fields and fells of Bleasdale, a 'closed' parish. The only public access is by footpaths and small access areas on Fairsnape (GR 591468) and Parlick (GR 596450) fells for which LCC compensate the landowners and tenants annually. The pattern of fields is fairly richly endowed with small plantations, often with a rhododendron understorey. These wooded areas are used to rear pheasants and such estates are used for pheasant and rough shoots as well as agriculture. Notice also the wooded valley of the River Brock which we will cross shortly.

Issues for discussion include i) What effect would a ban on shooting, as advocated by some bodies and political parties, have on the landscape in the long term? ii) Why should the owner permit access of the areas around Parlick and Fairsnape but not the moors to the west?

Leave the fell by the north-west corner and navigate down to Brock Mill car park and picnic site (GR 549431). This area of the River Brock is interesting scenically, for a physical geography resource and from a natural history point of view. The footpaths along the river are heavily used. The woodlands form part of a designated area of ancient and semi-ancient woodlands. Some deer are found in the area. The car park has been built in response to visitor pressure on the area.

Issues for discussion include i) What criteria should be used in meeting the demands of car-borne visitors in quiet areas of the countryside, ii) Should areas that hold such intrinsic, quiet interest be made accessible only to those under their own power?

Leave the car park by turning left up the hill, and drive back to Garstang.

Selected References

Anderson, M A (1981) *Historical perspectives on the role of AONBs; recreation preservation.* Wye College, Ashford.

Countryside Commission (1983) *AONBs - a policy statement.* CC, Cheltenham

Green, B (1981) *Countryside Conservation.* Allen and Unwin, London

Lancashire County Council (1985) *Forest of Bowland AONB - Statement of Intent.* LCC, Preston

Newby, H (1979) *Green and Pleasant Land?* Hutchinson, London

Shoard, M (1980) *The Theft of the Countryside.* Temple Smith, London

Shoard, M (1987) *This Land is our Land.* Paladin, London

Wyre Borough Council (1988) *Management Strategy for the Brock Valley.* WBC, Garstang

Appendix

Useful contacts include the following:

Forestry Commission: Forest Office, Dunsop Bridge, Clitheroe.
Lancashire County Council: County Hall, Preston.
North West Water: Pennine House, Stanley Street, Preston.
Wyre Borough Council: Civic Centre, Poulton-le-Fylde, Blackpool.

19 THE DOUGLAS VALLEY AT HAIGH: INDUSTRIAL ARCHAEOLOGY

Vivian Keyte
(Edge Hill College of Higher Education)

Outline: a study of the evidence for eighteenth and nineteenth century industrial activity in a wooded river valley on the outskirts of Wigan.

Starting point: A49 Wigan Lane at the Sicklefield footpath (GR 580080).

Finishing point: A49 Wigan Lane at the Plantation Gates (GR 585072).

Distance: 3.2 km.

Route: a walk of about 1.7 km on paths with some mud in winter; the remainder on surfaced roads.

Time needed: 2.5 to 3 hours.

Maps needed: OS 1:25,000 SD 40/50 Wigan; OS 1:10,000 SD 50 NE.

INTRODUCTION

Many people are surprised to find the scenic delights of this stretch of the Douglas valley within only 2 km of Wigan town centre. However, factories are hidden away here even today, and at the start of the Industrial Revolution this valley was a veritable hive of industry. Three elements combined to produce this activity - a stongly flowing river, plentiful local raw materials of coal and iron, and a talented and enterprising nobleman and entrepreneur.

The River Douglas

The Douglas valley seems to be of late glacial origin and it is incised through glacial till into the Middle Coal Measures. The overall gradient is approximately 1 in 240 (4 m per km), with fast flowing sections where the river is cutting into sandstone. The discharge would have been considerably greater before the Rivington and other reservoirs were built upstream in the mid-nineteenth century.

These physical conditions were very suitable for the early development of water power. Medieval corn mills existed at Worthington

197

(GR 580102), Standish (GR 581094), Haigh (GR 588071) and Wigan (GR 587066). By 1786, with the onset of the Industrial Revolution, this was one of the most intensively used stretches of river in Lancashire. Two new-comers were Brock and Leyland mills which, from 1788, formed the twin pillars of the Earl of Crawford's Haigh Ironworks enterprise.

Leyland Mill is the presumed site of an iron slitting mill which supplied the local nailing industry and was recorded in 1665. Brock Mill was first recorded in 1716 and it appears as 'Brock Forge' on William Yates' map of 1786. Both sites pre-date the Haigh Ironworks. As this enterprise came to dominate the valley for nearly 100 years, we must consider the role of the Haigh estate in the development of the valley.

The Bradshaigh family and the Haigh collieries

The Manor of Haigh came into the possession of the Bradshaigh family by marriage in about 1295. In 1538 John Leland wrote that "Mr Bradshaw hath a place called Hawe, a myle from Wigan, he hath found much canel like sea-coole in his ground, very profitable to him". In 1652 Sir Roger Bradshaigh was responsible for one of the major engineering works of his day - the Great Sough. This mine drainage tunnel took 18 years to construct by pick, hammer and wedge for a distance of 1 km from its outlet point at the Yellow Brook (GR 591072) north-east to Park Pit (GR 596079). A large area of flooded old workings and unworked coal was thus drained. The sough was eventually extended to Aspull Pumping Pit (GR 624081) in the mid-nineteenth century, a total distance of 4 km.

When the last Sir Roger Bradshaigh died in 1770 the estate and collieries were in a sadly run-down condition. This event neatly epitomises the end of the pre-industrial period at Haigh; it is touch-ingly commemorated by the block of almshouses known as the Recep-tacle (GR 588076). Haigh was inherited by Sir Roger's sister's grand-daughter, a child of ten, and eventually through marriage to her in 1780 by Alexander Lindsay, 23rd Earl of Crawford and Balcarres and Premier Earl of Scotland.

The Earl of Crawford and the Haigh Ironworks

Earl Alexander inherited an impoverished estate. He threw his consid-erable energy and talent into developing his collieries, improving mining methods and investing in the Lancaster Canal which opened in

1798 (see Excursion 12) and ran through the estate. In 1816 the southern end of this canal was incorporated into the newly completed Leeds and Liverpool Canal. In 1788, together with his brother Robert and the former owner of Brock Mill, he formed the Haigh Ironworks. These survived early difficulties to develop as a thriving concern under various ownerships, and later known as the Haigh Foundry, until 1884.

The ironworks initially comprised two blast furnaces at Leyland Mill integrated with the forge at Brock Mill. There was plenty of local coal to take advantage of the recent technological change from charcoal to coke as fuel. Ironstone was also obtained locally from 'blackband' nodules associated particularly with the Ince Seven Foot Mine (seam); this source was later supplemented by richer haematite ores transported from Furness via the Lancaster Canal. A small tub-boat canal and later a railway were constructed to bring these raw materials to Leyland Mill from local sources in the Whelley area (GR 5906). Stone and fireclay were also abundant; power for the blast and bellows, hammers and shears was provided by steam engines and three water-wheels. In the 1790s 400 people were employed here.

Early production concentrated on beam engines, rails, wagon wheels and so on (in demand for developing local collieries) together with edge tools, and shot for the Napoleonic Wars. In 1812 the Manager, Robert Daglish, built Lancashire's first locomotive called 'The Walking Horse', to Blenkinsop's patent design. From then to 1856 some 110 locomotives were produced at the works. Other products included sugar mills for the West Indies, paddle shafts for steamships, winding engines for collieries, and the swing bridge which still survives at the Albert Dock in Liverpool.

According to local tradition the world's largest water-wheel, the 'Lady Isabella' at Laxey in the Isle of Man, was also manufactured here. The balance of evidence, however, makes it more likely that the massive castings undoubtedly made at Haigh were for another slightly smaller wheel at Laxey, of which no trace now remains.

Since the closure of the Haigh Foundry in 1884 the two sites have continued in industrial use. Brock Mill became a dye- and print-works, then the headquarters of the local newspaper until 1984, and is now home to six companies ranging from engineering to a stained glass studio. Leyland Mill has a more extensive site on both sides of Leyland Mill Lane with a connecting under-bridge. Initially it provided prem-

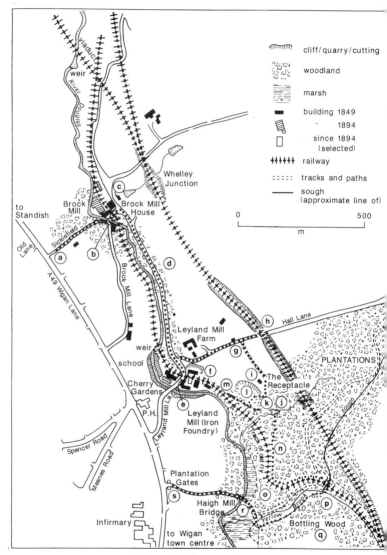

Figure 19. The excursion route.

ises for a large bedstead works, and the site of Haigh Foundy itself still supports an iron foundry. The name board at the site entrance proclaims today's other varied occupiers who include the biggest herbal suppliers in Britain and a firm specializing in boiler ignition systems for power stations and well-shutdown systems for North Sea oil rigs. The secluded Douglas valley has not been completely left behind by the march of industrial progress!

EXCURSION

The excursion begins on the A49 (Wigan Lane) at the inconspicuous Sicklefield footpath (580080), 200 m south of the Wigan Lane Service Station (Fina) (a on Figure 19). This is one of five routes converging on Brock Mill which must have brought workers trudging in from the surrounding countryside. Pause at the top of the steps to consider the physical features of the site and the buildings of the mill.

Brock Mill
Descend the 64 steps to the junction with Brock Mill Lane (footpath) and cross the footbridge over the old railway track. Beside it the old tail race from the mill entered the river, whilst a few metres downstream some girders are all that remains of a bridge for the railway which served the Brock and Leyland Mill sites from 1856 to 1909 - significantly, after the large-scale manufacture of locomotives ceased. Consider how they would have been conveyed to their markets beforehand.

From the entrance to the mill note the current uses of the various buildings. The Ordnance Survey map of 1849 shows the main building to have been in the front corner of the site (b). Across the road is the handsome stone Brock Mill House (c), bearing the plaque 'E.B. 1812' (Earl of Balcarres); this probably housed the manager.

Leave Brock Mill and walk southwards along Wingate Road. The steep bank to the left is pock-marked with old coal adits (horizontal workings) in the outcrop of the Ince Seven Foot Mine (d). Below to the right you will catch glimpses of the River Douglas, flowing placidly here between the rapid rock-cut sections at Brock (upstream) and Leyland (downstream) mills. After 600 m the road joins Hall Lane and descends to Leyland Mill Bridge (e).

Leyland Mill

This complex site is best viewed from the bridge parapet on the left-hand side, overlooking the foundry which nestles below the artificial cliff. This building occupies the site of the original foundry (f), traces of which can be seen in the form of masonry in the lower part of the cliff. The bridge on which you are standing crossed over the railway line but pre-dated it; near the lowest point on the road are two date stones on the right-hand wall which indicate that it was built in 1796 and repaired or rebuilt in 1846.

At the site entrance notice the name boards identifying the firms which now use the complex. Note also the cast iron gateposts, impressive survivors of the old ironworks. Listen for the rapidly flowing river below and to the right, where a newly constructed culvert (1987) underpins the old bridge. Finally, consider the steepness of Leyland Mill Lane, up which all the foundry's products had to be dragged by teams of up to 30 horses before rail access came in 1869. Tradition has it that in 1854 a hundred horses, mostly recruited from local farms, were needed to move the Laxey wheel! Consider how the relative accessibility of this site has changed from the early 1800s.

Now turn back, re-cross the bridge and turn right up Hall Lane. Notice that several of the old stone houses have metal tie-bars, evidence of mining subsidence (of which more later). The route follows the first track across the open field to the right (g), but you may like to walk the extra 100 m to the iron bridge which spans the track of the former Lancashire Union railway line (Whelley loop) (h). This was constructed in 1869 and served several local collieries as well as the Haigh Foundry by a short branch; it also acted as a necessary north-south bypass for Wigan during the period when most freight moved by rail.

The Receptacle

Retrace your steps and follow the track across the field (g), which leads to the Haigh almshouses quaintly known as 'The Receptacle' (i). Before you reach them notice the view to the left: you can see Haigh Hall, seat of the Bradshaighs (1295-1770) and of the Lindsays, Earls of Crawford from 1780 until Wigan Corporation purchased the estate in 1947.

The Receptacle (i) formerly comprised ten almshouses with an external staircase leading to those on the upper floor. It was renovated, cleaned, and converted into private dwellings in about 1980. It is a charming reminder of the passing of the old order on the eve of the Industrial Revolution. You might just be able to read the inscription, which runs: "This receptacle for ____ ____ of the worthy Poor was erected in 1772 at the expense of Dorothy Lady Bradshaigh, Relict of Sir Roger Bradshaigh, She thinking it the best way of showing her gratitude and to perpetuate the Memory of her affectionate husband whose Bounty enabled her to perform this act of charity so agreeable to his own good Disposition".

The path looks private but it is a public right of way. It curves towards the back of the building, then turns sharp left and descends into the Haigh Plantations.

The Haigh Plantations

Cross the wide track and climb up to the little plateau beyond (a minor spur covered by fine beech trees). On the further edge of this are two old coal workings (j), both sunk into the Ince Seven Foot Mine: to the left is a bell pit (shallow shaft) and to the right is an adit or 'day-eye'. These small workings are typical of the early nineteenth century, the Haigh Ironworks period. The latter overlooks a small pond (k), to which we shall return later.

Return to the track and turn left down it. On the right is an old quarry (l) known as Receptacle Delf, from which came sandstone for the later parts of Haigh Hall (Parbold quarry was the major source). In the quarry is the wooden headgear from the Gautley colliery in Orrell (GR 522029), re-erected here in 1978. It is the only surviving wooden pit headgear in Lancashire and dates from around 1890.

About 30 m beyond the headgear, turn right up a short flight of steps and proceed along the terraced bank for about 100 m. To your left the ground drops rapidly to the river Douglas; to your right is a linear depression some 3 m wide (m). This feature continues for another 100 m to Haigh Foundry. What do you make of it? It was a small tub-boat canal, of a type often constructed in mining areas during the pre-railway period, and dug here in the 1790s to bring coal and probably ironstone to the foundry from small mines in the Plantations.

Retrace your steps to the track and proceed up the steps opposite to rejoin the terraced bank which clearly pre-dates the drive. The paths in the Plantations, said to extend to over 60 km in all, were made by unemployed men during the Lancashire cotton famine of 1861-3, paid by James the 24th Earl. There was no unemployment benefit in those days!

The bank leads you to a small pond (k) where a minor valley has been dammed, presumably as water supply for the tub-boat canal. Continue along the bank as the ditch gradually disappears, then descend to a broader, gently inclined track which eventually obliterates the old canal. This carried the canal's successor, a railway (n) linking the collieries of the Whelley area to the foundry from 1856 until it was itself superseded by the Lancashire Union line in 1869.

The Great Haigh Sough

Continue along this contoured track around the spur (o). It is boggy in places, and an alternative route short-cuts the spur end by going through a cutting (now considerably infilled by slumped material and fallen trees) made for the railway. It is often possible to find nodules of impure ironstone in this area. In a further 80 m descend by some steps to the main Haigh Hall drive, across which more steps lead down to the Yellow Brook. Cross the footbridge and walk upstream to find the outlet of the sough beneath a sycamore tree (p).

The tunnel is protected by an iron grill; it consists of a 1m wide barrel arch of brickwork which continues in for about 250 m. The remaining 4 km is mainly unlined through hard rock. The sough has a discharge of about 2,250,000 litres per day. The Yellow Brook evidently takes its characteristic and name from this discharge, the discolouration being caused by deposits of complex iron oxides including forms of limonite (yellow ochre) created by the oxidation of pyrite and ironstones from old coal workings.

Leave the Great Sough and follow the path downstream along the left bank. This soon climbs up the valley side and passes an impressive bell pit with raised rim of spoil which is now sadly accumulating litter and rubbish. Bear right past further bell pits (q) until you meet the path which descends to cross Yellow Brook by a footbridge and causeway. The marshy valley floor is evidence of considerable mining subsidence, the effects of which are strikingly shown by Haigh Mill Bridge (r) over the Douglas which is reached by turning left along the main drive. Notice also the Douglas valley floor with levees, swampy backlands and dead trees. Altogether six seams amounting to 8 m of coal have been extracted from beneath this area since the 1870s, resulting in subsidence of about 3 m.

From the bridge walk up the main drive to the Plantation Gates (s) on Wigan Lane (GR 585072), pausing to admire the gates and ornamental ironwork which were cast at Haigh Foundry in 1850. The excursion ends here.

Selected References

Arthur, H H G (1957) *A History of Haigh Hall*. County Borough of Wigan

Birch, A (1953) The Haigh Ironworks 1797-1856. A nobleman's enterprise during the industrial revolution. *Bulletin of John Rylands Library* 35; 316-333

Grayson, R F and I A Williamson (editors) (1977) *Geological Routes around Wigan*. Wigan and District Geological Society

Grayson, R F, D Anderson and R E Fry (1979) *Mining and Geology Trail to Haigh Plantations, Wigan*. Metropolitan Borough of Wigan Department of Leisure

Harley, J B (1968) *William Yates' Map of Lancashire, 1786*. The Historic Society of Lancashire and Cheshire

Langton, J (1979) *Geographical Change and Industrial Revolution*. Cambridge University Press

Tupling, G H (1949) The early metal trades and the beginnings of engineering in Lancashire. *Transactions of the Lancashire and Cheshire Antiquarian Society* 61; 1-35

20 VEGETATION SYSTEMS AND THEIR MANAGEMENT ON THE WIRRAL PENINSULA

Jennifer M Jones
(Liverpool Polytechnic)

Outline: suggestions for the study of vegetation, habitat management in three sites in the Wirral - Bidston Hill, Dibbinsdale Local Nature Reserve and Thurstaston Common.

Starting point: Car park at Bidston Hill (GR 287897).

Finishing point: Thurstaston Common (GR 240850).

Distance: 40 km round trip taking in all 3 sites.

Route: Good road links to all sites. Easy walking on good footpaths except Bidston Hill where footpaths are not well-marked.

Time needed: One full day for all 3 sites. Individual sites could be covered in half a day each.

Maps needed: OS 1:50,000 sheet 108 (Liverpool), OS 1:50,000 sheet 117 (Chester).

INTRODUCTION

The Wirral peninsula is a narrow tongue of land 18 km long and 13 km wide, bounded to the east by the River Mersey and to the west by the River Dee (see Figure 20a). Major centres of population include Birkenhead on the western bank of the River Mersey (with Liverpool on the opposite bank) and Chester on the River Dee at the southern end. In addition, there are the smaller settlements of Bebington, Wallasey, Hoylake, West Kirby and Heswall.

Despite considerable urbanisation, the peninsula encompasses a remarkable diversity of natural and semi-natural habitats: estuary, heathland, salt marsh, ancient woodland, pond and river systems. In view of the proximity of the Wirral to the major conurbations of Liverpool and Manchester and North Wales, Cheshire and Lancashire it represents a remarkable educational resource which, to date, has

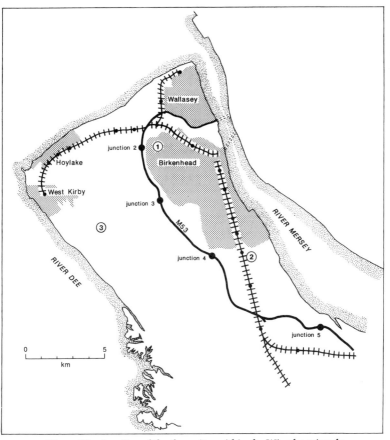

Figure 20a. Location of the three sites within the Wirral peninsula.

remained relatively untapped.

Three systems are described here: Bidston Hill, Dibbinsdale Local Nature Reserve (LNR) and Thurstaston Common/Royden Park. The Department of Leisure Services and Tourism (address in Appendix) produces leaflets for the Dibbinsdale LNR and Thurstaston Common sites which include site maps and suggested trails. Thus, supplementary information rather than suggested routes for these two sites are given here.

At all three sites access and parking are suitable for motor cars and minibuses but unsuitable for single or double decker buses. Theft from vehicles is also a problem at all the sites.

ENVIRONMENTAL SETTING

The solid geology of the Wirral peninsula comprises Triassic rocks, predominantly Bunter Upper and Lower mottled sandstone with the younger Keuper basement beds, waterstones and marls also featuring (Sheet 96, Geological Survey). Pebble Beds dominate at the southern edge of the peninsula. Much of the solid geology is overlain by drift deposits, mainly of till. The highest ground on the peninsula is formed by sandstone ridges both trending in an approximately NW-SE direction.

To the east one ridge extends from Birkenhead in the north to Eastham in the south, reaching a height of 70 m OD at Bidston Hill. The western ridge is more pronounced; it extends from West Kirby through Caldy and Thurstaston, ending south of Heswall. At Heswall Hills it reaches a height of 104 m OD - the highest point on the peninsula. Postglacial and recent deposits include blown sand and alluvium, both of which are mainly confined to the northern edge of the peninsula. Alluvium is also found in the valleys of the Fender and the Dibbin.

Soil formation on the peninsula is largely a function of geology and topography. Thus, freely drained conditions result in brown earths, with gleyed brown earths on lower slopes. Glaciofluvial drift parent material supports a range of soil types including groundwater gleys, gley podzols and surface water gleys.

There are two major stream systems on the Wirral: one, of which the Dibbin is the major tributary, drains into Bromborough Pool; the other is the Birket, with tributaries of the Fender and Arrowe Brook. The Dibbin drains a large area of the east of the peninsula, while the tributaries of the Birket drain the sand and boulder clay deposits in the north.

EXCURSION

SITE 1 BIDSTON HILL

Travel from Merseyside and the northern part of the region is via the

Kingsway (Wallasey Road) Tunnel. Exit the Kingsway Tunnel approach road immediately prior to Junction 1 of the M53 (Bidston Link Road), turn left into Hoylake Road (A553) and take the next left (Bidston Village Road). At the T-junction turn left into Boundary Road (B5151), continue across the junction with Vyner Road North and the entrance to the hill is opposite Flaybrick Hill Cemetery (close to the junction with the A5027).

Travel from Wirral, Cheshire or North Wales via the M53 taking the exit at Junction 1 onto Bidston Link Road and then as above. The driveway up to the car park is near to Tam O'Shanter cottage.

Taylor's Wood

Adjacent to the car park at Bidston Hill (a on Figure 20b, GR 287897) is a grassed picnic area with picnic benches and tables on the perimeter and litter bins provided discretely among the trees.

Follow the footpath across the picnic area into Taylor's Wood (b). This is an area of mixed deciduous-coniferous woodland with oak (*Quercus robur*) and pine (*Pinus sylvestris*). There is minimal management at this site and clear evidence of visitor pressure, particularly the extensive areas of bare ground caused mainly by motorcycling and tree climbing. Where ground cover has survived it is predominantly tufted hair grass (*Deschampsia caespitosa*).

Heathland

There is a gradual transition to heathland (c) as the tree cover diminishes and height increases. This juxtaposition of heathland and woodland is a feature of one quarter of the woodlands on sandstone substrata in Wirral. The heathland area at Bidston extends along the summit of the ridge, terminating just south of the Observatory. It is considerably fragmented and the lack of co-ordinated management has resulted in considerable encroachment from birch (*Betula*), so that views across to Liverpool and North Wales are obscured. However, despite this, it still represents a valuable resource with many heathland species present including ling (*Calluna vulgaris*), bell-heather (*Erica cinerea*), gorse (*Ulex* species) and, in particular, a diverse bryophyte flora (mosses and liverworts). Away from the woodland margins there is considerable microscale variation in vegetation in response to edaphic and hydrological controls.

The footbridge over Vyner Road North provides an excellent

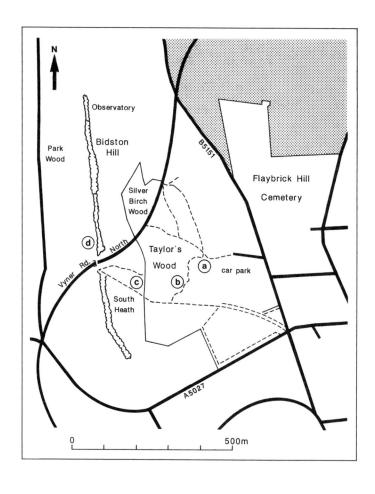

Figure 20b. Details of the walk at Bidston Hill.

vantage point (d) for observing the sandstone lithology. Closer examination is possible along the rock outcrop separating Park Wood from Bidston Hill. The footpath runs parallel to a sandstone wall a short distance from the footbridge on the Park Wood side. Known as Penny-a-day Dyke, this is the remnant of the enclosure of a deer park established in 1407. It may have encouraged the survival of the woodland.

SITE 2 DIBBINSDALE LOCAL NATURE RESERVE

Road access to Dibbinsdale LNR (GR 340825) is via the M53. Exit at Junction 4 and take the B5137 (Brimstage Road, leading into Spital Road). Turn right at the T-junction and proceed for 500 m (Figure 20c). The entrance to the Park is somewhat concealed, but it is marked by sandstone gateposts and signpost.

Rail travel is also possible to the site from both Chester and Birkenhead alighting at Spital station. The site is also served well by regular buses from Birkenhead, West Kirby and Chester.

Status and Habitats
Dibbinsdale LNR is located between the suburbs of Bebington and Bromborough and only 2 km from the banks of the River Mersey. It covers an area of 47.5 ha and lies in the valley of the Dibbinsdale Brook (Figure 20c). In 1978 the Nature Conservancy Council designated Dibbinsdale Site of Special Scientific Interest (SSSI); Dibbinsdale LNR is part of this SSSI. The site merited this status mainly because it represents the largest area of semi-natural 'ancient' broad-leaved woodland on Merseyside. In addition to this, the site includes reed swamp, fen pasture and neutral grassland. In 1983 Dibbinsdale was designated as a Local Nature Reserve. The trail detailed in the Reserve leaflet (details in Appendix) provides access to the varied habitats that Dibbinsdale offers: mature woodland, mixed age woodland, reed beds, neutral grassland and meadows.

Dibbinsdale Woodland
According to Peterken (1981), woodland may be considered 'ancient' if its origin pre-dates 1600 AD. Truly ancient woodland is rare within Britain today. Consequently, the term semi-natural 'ancient' woodland is more widely used to indicate woodland which has persisted for

211

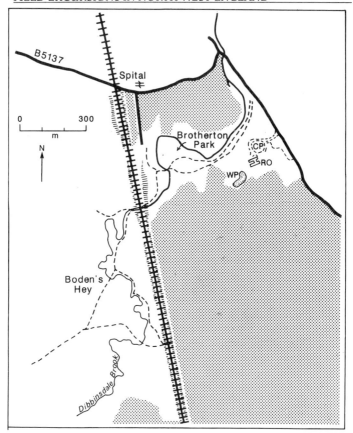

Figure 20c. Dibbinsdale Local Nature Reserve.

some considerable time but may be secondary in nature (that is, occupying a site which may not have been wooded continuously).

The origin and age of Dibbinsdale woodland are uncertain. According to the Nature Conservancy Council, woodland in the valley of Dibbinsdale has been recorded since 1818, although it is likely that some parts of the woods are much older than this. If it is assumed that the Wirral peninsula was almost continuously wooded in prehistoric

212

times, it is clear from the Domesday Book (1086) that woodland distribution was already reduced. According to Roberts (1974), the fact that Burdett's 1777 map does not record any woodland in Dibbinsdale may be an omission rather than a lack of woodland. This assessment is based on the fact that Greenwood's map of 1818 indicated widespread wooded areas in the Dibbinsdale Valley. Despite the dearth of reliable evidence, Roberts concludes that the woods of the Dibbinsdale Valley are some of the oldest on the Wirral peninsula.

Wetland - Reedbeds
The wetland areas of the Reserve have received considerable attention since early 1988 with the implementation of the Dibbinsdale Wildlife and Wetland Project. The reed swamp is quite extensive in places along the brook, and the intention is to manage the reed bed by cutting, raking and burning sections of the bed annually to prevent the build up of leaf litter. The proposed management plan aims not just to conserve the reed beds but also to improve the entire river corridor in order to attract wildlife.

The first stage of the project had been completed by the end of the summer 1984. This has involved the construction of three simple weirs to facilitate greater control over the water level. If such control is achieved it is anticipated that invertebrates, particularly damselflies and dragonflies, together with wildfowl and amphibians will use the water bodies so created in the valley bottoms for breeding.

Boden's Hey Meadow
Boden's Hey is of particular interest as it has been the focus for a meadow management scheme since 1986. The five hectare meadow has been ungrazed and unmanaged since the 1940's. However, in the summer of 1975 it was cut for hay. The following year saw a profusion of wild flowers such as lady's mantle (*Alchemilla vulgaris*), ragged robin (*Lychnis flos-cuculi*) and meadow cranesbill (*Geranium pratense*). The management scheme was implemented in order to preserve this old meadow and to encourage the growth of typical 'meadow' species. To achieve this it is necessary to impoverish the soil. Thus, management is based on the cutting, baling and removal of hay from the meadow annually.

By late 1988 there had been a marked reduction in the rank grasses while those typical of neutral grassland such as false oat grass

(*Arrhenatherum elatius*), common bent (*Agrostis capillaris*, formerly *tenuis*), Yorkshire fog (*Holcus lanatus*) and sweet vernal grass (*Anthoxanthum odoratum*) had survived. There was also the bonus of a display of common spotted orchids (*Dactylorhiza fuchsii*). Species characteristic of fen pasture are evident closer to the stream. These include floating sweet grass (*Glyceria fluitans*), creeping bent (*Agrostis stolonifera*), common nettle (*Urtica dioica*), meadowsweet (*Filipendula ulmaria*), soft rush (*Juncus effusus*), yellow loosestrife (*Lysimachia vulgaris*), marsh pennywort (*Hydrocotyle vulgaris*) and wavy bitter cress (*Cardamine flexuosa*).

Marford's Wood
At the southernmost tip of the reserve, Marford's Wood underwent some management by coppicing in 1987-8 in order to open up the canopy and favour the growth of ground flora. The regeneration of oak and ash seedlings has also been encouraged. As an addendum to this activity, it is proposed to lift some of these seedlings to supply the tree nursery established on the reserve at Woodslee. The aim is to use these seedlings not just to restock Dibbinsdale Wood but also to stock other locations in Wirral.

Wirral Wildlife and Countryside Project
Woodslee Cottages, which house the ranger offices, are also the location for the Wirral Wildlife and Countryside Project. The project, which began in 1986 under the aegis of the Community Programme of the Manpower Service Commission, comprised four components: Environmental Education, Estate Management, Ecology and Graphic Design. In the first year of its existence the Ecology branch of the project completed a Phase I Habitat Survey of the Wirral peninsula. As a result, a Phase II Survey of the project was implemented early in 1988.

The Phase I Survey outlined 106 sites on Wirral which were considered as ecologically important. The aim of the Phase II Survey was to study a number of these sites in detail. In addition to obtaining species lists for higher and lower plants, faunal species lists were planned with particular cooperation from entomologists. Basic soil analyses formed an important component of the study while factors such as slope, aspect etc. were also recorded. The overall aim was to obtain a detailed assessment of as many sites as possible primarily to provide valuable base level information. Following the introduction of Employment Training to succeed the Community Programme in September 1988, the future format of this work is being re-planned.

Although the Dibbinsdale reserve is staffed only by two full-time rangers, the management achieved is highly creditable. Over the last five years a rapport has been established between the rangers, schools and the local population. The provision of activities for children (eg pond dips, discovery walks) by Wirral Countryside Ranger Service together with close collaboration with voluntary conservation groups (such as Wirral Countryside Volunteers, Merseyside Nature Conservation Volunteers, Cheshire Conservation Trust and British Trust for Conservation Volunteers) have served to engender an enthusiasm which should ensure the successful management of this unique reserve.

SITE 3 THURSTASTON COMMON

For access via the M53, exit at Junction 3 and follow the A552 (Woodchurch Road) towards Arrowe Park. At the roundabout outside the park take the A551 exit (Arrowe Park Road), continue until the next roundabout, take the left exit (Upton by-pass) and at the next roundabout take the B5139 (Greasby Road). Continue for 3 km to Frankby Green. Turn left into Hill Bark Road (by Frankby Cemetery entrance) and continue to Royden Park gates (Figure 20d). Take care to follow the marked one-way system in the car park.

Conservation Interest
Within the British Isles the extent of heathland has declined markedly in recent years. This, together with the proximity of Thurstaston Common (GR 240850) to the Merseyside conurbations, serves to emphasise the value of these 100 ha of heathland and semi-natural and planted woodland.

Thurstaston Common was designated as a Site of Special Scientific Interest (SSSI) in 1984. It is jointly owned by the National Trust and the Wirral Borough Council, and is managed by the Department of Leisure Services and Tourism (through the Countryside Ranger service) primarily as a Countryside Area for informal recreation. However, the site clearly has an intrinsic conservation value and recent management proposals reflect this.

On the higher ground and steeper slopes, 'dry heath' is dominant

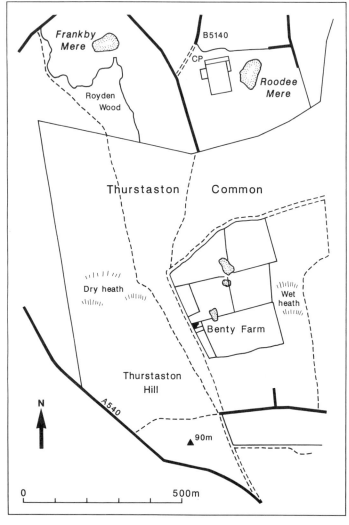

Figure 20d. Thurstaston Common.

with ling (*Calluna vulgaris*), bell heather (*Erica cinerea*) and gorse (*Ulex* spp.). The 'dry heath' areas are the most extensive, extending along the entire western margin of the Common. The areas of 'wet heath' are small by comparison, and they are confined mainly to the east of the Common between Benty Farm and Greasby Brook. Significant species on these more sensitive areas include cross-leaved heath (*Erica tetralix*), round-leaved sundew (*Drosera rotundifolia*), rushes (*Juncus* spp.) and bogmoss (*Sphagnum* spp).

Management Plan

In many areas of the Common invasion by bracken (*Pteridium aquilinum*) and birch (*Betula*) is a major problem. In response to this, and in order to preserve the character of the heathland, a management plan was drawn up in the early 1980s. The intention was to implement two major strategies: firstly, to clear birch, bracken and scrub from those areas in which the succession was most threatened and, secondly, to initiate a grazing experiment.

Clearance of threatened areas of open heath initially concentrated on the sensitive wet heaths. Here birch was cleared and the stumps were treated with a selective herbicide to prevent regeneration. Subsequently it was observed that, in addition to birch, some of the drier areas of the site were under threat from gorse (*Ulex* species), bramble (*Rubus fruticosus*) and rosebay willowherb (*Epilobium angustifolium*).

Heather Regeneration

The grazing experiment was initiated with the aim of stimulating heather regeneration, initially by heavy grazing. The experiment involved agreement between the National Trust, the tenant of Benty Farm and the Nature Conservancy Council. The grazing activity is overseen by the Countryside Ranger Service and they monitor the results together with the Nature Conservancy Council.

The area to be grazed was sub-divided into three 'paddocks' to facilitate manipulation of grazing rates and allow for rotation to permit some areas to rest. Temporary fencing with stiles was erected, together with signs explaining the aim of the experiment to the public. Heavy grazing of the paddock continued until 1983 to ensure removal of species such as purple moor grass (*Molinia caerulea*) and birch (*Betula*) seedlings and stimulate heather regeneration. Two years later the extent of regeneration was seen to be encouraging, although there was concern that the *Calluna vulgaris* and *Erica tetralix* seedlings should be fairly well established before further grazing was allowed. In the subsequent two year period (1985-1987) sheep were grazed at stocking rates of twenty to thirty ewes from April to June with the aim of controlling the early flush of *Molinia caerulea* and again during August and September to control *Betula* seedlings.

Ironically, early in 1987 the regenerating heather was itself seen to be a threat to *Drosera rotundifolia*. The life cycle of *Calluna vulgaris* comprises four stages: pioneer, building, mature and degenerate (Gimingham, 1972). As a result of the grazing experiment at Thurstaston, the heather was making a rapid transition from the open pyramidal growth form of the pioneer stage to the bushier growth form of the building phase. Consequently, the rapid reduction in available light to the surface was detrimental to the survival of *Drosera*. To overcome this, areas of bare ground were created by disturbing the heath 'turf' to encourage regeneration of *Drosera* (Hose, 1988).

In some parts of the Common it is evident that the heather is not healthy. The symptoms are mainly of 'scorching' or in more extreme cases of dieback. Reports of similar observations at other heathland areas on the Wirral (eg Heswall Hills and Caldy Hill) and in North Wales (eg Denbigh Moors and Clwydian Hills) suggest that this is not a localised phenomenon. Although micrometeorological factors were thought to be implicated initially, the Ranger service is now considering the possibility that infestation by heather beetle may be the prime cause.

PROSPECTS

It is clear that many of Wirral's vegetation systems are being managed successfully for both informal leisure and conservation purposes. Further, there is obviously good liaison between the ranger services, conservation organisations and the public. There is a wealth of habitats on the peninsula; the three sites detailed here serve only to illustrate the variety both in terms of structure and function and management strategy.

Clearly, from an educational point of view, the sites offer considerable potential. All could provide useful sites for simple vegetation analysis to give novices valuable experience in species identification.

There is potential for both intra- and inter-site comparisons of dominant species. The influence of vegetation type on soil properties could be studied employing simple variables such as depth of litter layer, pH of different horizons and depths of horizons. The wooded areas of all sites would be conducive to the study of tree age and woodland structure eg. girth at breast height, tree height (using an Abney level), distance to nearest neighbour of the same species, distance to nearest tree of any species and evidence of woodland management (eg. coppicing or pollarding).

There is clearly tremendous scope for comparing impact of visitor pressure and management implemented to cope with this. Thus, for example, the lack of well-defined and constructed pathways at Bidston Hill is reflected in the considerable areas of bare ground. This contrasts markedly with the well-defined but relatively unobtrusive pathways of Thurstaston Hill which differ again from the constructed pathways of Dibbinsdale LNR where a need to ease pressure from sensitive 'ancient' woodland and wetland areas is essential.

Selected References

Gimingham, C H (1972) *The Ecology of Heathlands.* Chapman & Hall

Hose, S V (1988) *Vegetation communities of the wet heath area of Thurstaston Common.* Unpublished BSc undergraduate dissertation, University of Lancaster

Peterken, G F (1981) *Woodland Conservation and Management.* Chapman & Hall

Roberts, J (1974) *The distribution and vegetation composition of woodland on the Wirral peninsula.* Unpublished PhD thesis, University of Liverpool

Some Useful Field Guides

Fitter, R, A Fitter, & M Blamey (1974) *The Wildflowers of Britain and Northern Europe.* Collins

Fitter, R, A Fitter, and A Farrer (1984) *Collins Guide to the Grasses, Sedges, Rushes and Ferns of Britain and Northern Europe.* Collins

Jahns, H M (1987) *Collins Guide to the Ferns, Mosses and Lichens of Britain and Northern and Central Europe.* Collins

Mitchell, A (1988) *The Trees of Britain and Northern Europe.* Collins

Appendix

Useful addresses include;

Bidston Hill, Tel: 051 653 9332

Department of Leisure Services & Tourism, Westminster House,
Hamilton Street, BIRKENHEAD L41 5FN. Tel: 051 647 2366

Dibbinsdale LNR, Spital Road, BROMBOROUGH, Wirral, L62 2BJ.
Tel: 051 334 9851

Royden Park & Thurstaston Common, Tel: 051 677 7594

Wirral Country Park Centre, Station Road, THURSTASTON, Wirral
L61 OHN. Tel: 051 648 4371/3884

Wirral Wildlife & Countryside Project, 3 Woodslee Cottages,
Dibbinsdale LNR, Spital Road, BROMBOROUGH, Wirral
L62 2BJ. Tel: 051 334 6227

Acknowledgements

Considerable assistance in the compiling of this chapter was given by
Rob Daniels and Vicky Hose of Dibbinsdale LNR and Keith Norton
formerly of Dibbinsdale LNR.

21 THE PLEISTOCENE DEPOSITS AT THURSTASTON, WIRRAL

Arnold Jones
(Liverpool Polytechnic)

Outline: a detailed examination of a Pleistocene sedimentary sequence which reveals evidence of patterns of ice movement in the Wirral.
Starting point: Thurstaston Hill (GR 245846).
Finishing point: Thurstaston Country Park Centre (GR 239835).
Distance: 4 km.
Route: by vehicle between sites, on foot within sites.
Time needed: 3 hours minimum.
Maps needed: OS 1:250,000 map, North West England and North Wales (regional setting); OS 1:50,000 Landranger Series, Sheet 108; OS 1:25,000 Series, Sheet SJ28; OS 1:10,000 Series, Sheet SJ28SW

INTRODUCTION

The cliff section that extends along the south-west coast of the Wirral Peninsula, from West Kirkby to Heswall (Figure 21), is probably unique - it is the only continuous section of presumed Late Devensian glacial deposits in North-West England. The topography of the area, the trend of the glacial striae and the provenance (source) of the erratics in the drift suggest that it was once covered by an ice sheet which extended south from its source area in western and southern Scotland across the northern Irish Sea Basin, before being split by the barrier created by the Welsh mountains and an associated Welsh ice cap occupying the Vale of Clwyd and the Conway Valley. It is believed that the ice sheet which was responsible for the Thurstaston deposits extended southwards as far as the West Midlands.

In 1954 the Dee Estuary was declared a Site of Special Scientific Interest (SSSI) because of its international importance as a feeding place for wading birds and wildfowl, and for the flora of the salt marshes which border the estuary (see Excursion 20). In 1979 a 53 ha

221

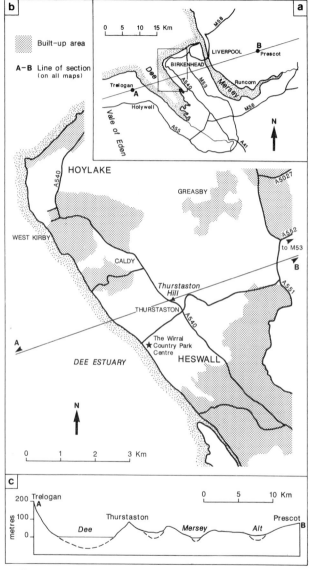

Figure 21. Regional setting (a), location (b) and cross-section (c).

strip of the cliffs centred upon Thurstaston was also declared an SSSI; combining its physiographic and geomorphological interest with its value as a botanical site. Cheshire County Council designated part of the area centred on the abandoned railway line from Hooton to West Kirby 'The Wirral Country Park' in 1969. The administration of the Park was taken over by the Metropolitan Borough of Wirral in 1974.

The complete section stretches from West Kirby Sailing Club (GR 216859) to Heswall Sailing Club (GR 253815), a distance of almost 6 km, but much of the section is either obscured by mass movements or coastal defence structures. Throughout its length it is being actively eroded by the tides and currents of the Dee Estuary; fresh sections are constantly being exposed as a result. The most accessible section extends for almost 4 km from 100 m north-west from Caldy Steps (GR 222848) to GR 246823. Recent cliff recession of about 1 m a year has been indirectly measured at Thurstaston.

Thurstaston is reached either through the Mersey Tunnels, or from Chester and the M56 via the A540 through Heswall.

There are three possible access points to the section where car and coach parking facilities are available - at Caldy Station (GR 223850), at the Wirral Country Park Centre at Thurstaston (GR 239835), and at Heswall (GR 255815). All these points can be reached from the A540 West Kirby - Chester Road. From Thurstaston Hill drive to Caldy Station (GR 23850). From Caldy Steps the route lies entirely along the beach. If desired, after visiting Sites 2, 3 and 4, vehicles could transport the party to the Wirral Country Park Centre at Thurstaston (GR 239835) to visit Sites 5 and 6.

Access to the beach is easy at Caldy and Heswall (where the cliffs are low), but the cliff paths are steep at Thurstaston (where the cliffs are at their highest). It is advisable to contact the Wirral Country Park Ranger Service (address in Appendix) before visiting the site. Since the section has the status of an SSSI, collection of samples and digging along the section are prohibited unless prior permission has been obtained from the Nature Conservancy Council (see Appendix for details).

EXCURSION

Site 1. Thurstaston Hill (GR 245846)
This is an excellent viewpoint at 90 m OD from which to view the to-

pography of the area. The bedrock surface is believed to be the result of intense glacial erosion by an actively moving ice sheet. A series of NNW/SSE trending Triassic Sandstone ridges can be seen, separated by intervening depressions where the bedrock surface is often below sea level. A bedrock profile from Prescot to Holywell Mountain (Figure 21b) passing through the viewpoint, demonstrates how the ice sheet selectively carved out the alternating series of valleys and hills.

It is known that bedrock extends at least 45 m below sea level underneath the estuary. The deepest part of the valley has been reported upstream at Sealand, where depths of 78 m have been recorded. All the valleys are infilled with glacial drift and alluvium. The drift can be seen to be draped along the south west side of Thurstaston Hill, producing the cliffs, which rise from sea level at West Kirby to 40 m at Thurstaston before falling to sea level again at Heswall.

Sites 2 and 3   Caldy Steps

The easy access to the beach at Caldy Station allows examination of two sites. Site 2, some 200 m north-westwards towards West Kirby, illustrates how active erosion is exposing the upper part of the sequence. Above the till there is orange sand up to 1 m thick.

At Site 3, south-east of Caldy Steps, a 400 m section of till is exposed above laminated sands which can be seen at several places at the base of the cliff. The stratified sequence gradually increases in thickness to over 3 m while fine and medium gravels can also be seen. The overlying base of the till is seen to dip to the north-west.

From this point to the Dee Sailing Club there are no exposures, partly due to slumping but also due to coastal defence works which have graded and protected the base of the cliff.

Sites 4, 5 and 6   Thurstaston

At a point about 100 m south-east of the Dee Sailing Club Causeway (Site 4), the stratified succession can be seen above and below till. It would appear, however, to be very localised and there is evidence of at least one channel cut into the lower till, which has been filled in with cross-bedded sand. Some 100 m before the Shore Cottages is the site (Site 5) where Lee (1979) discovered a 'loess' bed in the stratified series, and Pitts (1983) described shear structures and faults. The beach is formed of till, which lies below the stratified deposits; geophysical methods have demonstrated that it is at least 50 m thick at this point.

To the south-east of the Thurstaston steps the cliff is often difficult to get access to and mass movements are common. But 100 m further along (Site 6) the best exposure of the lower till can be seen, with lenses of sands and gravels and a plane separating it from the upper till.

INTERPRETATIONS OF THE SUCCESSION

The occurence of glacial striae in the area was first noted in the Liverpool area by Morton in 1859. But the earliest synopsis of the evidence was produced by Strahan in 1886, who produced a map and diagrams to illustrate that the predominant ice direction was between N2OW and N4OW. The erratic evidence was summarised by Mackintosh in 1879, who identified abundant Criffel Granite and Scottish 'greenstone', Eskdale Granite and Lake District volcanics on the beach, where they had been washed out of the Lower Boulder Clay. He also briefly described the section, which was summarised by Lamplugh in 1923, in the Memoir of the Geological Survey to Sheet 96 (Liverpool):

> 3. Upper Boulder Clay - up to 6 m of a dull red-brown clay with ashy gray facings and vertical joint planes, much less stony than 1, which appears to be draped over the underlying surface.
>
> 2. A stratified belt up to 6 m thick, tapering laterally, of yellow sand and gravel, loam and laminated clay.
>
> 1. Lower Boulder Clay, unstratified, red, tough, homogeneous clay, with Lake District and Southern Scotland erratics, but with 5-10 per cent locally derived Triassic bedrock. The top surface is uneven and hummocky.

In 1929, Slater agreed with this subdivision, and indicated locations where the different beds could be seen. He suggested that the Lower Boulder Clay was a streamlined drumlin, formed below a thick ice sheet moving down the Dee Estuary. The overlying Sands and Gravels were thickest on the northern side of the drumlin, where they dipped to the north; they were thin or absent on the southern side where the dip was to the south. Slater also provided more detailed sections of two of the best exposures, immediately to the north-west and south-east of

225

Thurstaston Station.

At that time most workers believed that this three-fold succession, which could be identified at many locations in north-west England, indicated distinct phases of deposition. Slater followed this ruling hypothesis but also made several interesting comments. He noted that the Lower Boulder Clay was deposited under considerable pressure. He doubted whether many of the Sands and Gravels were in situ, and noted that "lenticles of sand and gravel were incorporated in the Upper Boulder Clay". Subsequently, marine shells found in sands at Sandiway in North Cheshire were radiocarbon dated at 28,000 BP (years before present) and organic deposits at the base of a kettle hole in the Delamere Forest were dated at 12,000 BP, suggesting that the Upper Boulder Clay at least was Late Devensian in age.

Boulton and Worsley (1965) proposed that this interpretation of the succession was too simplistic, causing a reinvestigation by Brenchley (1968) who used standard techniques of particle size and shape analysis, provenance studies of erratics and fabric analysis.

Brenchley's (1968) study was confined to a 1 km stretch of cliff immediately below the road leading down from Thurstaston village. He indicated problems with examining this succession - inaccessibility, a crust of mud washed down the cliff face to obscure the drift, and the differing appearance of the drift depending upon whether it is dry or wet. He agreed that the three lithologies could be distinguished, but noted that they were not always clearly differentiated. He also pointed out that the Lower Boulder Clay contained lenses of bedded sand and gravel; the clay was partially cemented by calcite, thereby hardening it; the top of the clay sometimes formed a shelf; and the boundary between the Lower Boulder Clay and the overlying sands was very irregular.

Brenchley agreed with Slater that the thickest part of the sand succession was on the northern limb, often up to 11 m thick and often exposed at beach level. At several places a lateral change could be identified where cross-bedded sands gave way laterally to clay, suggesting channel fill deposits. He identified a location where channel walls had collapsed. In the south the sands were very thin, and could best be seen as an almost plane surface about 5 m above the beach. Finally, he noted that the Upper Boulder Clay also contained occasional sandy lenses, had far fewer erratics and weathered to a characteristic blue grey colour on joint faces.

Extensive sampling of the erratics suggested that the only significant difference between the provenance of the two units was that "the Upper Clay had occasional whole marine shells, while the Lower had only comminuted debris". He accepted a northern origin for the granites and garnet bearing lavas and 'streaky' ingnimbrites, and hematite impregnated limestone; while he believed that the flint, gypsum and marine shells must have come from the floor of the Irish Sea. Many of the erratics displayed faceted sides with scratches. Pebble shape analysis between the erratics in the Lower and Upper Boulder Clay failed to make any distinction. The gravels generally displayed more rounding consistent with water transport. He noted that the upper layers contained greater amounts (40 per cent) of locally derived material. Brenchley suggested that this could be due to the fact that the local hills were ice free. Particle size analysis on the fraction finer than 2 mm showed that the Lower Boulder Clay contained more sand and less clay than the Upper Boulder Clay, ie it was coarser. Fabric measurements taken from the Lower Boulder Clay suggested that there was a preferred orientation from the north-west.

He concluded that while the Lower Boulder Clay was probably the result of ice deposition (albeit in close association with running water) and was followed by the deposition of waterlain sands and gravels, the Upper Boulder Clay presented a problem. He proposed a lacustrine origin, and suggested that the scattered stones could have been deposited from floating ice. He noted that imprints of fossil leaves had been found in brown clay at the base of the cliff, which resembled the Upper Boulder Clay. He added that these leaves would be unlikely to be preserved in a deposit formed at the base of a moving ice sheet.

Brenchley also pointed out that a stoneless clay and bedded sands could be identified above the Upper Boulder Clay at the north end of the section, suggesting that they could either represent "the bedded upper part of the lacustrine deposits" or "sediment deposited by water on top of ice deposited boulder clay".

Since that time there has been considerable review of glaciogenic processes from a wide range of arctic and sub-arctic environments, and there have been several attempts at re-evaluation of this critical succession. Distinctions have been made between overconsolidated tills (laid down at the base of a glacier) and unconsolidated tills (produced by melt out and flow processes). In 1979, Lee claimed that a silt which was exposed between the tills at the base of the cliff in 1975 was loess (fine wind-blown sediment). He stresses that it is difficult to conceive of any other alternative than a sub-aerial phase following the deposition of the Lower Till. However, the exceptionally isolated nature of this exposure and the lack of any other confirmatory evidence would suggest that the loess could have been ice rafted into the area by the ice sheet, and that its exposure at this site is entirely fortuitous.

Pitts (1983) also examined part of the stratified sequence which was exposed at the base of the cliff in 1976 and 1977-78. He suggested that they belonged to a subglacial/proglacial land system and sediment association. He described eleven recognisable units in the bedded sequence, including a shear zone between Units 6 and 8, and faults in Units 1 and 6. He concluded that since the overlying till is non-consolidated, the shear plane sand faults must be the result of "rapid loading of a saturated succession of limited mass permeability". This he suggests is a flow till. Another interpretation which more reasonably fits the observed facts is that the Upper Till is a melt-out till, which would be highly saturated and would produce the same effect.

CONCLUSIONS

The fragmentary evidence available from these cliffs suggests that the sedimentary sequence was laid down by a single glacial episode. The basal till is a classic overconsolidated lodgement till, possessing a fabric which is in agreement with the NNW/SSE trend of the drumlinate structure as defined by Slater (1929). The occasional sand lenses are evidence of the close association of flowing water in a subglacial environment. The ice mass would be wet based and flowing relatively freely. It is not unreasonable to suggest that this episode dates from 18,000 BP, when the Late Devensian ice advance reached its maximum limit in the West Midlands.

The overlying stratified sequence is best developed on the northern side of the structure, where it is up to 3 m thick. It appears to be associated with a sub-glacial meltwater system flowing in a southeasterly direction. It is probable that contemporaneous melting of the ice sheet produced the overlying till (a melt-out till) which could explain the structures outlined by Pitts (1983). A problem still remains with the loess as defined by Lee (1979), but it is possible that such a deposit could be transported from the surrounding ice free slopes.

Selected References

Brenchley, P (1968) An investigation into the glacial deposits at Thurstaston, Wirral. *Amateur Geologist* 3; 27-40

Boulton G S and P Worsley (1965) Late Weichselian Glaciation of the Cheshire Shropshire Basin. *Nature* 207; 704-706

Lee, M P (1979) Loess from the Pleistocene of the Wirral Peninsula, Merseyside. *Proceedings of the Geological Association* 90; 21-26

Mackintosh, D (1879) Results of a Systematic Survey, in 1878, of the Directions and Limits of Dispersion, Mode of Occurence, and Relation to Drift Deposits of the erratic Blocks or Boulders of the West of England and East of Wales, including a Revision of many Years' previous Observations. *Quarterly Journal of the Geological Society of London* 35; 425-452

Pitts, J (1983) Faults and other shears in bedded Pleistocene deposits on the Wirral, United Kingdom. *Boreas* 12; 137-144

Slater, G (1929) The Dawpool section of the Dee Estuary, Cheshire. *Proceedings of the Liverpool Geological Society* 15; 134-143

Strahan, A (1886) On the Glaciation of South Lancashire, Cheshire and the Welsh Border. *Quarterly Journal of the Geological Society of London* 42; 369-380

Appendix

Assistant Regional Officer, Nature Conservancy Council, Blackrod Council Offices, Church Street, Blackrod, Bolton, Lancashire. Telephone 0204 693800

The Chief Ranger, Wirral Country Park, Thurstaston, Wirral. Telephone 051 648 4371

22 LAND RECLAMATION FOR RECREATION IN THE URBAN FRINGE

John Boothby
(Liverpool Polytechnic)

Outline: a study of the problems and opportunities of land reclamation at three sites - Pennington Flash Country Park (near Wigan), Culcheth Linear Park (near Warrington) and Risley Moss Nature Reserve (near Warrington).

Starting point: Pennington Flash Country Park, Leigh (GR 643985).

Finishing point: Birchwood, Warrington New Town (GR 665922).

Distance: 15 km by road, with approx 3 km walking at each site.

Route: by vehicle between sites, on foot within sites.

Time needed: one full day.

Maps needed: OS 1:50,000 sheet 109 (Manchester).

INTRODUCTION

George Orwell was a close observer of the North West in the late winter of 1935/6 and describes the area in The Road to Wigan Pier (1962 p.94-5): "For some reason .... Wigan has always been picked on as a symbol of the ugliness of the industrial areas". He continues his description in detail:

> "all around was the lunar landscape of slag-heaps ... the factory chimneys sending out their plumes of smoke. The canal path was a mixture of cinders and frozen mud, criss-crossed by the imprints of innumerable clogs, and all around, as far as the slag-heaps in the distance, stretched the 'flashes' - pools of stagnant water that had seeped into the hollows caused by the subsidence of ancient pits. It seemed a world from which vegetation had been banished; nothing existed except smoke, shale, ice, mud, ashes and foul water."

This "real ugliness of industrialism" has played an important and in-strumental part in the quality of life of the region and in the regional

230

image farther afield. Industrialism, recession, the long-term decline of staple industries have left parts of this region with a legacy of derelict land and buildings. Such land ranges from abandoned mineral workings to cotton mills and steelworks, from disused railway lines and dockland to factories and airfields.

However, much has changed in the North-West in the 50 years since Orwell's commentary. Some of the eyesores have been redeveloped to national acclaim: Albert Dock, Liverpool and Wigan Pier provide two outstanding examples, attracting between them some 2.5 million tourist visits in 1986. This excursion is concerned with environmental quality in the boroughs of Wigan and Warrington. The projects described here are on a smaller scale than the two examples above; but each is an example of the positive use of derelict land, where the 'symbols of ugliness' have now become the symbols of an enhanced environmental quality and of the positive facet of regional image and quality of life. Certainly the local authorities, concerned to attract new industry, see environmental improvement as their objective, though the impact of recession from the late 1970s faced them with an increasing area of derelict land, as the figures for Wigan MBC demonstrate (Table 22.1).

Table 22.1 Derelict land and reclamation, Wigan MBC

	Year	Area (ha)	Notes
Derelict Land	1974	1045	
	1982	1342	
	1987	885	
Land reclaimed (actual and projected)	1974/87	{331	(Wigan MBC)
		{497	(Greater Manchester County)
	1987/88	159	(11 schemes)
	1988/89	117	(3 schemes)
	1989/90	114	(4 schemes)
	1990/91	84	(5 schemes)

Source: Data from Wigan MBC, Department of Technical Services

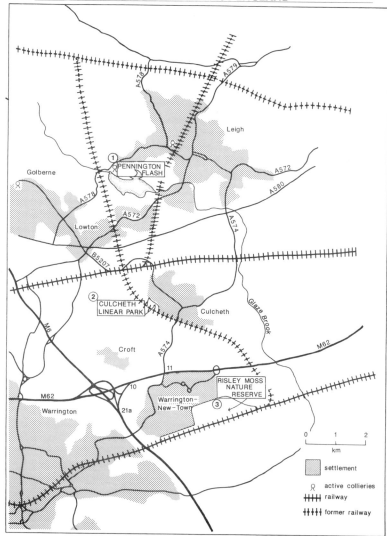

Figure 22a. Location of the three study sites.

EXCURSION

The route and locations are shown in Figure 22a.

SITE 1 PENNINGTON FLASH COUNTRY PARK

This site is also described in detail in Excursion 23; site details (including access and permission) are given in the Appendix.

Coal mining has left the area around Wigan with several flashes - subsidence areas, now flooded, following coal extraction. For many years, these areas were seen as a liability - wet, marshy, evil-smelling. The best use for such areas was felt to be waste disposal, and it was only from the late 1960s that alternative, positive uses began to be considered. Barr (1970 p.33) states clearly the common view: "the easiest and cheapest way to dispose of refuse is to find a large hole in the ground, empty the rubbish into it, and beat a hasty retreat."

At Pennington Flash (Figure 22b) the site was used for extensive disposal of household waste between 1971 and 1985, though several sailing clubs had been established for many years, as the Flash offered one of the few accessible stretches of open water in the north-west in the days when public use of reservoirs was scarcely possible. The water quality , though formerly rather poor, did not significantly detracted from its potential for sailing, fishing or wildlife.

The site was formally opened as a Country Park in 1981, jointly managed by Wigan Manchester Borough Council (MBC) and Greater Manchester Council. But active coal mining (at the Bickershaw Colliery complex) and the on-site disposal of household waste were to continue. The main works carried out in the programme of land reclamation/improvement have been:

   (i)   the covering of landfill
   (ii) landscaping, seeding etc
   (iii) tree planting
   (iv) path building
   (v) fences, signposting, bird-hides
   (vi) stabilisation of shoreline
   (vii) provision of visitors' centre
   (viii) nine-hole golf course
   (ix) nature-reserve construction
   (x) car parking (150 spaces)
   (xi) provision of warden service

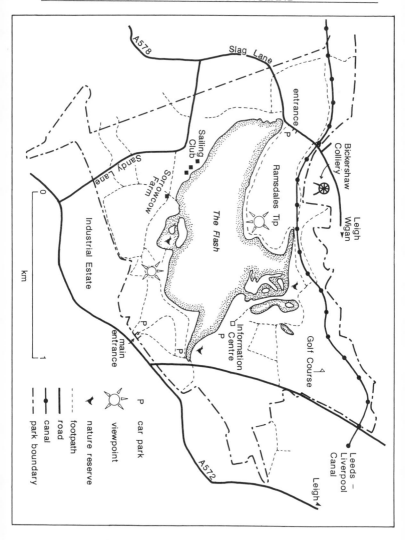

Figure 22b. Pennington Flash Country Park.

As a Country Park, Pennington Flash has been designed to maximize its visitor numbers within the limits set by its conservation objectives. Its paths have been built using crushed stone to handle large numbers of people - more than 250,000 visitors use the Park each year. Although these designated pathways are heavily used, the public can roam freely over the Park area, with the exception of the fenced-off plantation areas and the nature reserves. Extensive numbers of wildfowl breed in the latter, over 200 species of bird have been recorded in the Park, ranging from resident breeding species such as Kingfisher, Great Crested Grebe, Grasshopper Warbler and Tawny Owl, to less common visitors (such as Snipe, Cormorant and Woodcock) and the even rarer visits of Bewick's Swan, Great Northern Diver and Osprey.

Informal recreation is the most common activity - bird watching, walking, pony riding and nature study, though the more 'formal' activities of golf and sailing are also important: there are three sailing clubs based here. The resident wardens also organise a programme of activities including guided walks and events. Even though informality is the hallmark of this site, it is quite clearly not wild countryside; it is not possible or desirable to avoid sign-boards, notices and other aspects of formal management. In spite of this, however, it is a tribute to the design and operation of the site that a large part of management is 'invisible'.

The best way to see the Park is to complete the circular walk around the Flash (Figure 22b) which at Sorrowcow Farm becomes a permissive right of way. This walk enables you to see the range of reclamation works, the wildlife, and the successful attempts to achieve a natural landscape. There are a number of good vantage points accessible by a short walk from the car parks.

SITE 2 CULCHETH LINEAR PARK

In 1963 the Beeching Report recommended the closure of uneconomic railway lines. Indeed, between 1948 and 1968, some 9,000 km of railway line were abandoned, some of it to be purchased for new uses, including refuse disposal, car parks, agriculture or industry. In some cases, local authorities (and other bodies) have been instrumental in creating nature reserves and footpaths, in some instances up to 25 km long.

In general, the potential use of a disused line depends upon a number of physical characteristics - areal extent, gradient, curvature, relationship to adjacent land surface, condition of the trackbed, and guage. Specific considerations for informal recreational use include drainage, scrub clearance, landscaping, bridge maintenance, access and car parking, and the site location in relation to its potential users. Linear parks are, area for area, more expensive undertakings than more conventional developments.

As a commuter settlement lying between Manchester and Liverpool, Culcheth is an ideal location for the development of the informal recreation facilities provided by the linear park (Figure 22c; site details in Appendix). The urban fringe surrounding Culcheth is typical of its kind, in which farming has to cope with pressure from a variety of competing land uses, especially those with extensive space demands. The area immediately surrounding the park contains, in addition to housing, a golf-course, a school, and buildings used by the United Kingdom Atomic Energy Authority (UKAEA). The outskirts of Culcheth also contain a large hospital and the underground chemical store of ICI (Glazebury Depot).

The rural landscape of the fringe is also the focus of increased demand for recreational access to the countryside, which can have an adverse impact on the farmed landscape. In particular, it is the difficulties of access which have typified the problem of fringe; the footpath network, created for agricultural purposes, is no longer suitable for the other recreational demands. The footpath/bridle-way network has often degenerated, is often poorly signposted and way-marked, and there may be inherent conflicts between walkers and riders.

At Culcheth, the transformation of the abandoned line began with its acquisition by Warrington Borough Council in 1974. Before this, it had been derelict for several years, used for unofficial access or for fly-tipping of domestic rubbish. The works carried out in the conversion have included:

      (i)   landscaping
      (ii)   tree, flower and bulb planting
      (iii) drainage maintenance
      (iv) bridge-building
      (v)   installation of steps
      (vi) way marking
      (vii) provision of benches

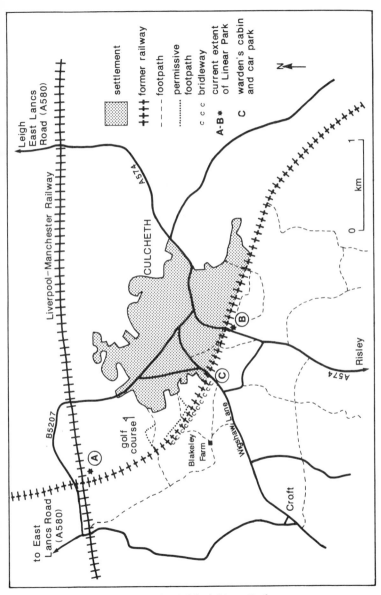

Figure 22c. Culcheth Linear Park.

(viii) creation of footpaths and separate bridle paths
(ix) scrub clearance
(x)   habitat creation and management
(xi) provision of picnic site
(xii) car parking
(xiii) warden services

The linear park intersects the existing footpath network (Figure 22c) and with the provision of "permissive" rights of way, the area is now more accessible to both walker and rider. Liaison with local farmers has ensured a more sympathetic use of the footpath network, which is now waymarked and for which leaflets are provided. This strategy is actively promoted by the Mersey Valley Partnership as part of a wide programme of environmental improvements.

Access to the linear park can be made from the existing footpath network, but a small car park is provided at the site of the former station on Wigshaw Lane; in common with other linear park developments, this limited car access presents difficulties. The northward line of the park has segregated routes for walkers and riders, and the former have a variety of footpaths for their use, some built into the side of the old embankment. It is also valuable as a walk in its own right especially because its hard surface makes it more accessible to the elderly and infirm and those with small children. It is limited at its northern end by the cutting of the Manchester-Liverpool railway. The former bridge has now been demolished, but the abandoned Culcheth line continues towards Pennington Flash some 3 km further on.

Southwards, the reclamation has proceeded only part of the way towards the M62. Clearly, attempts to use such lines in a wider regional network of footpaths or cycle ways must remain a long-term objective. As Wallwork (1974) observes, "many potentially fine recreation routes have been ruined by the practice of dismantling bridges and selling sections of the route piecemeal before the possiblity of systematic restoration has been canvassed". More recent attempts to use abandoned lines, for example, the Liverpool Loopline (see Excursion 26) redevelopment by Sustrans Ltd attempts to make the best use by systematic restoration.

Use of the Park is overwhelmingly for informal recreation and habitual local users are the most common. Additionally, the warden service has involved schools and children in the work of habitat management. The visitor can gain a clear impression of the site by following the track to its northern boundary, turning off to visit Blakeley Farm. This diversion provides interesting insights into the nature and problems of farming in the fringe (changing importance of field boundaries; "horsey culture") and gives some indication of the liaison work that has taken place with the farming community.

SITE 3 RISLEY MOSS NATURE RESERVE

Risley Moss (Figure 22d; site details in Appendix) opened as a Nature Reserve in 1980 though there is public access to about a third of the site. The main part of the 84 ha site is established on the peat mossland of the Mersey corridor on the edge of Warrington New Town. Before designation, much of the site had been used as part of the wartime Royal Ordnance Factory, and the vegetation had become overgrown. The peat mossland itself presents an interesting and unusual resource with high educational potential and recreational possibilities. In development, a balance had to be found between people enjoying themselves with a minimum of restrictions, whilst safeguarding the conservation value and semi-natural character of the site. This has been achieved in two ways:

Zoning; Risley Moss is naturally divided into two distinct areas by ground conditions and vegetation. Open mossland on peat covers 70 per cent of the area, and birch and mixed woodland on a clay ridge accounts for the rest. Conservation is the dominant objective in the mossland with supervised access only; informal recreation (picnics, nature study, walking) has been developed in the woodland. The whole site is based around the visitor centre, close to the car park (with space for 100 vehicles). This natural zoning has been reinforced by the design and operation of the site, using fencing, ditches, closed access, and the general approach to visitor management. The general visitor is confined to the woodland zone, though he/she will probably be unaware of these restrictions;

Design and Management; The site is designed and managed in detail with several identifiable themes:

a) Sensible design and robust construction: for example, many of the paths are artificially constructed, and must be kept regularly surfaced.

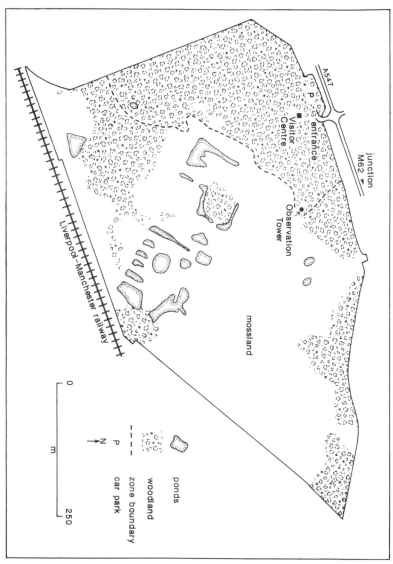

Figure 22d. Risley Moss Nature Reserve.

Ponds in the woodland zone have stoned-lined edges to protect from erosion; many of the ponds themselves are artificially created and lined with waterproof material. Sign-posting around the site is designed to ensure 'correct' use by visitors.

b) Wildlife conservation: the site is only semi-natural, having had a variety of earlier uses, many of which are explored at length in the visitor centre display. A gradual management of the wooded areas had begun to limit rhododendron growth, and the trees and saplings have been extensively thinned. Native plant species have been introduced, and on the moss proper, the artificially heightened water level has now begun to show results in the re-growth of the peat and its associated fauna and flora;

c) 'Invisible management': Risley Moss is a tribute to thoughtful and unobtrusive management: examples include fencing hidden in the undergrowth to enforce the zoning; regular lime and fertilizer treatment to the grassland to maintain a suitable pH for growth; use of dead timber and brashings to aid in habitat creation; differential mowing to create woodland glades and relatively impassable areas;

d) Maintenance of standards: the site has a clear identity, summed up in its dragonfly logo. The wardens maintain a clean and attractive site, in spite of a very high level of visitors in a small area. In part, this public acceptance of the site and its aims is encouraged by the environmental education functions - a wide programme of regular and occasional events attracts many visitors on a regular basis. The visitor centre plays a key role in this, and the excursion should allow time to view the tape-slide presentations, the varied displays of mossland artefacts and the interpretative exhibition.

CONCLUSION

The three urban-fringe sites visited on this excursion all have recreation and convervation objectives. They also have in common their fringe location, their type of visitor, and their origin as derelict land.

There are, however, some interesting bases for comparison, raising several issues. For instance: What influence does the original land use have upon today's resource? Are there any conflicts (potential or realized) between the recreational and conservation objectives of the site? How are these conflicts to be resolved? How overt are the design features of each site? To what degree is there "invisible" control of visitors? Does the site direct, control or persuade its visitors?

A wider appreciation of the industrial heritage and the importance of urban regeneration can be gained by visiting the Wigan Pier complex, which offers an interpretation of the industrial and social development of the district. The visit to Risley Moss could usefully include a tour around the adjoining suburbs of Warrington New Town including the Science Park which illustrates the 'hi-tech' face of the regional regeneration.

Selected References

Appleton, J H (1970) *Disused railways in the Countryside of England and Wales.* Report to the Countryside Commission, HMSO

Barr, J (1970) *Derelict Britain.* Penguin

Cooper, G and A P Hull (1978) Managing a Linear Country Park. *Town and Country Planning* 46; 168-172

Countryside Commission (1981) *Countryside Management in the urban fringe.* Countryside Commission

Hanna, M (1988) Sightseeing in 1986. *Tourism* 57; 5

Ministry of Transport (1963) *The Reshaping of British Railways (Beeching Report).* HMSO

Orwell, G (1962) *The Road to Wigan Pier.* Penguin

Palmer, C (1983) Recreation Design: Risley Moss, Warrington. *Landscape Design;* 8

Somerville, C (1979) *Walking Old Railways.* David & Charles

Wallwork, K L (1974) *Derelict Land: Origin & Propects of a land-use problem.* David & Charles

APPENDIX

Pennington Flash (GR 643985)

Owner/operator: Wigan MBC

Site 'phone: Leigh (0942) 605253

Location: 2 km SW of Leigh, entrance on A572 opposite 'Railway' public house. Consult with wardens before making organised visit, for which a small charge may be made if warden services used.

Culcheth Linear Park (GR 648940)

Owner/operator: Warrington BC.

Site 'phone: Culcheth 5064

Location: 8 km NNE of Warrington, entrance off Wigshaw Lane, off A574.

Restricted Parking: warden service on site (1989), no charge for visit.

Risley Moss Nature Reserve (GR 665922)

Owner/operator: Cheshire CC.

Site 'phone: Padgate (0925) 824339

Location: 6 km NE of Warrington, 1 km from M62 Junction 11, off Ordnance Avenue, Warrington New Town. Coaches by arrangement; resident wardens; small charge for use of lecture room and warden services. Advance booking necessary for parties. Closed Fridays.

23 DEALING WITH DERELICTION: PENNINGTON FLASH, LEIGH

John Boothby
(Liverpool Polytechnic)

Outline: a study of the potential use of derelict sites left after coal for recreation use, based on a case study of Pennington Flash.

Starting and finishing points: lakeside car park, Pennington Flash Country Park (GR 643985) Entrance on A572, 2 km SW of Leigh.

Distance: about 5.5 km (depending on specific route chosen).

Route: a circular walk, including surfaced and unsurfaced footpaths, often fairly damp.

Time needed: half a day.

Maps needed: OS 1;50,000 sheet 109 (Manchester).

Access: The site is owned and operated by Wigan Metropolitan Borough Council (MBC), and the warden service can be contacted on site (tel: 0942 605253).

INTRODUCTION

This excursion focuses upon the development of derelict land, its treatment, and ultimate use. Derelict land has been defined as "land so damaged by industrial or other development that it is impossible for beneficial use without treatment" (DOE 1975, vi). The variety of problems at Pennington Flash poses a number of choices for reclamation. The ultimate use for recreation and the important conservation value of the site provide interesting lessons in the problems and prospects of dealing with derelict land.

Coal extraction and subsidence

Pennington Flash (Figure 23; see also Figure 22b) has been formed by subsidence caused by coal extraction, largely since the turn of the century. In the 1800s, the area was agricultural land. Some thirteen separate coal seams were worked beneath the area and subsidence, together with consequent changes in the drainage pattern, have led to flooding. By 1905 the flash had been created, overcoming two farms,
244

and forming an area of some 70 ha of open water. Around this area ran several railway lines and the Leeds-Liverpool Canal (Leigh Branch).

The period 1871-1920 was a formative one in the development of derelict mining areas nationally; several technical innovations were introduced, such as mechanical mining using longwall methods, mechanized tipping and deep working. Most of the still derelict mine sites pre-date the formation of the National Coal Board (NCB) in 1947; private mine owners before that were generally not required, unlike the NCB, to make restoration of despoiled land. The area is still subject to subsidence and land at the outflow of the area is becoming progressively marshier.

Although mining continues at the Bickershaw Colliery Complex, there is currently no active extraction from beneath the site. Mining in the last phase of extraction (1979-1981) resulted in subsidence of up to 800 mm; this phase of subsidence led to the flooding of large areas of the golf course and is the subject of claims for compensation between Wigan MBC and British Coal (successor to the NCB).

The impact of deep extraction can be best seen by the example of the canal, which runs through the park on an embankment, and which is described by British Waterways Board as "probably a unique example of the effects of subsidence on a working waterway". Mining from an in-situ vertical coal thickness of over 20 m has resulted in considerable subsidence: the canal water level is now 4.6 m below its original level. The canal embankments adjacent to the golf course are about 9 m high; this represents the amount of subsidence which has occurred this century. The recent mining activities (1979-1981) needed extensive preventive and remedial work, including raising the concrete walls at the water's edge, raising and buttressing the embankment, and in-filling the canal channel to remove depth, all over a linear extent of some 800 m. Wigan MBC have also carried out some buttressing works (Figure 23).

Much of the subsidence occurred when the canal was still a busy commercial waterway. Even up to 1972, there were 100 coal barge movements per day between Bickershaw and Westwood Power Station, Wigan. The canal now has significant recreational value; estimated annual boat numbers, now solely of pleasure craft, have risen from 520 in 1974, to 1,000 in 1977, to 1,500 in 1987. Like the flash itself, the canal is used extensively for competitive and recreational angling. Plans for the regeneration of the Leeds-Liverpool Canal Corridor also

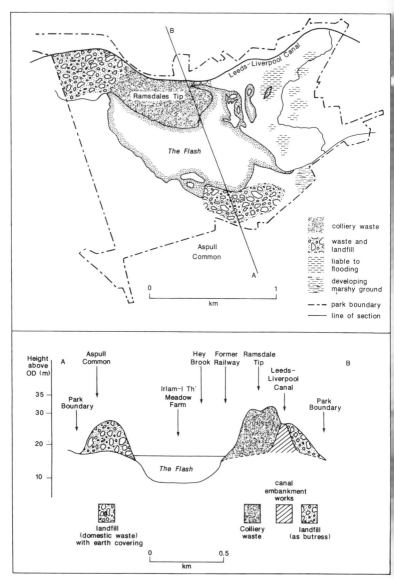

Figure 23. Pennington Flash.

envisage environmental improvements at the nearby Leigh basin. Visually, the most impressive by-product of mining activity - colliery waste - can be seen in the Ramsdales Tip, which rises some 16 m above the level of the flash which it overshadows. The tip comprises around 6,000,000 m³ of waste material; it is largely unvegetated, loose, and extensively gullied. The problem of this tip is dealt with below.

Waste disposal
In common with many other derelict areas, Pennington Flash offered, in the 1960s, an 'ideal' site for waste disposal. The urgent need for waste disposal sites for the conurbations and towns of the region is long-standing. Table 23.1 shows the scale of this demand for the county area of Greater Manchester alone, of which Wigan MBC was a constituent authority.

Table 23.1   Waste disposal in Greater Manchester

Type of waste	Tonnes	
	1985/6	1986/7
Household	682,300	786,020
Trade/commercial	189,867	74,246
Building/amenity	275,000	320,000
TOTAL	1,147,367	1,180,966

Source; Greater Manchester Waste Disposal Authority, *Annual Reports* 1986 and 1987

Well in excess of one million tonnes of waste are disposed of annually, most of which is domestic waste. Wigan, which is not now a member of the GMWDA, disposed of 164,426 tonnes in 1986/7. Waste disposal has taken place at the site since the early 1970s. This has comprised household and industrial waste, tipped in layers to aid decomposition and help prevent the migration of leachate. The control of leachate and methane gas are the two main post-disposal problems of waste sites. At the Plank Lane site, completed in 1985, some 600,000 m³ of waste is contained within a bentonite diaphragm wall and leachate is channelled for sewage disposal. Full monitoring is made both of the leachate and the methane, which is vented from the site. To assist in venting and drainage, the waste is typically formed into mounds up to 10 m above original ground level (shown in cross-section in Figure 23).

Domestic waste tips consist mainly of rubble and household refuse. They are rich in organic matter chiefly derived from waste-foods, paper, cloth and wood - high in plant nutrients though not always in available nitrogen. Heat, methane and hydrogen sulphide are typically generated, all of which may cause vegetation death, though long term plant growth is guaranteed. The incorporation of hazardous industrial wastes (eg metallic compounds; tarry wastes) present specific problems of their own in the control of leachates, though their presence in tips formed largely of household waste is not considered to present any extra problems.

CREATING THE COUNTRY PARK

The creation of the Country Park was a joint decision between Wigan MBC and Greater Manchester CC. It was formally opened in 1981, but the derelict site had been used for many years, for fishing, boating and wildfowling. It covers 445 ha, most of which is owned by Wigan MBC; other areas are owned by British Waterways Board or in private ownership.

Following the abolition of the Metropolitan Counties in 1985, the park is now the sole responsiblity of Wigan MBC. Nevertheless, the park operates as a regional recreational facility, and the local plan (Wigan MBC 1986) foresees the acquisition of additional land. In particular, the park will operate as a key node in a wider programme of developing a 'Greenway' system which aims "to preserve and create footpaths ... cycleways and bridlepaths with attractive adjoining landscapes and features" (Policy E9).

A Country Park is defined in the 1968 Countryside Act as "a park or pleasure ground in the countryside which by reason of its position in relation to major concentrations of population affords convenient opportunities to the public for enjoyment of the countryside or open-air recreation". Such parks are grant-aided by the Countryside Commission, and were clearly intended to provide recreational facilities in the immediate urban fringe, where almost 60 per cent are located. At a strategic regional level they have also been given the role of 'honey pots', relieving pressure from the National Parks by attracting visitors who might otherwise have travelled to the more remote countryside.

THE PARK IN OPERATION

Research elsewhere suggests that the typical visitor to Country Parks is likely to be local and habitual. Many visitors will arrive on foot, but car ownership amongst visitors will be high; weekends are popular visiting times, especially amongst family groups who form a significant proportion of all visitors. Visits may be of only short duration (two hours or less) but are likely to be of high frequency.

In short, parks provide recreation with a mixture of resource-based and user-based facilities often used on a regular, repetitive basis by local residents. This usage, these facilities, are possibly better suited to the geographical circumstances of the UK than the borrowed notion of the National Park.

For recreation planners, Country Parks present a number of choices, such as the following:

(i) What facilities should be provided? In part, this depends upon the mix of activities to be catered for, along with an appreciation of their possible conflict. The choice is also constrained by the suitability of the site (soil, terrain, water table etc) to sustain the proposed activities; the park must also be a "good neighbour" in its locality;

(ii) What should be the scope for nature conservation? The choice of recreational provision has a direct bearing upon the maintenance, enhancement or limitation of the conservation value of a site. Some zoning of the site may be called for to separate the more intrusive activities from the nature reserve areas;

(iii) What should the overall appearance of the park be like? In part, this decision will turn upon (i) and (ii) above, but management have considerable scope to affect this by attention to detail - way-marking, quality of site 'furniture', interpretation, warden services.

At Pennington, careful management is required to ensure "that development of recreation is in sympathy with the conservation, enhancement, and protection of the ecological value of the area" (Pennington Flash Joint Committee, 1985). Three specific aims were identified within these broad objectives:

(1) increasing educational use;

(2) influencing attitudes in favour of conservation;

(3) maintaining the wildlife conservation areas in an undisturbed state. As noted in Excursion 22, the bird population of the park is of prime importance.

FUTURE DEVELOPMENTS

In a 1974 survey, Greater Manchester was shown to have, after Cornwall, the largest county area covered in 'spoil tips' and almost 22 per cent of land in England "justifying treatment" (Chisholm & Howells, 1979). It is perhaps not surprising that reclamation of the Ramsdales tip remains the last major task of reclamation within the park.

There are examples of coal tips undergoing natural recolonization by plant species but this is usually a very slow process and depends upon ground and environmental conditions - texture, composition, organic content, exposure, stability, nutrient content, pH, toxic concentrations, surface temperatures and water supply. Acid conditions are often critical in controlling germination of seeds; however, application of lime/limestone can significantly ameliorate conditions in the surface layer, though up to 25,000 kg per ha may be needed. In reclaiming a spoil tip, intervention will usually produce results more rapidly, provided that a number of basic steps are taken:

(i) neutralize any acidity;
(ii) break up coarse material, maximizing particles in the 2mm - 0.002mm range;
(iii) build up organic content;
(iv) develop soil structure.

In the case of Ramsdales, it is quite likely that reclamation will be preceded by coal recovery. Such spoil tips may contain up to 10 per cent recoverable coal, and recovery may be economic at concentrations as low as 4 per cent. Should such recovery be carried out here, a rolling programme of reclamation will be instituted which could extend to ten years.

Following coal recovery the remaining heap, little reduced in height, will be graded. After treatment according to the basic steps above the heap will be planted with trees in a manner similar to the existing areas of the park, creating pathways and hay meadows and using the height of the tip to create viewpoints over the park. It is possible, but not yet certain, that some of the site will be used for intensive recreation; suggestions have included a BMX track, a dry ski-slope and a site for touring caravans. It will be possible to retain existing vegetation along the water-side; it may also prove useful to retain some unreclaimed segment of the tip which would have distinct educational and interpretive value. Extension to the wildfowl area by the creation of further islands is also possible.

Coal mining operations will also condition the scope for future development. Although there is no current or projected mining beneath the Flash, there is still coal to be mined. The last major period of subsidence provided severe problems for the golf course; any proposal to extend the golf course to 18 holes will be held in abeyance until the reclamation work at Ramsdales is complete.

Postscript

Wigan MBCs rolling programme of derelict land reclamation for 1987-1991 includes the reclamation of two further large areas of flashes - Scotsman's Flash and Pearson's Flash, as well as unused power stations, abandoned railway lines, and colliery spoil areas. From these, further areas of Country Park will be constructed and large amounts of public open space created.

It now seems possible that the tide of dereliction may have been stemmed. The legacy of the nineteenth century has been consistently attacked, and the impact of the 'new landscapes' is now present for all to see.

Selected References

Barr, J (1970) *Derelict Britain*. Penguin

Chisholm, M and J Howells J (1979) Derelict land in Great Britain : a context for the lower Swansea Valley in RDF Bromley and G Humphreys (eds) *Dealing with dereliction*. University College, Swansea

Department of the Environment (1975) *Results of the 1974 Survey of derelict and despoiled land in England*, 3 volumes. DOE

Department of the Environment (1978) *Cooperative programmes of research on the behaviour of hazardous wastes in landfill sites: Final report of the Policy Review Committee.* HMSO

Goodman, G T and S A Bray (1975) *Ecological aspects of the reclamation of derelict and disturbed land.* GeoAbstracts, Norwich

Jones, P (1987) The Leeds - Liverpool Canal corridor programme. *Planner* 73 (1); 35

Pennington Flash Joint Committee (1985) *Pennington Flash Country Park: Interpretive Plan.* PFJC, Manchester

Richardson, J A (1976) Pit heap into pasture. in J Lenihan and W W Fletcher (eds) *Reclamation.* Blackie

Wallwork, K L (1974) *Derelict land: origins and prospects of a land use problem.* David and Charles

Wigan MBC (1986) *Leigh Local Plan: Written Statement.* Wigan MBC

Wigan MBC (1987) *Annual Report and Accounts 1986/7.* Wigan MBC

Stephen Jackson and David Stenhouse
(Liverpool Polytechnic)

Outline: a tour of three Victorian factory villages which illustrate
    themes relating to the morphology and planning of 'model'
    communities and introduce ideas about paternalistic styles of
    business management and experiments in social reform.
Starting and finishing points: central Liverpool (GR 338905).
Distance: about 30 km.
Route: coach or mini-bus tour.
Time needed: half a day.
Maps needed: OS 1:50,000 sheet 108 (Liverpool).

INTRODUCTION: MODEL INDUSTRIAL VILLAGES

The building of accommodation for employees on or adjacent to the
sites of factories, mills or collieries was a feature of many of the
industrializing areas of nineteenth century Britain. Early examples of
factory colonies can be found in the hills of east Lancashire where
problems of access and dispersed rural population necessitated the
provision of housing to ensure a stable workforce. Similarly the
expansion of mining on the major British coalfields led to the spawning
of many small communities tied to individual collieries and run by
owners and agents.

The villages illustrated in this tour are not, however, creations of
economic necessity. They are essentially the products of philanthropy
and idealism: attempts to demonstrate how working people could be
housed, and their needs and aspirations catered for, within the context
of a better living environment. In this respect they represent examples
of community building and statements of an alternative life-style to
that which prevailed in the industrial towns of Northern and Midland

253

England. In this way a paternalistic employer could repay the costs of labour by improving the material and moral conditions of life of his employees. The ethos of these communities was firmly based on Christian principles and emphasis was placed on such virtues as sobriety, thrift, self-improvement and rational recreation. To this end most community builders provided generous social amenities as part of their new villages (village halls, institutes, allotments etc) which provided a focus for community life.

The best examples of this type of community are fairly well known; from the early developments of Robert Owen at New Lanark (1799) to Titus Salt's Saltaire outside Bradford (1853), Port Sunlight (1888), Cadbury's Bournville (1895) and Rowntree's village at New Earswick (1903). But there were many other smaller scale developments and experiments in the building of 'model housing' which collectively contributed to this tradition of humanitarian social provision. A visit to these villages is valuable because they illustrate these points and provide an indication of contemporary nineteenth century attitudes towards the problems of working-class housing and urban deprivation. Also, more generally, they provide an insight to the development of paternalistic styles of business management.

These communities are also significant because of their influence over the development of town planning in Britain during the twentieth century. The principles of urban design and layout, which were reflected in the semi-detached suburban expansion of the inter-war years and later in the planting of new towns around the major metropolitan centres, originated from the enlightened views of the developers of these model communities and the related 'garden city movement'.

EXCURSION

The three villages covered here are of different sizes and represent different stages in the development of model communities. For the purposes of a field visit either all three could be taken in on a half-day trip or it may be desirable to combine a visit to one or all of them with the urban trail around central Liverpool (Excursion 25).

HARTLEY'S VILLAGE, AINTREE

This compact little community (Figure 24a) was built by William

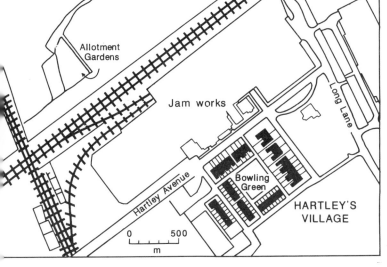

Figure 24a. Hartley's Village.

Hartley in 1888 to accommodate workers in his adjacent jam factory. Hartley originated from Colne in Lancashire where he started his jam making business. In 1874 he transferred to Bootle on Merseyside to take advantage of a location close to the port facilities (for the importation of fruit and sugar) and well connected to the communications network for the distribution of his products. Continued expansion of production, resulting mainly from Hartley's success in the branding of jams and marmalade, required an extension of premises. A green-field site was chosen at Aintree which provided ample space for the layout of a new, efficient production unit and which had direct access to the Cheshire lines and Lancashire and Yorkshire railways.

The railway connections were particularly important to the business. Hartley owned his own farms in Bedfordshire, which provided much of the soft fruit, but he also brought in produce from many other parts of the country. Most of the fruit was carried in his own special trains and to maintain freshness and quality the processing was always completed on the day of arrival at Aintree (producing

255

a maximum turn-round from picking to packing of forty-eight hours). Because of this, work in the factory was highly seasonal; up to 2,000 people were employed during peak production in the summer season. The majority of these were women recruited locally on Merseyside. Outside the main season a smaller workforce of approximately 600 were employed mainly on the bottling of marmalade.

The village, planned and developed at the same time as the construction of the new factory, was primarily intended to house the nucleus of permanent skilled labour. It was designed by W Sugden & Son of Leek, who won the advertised competition to select the best design. Their plan was focused around a central recreation green of approximately one acre (0.4 ha, now a car park) and comprised seventy-one houses and five shops. The houses were graded into three types: Class A, Class B and Cottages, reflecting the varying status and family sizes of occupants. Rent varied from two-shillings-and-sixpence (£0.12) to three-shillings-and-sixpence (£0.17) per week; some of the houses were sold, at cost price, to working men at 3.75 per cent interest.

Commenting on the design of the village, *The Builder* (1888) stated: "The architects have endeavoured, in the arrangement of the village, to obtain a certain degree of picturesque effect without eccentricity, and have designed the cottages in conformity with the old domestic buildings indigenous to the district and avoiding all flimsy and supposed 'picturesque' ornamental additions - for which they are entirely to be commended".

There was a close association between the village and the activities of the company. The streets and rows of cottages were named after the materials used in the manufacture of jam (Sugar Street, Red Current Court, Cherry Row etc) and Hartley's name and monogram are much in evidence. Apart from the housing, Hartley introduced many other amenities for his workpeople, including a dining hall, an institute and medical facilities at work. He was an enlightened employer and a genuinely generous man. He paid wages up to 40 per cent above those of his local competitors, and he introduced a profit-sharing scheme and a non-contributory pension fund. Much of the motivation for this derived from his strong religious convictions. He was a leading Primitive Methodist and it is reported that he devoted up to one third of his total income to religious and charitable causes.

The jam factory is no longer in production. Hartley's 'New Jam' is now part of the Cadbury-Schweppes Group and operations are based in London. The site is used by a variety of different enterprises and some elements of the factory buildings remain intact. The village is more or less complete, although the principal house 'Inglewood' has been demolished. The whole complex of factory and village is looking neglected and run down. Unlike the other two communities covered in this excursion, Hartley's village is not protected by conservation area status.

BROMBOROUGH POOL

The village of Bromborough Pool (Figure 24b) was built by 'Price's Patent Candle Making Company' in 1853 to house workers for their newly established factory. The development was an off-shoot of Price's London based operations and the choice of the location on Merseyside was mainly for reasons of trade. The company was diversifying away from candles and into industrial lubricants, the main markets for which were the textile towns of Lancashire and Yorkshire. Also many of the basic raw materials (especially vegetable oils) were being imported through Liverpool.

The planning and development of the village, however, were not concerned simply with the provision of basic accommodation. The Directors of Price's had professed ideological motives for improving the conditions of their working people and during the 1840s they had introduced a number of social initiatives in their works at Battersea. They thought the new factory would offer an opportunity to experiment with community design and allow them to put into practice their ideas for a better living environment for their employees.

The physical development of the village reflects this management philosophy. The houses were generously apportioned, laid out in spacious gardens and with additional areas set aside for allotments. Social amenities provided included a village hall, which was also used as a chapel and school, an isolation hospital and a shop. The Bromborough Branch of Price's 'Mutual Improvement Society' was established to oversee the everyday life of the community. This had the express objective of promoting the "intellectual, moral and social advancement of all its members" and from the outset it acted as an umbrella organisation for a range of different clubs and societies. Central to the village was the cricket pitch. The company had a particular attachment to cricket, fostering it not only for its recreational pleasures but also for the virtues of team spirit and camaraderie that it engendered in the

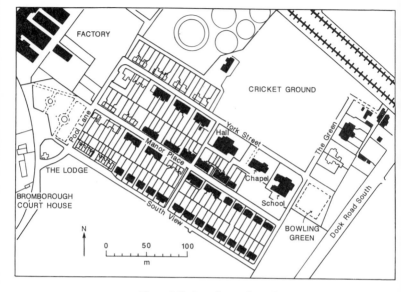

Figure 24b. Bromborough Pool.

factory.

The village grew rapidly following the opening of the candle factory. The first street of cottages, York Street, was completed in 1854 and the first residents moved in during the January of that year. By 1856 another row of cottages, Manor Place, had been added and by 1858, when the village hall was built, the community had 76 houses with a population of 460.

The original cottages, designed by Julian Hill (also the architect of the factory and village hall), were advanced for their period. Arranged in blocks of four, the accommodation comprised a living room, a scullery and kitchen and two bedrooms: each house had water-borne sanitation. In addition, there were two pairs of semi-detached villas and a separate 'Lodge' provided for the members of the company's management who resided in the village. These were discreetly separated from the artisans' cottages.

258

In the 1870s the company built more houses, adding fifteen to Manor Place as well as a new road, South View, which had two blocks of six cottages by the end of the decade. By 1877, the village contained over a hundred houses and had further expanded its social facilities. The company's fortunes appear to have been cyclic during the second half of the century: the 1850s, 1870s and 1890s were periods of prosperity, the intervening decades times of recession. The development of the village matched the periods of prosperity and the last phase of growth came in the final years of the century with 24 houses being built in Manor Place and South View, as well as a further development of communal buildings with a new school, hospital and church. Except for minor amendments, the village's physical growth ceased in 1901, by which time it contained 142 dwellings with a population of 728.

In recent years the village has suffered from neglect and some of the early housing has been demolished. However, in 1987, partly in recognition of its historical significance, the whole site was given conservation area status. The management of the community was also handed over from the firm (by this time UNICHEMA, a subsidiary of the UNILEVER Group) to a Housing Trust (Merseyside Improved Houses), who have since embarked on a progressive policy of rehabilitation of the cottages and general improvement of the village area.

Also worth a visit is the site of Bromborough Court House (see Figure 24b). This was originally a medieval moated manor house. At the time of the building of the factory the then existing Court House and adjacent farm buildings were incorporated into the village and part of it was used as a hostel for apprenticed labour. Unfortunately the seventeenth century brick built Court House was demolished in 1969 but much of the earlier medieval site is still visible and has recently been exposed by a landscape improvement scheme.

PORT SUNLIGHT

Port Sunlight (Figure 24c) was possibly the finest of all the model factory villages. It was certainly one of the most ambitious and elaborate projects, containing not only spacious accommodation in a landscaped setting, but also many fine public buildings and social amenities. It is a much larger development than either Bromborough Pool or Hartley's Village and it is worth allowing sufficent time to see all the village has to offer.

Port Sunlight is the creation of William Hesketh Lever, a man of considerable business ability and personal fortune, who used his wealth and influence to demonstrate his own beliefs about social change and the desire for reform. Hence the village was more than just a community for the employees in his soap factory. It was intended to be a statement of Lever's vision of the future, a solution to the problems of deprivation in urban areas and a way forward in social relations between employers and working people.

Work began on the factory and the housing in the same year that Hartley was building his village at Aintree (1888) and the first stage of the developement was completed by 1890. The site was later extended to 130 acres and the whole complex of buildings was not finally completed until the 1920s. By that time the village contained approximately 3,000 people in 900 houses, with an average density of seven houses per acre (0.4 ha). The style of the architecture was varied, reflecting a mixture of traditional English vernacular cottage designs (the earlier houses were fairly plain and simple, but later plans were more elaborate and fanciful) and the Edwardian 'Beaux Arts' influence, particularly in the public buildings and the formal street layouts. Many architects were employed in the design of the individual buildings although the most significant were William Owen (responsible with Lever for the initial layout of the village), Douglas and Fordham, Grayson and Old, J J Talbot and J Lomax Simpson. Such a large number of contributing architects has produced a wide variety in the detailed styles of buildings, but the whole development has a certain unity of scale and proportion and fits together reasonably well.

Nevertheless, the lasting impression of the village is, perhaps, that the whole project was a little overdone. The cottages are quaint rather than attractive; the public buildings tend to be excessively large and imposing; everywhere there are frequent reminders of the founder. His personality is firmly imprinted on the place and for those who lived in the community there was no escape from the presence of the workplace or from the oppressive benevolence of Lever. The benefits of material comfort and enhanced living conditions were, after all, paid for by the adoption of a life-style that was decent and deferential and, to a certain extent, cut off from the outside world.

There are many buildings to see on a walk around the village. The best place to start is the Heritage Centre, near to the entrance to the factory. This contains full details of the building of the village as well as an explanation of the manufacture of soap and the development of

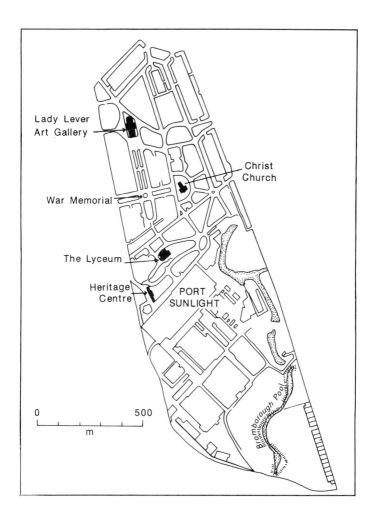

Figure 24c. Port Sunlight.

Lever Brothers (now UNILEVER). A brief selection of other buildings which should not be missed include:

(a) THE LADY LEVER ART GALLERY: provided by Lever as a memorial to his wife, it contains part of his very extensive collection of art treasures, including English period furniture, paintings of the British School, Wedgewood ware and Chinese pottery and porcelain. The building itself is impressive; it was designed by William and Segar Owen in the classical tradition and built of reinforced concrete, clad in Portland stone.

(b) CHRIST CHURCH: also designed by the Owens and built in Late Perpendicular style. Lever was a Congregationalist, but nonetheless provided the church as an inter-denominational place of worship. It was built to very generous proportions (seating over 1,000) and contains inside a wealth of furnishings in English oak as well as marble flooring and number of notable stained glass windows.

(c) WAR MEMORIAL: designed and sculpted by Sir William Goscombe John (1919-20), not simply as a memorial to those who lost their lives in the Great War, but also as a statement of the values and principles that they had fought for. The theme is defence of the home, with soldiers protecting a wounded comrade and groups of women and children "...a rare example of a war memorial which is genuinely moving and which avoids sentimentality" (Pevsner and Hubbard, 1971).

(d) LYCEUM: built 1894-6; originally designed by Douglas and Fordham as a village school and chapel, later it acted as a staff training college and Port Sunlight Men's Club. It overlooks the dell, a former tidal inlet of the Bromborough Pool that has been drained and landscaped.

It is difficult to do justice to Port Sunlight in a short guide like this, but fortunately there is no shortage of published material on the village. The best books are undoubtedly the Cheshire volume of Pevsner's Buildings of England series and Hubbard and Shippobottom's Guide to Port Sunlight Village.

Selected References

The Builder (1988) Design for model village, Aintree., August 25

Hubbard, E and M Shippobottom (1988) *A Guide to Port Sunlight Village.* Liverpool University Press

Merseyside Archaeological Society (1978) *Bromborough Court House: a Survey of Evidence.* Institute of Extension Studies

Peake, A S (1926) *The Life of Sir William Hartley.* Hodder & Stoughton

Pevsner, N and E Hubbard E (1971) *The Buildings of England: Cheshire.* Penguin

Reynolds, J (1948) The model village of Port Sunlight. *Architects Journal* May; 492-96

Sellers, S (1988) *Sunlighters: the Story of a Village.* Unilever PLC

Tarn, J N (1971) *Working Class Housing in Nineteenth Century Britain.* Lund Humphries

Watson, A (1966) *Price's Village: a Study of a Victorian Industrial and Social Experiment.* Price's Chemicals, Bromborough

25 LIVERPOOL CITY CENTRE URBAN TRAIL

Stephen Jackson and Jane Springett
(Liverpool Polytechnic)

Outline: a series of views of the centre of Liverpool which illustrate the commercial expansion of the port in the eighteenth and nineteenth centuries, and the creation of a townscape epresentative of the city's achievements. Attention is also focused on post-war redevelopments and more recent attempts to revitalise parts of the city centre.

Starting point: Liverpool Museum, William Brown Street (GR 348908). Park in Queen Square car park by St John's Gardens.

Finishing point: Albert Dock (GR 341987).

Distance: 3 km.

Route: walking through town.

Time needed: 2 hours.

Maps needed: OS 1:10,000 sheet SJ 39SW.

INTRODUCTION

Like all cities, Liverpool is a place of contrasts. There are contrasts between the immense wealth of the merchant elite, who for many years controlled both the economic and political life of the city, and the severe poverty which has remained a persistent feature over the past three centuries. There are also contrasts between the elaborate and ostentatious public buildings of civic pride and the mean squalid areas of urban deprivation. Further contrasts exist between the elegance of its historical buildings and the functional blandness of its mid-twentieth century developments.

It is impossible, in a short urban trail, to fully appreciate the richness and wealth of the city's heritage. Liverpool needs to be seen not - as it commonly is today - as an ailing regional centre on the edges of a European economy, but as a world port at the hub of international trade, with a thriving commercial economy and servicing England's principal nineteenth century industrial regions in the North and Midlands.

The city's former significance is crucial in understanding its structure and character. The splendour may have faded and Liverpool has suffered more than most from Second World War bomb damage and city centre redevelopment. But nonetheless it still contains one of the finest collections of commercial architecture in Europe and the townscape provides lasting reminders of the dominance and self confidence of the city during the Victorian and Edwardian periods. The contemporary landscape needs to be seen not only as a relict of the past and a reflection of past ideologies and power structures, but also as a product of contemporary forces of economic and social change.

MAIN THEMES

The trail focuses on three principal themes:

    i) the evolution of the morphology and structure of the city centre and the identification of the stages in the city's development (Medieval, Early Modern, Georgian etc)

    ii) the impact of the commercial economy of the city in the late Victorian and Edwardian periods as represented by the development of the central business district, and

    iii) the rebuilding of the city centre in the period 1945-1980 and the dominance of the ideology of corporations over individual expression. Also the failure to fulfill the optimistic expectations of the sixties.

Economy, townscape and planning

The early history of the port of Liverpool is unspectacular. The old Medieval town was granted a charter by King John in 1207 when it was primarily a staging port for Ireland, overshadowed by Chester as the major port for north-west England. The conditions were far from favourable for a harbour. The Mersey has a high tidal range and the moorings were too exposed in winter for the handling of larger boats. Development of the port began in the early eighteenth century, with the opening of the first enclosed dock in 1715 and the subsequent expansion of trade across the North Atlantic. In this initial phase, Liverpool's merchants were involved in the importation of commodities from Africa and America as well as the trade in slaves. Undoubtedly the foundations of the port's subsequent prosperity were laid during this period.

However, by the mid-nineteenth century its port economy had

broadened and was based more securely on the shipment of goods from its expanding industrial hinterland and on the processing of imported raw materials. Tertiary activities, most notably in the financial and trading sectors, grew rapidly during the Victorian period to complete the tripartite base to Liverpool's economy (international commodity trading, port processing and financial services). Apart from brief periods of economic revival, the fortunes of the port, the city and its industrial region have all been in general decline since about 1914.

The immense wealth of the city during the nineteenth century provided capital for the creation of a townscape which reflected the status and achievement of its ruling merchant elite. Some of this investment came from ratepayers, but there was also considerable direct support from prosperous individuals. Schemes such as St George's Hall, which were very expensive (over £300,000) were largely financed by public subscription; consequently they display not only the collective ideology of new civic authority but also the success of individual enterprise. For many the new buildings of the city centre were a mark of cultural identity as well as commercial accomplishment - they represented a 'second Renaissance'; the flowering of a new urban era in which art and architecture were expressions of the intellectual advancement of the modern industrial city and an outward display of ostentatious wealth tempered by good taste. Considerations of the utility of these buildings were never very evident. Neither was there much comment on the paradox of excessive expenditure on noble buildings at a time of worsening environmental conditions in the poorer areas of the city centre.

Post-war change

Many of the buildings of civic pride remain and have escaped the excesses of more recent redevelopment. But the form and character of the city centre as a whole has been strongly influenced by twentieth century changes. Partly this has been a consequence of destruction and damage during the war years (1939-1945), most notably in the area between the shopping centre and Pier Head (Lord Street, Derby Square). The replacement buildings reflect the austerity and functionalism of the forties and fifties, maintaining the basic proportions of the pre-existing buildings but totally lacking in aesthetic quality or physical presence.

But if the developments after World War II were bland, the more wholesale attempts to replan the city centre in the sixties were far more ambitious and arguably more detrimental to the city's townscape. This was a period of great optimism and new beginnings when city authorities had the self-confidence and resources to tackle the deep-seated problems of poor quality housing and degraded residential environments, and to embark upon the reshaping of a new city.

The city centre plan of 1965 involved such things as an inner motorway box, a complete separation of traffic from pedestrians by the building of a complex walkway system at first floor level and the resiting of the municipal offices and the law courts in a 'brilliantly-conceived' civic centre masking the Mersey Tunnel entrance and decking over St John's Gardens (below St Georges Hall). In additon, there were many new buildings in the retail sector (including the St John's Precinct complex) and attempts at revitalising the office sector. At the time these plans were received as radical and exciting. Liverpool was described as 'a city of change and challenge' turning the corner after the long years of post-war lethargy into a new era of prosperity and hope.

The reality of the city's experience in the succeeding twenty years is one of partial development and unfulfilled expectations. Tha architectural style of buildings like the St John's Precinct or Wilberforce House (City Planning Offices) has proved to be less impressive and less enduring than earlier traditions and the buildings themselves - paying scant regard to existing proportions or street alignments - sit unconformably with the other elements in the city's townscape.

More recent attempts at redevelopment have been rather more sympathetic. The Cavern Walks complex (Matthew Street) is unobtrusive and displays detailed features that reflect the dominant style of what was formerly an area of warehousing. The biggest single project of recent years has been the redevelopment of the Southern Docks under the auspices of the Merseyside Development Corporation.

There has been considerable investment (over £100 million) directed at regenerating the derelict dock estate and the show-piece complex of the Albert Dock has attracted much critical acclaim. This type of development is again reflective of underlying ideologies and new attitudes towards the revitalisation of the city. Unlike the corporate idealism of the sixties, the Albert Dock represents the enterprise culture of the eighties. It is not an attempt to solve old problems but to

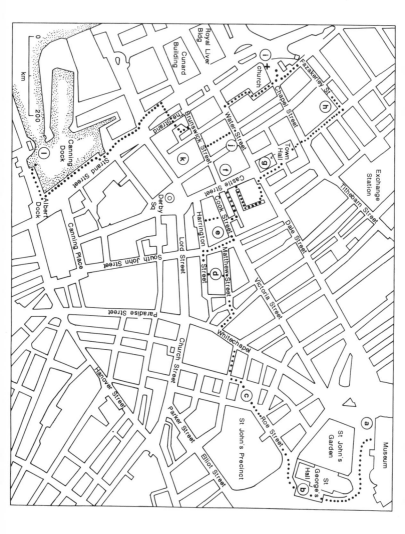

Figure 25. *Liverpool City Centre Urban Trail.*

introduce new dimensions to the city's economy and culture. The emphasis is on leisure, tourism and the heritage industry, with the expectation that the rapid expansion of this sector will, in part, compensate for the irreversible decline of other elements of the city's economy. It remains to be seen if this regeneration of the dockland area will spread into other parts of the city, or whether sites like the Albert Dock will persist as islands of modern development.

EXCURSION

These general issues set a context for, and should help, the interpretation of the townscape of central Liverpool. The urban trail (Figure 25) has been designed not so much as a stop-by-stop wander through the street but as a series of views of the city. However there is a suggested route to follow, covering the main elements of the centre. There is a lot more to see than can be included on a single route and the references at the end may be useful if you wish to plan a more exhaustive exploration of the city.

The following notes describe some of the more important features and buildings on the trail. But there is no overall rationale or historical sequence for the order in which they come, hence no requirement to stick rigidly to the route as described (Figure 25).

(a) Museum Steps
Note the view of the medieval town, built on the ridge between the Mersey and the Fleet. The former high water mark of the inlet was approximately where the flyovers are now; the line of the water course can be seen down Whitechapel and Paradise street. The stream was drained when the first dock was built at Canning Place. William Brown Street (in front of you) contains a fine collection of Victorian municipal buildings, including: the Museum (1860), the Walker Art Gallery (1877), Picton Library (1879), the Session House (1884) and the College of Technology (1902). Walk eastwards along William Brown Street, turn left into Lime Street and stop at St George's Hall (on your right).

(b) St George's Hall
The Hall was described by Quentin Hughes (1964) as "...the greatest classical monument of the nineteenth century and the finest work of architecture in the North of England." It is an impressive building that

269

epitomises early Victorian expressions of civic achievement. It was designed by Harvey Lonsdale Elmes and opened in 1854. The building contains a concert hall and assize courts, both now redundant. The interior is almost as spectacular as the exterior, particularly the small concert room (the work of Charles R Cockerell). Cross over St John's Lane at the southern end of St George's Hall and walk down Roe Street with St John's Precinct to your left.

(c) Williamson Square

The square was developed in the early eighteenth century as a select residential area. By 1900 it was the main centre of vice and crime. Note the Playhouse Theatre, built in 1865 as the Star Music Hall and rebuilt as a theatre 1912-13 by Stanley Adshead. The New extension was added in 1967 by Hall, O'Donahue and Wilson. St John's Precinct is one of Liverpool's best examples of sixties neo-barbarism - "... a highly original complex of shops, market, car park and hotel, straddling the site of the old St John's market" (Willett, 1967). Walk down Whitechapel, then right down Stanley Street then left into Matthew Street.

(d) Matthew Street

This is Beatles country! Cavern Walks was built on the site of the former Cavern Club; it opened in 1984. Subsequently much of this part of the city centre, which had been a run-down warehousing district, has been gentrified. Leave Cavern Walks at Harrington Street; then turn right along North John Street and take the left turn into Cook Street.

(e) Cook Street

You are now in the zone of transition between the retail sector and the Central Business District. Of particular note is No 16 by Peter Ellis (1866), an original building with an imaginative use of glass panelling - notably on the rear elevation. Cross Cook Street, take the street straight ahead of you (Union Court), and follow it round to the left. You will emerge on Castle Street; turn right.

(f) Castle Street

This is "one of the finest Victorian commercial streets anywhere in the country" (Hubbard & Vaughan, 1986). Noteworthy buildings include the National Westminster Bank (Norman Shaw, 1898), Nos 34-6

(Grayson & Ould), Co-operative Bank (Caroe, 1892-4) and the Branch Bank of England (C R Cockerell, 1845-8). Cross over Dale Street to the Town Hall. This was originally built by John Wood (1749-54), and was rebuilt after a fire in 1795 by James Wyatt. The portico was added in 1811. Walk around the outside of the Town Hall to the Exchange Flags behind.

(g) Exchange Flags

This area was originally laid-out by Wyatt when the Town Hall was rebuilt. It was the meeting place for merchants and cotton brokers. Note the Nelson memorial (1813), designed by M C Wyatt. The drum acted as a ventilation shaft for bonded warehouses below (now a car park). Follow the route across Exchange Flags to Chapel Street; walk northwards up Old Hall Street to its junction with Fazakerley Street.

(h) Old Hall Street

This street was named after the Medieval house of the Moore family. It was formerly a high class residential area, and was redeveloped as the central business district expanded. Note the Albany (1856) by J K Colling; the complex of company offices and warehousing arranged around a spacious courtyard; and the Cotton Exchange (1906) built to house the Liverpool Cotton Market. All that remains of the Exchange are the side and rear elevations plus stone figures (Science, Industry and Commerce) which once formed part of the towers on the original facade. The City Building (1906) is noteworthy for its glass and cast-iron frontage. Turn left down Fazakerley Street, continue to the end, then turn left and walk down towards The Atlantic Towers Hotel.

(i) Parish Church

This has been Liverpool's parish church since 1699 (it was originally founded in the fourteenth century). The church was destroyed during World War II and the present building was completed in 1952. Note the Tower Building (1908) by Aubrey Thomas. It is an early example of a steel-framed building with large windows and clean white-glazed exterior. Continue to the left of the Church and walk down to Water Street. Turn left up Water Street and head towards the India Building.

(j) Water Street

Note the Oriel Chambers (1864) by Peter Ellis. It is both elegant and functional; Pevsner (1969) describes it as "one of the most significant buildings of its date in Europe". Note also the courtyard at the rear. Here you can also see the India Building (1924-32) built by Herbert Rowse for Holt's Blue Funnel Line. Follow through the impressive tunnel vaulted corridor to Brunswick Street. Turn right on Brunswick Street, walk past Drury Lane and cross over into Goree Piazza.

(k) Goree Piazza

Note Wilberforce House, the City Planning Offices with a permanent exhibition of recent developments in the city and other displays. The building itself is a fitting testament to the 'civic barbarism' of the sixties. Note also the 'buckets sculpture' by Richard Huws, a novel structure which no longer works and now looks rather derelict. Cross the Strand by the footbridge, then walk southwards along the ring-groad, past Canning Dock, to Albert Dock.

(l) Albert Dock

The dock was designed by Jess Hartley and opened in 1845. It is enclosed, with warehousing on all four sides. The design is powerful and impressive. Pevsner (1969) comments that "for sheer punch there is little in the early commercial architecture of Europe to emulate the Albert Dock". The whole area is now happily accessible due to redevelopment, although it has been somewhat emasculated by its new role.

Selected References

Hubbard, E and J Vaughan (1986) *Liverpool. Victorian Society Walks No. 5*. Victorian Society, London

Hughes, Q (1964) *Seaport: Architecture and Townscape in Liverpool*. Lund Humphries

Liverpool Heritage Bureau (1978) *Buildings of Liverpool*. Liverpool City Planning Department

Lloyd-Jones, T (1974) *Know Your Liverpool: Walks in the City Centre*. Workers' Education Association

Pevsner, N (1969) *The Buildings of England: South Lancashire*. Penguin

Willett, J (1967) *Art in a City*. Methuen

26 PUBLIC PASSENGER TRANSPORT PROVISION IN MERSEYSIDE

David Halsall
(Edge Hill College of Higher Education)

Outline: some ideas for using the public transport system in
Merseyside as an aid to understanding how and why it has
evolved, what problems it faces, and how it serves the public.
Distance and route: variable, depending on the excursion chosen.
Time needed: one day.
Map needed: OS 1:50,000 Landranger Series, sheet 108 (Liverpool).

INTRODUCTION

Public passenger transport is one segment of the total transportation
system which links where people live with where they work, seek
services and other activities within modern city regions.

Patterns of travel behaviour and the effects of varying opportunities and constraints upon movement are of particular interest to geographers. Four key elements affect travel behaviour within conurbations: the decentralization of population, car ownership rates, rising
standards of living and transport costs.

Population and Employment

Recent trends in Merseyside, as in other conurbations, show decentralization of population and employment. The population of Liverpool has declined markedly, from 745,000 in 1961 to 510,000 in 1981.

All districts of the former County of Merseyside are characterised
by declining birth rates and continuing out migration. The percentage
fall in population between 1961 and 1981 was greater in Merseyside
than in the other counties in the north west. In fact, Merseyside had the
greatest decline in population of any of the Metropolitan Counties
between 1971 and 1981 despite remaining third in rank of population
density of all the counties of England and Wales.

Increases in population in outer areas such as West Lancashire,
Ellesmere Port and Neston are insufficient to compensate fully for

273

overall migration loss.

Similarly the decentralization of services (especially retailing) is increasing, and jobs have declined markedly, particularly in the central area.

Car ownership rates

Car ownership rates have risen in all British conurbations but the rate of growth in Merseyside is less than the British average. In 1981, 39.5 per cent of British households had no car (37 per cent by 1986). In Merseyside 50.1 per cent lacked this facility. Central areas show the lowest figures whilst outer areas (in adjacent counties) show highest rates of ownership and change.

The overall figures conceal the lack of access to cars for mobility deprived groups and individuals, many of whom live in car-owning households but cannot drive. Access to the car depends upon licence holding by adults and daily patterns of usage. Of those of eligible age, women and manual workers are notably under-represented in licence holders.

Rising standards of living

Rising ownership rates of cars, freezers and fridges have reduced the frequency of shopping trips and encouraged bulk purchases. Negative changes in employment levels tend to smooth daily variations in trip generation, reducing the dominance of peaks.

Transport costs to the consumer

The discrepancy between rises in motoring costs and public transport fares (8 per cent and 20 per cent respectively above inflation, 1982) is considerable. The standardization of fares and simplification of the Merseyside fares system and increasing use of subsidies allowing fares reduction, 1981-83, helped reduce this detrimental relationship.

THE PUBLIC TRANSPORT PROBLEM

Thomson (1977, 60-61) stresses that the transport problem is economic and exonerates "the car from much of the blame that has been piled upon it", "pinpointing the growth of affluence" whilst acknowledging that "this too is an inadequate explanation". Changes in population patterns, employment availability and distribution and car ownership rates have created problems for public transport provision. Services "face the difficulties of widening gaps between costs and revenue and between the areas and population they are required to serve" (Halsall 1982, 69): numbers of passengers fall, but simultaneously the areas needing public transport widen (Merseyside County Council 1980, 5)

There have been few attempts by central government to develop national policies to integrate transport provision except for the Passenger Transport Authorities and Executives in the English Metropolitan Counties and the Scottish Region of Strathclyde between 1968 and 1980. Such policies are being systematically destroyed by contemporary privatisation and deregulation, most notably under the Transport Acts of 1980 and 1985. These are obliterating "the purpose of securing the provision of a properly integrated and efficient system of public passenger transport to meet the needs of that area" by the PTAs (Swallow 1988).

Existing problems of public transport provision in these areas are now compounded by changing policy emphases. These have introduced "a loss of stability, constant changes in service pattern and unfamiliarity for the passenger" (Swallow 1988), which are likely to intensify with privatisation of the municipal bus companies and the disbandment of the PTAs. The current debate over the future of British Rail and individual lines adds further uncertainty to a situation of conflict betwen local authorities and central government in which perceived merits of competition or co-ordination underline differing party approaches. Thus the contemporary situation is transitionary: the effects of deregulation have started but the full consequences of privatisation and competition have yet to emerge.

EXCURSION

Four routes show selected results of changing transport policies within Merseyside since 1968, emphasizing the impacts of integrative, and since 1986, competitive aspects of a network still based upon older rail, road and ferry services. The itinerary utilizes railway corridors allowing fast transit between specific locations. Use of the presently available (1990) all-modes Merseyside 'Saveaway' ticket gives an insight into a major element of integration. A balance between road, rail and river transport is intended. Use of the facilities themselves gives an understanding of the levels of provision (Figures 26a and b)

The specimen schedule (Table 26.1) is based upon summer 1989 timetables.

Table 26.1 Excursion schedule (based upon summer 1989 timetables)

ROUTE 1

Liverpool Central Low Level	
(Northern Line)	dep 0941
Kirkby	arr 0957 Visit Kirkby
	dep 1017 Interchange
Liverpool Central L L	arr 1033
	dep 1045
Garston	arr 1056 Visit Garston
	dep 1109 Interchange
Liverpool Central L L	arr 1120

ROUTE 2

Walk to Liverpool Lime Street station: turn right into Ranelagh Street and left into Lime Street. Station is on right.

Liverpool Lime Street	dep 1135	1147	1150
(City Line)	(to	(to	(to
	Manchester)	Crewe)	Wigan)
Edge Hill	arr 1139	1151	1154

Leave Edge Hill station, turn right into Tunnel Road and left into Wavertree Road: catch one of the following buses - Merseybus 76, 78, 79, 178, 209, 402 (via Brownlow Hill) or Crosville H20, H21, H24, H30, H31 (via Mount Pleasant) to the south side of Gyratory.

ROUTE 3

Return to Central Station

Liverpool Central Deep	
Level (Wirral Line)	dep 1326

Hooton   arr 1348

                                      dep 1355

Birkenhead Hamilton Square   arr 1413

Walk to Woodside Landing Stage.

Ferry for Liverpool   dep. 1435 or 1455.
Liverpool Pier Head - view Landing Stage and Pier Head Bus
                     Station.

ROUTE 4

Pier Head Bus Station - walk to Goree, cross by St. Nicholas'
Church and turn right into Chapel Street (becomes Tithebarn
Street). Visit Mercury Court (facade - former Exchange station)
and turn right into Moorfields, pass station and turn left into Dale
Street and right into Stanley Street. Turn right into Whitechapel
and continue across Lord Street into Paradise Street - turn right,
walk through Central Bus Station, turn right into South John
Street and left into Lord Street, continuing into James Street -
station is on right.

James Street (Wirral Line)   dep. at 5 minute intervals
arrive Liverpool Central, via Moorfields, Lime Street

A Merseyside Passenger Transport Executive Saveaway ticket
should be purchased at transport stations or Post Offices. It is
part of the MPTE integrated fares system, and is relatively cheap
and saves multiple booking for multi-mode journeys. Merseyside is divided into thirty seven zones grouped into four areas -
Wirral, Liverpool, Southport and St. Helens - for a system of
season and day tickets which ease inter-modal transfer and fulfill
complete integration.

Financial pressures on bus companies since deregulation have stimulated other ex-PTE bus companies to produce separate bus saver
tickets or cards. It remains to be seen how long Merseyside will retain
the greater degree of integrative ticketing.

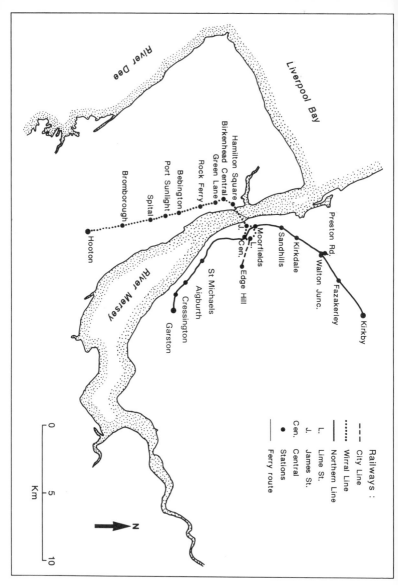

Figure 26a. Railways from Liverpool to Edge Hill, Garston, Hooton, Kirkby (Routes 1, 2, 3)

ROUTE 1 LIVERPOOL-KIRKBY-GARSTON

MPTE initially planned to improve the suburban rail network, investigate bus-rail and car-rail integration and optimise bus services. This route demonstrates the 'Link' line of railway opened in 1977-78. The Kirkby line and existing electrified lines to Ormskirk and Southport were joined to the re-opened Garston line (which was subsequently extended to Hunts Cross to connect with Manchester services previously running from Lime Street) via the new connecting 'Link' beneath central Liverpool (Northern Line). The line successfully generated new traffic, reversing trends of decline; increases in passenger numbers also resulted from bus service rationalisation (including withdrawal of the competing 500 route, Speke - Kirkby), the integrated fares policy and fare reductions. Deregulation has returned bus/rail competition.

Liverpool Central Low Level Station (Figure 26b) was originally the Mersey Railway terminus: the first 0.8 km northwards of the 'Link' utilizes the original Wirral route which diverges at Paradise Street junction to join the 'Loop' for maintenance purposes. The 'Link's' twin tubes cut through mainly Triassic sandstone 10.7-18.29 m below the surface.

Moorfields station (Figure 26b) replaced Exchange terminus. The line joins the original alignment via a 3.7 per cent gradient replacing the partially demolished viaducts to the east. The line runs parallel to the northern docks through Sandhills where the expansive Huskisson goods station lies derelict at lower level to the east.

Liverpool's stagnant economy has hindered reclamation of the city's derelict railway land. Sandhills maintenance depot, built for the new trains, is on the site of older locomotive and carriage servicing facilities. Derelict trackbed to the east at Kirkdale was the line to Huskisson; an important dock connection runs beneath. Kirkdale cuttings and two tunnels formerly carried quadruple track, segregating Wigan and Ormskirk services which still diverge at Walton Junction. The line passes through early- to mid-twentieth century industrial and residential areas to Kirkby, "in the 1950s the major overspill area" characterised by "high birth rates .... a youthful population" and subsequently "a major juvenile unemployment problem for this largely working-class community" (Lawton 1982, 155).

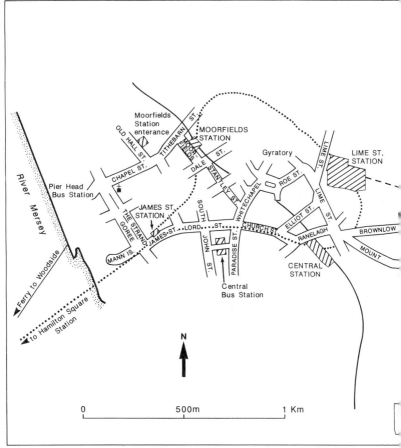

Figure 26b. Details of the Liverpool city centre bus and rail facilities.

At Kirkby interchange, electric trains from Liverpool connect with diesel services to Wigan, Bolton and Manchester. The car park here is well patronised and Merseybus (ex-MPTE company) continues to use the facility. New services by Fareway (the first new company in Merseyside after deregulation) and other smaller operators pass by. Fareway competes with Merseybus and BR, further upsetting MPTE

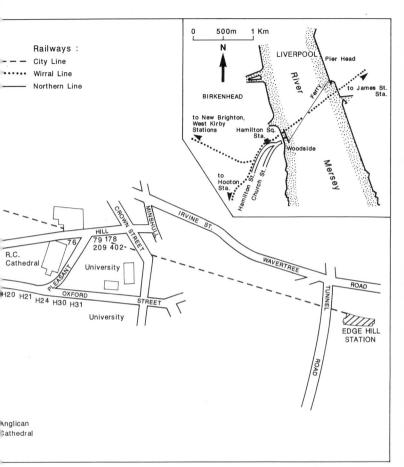

co-ordinative policies since 1987. It now operates over 50 buses on 4 routes to Kirkby.

South from Liverpool Central Low Level a new tunnel connects with the original surface line to Garston, which was reopened in January 1978. The blind tunnel bore is for a possible extension via the University to Edge Hill thence to St. Helens via the existing City Line which would be electrified and replace present services from Lime

Street. The line passes the defunct south docks and the 1984 Garden Festival site (to the west), as well as the renovated Cheshire Line's Committee stations at St. Michaels, Aigburth and Gressington. Garston is an older working-class community than Kirkby. Its interchange is simple - buses stop on the access road outside the station. Merseybus operates connecting services to Speke. Airport services are provided by a local minibus.

ROUTE 2 LIVERPOOL-EDGE HILL

Lime Street station (Figure 26b) accommodates Inter-City and local City line services, the latter serving St. Helens, Wigan, Manchester (diesel) and Crewe (electric). The Deep Level station is on the single bore one-way 'Loop' opened with the 'Link' and replacing the Central - James Street direct line. It thus gives Wirral passengers access to the central office, financial and retail areas, Inter-City services and local Northern and City lines through connections at Moorfields, Central and Lime Street. The 'Loop' cannot be used 'in reverse' from Central to Lime Street, a problem for passengers with luggage who originate on the Garston line. Concentration of Inter City services into Lime Street enabled closure of Central High Level and Exchange stations in the 1970s. Lime Street's new concourse opened in 1984, although the Gothic North Western Hotel facade awaits re-use.

The dramatic succession of cuttings and tunnels through the Triassic sandstone ridge climb a 1.1 per cent gradient to Edge Hill, and result from the Liverpool & Manchester Railway's extension to a more central terminal than Crown Street in 1836. Edge Hill Station, largely original, was renovated for the 150th anniversary of the LMR in 1980.

The return trip by bus to Gyratory (Figure 26b) demonstrates the differing route and journey time of bus services and the modal interchangeability of the Saveaway ticket. Gyratory is constructed around the service entrance for the St. John's Precinct. The variety of buses contrasts with the situation before deregulation when Merseyside was served by the MPTE (now Merseybus) with additonal services operated by the National Bus Company's subsidiaries Ribble (now North Western) and Crosville, and some Greater Manchester buses.

There was little competition immediately after deregulation on 26 October 1986. By August 1988 there were 25 bus operators running commercial and subsidised services. Merseybus remains dominant with about 70 per cent of the total bus mileage. Notable new operations include North Western's two minibus services to Huyton, Crosville's Albert Dock minibus services, Fareway's competition on the Kirkby corridor, incursions by Red Rover Potteries Motor Transport (ex-NBC), and recent (since April 1988) competition on south Liverpool services by Liverline. Merseybus has retaliated to competition from Fareway and Liverline by lowering fares on affected routes from mid-August 1988.

ROUTE 3 LIVERPOOL-HOOTON

The 3.2 km 'Loop' branches from the original Mersey Railway alignment beneath Mann Island, Pier Head and cuts through mainly Triassic sandstone at 17.6-37.8 m below the surface. New stations were built at Moorfields, Lime Street and Central (Figure 26b) and those at James Street and Birkenhead Hamilton Square were enlarged, the latter in connection with a new burrowing junction to segregate New Brighton and West Kirby trains from Hooton traffic. This permitted a 50 per cent increase in frequency of trains, which has not been fully utilized, through the Mersey rail tunnel.

Until 1986, the MPTE shielded the cross river railway from bus competition. Now Merseybus run competing services through the 1971 road tunnel. Extension of electrification to Hooton in 1985 leaves the Bidston - Wrexham services as the only ones propelled by diesel traction in Wirral. Electrification to Chester and Ellesmere Port/Helsby is proposed. The journey along the eastern side of Wirral demonstrates the outward growth of suburbs and industry along the Mersey. Lever's model industrial settlement at Port Sunlight is notable (see Excursion 24).

Return by train to Hamilton Square (Figure 26b) and then ferry, walking past the former Mersey Railway power and pumping station, preserved in 1988, at Shore Road. Woodside bus station is a similar but smaller connection between road and ferry to Liverpool's Pier Head. Merseybus and Crosville routes radiate outwards. The derelict site to the south was Woodside railway station, from which Great Western Railway trains formerly competed for London and Birmingham traffic with the London & North Western Railway (later the London Midland & Scottish Railway) from Lime Street until main line electrification in 1965. The Woodside line joined the existing railway at Rock Ferry.

Only the Woodside and Seacombe ferries remain from a series of long established Mersey crossings. By 1981 the ferries' share of cross river trips was less than 10 per cent and public support in 1978/79 cost £1 million. The ferries are a costly anachronism, which cannot compete with two road and one rail tunnels. But they are a valued leisure and educational resource. Both scheduled services and cruises offer superb views of the river and its facilities and the urban areas. The floating landing stages at Birkenhead and Liverpool have been renewed, the latter with assistance from the Isle of Man government to aid the island's shipping link.

Liverpool's Pier Head bus station is the main terminal for local services. Merseybus, North Western, Crosville and Fareway operate from here.

ROUTE 4 PIER HEAD-MOORFIELDS-CENTRAL BUS STATION-JAMES STREET-CENTRAL RAILWAY STATION

Buses for northern destinations use the Chapel Street - Tithebarn Street axis, passing the Moorfields station entrance in Old Hall Street (which is linked to the main station by walkway) and the Mercury Court Offices which incorporate the facade of the Lancashire & Yorkshire Railway terminus, Exchange. Note the bust of John Pearson (Chairman 1883-1887). Moorfields station entrance was designed to lead onto an elevated walkway through the office zone. The scheme was abandoned before completion.

The eastern part of Lord Street is pedestrianised since July 1988, linking with existing pedestrian areas around Church Street. The project has diverted bus routes, some of which now terminate at Central Bus station rather than Pier Head. The scheme is intended to stimulate redevelopment and employment in the retail centre, and to create a safer and more pleasant shopping environment. North Western's Huyton minibuses, Merseybus, Fareway and Liverline services operate from Central Bus station.

The return rail journey from James Street to Central Deep Level completes the circuit of the 'Loop' commenced earlier, beneath office, commercial and retail areas of the central area.

CONCLUSIONS

Since 1968 much change in Merseyside's transport infrastructure and services has accompanied socio-economic and political transition. These have not always been synchronised. Most transport innovations have aided individual mobility although many realities of personal mobility and mobility deprivation remain unknown.

The mainly electric suburban rail system with frequent interval services became "a backbone to public transport services ... which enables measures to integrate bus and rail transport" (MPTE 1981, 7) at a series of interchanges upon which revised bus services focused, serving suburbs without direct rail communications. The investment into the rail corridors thus benefits much more than the city centre.

Overall these improvements are effective despite the limitations already noted. Returns from individual stations vary considerably. By 1981 MPTE foresaw annual savings and increased revenue from bus-rail integration. In 1984-85 Merseyrail passenger traffic totalled 307 million passenger miles (494 million passenger km) and required a subsidy of £14.3 million. Whilst the Northern line showed marked improvements, Wirral Line services took nearly half the revenue support for rail to support a quarter of the rail passenger traffic.

Transport innovation is closely linked to shifts in transport policy, products of swings of the political pendulum and "continuing failure to resolve the urban transport problem arising from the vicious circle of increased car use threatening the viability of more environmentally acceptable and socially necessary public transport operations" (Hill 1986, 87). Since deregulation, revival of bus competition has not always shown success (for example between bus and rail between Liverpool and Southport), fewer buses call at some interchanges (notably Waterloo), and rising fares on commercial services, unreliability and instability of bus service patterns have contributed to a 12.5 per cent increase in rail patronage (around five million journeys a year).

Bus use had grown between 1981 and 1986. Bus patronage is now at its lowest: it sunk by 29 per cent 1986-87, a reduction of around 90 million passenger journeys a year (far greater than the rise in rail traffic). MPTE stresses that "this represents a significant reduction in mobility particularly for those least able to pay the higher fares". This conflicts with government optimism for the 1985 Act stimulating "good bus services" aimed at "the 39 per cent of households ...who do not have the regular use of a car" (Department of Transport et al 1984, 1) Fares have not been reduced, nor usage increased, as intended. On commercially viable services (79 per cent) fares have risen considerably although MPTE is allowed to continue to subsidise socially necessary but loss making services (21 per cent) costing around £10 million (budget £12 million). The government emphasizes that it "does not regard ... big metropolitan subsidies as necessary or unavoidable". (ibid, 3).

In Merseyside, it does not appear that the strategy of competition is providing "lower fares, new services, more passengers" (ibid) overall. Fareway has expanded; Liverline and PMT may follow. Merseybus' concern is indicated by fare reductions in August 1988 on their routes competing with Fareway and Liverline. Minibuses are well established specialist elements such as the 'Merseylink' scheme for the disabled, or relatively small scale and localised, reflecting problems of their use in large cities.

Within the economic situation of Merseyside many people are particularly sensitive to fare increases and reduce their trips accordingly. The danger is that necessary trips will be cancelled by those least financially able but most needy of services. Full privatisation, plans for BR and further financial measures will inevitably further affect service provision.

Selected References

Daniels, P W and A M Warnes (1980) *Movement in cities*. Methuen

Department of Transport, Scottish Office and Welsh Office (1984) *Buses, Cmnd 9300*. HMSO

Department of Transport, Scottish Development Department of Transport, Welsh Office (1987) *Transport Statistics, Great Britain 1976-1986*. HMSO

Farrington, J (1985) Transport geography and policy; deregulation and privatisation. *Transactions of the Institute of British Geographers* NS 10; 109-119

Hall, P (1980) Transport in the conurbations. 146-171 in G Cameron (editor) *The future of the British conurbations*. London

Halsall, D A (1978) Rapid transit in Merseyside. *Area* 10, 212-216.

Halsall, D A (1982) Transport issues and policies. 69-82 in W T S Gould and A G Hodgkiss (editors) *The Resources of Merseyside*. Liverpool University Press

Halsall, D A (1985) Rapid transit in Merseyside: problems and policies. 76-91 in A F Williams (editor) *Rapid Transit Systems in the UK*. Institute of British Geographers, Transport Geography Study Group

Halsall, D A (1988) The minibus revolution. *Geographical Magazine* LX/6; 38

Hill, R (1986) Urban transport; from technical process to social policy. 85-106 in P Lawless and C Raban (editors) *The Contemporary British City*. Harper & Row

Lawton, R (1982) The distribution and structure of population since 1951. 147-162 in W T S Gould and A G Hodgkiss (editors) *The Resources of Merseyside*. Liverpool University Press

Merseyside County Council (1980) *Plan (Written statement)*. MCC, Liverpool

Merseyside Passenger Transport Executive (1981) *The Merseyrail projects: a monitoring report*. MPTE, Liverpool

MPTE (1985) *Passenger Transport in Merseyside 1969-1986*. MPTE, Liverpool

Paul, A H (1980) Vanishing railways and the urban scene: the case of Liverpool. *Geography* 65; 119-124

Swallow, K (1988) The new PTE scene. *Buses* 40; 12-13

Thomson, J M (1977) *Great cities and their traffic*. Victor Gollancz

Whitelegg, J (1985) *Urban Transport*. Macmillan

Acknowledgements

I am most grateful for help from Mr A H Coleman of the MPTE for the provision of MPTE data and material, and to Edge Hill College for financial assistance in the preparation of this article.

Text pages printed by Martin's of Berwick Ltd.

en I'll see ya around. When you're ready to fly, let me

choked on a sob. "Raven—"

cut her off. "Do me a favor?"

nodded. "Anything."

n't tell anyone I was here."

hat?" Confusion scrunched her face, adding a new
sion. It was better than the pain so evident a moment

I'm going, I'd just as soon they continue thinking I'm

ven, I can't lie." The wind caught Nikki's hair, and he
ot to notice the strands dancing around her shoulders,
against her upper arms.

u don't have to. It's what they already think."

, it's not. They all think you're alive and just playing the

t shouldn't hurt, but it did. "There's just no loyalty at all,
?" he mumbled.

ase stay." He knew it was her last-ditch plea.

he countered with one of his own. "With you?"

," she whispered.

e I said, when you're ready, you know how to find me."
frowned. "No, I don't."

u found me tonight. Follow your heart, Nikki. No mat-
re it roams, it'll always lead you back to me, because my
always calling to yours. You can choose not to listen for
, but eventually you'll go where it's leading you." And
stepped close and kissed her.

188

She stiffened. "You mean away from Mace." Did he really
expect her to just run away? Maybe running was what Raven
did best. In the amount of time it took lightning to flash,
Nikki's emotion toward Raven shifted. "I'd never walk away.
I owe them." The pain materialized in his gaze, and she could
almost hear his thoughts. She squeezed her eyes shut, hoping
he wouldn't give those words voice. But of course he did. This
was Raven, after all.

"What about the guy who was willing to die for you?"

It sounded like such a self-serving comment, the kind of
bargain small children make. *You do this for me and I'll do that
for you.* "Don't do this, Raven, please."

"You say you want a stabilizer, Nikki. But I know you. You
don't want safe ground. You want castle ruins where you can
stand on the edge, where maybe it will stay firm and maybe it
will crumble." He let his hands roam over her arms, her back.
"How long will it take before you're bored out of your mind? How
long until Mace's firm foundation closes around you like a cage?"

Part of her wanted to shut him out completely, but part
wanted to agree. If there was one thing Nikki'd always feared,
it was being trapped. So much so she'd dreamed about it as a
child: the cold, unforgiving floor, the bars where she pressed
her face, the desperation to feel the air beyond the stifling confines of the prison. She shook her head against the memory,
but the gilded cage would not dissipate. "I don't know. Okay? I.
Don't. Know. Can we please just give this more time?"

He dropped his hands from her with chilling reserve. "Why?
You've made your choice. And as I recall, giving you time didn't
work out so well for us." Raven took a few steps back.

This is for the best. She pulled a shaky breath, released it
slowly. "Yes, I have made my choice."

185

"You know I'm not going to sit around and watch. You don't expect me to, right?"

Fresh waves of panic unfurled in her chest. "What do you mean?"

He shrugged. "It doesn't matter. Come on, I'll take you home."

The garage door was open, but Raven stopped a distance away from it and got off the bike.

Nikki stared at him, questions glistening in her night-darkened eyes. Lights from Viennesse illuminated the grounds, giving it a homey glow. He wouldn't let the image take root in his psyche. It was hard enough leaving already.

Off the motorcycle and standing beside him, she tilted her head. "Why didn't you ride on into the garage?" Apprehension captured her voice.

"I'm not staying." *His* voice was solid. Solid as a rock.

"What? Where will you go?" She started to reach out.

Raven stepped back, erecting an invisible wall between them. It's what he had to do to survive this. "I still have work to do at the lab in Arkansas."

"So you *were* the one sending information to Zero."

"Yeah." Raven ran a hand over the smooth gas tank. A lone bird in flight. Just like him. Nowhere to rest, nowhere to call home. And no one along for the ride. Nikki would drive the motorcycle in and cover it with the lifeless tan tarp. There his bike would wait in lonely silence and fading hope, perhaps forever like some of the others.

"Have you been in the lab this whole time?" Concern filled

her words, along with a little bit of …
eager to keep him talking, keep him er
Keep him there. But that didn't matter.

"In and out. The air vents there are
during the day, and nights I've stayed ir

"Isn't there a guard?"

"Yeah, I guess you could call him
more information to obtain and now is
hardly anyone in the lab. It's like ther
or something. I think they routed ever
when they hired the new geneticists."

"When you're done there, then you'
that hope blooming in her? He almost
it. Until her eyes found his. There, tra
moonlight, was his Nikki—hands clas
of her, teeth nibbling on her bottom li
on countless occasions, the one who th
neck and squealed at the chance to feed
loved him. And the one who was just
truth attached to those feelings.

Her eyes swam in fresh pools of
that much harder. "No. I'm not com
impossible.

"Raven, please. Stay here. Don't g
grabbed his arms in a vice grip. "Som
happen."

He cocked his head like the defiant
stay here, it's with you."

The moisture in her eyes shrank
sensed her resignation rise slowly as sl
his fierce inflexibility. Nikki shook he
fall to her sides—she was stubborn too

Raven's lips roamed lightly over hers until she responded. Again, her body reacted without her mind's consent. A moment later she was lost in a spinning, sinking whirlpool of wonder and magic. His lips were alive against hers and a million butterflies seemed to take flight everywhere their skin touched. Gentle electricity tickled over her flesh, causing the strangest sensation. *A roller coaster submerged in honey.* Utterly trapped by the world below, then careening over hills and into valleys as if free, every motion thick and sweet. His hands were flattened against her back, just as he always did whenever … whenever she needed him. Fear lit a fire in Nikki's veins, and it burned like a match that ignited her blood. With it, a realization she couldn't bear to face.

She needed him.

The press of her mouth intensified against Raven's. A tiny cry escaped.

I need him. And he's leaving.

Nikki wound her arms around his neck in a useless attempt to keep him, but a violent conflict raged within. She could have him and lose Mace. Or she could let him go. As if he heard the battle, understood her struggle, Raven broke the kiss.

When he did, her fingertips flew to her mouth, desperately ashamed of her actions and desperately trying to retain the feel of his lips on hers—both emotions wove together as he took a step back. Her hand stretched to stop him, but her legs were still stuck in the rich honey that had poured from his kiss.

Through his long bangs, one eye winked. And for the first time ever, Nikki couldn't read the story swimming in his midnight-blue eyes. He'd masked what he'd always shown her—his truest feelings, deepest emotions. Gone. Hidden from her.

He shot a look up to the sky, gaze flittering from star to star. "When you're ready to fly …"

Then he took one more step back, snapped his wings open, and leapt.

Nikki stood for a long time gazing at the night he'd disappeared into. Over and over his words echoed in her head. *When you're ready to fly ...*

"I'm sorry, man," Gearhead mumbled as they watched Nikki.

Mace's jaw ached; this was the third time he'd seen Nikki and Raven kiss. *Doesn't get any easier.*

"I thought you and Nikki were—" Gearhead glanced at him in the garage's dim light.

Mace hardened. "We were."

Gearhead wiped his hands on the shop towel he kept tucked in his waistband. "Look, I'll give you two some space."

Mace thrust out a hand as the mechanic passed. "Don't bother."

"You couldn't hear what they were saying, and things aren't always the way they look."

Mace glared.

"Yeah, okay, that *was* pretty obvious."

"Ya think?" Without another word, Mace crossed the garage and headed back into the main house, wondering if he'd already lost the girl he'd recently reclaimed.

Chapter
17

"Hi," Nikki said, peeking her head into Mace's room.

Back to her, he shoved something into a bag with so much force it made her jump. He didn't answer her greeting.

"Can I come in?"

"Sure, but I'm on my way out," he said, words clipped.

Nikki frowned while he manhandled the zipper of the backpack, as if he had some personal vendetta against it. "Where are you going?"

He finally relented when the zipper stuck. He huffed out an angry breath and left it half open. "Some of the guys are going to a friend's house to hang out for a few hours."

Okay, everything was wrong with that statement. First of all, Halflings didn't just go to friend's houses to hang out. So where was he *really* going, and why was Mace acting like he'd eaten nails for breakfast? "Who's the friend?"

"You don't know him."

She chewed her lip. "Is it close?"

"Across the Rhine Valley, in France."

When she dropped her gaze to the floor, he exhaled. "It's at another ancestral home. A group of Halflings lives there. We won't be gone that long."

"Is it similar to the one here?" She wanted him to keep talking. Maybe if he did, she'd break through that tough shell of … well, of whatever it was.

"Yup."

"Is it the only one in France?"

"That I know of. But I don't know where the females hang out when they aren't infiltrating our domain." On Will's instructions, Winter, Vegan, and Glimmer were staying at Viennesse in case something happened.

Nikki thought back to the first conversation she and Mace had about Halflings. They'd sat on the back porch of the two-story house Will and the boys had rented in her hometown. "That's right. Until this journey, you hadn't met any female Halflings." Raven, on the other hand, seemed to know them and know them well. Of course, Raven had been on more journeys than Mace, and was the kind of guy who had no problem chatting up girls.

A muscle in Mace's cheek twitched. "So, I'll see you later," he said, and started to step past her.

Nikki glanced outside at the bright morning sun spilling through the window. "But it's supposed to be really nice out today, and I thought maybe we could take one of the cars and see the countryside."

He spun on his heel just as he reached the door. "Haven't you seen enough of it?"

What did that mean? She hadn't been outside the castle walls other than their picnic and her trip last night.

Fear filled her system.

Could he know about that? "Mace, I need to talk to you about something."

The only acknowledgement he'd even heard her was the quirking of his brows. Those cerulean-blue eyes she usually found comfort in were brimmed with tension and bore into her. At last he looked away, focusing on the wall by the window. She could almost feel his pain reaching its hungry fingers toward her.

"I did something last night."

His head tipped back a degree as if readying for a punch he'd seen in advance. "What?"

Nikki rubbed her hands together, nervous energy seeking escape from her body. "I took Raven's motorcycle."

His mouth hardened. "What happened?"

She forced a steadying breath and leaned her weight against the wall alongside the open door for support. "Well, I thought if I went to the castle ruins, maybe I could help him. Zero thought Raven was sending information, but then Zero also said he thought Raven could be dead, and—" She shook her head. "I don't know. I was really confused. So I went."

He crossed his arms over his chest. "And?"

She blinked, frowned. "And I shouldn't have done it."

The muscle in Mace's jaw tightened, highlighting the usually smooth lines of his face. He stood there, unwavering. Very Mace-like. But he had an edge as well. An unfriendly, almost mean edge that was most *un*-Mace-like. "That's all you have to tell me?"

A battle was laid out before them, but neither seemed ready to fire the first shot. If she told him Raven had been there, she'd be breaking a promise. Maybe the last promise she'd ever make to Raven. After all he'd done for her, it didn't seem right to divulge his secret. Even to Mace.

The uneasy nod of her head broke their stalemate.

Suddenly, the backpack's stubborn zipper was forced to absorb the full impact of his frustration. He launched into a furious fight with it while she watched, mouth gaping.

After a few awkward moments, she stepped to him and took the backpack into her own hands. "A bit of the material is stuck," she whispered so as not to disturb any more of the hornets needling his flesh. Using soft back-and-forth motions, she worked the zipper until the cloth was freed.

"Thanks," he muttered.

She held the bag out to him. When he reached for it, his hand fell against hers, but he snatched it away from her touch. "Mace, what's wrong?"

He became deathly calm as he fingered the now-functioning zipper. "You've got some things you need to figure out, Nikki. Being in a relationship with someone means there are certain boundaries. I'm not really sure how you feel about Raven or about me. But you can't feel the same for both of us, so you're either lying to yourself about me or you're lying to yourself about him. Either way, you're intentionally fooling yourself. You need to make a choice. Then you need to stick with the rules, because I'm sick of feeling like this." Before she could answer, he stepped past her and left the room.

Nikki blinked when the door closed. "I have made a choice," she whispered to the empty space. It felt like tiny needles pierced her heart. But with that sensation an unsettling irritation formed. *Stick to the rules? Was he kidding? What rules are there anymore?* She didn't want to hurt Mace, ever. But she'd stared death in the face over and over, and had been spared by either him or Raven. *A person can't just flip a switch and expect to be able to sort through the emotions that causes.*

What did she know about love, anyway? All she knew was how she felt, and that was an untrustworthy measuring device to be sure. The girl who'd never had a boyfriend was now surrounded by tall, beautiful angelic beings compelled to protect her.

Unsteady legs carried Nikki to the window. The wall clock ticked. A bird sailed past the stone opening, pausing in mid-flight. She watched its effortless movements as it gathered speed for a nosedive toward the courtyard. A smaller bird followed, unsteady, less fluid than the first. "Learning to fly?" she uttered, but as the question left her mouth, the reference to Raven's last words to her rushed fresh and blistering in her mind. She stepped away from the window ... and saw the opening resembled a cage. Nikki ran out of the room, rejecting the notion that her stone palace was quickly becoming her prison. And that maybe Raven really was the only one with a key.

After Mace left to go "hang out at a friend's house," Nikki made her way to the girls' room. Glimmer and Vegan shared a room, while Winter had her own. But more likely than not, the three were together in their own little clique. If not gathered in Winter's domain, than in the other room. Nikki wasn't used to searching out camaraderie, but after her argument with Mace, she needed a friend, maybe three.

Winter's room was empty, so she traversed the hall, walking slowly and thinking how out of character it was for her to search out support from other girls. A huge part of her wondered who she'd become. When she made it to the door, she could hear the females talking on the other side. Even through the thick mahogany, their words rang clear. She lifted her hand to knock, until she heard Glimmer say her name.

Nikki's hand froze in midair.

"I can see her messing around with Raven—I mean, he's always got one foot in the dark side, but I'm surprised she and Mace are taking such a risk. It's not like him. He knows better, and to throw away your eternity for a human—it's beyond stupid. That's not the kind of thing Mace does. And I can't believe she's letting him! They're walking around here like teenagers in love. Please. Happy today, eternity in hell tomorrow. Like she's worth it. Like *any* human is worth it."

"Relax, Glimmer," Vegan's voice soothed. "We haven't really known Mace that long, certainly not long enough to make judgments about him."

"I think his eyes have gotten darker. We all know what *that* means.'"

Nikki's hand fisted. When Halflings' eyes darkened, it meant they were giving in to evil. Was Mace slipping into darkness because of her? She hadn't noticed any changes …

Glimmer continued. "Mace is awesome, and there are plenty of Halfling girls who would love to have him fawning over them like that. Girls who understand him and his life, girls who can fight shoulder to shoulder with him."

"Are you volunteering?"

"No. I've actually got my eye on Raven right now. Provided he gets back here soon. I'm not going to wait forever."

"You change crushes like Zero changes flash drives," Vegan said.

"And who is Raven crushing on? *Nikki*. It's pathetic. What

do they see in her?" Glimmer's voice cut like a stiletto blade, each word stabbing harder and deeper into the same wound.

"She's a bit of a warrior herself. If I was a guy, I'd like her." Vegan again.

"Right up until Satan ushered you into hell. This infatuation with humans is all wrong."

"Glimmer's right." That one was Winter's voice, and hearing it made Nikki sink a little deeper into despair. "What Mace is engaging in is dangerous. Deadly dangerous."

Nikki thought she heard Vegan sigh. "Maybe Nikki doesn't know. Maybe she doesn't realize ..." But the girl—Nikki's supposed friend—held zero conviction in her words.

"If she loved him, she'd leave."

"Glimmer!" Vegan gasped.

"Well, if he's too stupid to leave her alone, she should take matters into her own hands."

"Winter, surely you don't agree with this."

Long pause. "I don't know."

"I can't believe you two. We've been commissioned by the Throne to protect Nikki. And you would have her leave?"

"Protect her from what?" Glimmer spat. "Nothing man or demon has made any kind of attempt on her since we all left Missouri. Nothing. Not even a sideways glance from an angry human. Nikki is fine. She just needs to go away for a while."

Nikki waited for Vegan to come to her defense again, but no words followed. In Nikki's heart she knew the other girls agreed. They may not have voiced it, but they thought the things Glimmer dared say. Sorrow wound around her and squeezed.

She needed to find Will. He'd make sense of all this. He'd remind her in that booming voice filled with years of authority that her safety was vital. Even key to protecting the plan handed down throughout the ages by the Throne. Will put things in perspective by reminding her that what the Halflings were doing was about more than a girl. It was destiny, and it was ordained by a power she could only hope to one day understand. Will made things better ... by making her smaller. And right now, that's exactly what she needed, because the females had made her feel like a giant problem able to wreck both lives and eternities.

Nikki tiptoed away from the door and headed down the stairs, her heart feeling like a twenty-pound anchor. At the end of the long hall she noticed Ocean just as he entered Will's room. He hadn't seen her, so she took her time, putting one measured foot in front of the other. Like a prisoner on death row, each step felt like it was taking her to something she didn't want to face.

She started to go inside, but paused. What would she say? *Sorry to interrupt you, but I could use a pep talk right now.* No. She squared her shoulders while trying to force Glimmer's harsh words from her head. *Ugh. Why do things hurt so much when you aren't expecting them?* She hadn't planned on being chucked under the bus by the trendy Halfling with the curly bob. A few weeks ago? Sure, Glimmer would have gladly hacked her to pieces with her sharp tongue. But now, they'd become close—a huge mistake on Nikki's part. Because now there was no defensive shield, no armor, allowing the words to cut right through her.

Deeper in Will's room, she heard voices. They must be on the balcony.

"You can't sit around like a lifeless rock, Will." Ocean was standing beside the angel as they both stared out at the sky.

"I am not equipped with fear, and yet it grips my heart."

"It's Mace, isn't it?" At Ocean's words, Nikki sank to the floor.

Silence.

She squeezed her eyes shut. *No, no, no. Please, no.*

"My apprehension about this journey grows exponentially. As time careens toward its conclusion, I know the training of my Lost Boys was inadequate in the most elemental of areas."

Ocean shifted his weight. "Will, God was the perfect father, yet Adam still chose sin."

"Yes. For a woman."

"Mace is strong. In the end, he'll make the right choice."

"It is foolishness to question the Throne's judgment. But in my heart of hearts, I wish we'd never met Nikki Youngblood."

Icy-cold talons seized Nikki. Her mind blackened and the rope around her heart released slowly, leaving her chest empty and hollow.

Movement was difficult, but she managed to stand and trace her steps back to the staircase. Fingers closed on the railing while she paused. There was nothing else for her to hold on to—no thoughts, no words, no anything. Just emptiness like she'd only felt once before; when a police officer arrived to tell her of her parents' death.

Somehow, she made it to her room and locked the door. But the rock walls and high ceiling offered no sanctuary. They loomed, staring at her with accusing eyes.

Sensei Coble's voice echoed in her head. "Always find an ally." But there were none here. Not the females, not Will, certainly not Mace. "And when there is no ally, embrace the universe's decision to move you. For you will never be left without a companion."

Was that it? Was the "universe" moving her? Nikki'd never bought into the spiritualism Sensei Coble subscribed to. She crossed the room and dragged open her top drawer. There, in the corner, her cell phone rested against the clothing she'd purchased with the females. She didn't want to look at the garments she'd once associated with happiness. She'd allowed the girls to suck her in with the promise of friendship when, really, they wanted her gone. Nikki shoved the clothes away from her cell.

The slam of the drawer rocked the whole chest, no easy feat for the mammoth block of carved wood. Frustration flew from her fingers as she turned on her cell and stared down at the screen. It blurred. *Gah. Stupid, stupid tears.* She scraped at her eyes with the palm of her hand while the cell powered up.

Sixty-six missed calls. All the same number: Damon Vessler. Nikki found the open window and looked out on the rolling landscape. What was she doing here, in this dream turned nightmare? How could she go downstairs and sit at dinner and chat about the day when she knew what they were all thinking? She hit the button to listen to her messages, hoping the phone would work so far from home.

They were all the same; Damon pleading with her to come home. Hot tears scorched her cheeks as she listened to him speak of her parents' things. He kept reassuring her everything was safe and sound and in the lower level of his home. Waiting for her.

He'd set up an art studio for her in one corner. And if she chose, they'd keep everything that belonged to her mom and dad. Each message ended with "Nikki, come home. Please, come home."

Four hours later she'd nicked the keys to the Kawasaki, purchased a phone card with some of the "Throne funds" she'd been given, and punched the numbers into a phone in a hotel lobby somewhere in France. She felt slightly guilty for leaving everyone behind, but knew she couldn't call Damon from her cell. The Halflings didn't trust him, and to divulge their location would be wrong. If he pressed, she'd tell Damon she was in Europe. But she needed to hear his voice. Needed to see if he still wanted her back, because Glimmer was right about everything. Even about the lack of threats. In the four hours Nikki'd been gone, nothing had happened. No hell hounds, no crazed hate-filled humans. Maybe she wasn't even in danger anymore.

Yet that far-off voice beckoned to her. Something evil would find her. Very, very soon.

Chapter
18

"Damon?" She cradled the phone for support. "It's me, Nikki."

His words rushed out after a relieved exhale. "Oh, Nikki. I'm so glad you're all right. Please come home."

"I— I don't know that I should." What was wrong with her? This was what she wanted, right? But everything in her screamed against it.

"I have some new information about your parents. If you come back, I'll go after the guy who killed them. But it's somewhat costly. I have to know you're invested. I have to know it matters to you."

She hadn't expected this, and had to shake her head to sort it out. "You think it wouldn't matter to me?" Through the hotel lobby window, Nikki watched a young man sit down at an outside café. It was an inviting kind of place with streams of vines and flowers flowing from the transom above the doorway.

"Sweetheart, you ran away. How important could it be?"

"Damon, I didn't run away. I was—" What could she say?

"It doesn't matter, Nikki. Just come home. We can start fresh."

It sounded good, but impossible for her; the wounds she'd suffered were too deep for new starts.

"I've got everything organized downstairs. We need to go through your dad's things. My whole basement smells like them, you know. I walk down there and expect to see their faces."

Her eyes closed in an attempt to remember the scent of her parents. But only unfamiliar smells filled her nose. "I may not be safe."

"You're safe with me, Nikki. I have the best security men in the world. Nothing will hurt you. There's no demon in hell that can get to you if you're with me."

Was that a hypothetical statement? His voice suggested not. "What do you mean?"

"I mean there are forces around us that aren't human. And they can't be allowed to run rampant. I have in my employ some of the best monster hunters on the planet. You probably think that's silly, but I've traveled the world and I can tell you there are beasts, creatures unlike anything you've ever seen. Straight out of the pit and ready to kill. But I know their secrets, Nikki." He laughed. "I'm only divulging this to you so you understand the depth of my commitment to your safety. *This* is where you belong. Can't you feel that?"

She squeezed the phone tighter. She did feel it. She belonged somewhere, surrounded by her parent's things. Those items were all she had left of them. Didn't she owe it to them to go back?

Could Damon really protect her? He certainly sounded

like he could. "I guess I could come back long enough to sort through Mom and Dad's things. But I can't make any promises after that. And I really have to know I'm safe there." If today's journey out alone was any indication, there was nothing to worry about. As long as she didn't draw, she was fine. Ever since Will had taught her how to recognize when she was tapping into the realm of the spirit and how to avoid it, she'd been strong. She'd learned. What harm could there be in going home for a time? Vessler's house was safe. And maybe she'd even have time for the wounds—the ones inflicted by Glimmer, Will, and especially Mace—to heal.

"Where are you, Nikki? I'll come get you."

"Uh." She couldn't divulge where she was. No way. Too close to the Rhine Valley, the location of an ancestral home. As angry as she was, she couldn't rat out the Halflings. But Europe was small, and public transportation could take her anywhere. "I'm in Paris." She'd hop the train and leave the bike. Later, much later, after she was long gone, she'd get a message to Viennesse about the motorcycle.

"Uh-huh." He didn't believe her, she could tell. "How on earth did you get there?" Other questions drifted in the silence around his words.

"I climbed aboard a ship." Not a lie.

"I'll charter a jet to get you home. I'll text you information on which airport. We'll have to see what's available on such short notice."

Nikki pulled the cell phone from her pocket. "Damon, I'm using a phone card. My cell doesn't work here."

"Yes it does, my lady. I've already activated international service on it."

Trepidation gnawed in her gut. She ignored it. "Why did you do that? What made you think I'd leave the country?"

"A hunch. Nikki, promise you won't run away again."

"I didn't ... and I promise."

The following day she was home. Or as close to a home she had. She'd gone to sleep on a bed of silk after Damon met her at the door and held her for so long it seemed he'd never let go.

She'd wanted to go straight to her mom and dad's things, but he said no. "Sleep, Nikki. Tomorrow morning, we'll go downstairs together."

She woke to the smell of freshly toasted bread and the realization someone had entered her room. She heard their whispered steps and the sound of their breathing, and she sensed them as well. Through her barely opened eyes, Nikki watched Anya, Vessler's housekeeper, pour a cup of coffee from the silver carafe, dump in a bit of cream and sugar, and stir the concoction vigorously. She breezed out of the room and the door clicked behind her.

Nikki leaned onto her elbows and stared at the tray of breakfast like it was a snake. Her mouth watered, but something in her begged not to trust what was in front of her. Not to trust any of this.

She threw the covers back. "That's ridiculous," she mumbled and sailed to the tray, taking a bite so big the bread barely fit into her mouth.

A knock caused her to jump.

"Come in," she said in a muffled voice, tongue maneuvering around the half-macerated bread.

Damon slid the door open. His dark eyes widened, brows raised high. "Glad to see you have your appetite."

She swallowed, wished there'd been a little more butter on the toast, and reached for the coffee.

With a mega-smile, he moved with the fluid motions of a man with years of martial arts training. He paused at the table, reached for the delicate pat of butter, and smeared it on her bread. Another devastating smile as he held it out for her to take a bite.

She froze. Did he actually expect to feed her? *Okay, that ranks pretty high on the creepy, possible-pedophile scale.* Her eyes cut from him to the butter-gooed bread, and noticed a stream of spread ran along the edge of the toast. She grabbed it from him and took another bite, making sure she caught the buttery river while stepping a good foot away.

The air kicked on and Damon's scent of clean linen and expensive cologne surrounded her. He always smelled so good. She took in the room, the *bedroom*, and again everything felt wrong. Very, very wrong.

Damon lifted his hands and bowed. "Forgive me. I know this must seem strange to you, Nicole, but it feels perfectly natural to me. In many ways I feel like you're my own daughter." His gold chain twinkled, catching the light in the hollow of his throat where the V of his designer shirt framed his tan neckline.

His own daughter? Well, that leveled the freak flag, but raised the *alarm* flag to full mast. "I barely know you," she uttered. Oops. She'd only meant to think that, not say it.

"But I know you, my dear. Through your parents, I shared every moment of your life. I know about your first bicycle wreck, your first B on a math assignment." He led her to the window and opened the curtains wide. Below, on a smaller hillside, her house sat nestled inside the neighborhood of smallish homes where she grew up. "I've kept a watch over you. And as long as you'll let me, I promise to do so forever."

Great. Just what she needed right now: another guardian. But this one wasn't trying to toss her into an epic war, this one wasn't trying to dictate her life; this one cared simply because he cared.

"You got a lovely tan on the, uh, *ship*, was it?"

She focused on the windowsill. *Here it comes. The third degree about where I was and why, and I don't have a clue how to answer any of it.* She steeled herself. "Yes, it was a ship."

"The sun agrees with you. I wouldn't have thought it possible to make you any more beautiful, and yet you are."

Uh-huh. "Thanks," she said, more of a question than an answer. "I guess I should explain." She pivoted to face him.

"No, you shouldn't."

"Wha—what?"

"You've nothing to explain to me. You're an adult now, Nikki. You don't have to answer to anyone anymore."

Huh. She hadn't thought of that.

"In fact," Damon continued, "I forbid it. No talk of where you were and what you were doing."

Her eyes narrowed playfully. "If I've no one to answer to, then how can you forbid it?"

His smile was slow, alarmingly so, and it caused the blacks of his eyes to twinkle like quartz dazzled by sunlight. "Exactly." He rested his hands on her shoulders, and with a gentle press urged her to gaze out at the world beyond the window.

A few houses over, a small boy helped his dad rake leaves while a lady rocked in a porch swing. If Nikki really tried, maybe she could forget all about demons and angels. Maybe, just maybe, Damon Vessler was her one shot at a normal life.

"Okay," she agreed, and felt the tips of his fingers throb where they rested lightly against the T-shirt she'd slept in. Why her awareness of his reaction caused alarm, she couldn't say. She pushed the sensation aside. If Will and Mace and Raven had taught her one thing, it was that she had no right to trust her feelings.

Tears kept her company as she journeyed through her parents' life. It seemed so strange that her mom and dad could be reduced to a basement full of quiet, lonely objects. What had once brought her joy—seeing the counter filled with a mix of Mom's baking dishes on a Saturday morning—now only added to her suffering. Those things sat patiently in a cardboard box waiting for her to choose one. But she never would. Nor would her mom ever tap her finger against her chin and say, "Hmm. I think a glass pan will work best for this." Each item was just an echo of the lives they represented. And echoes became quieter and quieter as time passed.

Damon had walked her to the foot of the stairs that first morning, but when he reached for the first box, one marked *Dale's Garage*, she'd gently placed a hand on his and shook her head.

He'd understood completely. Damon had nodded, taken a breath so deep she thought he'd pop the buttons on his expensive linen shirt, and given her a quick smile that conveyed more than words. And then he left. Simple as that. She'd once thought Mace understood her, then thought Raven better fit that role. Maybe *Damon* was the only one who understood her. The only one left, anyway.

In the days that followed, life became a solemn routine of working through her parents' things, practicing her karate, and spending evenings with Damon, who gave her space, who didn't coddle, who left her alone. And that's all Nikki really needed. To be left alone. She should have contacted Krissy, but even the guilt over not letting her best friend know she was back began to fade with time. It was like that part of her life died alongside her mom and dad.

But after a few weeks, the loneliness intensified, and a tiny part of her searched for something, anything, to replace the utter nothingness. Only a month ago she'd been so surrounded by life and noise and people. Now emptiness filled her, refusing to leave her unaccompanied for long.

Something was growing within her soul, something cold and black and deadly. She found it easier and easier to get rid of items her parents once cherished. Some things she kept, for one reason or another, but the reality of sorting had hardened her. People who are dead have no use for items. People who are dead don't come back.

Damon said the lead he'd had on the killer had gone cold. "Maybe if you'd been here ..." But he'd stopped himself. He hadn't needed to say more. She understood, and it fed the black thing growing in her stomach.

She sat before a box of old books, some of which her dad had purchased as research. *A robbery. My parents died in a robbery.* A handful of antique swords, possessions they'd gained by chance, led to the forfeit of their lives. She'd give the world to have them back, yet they died over a bundle of inanimate objects. Irony was an angry witch, a witch with sharpened claws.

It didn't matter anyway. Nikki'd reached a decision. Once she was finished with her parents' things, she'd go after the guy herself. And she'd do to him every horrible thing he'd done to her parents before he stole their lives.

Chapter
19

She'd stopped doing her classwork somewhere along the way. When she told Damon it was probably time for her to get back to school, he'd shaken his head. No need. He'd done some checking and learned she had enough credits to graduate two years early. Principal Schmidt apparently hadn't liked it, but had agreed under the circumstances. After all, Damon could be quite persuasive. Nikki'd tried to voice her concerns about the credits, about going from a junior to a high school graduate, but Damon shut her down.

No more chemistry tests, no more sweaty locker rooms, no more friends. Guilt over Krissy slinked back into her mind. She hadn't even called her best friend once since she'd returned from Germany, mostly because Krissy represented everything that no longer was. And Krissy—best friend extraordinaire—would be full of questions Nikki couldn't answer now or ever. When Mace, Raven, and Vine started attending her school—oh, so many innocent days ago—it was Krissy who first encouraged Nikki to get to know them. She was something of a bridge between Nikki's two worlds. And Nikki didn't need a bridge—she needed dynamite to blast the whole thing to dust.

So when Damon informed her she'd graduated, Nikki accepted it like she had everything else in her new world. He held an intimate ceremony in her honor and gave her the title to the Ducati concept bike he'd purchased from a doctor in Florida. Life should be good. But the walls, though soaring and palatial, were closing in around her.

"I've arranged for us to spend a few days at my beach house. And I have a surprise for you when we get there," Damon said. He handed her a fresh bottle of water. He was always doing that. Encouraging her to eat, making sure she had coffee in the morning and water throughout the rest of the day.

She turned from the library window. She didn't open the window in her room anymore, as she'd lost all interest in looking over to the house that had once been her home. But here in the library, she enjoyed the vivid view of a meandering garden. It reminded her of Viennesse. "Oh?"

"Yes, I thought a change of scenery would do you good."

Sunshine, beach, sand sifting between her toes. Too bad it sounded dead.

"Thought it would cheer you. And even if the setting doesn't, the surprise is sure to."

She didn't expect to experience cheer again. Even when he gave her the keys to the bike, a prize she'd once only been able to dream of, there'd been no delight. Waking, sleeping, she was a zombie. An undead. She felt nothing. Not pain, not joy. She couldn't remember what it was to smile, to laugh. She felt old, finished.

No. The beach held no appeal. She could just as well stay right here. "Do we have any news on the killer, Damon?"

"Ah," he said. "A spark of life."

True. The desire to see the monster brought to justice was the only thing that kept her heart beating. Black vines twisted in her chest and offered perverted comfort. She accepted their embrace. It was growing easier and easier to do so.

Damon maneuvered around a table and came to rest behind her. He placed his hands on her shoulders and kneaded with a gentle touch. "I *will* find him. I gave you my word. We even have a new lead." He leaned closer. "Nikki, what are your wishes when we locate the assassin?"

She spun to face him. "I want him to suffer like my parents suffered."

He seemed to fight a smile. "It's justice. An eye for an eye. It's the only way you'll ever be able to move on. To get closure."

Deep within her a still, small voice whispered revenge was not the answer. She smothered it and clung to her dream. Because revenge—right or wrong—had become her closest companion. Oftentimes, her only companion.

And Damon was going to help her accomplish it.

Nikki threw a punch into the heavy bag hard enough to double it. Damon had arranged for her karate instructor, Sensei Coble, to continue private classes at the mansion. "I want to learn KravMaga," Nikki said. "Are you familiar with it, Sensei?"

Damon had become her sparring partner, as her ability was quickly eclipsing her sensei's. Damon was a specialist in several fighting styles and the first to mention the style taught to the Israeli Special Forces.

Concern washed across Sensei Coble's usually calm veneer. "It's a brutal style, Nikki."

She punched again, embracing the sudden sting of the heavy bag against her fist. "Exactly." She downed half a bottle of water and felt the tightness of the tape around her hand. Nikki'd stopped wearing gloves while training, but Damon insisted she cover her knuckles to avoid cutting them.

"You'll be banned from tournaments. It's too deadly."

She turned on him. The anger gurgling in her belly boiled over in one quick gush. "Do you think I care about tournaments right now?"

He stood firm, but she thought she'd seen a flash of fear in his gaze. She tried not to enjoy it. "No, not now. But eventually you'll want to compete."

"My competing days are over."

It seemed to sadden him. He stepped from the bag then held a hand towel in her direction.

She snatched it from his fingers. Blotting her face, she pressed her taped hands to her cheeks, keeping her eyes trained on her sensei.

He frowned, probably noticing she'd continued to look at him.

Never take your eyes off your enemy, Damon had taught her.

As a show of trust, Sensei Coble turned his back to her and wiped down the heavy bag with another hand towel. When finished, he held the fabric out to her and nodded to the linen basket behind her. He was trying, with little success, to be passive about the whole thing, but it tasted like a lie. His motions were a little too drawn out, his brow a bit too furrowed, his eyes a bit too suspicious.

She understood. Master and student were close as father and child. She'd enjoyed a great relationship with her sensei for years, but she'd outgrown him. And one valuable lesson

Damon had taught her was to trust no one, especially those who know your weaknesses. Nikki challenged him with a look and snatched the towel from his hand. But rather than turn and walk to the laundry basket, she took two steps backward and half-turned. Gaze still locked with Sensei's, she tossed the first towel behind her.

His eyes widened and she knew she'd hit the target. That's another thing Damon was teaching her—how to shoot. She'd never known much about guns, but in going out to his firing range she'd discovered a fresh new appreciation for firepower. And aim. She wadded the second towel and tossed it into the basket. Of course, the wastebasket and the towel were far different from the Smith and Wesson she'd been firing, but aim was aim. And hers was dead-on.

"Good shot," Sensei said.

She didn't bother hiding the smug little smile.

"You're training so hard. I thought maybe you hoped to throw yourself into competing as a sort of therapy."

She laughed without humor. A corner of tape on one hand had lifted. She absently picked at it. "Only one thing will be therapy for me." She motioned for him to steady the bag again.

With a sigh, he pressed his shoulder to the canvas. "Do you remember when you were very small and I first began training you?"

Slowly, her hands dropped. It seemed a lifetime ago. Almost as if those memories belonged to someone else and she'd watched a movie of it. "Yes, I remember."

"I made you promise that you'd stay committed. You were too young to begin training, but I sat you down—"

"Yeah," she said, irritation edging her voice. "I remember. I told you I was a person of my word, and you had me promise to continue in training and tournaments."

"Exactly. You gave me your word."

Really? Was he *really* trying to do the whole psychology thing on her? Nikki challenged him with another hard look. His eyes softened on her, causing a spasm of guilt. Why was she being so mean to Sensei Coble? He'd always wanted the best for her. She loved him, sort of thought of him as the uncle she never had. She wasn't herself right now. That's all. But as she tried to reason away her attitude, she realized *why* she was angry at him. And both the thought and its implication made her sick, maybe a little more dead inside.

She was mad at Coble because he had nothing left to teach her. What was happening to her? She wasn't the type of person to use someone only to throw them out like yesterday's pizza box. She opened her mouth to apologize, but heard herself saying, "I'll never set foot in a karate tournament again. *I give you my word.*" Driving through, she doubled the heavy bag, jolting her sensei and erasing the hope that had moments ago lit his eyes.

Without ceremony, she turned, grabbed her water bottle, and left the exercise area to search for Damon.

Lying flat on his back atop his bed, Mace quieted his mind. He prayed for wisdom and thought about Nikki. "Where are you?" he whispered to the darkness. Will had moved the boys and females back to Missouri when Raven contacted Zero and informed him Nikki'd returned, and they'd spent the last three weeks reunited at the two-story house on Pine Boulevard. All except Nikki. Which meant the house was empty as far as Mace was concerned.

Every night he'd sat at the gate to Vessler's mansion. It was all he could do to keep from leaping inside the giant house to find her. But he knew that wouldn't work. He'd even gone to the door on several occasions to inquire about her, but the answer was always the same—she wasn't taking visitors. Nikki had things to sort through, he knew, and he'd pushed her away when she needed him the most. He'd accused her of having her loyalty in the wrong place when it was Mace who'd needed the lesson.

He'd watched her kiss Raven. Big deal. Raven had confirmed it was a good-bye kiss that meant she'd made her choice. But how had he responded? By pushing her away, giving her an ultimatum. Her whole world had crashed around her and he'd done nothing but throw dirt on the stones that had once been her life.

Help me.

He sat up, eyes fully focused in the dim light. Fear clamped its fingers around his throat. The words, *Nikki's* words, had been so real, so close, he thought she might be standing in the room. She wasn't, of course. But that didn't stop his eyes from roaming the empty space. Mace mopped sweat from his forehead. The perspiration had appeared as quickly as the plea. Dread pressed as the words dissipated into the air, and he had to wonder if he'd imagined her voice.

No. He hadn't. Mace closed his eyes and drew on the strength of the One he served. Waves of peace crashed over him. "Where are you?" he asked.

Drawing deeply on the presence of all power, he lay back, tuning in to his own breathing. For a few moments there was nothing. And his very being pressed him to get up. Do something. Instead he quieted his heart and listened with his spirit.

There. Eyes closed, he saw it. An airplane turning into the setting sun, golden rays glinting off the tilted wing. A shoreline. A concrete palace sitting on the beach. A green sign. Casey Key.

Mace bolted from the bed.

He ran down the steps and flipped on the kitchen light as he entered. Will sat over a cup of coffee, reading a book. He smiled as Mace approached.

"You shouldn't read in the dark." Mace took the cup from Will's massive hand and drained the lukewarm liquid. "Yuck. You know microwaves were invented for stuff like this."

Will turned to the stove clock. "It's three in the morning. Can't sleep?"

"No. In the weeks since Nikki left, I've discovered how little sleep we actually need."

"Have you seen her at all?"

"I met her best friend Krissy for lunch a week ago. She didn't even know Nikki was back here." He shook his head and sank onto the barstool beside Will. "I've gone to the door of the mausoleum that freak Vessler calls a house, but each time I inquire someone makes an excuse. I can't seem to permeate the atmosphere around Vessler's house. It's like there's this ..."

"Evil?"

Mace nodded. "Yes. She refuses to see me. But if she'd go outside into the gardens or something, I could see her, talk to her."

"Every man must choose his path. Light, dark. Forgiveness, revenge."

"But Will, she's like a pawn in this horrific chess game." That much was true. Zero had found another mention of Nikki in an encoded computer file from Omega. The word *surgery* was paired with her name.

Will's clear-blue eyes were troubled. "I wish she was simply caught in the middle. You can only help those who want it. I feel I owe you an apology."

"What? Why?"

"Words hold the power of life and death. It is what we speak that can rescue ... or condemn us."

Mace felt for Will. So much wisdom confined in a being who's bound to the earth. "I'm not really following you, Will."

"I wished Nikki gone."

"You're not a genie, so I don't think that's possible."

"Mace." Will pivoted and dropped a giant hand onto Mace's shoulder. "I was concerned for you—about your feelings for her. And that concern caused my faith to falter. The Throne's judgment came into question and the seed of my fear grew."

Heart pounding, Mace tried to swallow. "Did you tell Nikki to leave?"

Will brushed a hand through the air. "No. Of course not. But in my heart I wished you'd never been called to this journey."

Mace tried to fight the anger now growing within him. "That's not your decision to make."

"I know. Believe me, I've been scolded for it." Will ran a hand through his curly hair. "So often I don't understand the Throne's decisions. His plan is perfect. It is only we who get in the way. And that's what I did. I just hope it can be repaired. The last time I got in the way of the plan, a human died. I was banished for it."

"Well, confession is good for the soul, right? Or as you like to put it, 'It ain't over 'til it's over.' Zero is still looking for a way to link Vessler to Omega. If he finds it, Nikki will know what her godfather really is."

"*If* that's what he is. We have no proof."

Mace nodded in reluctant agreement.

A slow smile formed on Will's face. "I should have warned you about ... love. But I must admit, I don't understand attraction between sexes."

Mace slapped Will on the back. "Maybe I should have warned *you*."

Will sighed. "You said Nikki was a pawn. If that were true, this journey would be much less complicated."

Mace shook his head. "What role do you think she plays?" When Will failed to answer, Mace's voice rose. "What role do you think she plays, Will?"

"Not that of a pawn. Possibly that of the queen." He paused. "I see her slipping. You must reach her, Mace. So much rests on the edge of the blade."

Mace nodded. "And the blade is already tipped in the wrong direction?"

"Yes, thanks to my interference and lack of faith. This could have eternal consequences for countless people. But right now, my thoughts dwell with Nikki. Saving her."

"I'm working on that."

"What do you plan to do?" Will shoved back from the counter.

"Go to Casey Key. As soon as I figure out where it's located."

Will frowned. "I don't know." He thought a moment. "And why?"

"I think she's going there, or maybe she's already arrived. Wait a minute," Mace said with a flat stare. "You've lived for millennia and you don't know where Casey Key is located?"

He shrugged. "Sorry. Is it in Florida?"

Mace grabbed his laptop from the kitchen table. "Let's find out."

Within a few minutes, they discovered Casey Key was a five-mile stretch of beachfront on Florida's Gulf Coast. Mace read, "Pristine and exclusive, it's touted as one of the most beautiful in the country. If one so chose, they could purchase a one acre piece of beachfront for a mere $3.8 million."

"Pricey." Will whistled.

"Just the kind of place a snake like Vessler would hide."

"You have no love lost for the man, do you?" Will scratched his head. "I have to admit, I never understood that phrase. Just seems like a confusing way of saying, 'I don't like him.'"

Mace closed the laptop. "No love lost. I don't like him. I don't trust him. Take your pick. Each one fits Vessler."

"How does he play into this journey, Mace?"

"I'm not sure, but the longer I spend away from Nikki, the more danger I feel she's in."

"I've sensed no attacks from the supernatural realm," Will said.

"Exactly. Don't you think that's weird? When we first met Nikki, both humans and demons were after her. Then her parents died at the hands of a thief, not to mention her dog was killed by a hell hound. Now nothing."

"What are you suggesting?"

"That she's played right into the enemy's hands. If not, he'd be attacking her. What do you see, Will? Is she physically in danger, or is the danger actually worse than that?" Mace asked.

"Sometimes heaven whispers and I'm alerted to physical attacks. I'm not told everything, Mace. Just bits and pieces, scattered like salt across a table. And with my recent breach of faith in the One, my vision is dim."

"What about psychological attacks?" Mace said.

"What do you mean?"

"I think Vessler is poisoning her mind. At the police station—back after her parents were killed—I heard him whisper to her that he would find the killer. He'd make the man pay. I think the thought of avenging her parents could be blinding Nikki to everything else. Hate is a deadly enemy to fight."

Will nodded. "Hate has only one nemesis able to conquer it."

"What's that?"

"Love. Go to her, Mace. Bring her back into the light."

Chapter
20

"Surprise!" Krissy screamed, jumping from behind the drapes and landing on the bed.

"What?" Nikki sat up, rubbing the sleep from her eyes. "Krissy? How—how'd you get here?"

"I snuck in with your breakfast."

Nikki had arrived on Casey Key late the night before, and Damon sent her directly to bed. Exhausted, she hadn't argued. Waking in a sundrenched room infused with the scent of coffee, warm blueberry muffins, and saltwater boosted her dismal outlook somewhat. A petite woman dressed in a black-and-white uniform had knocked gently a few minutes ago, deposited breakfast in the nook, and pulled the gigantic shade open. *But the best friend springing up and down like Tigger Junior on the corner of the bed must be ... a mirage?* Nikki stared at the door, the curtain where Krissy'd been hiding, and then at her friend.

"Don't look so befuddled. We're going to have so much fun!"

Krissy bounced, screamed, clapped, hugged her, and bounced some more.

Did she just say befuddled? Nikki reached to hug her again, since she'd missed the first one. Krissy *felt* real enough. And no self-respecting figment of one's imagination would use a word like befuddled. Yes, this *must* be her best friend. "What are you doing here?"

"Mr. Vessler didn't want you to be here alone, and he'll be gone for a couple of days. So, ta-da! Best-friend weekend. Yay! I've been here for three days."

"What?"

Krissy's eyes rounded. "Yeah, I know, right? Crazy. Mr. Vessler actually owns the company my mom works for. Isn't that bizarre? But I mean, not *that* weird, right? Seeing as he owns half the world."

Nikki rubbed her eyes again as if continuing to do so would clear things.

Krissy cocked her head. "Four days ago, he shows up at my house and says he wants to bring you and me here, and my parents are like, 'Sorry, no way are we sending our daughter, blah, blah, blah.'" Krissy hopped up and went to the breakfast tray, grabbed a strawberry from the selection of fruit, and popped it into her mouth. Talking between chews, she continued. "Within less than an hour, he'd arranged for my mom to have a few days off, *and* my dad is working on a real-estate deal for him. My dad is brokering the *very* property Mr. Vessler wants to purchase." She pumped her fist. "Oh, yeah, Dad will be the listing *and* selling agent for the half-million dollar property, so that doubles his commission. Do I look tan?" She did a pirouette.

"You look gorgeous," Nikki responded, but her heart thudded. Everything—abso-stinkin-lutely *every little thing*—worked out the way Damon orchestrated. The realization burned like a chili pepper, though she didn't know why. After all, this entire trip and everything that went into it was for her. At the same time, she knew the exact reason Damon's dealings rankled her. If he couldn't have something, he'd just manipulate things, people, and circumstances to his liking. He was a puppet master and the rest of the world his wooden dolls. Except her. He treated her like a queen. Even called her *my lady.* Well, Nikki knew Krissy's parents, and they'd never send her off with some strange guy, no matter how handsome, how charming, how irresistible, or how rich. She found a trace of comfort in that fact.

Nikki shrugged out of the covers and met her friend at the silver breakfast tray. She needed to sit Krissy Doll's folks down and have a chat with them. Find out what they thought of Damon, what they *really* thought. "Can your mom and dad meet us up here for breakfast? We can sit out on my balcony."

"Uh, that would be difficult, because they're on a plane right now headed home."

A slow molasses drip of alarm released into Nikki's body.

Krissy tipped out her bottom lip. "Don't be sad, Nikki. You're gonna love the beach house. This is the kind of place we've always dreamed about."

Was it? Nikki no longer remembered her dreams. She'd become more of a nightmare kind of girl lately.

Krissy was chatting on like one of those chipmunk characters that were supposed to be adorable, but who just gave Nikki a headache. "Remember when I had that ridiculous crush on Joe Jonas and you— Well, you really didn't ever crush on anybody except maybe Josh Nolens, but we'd talk about awesome houses in the Hills and throwing parties for celebrities."

225

"Those fantasies were all yours, Krissy. Not mine." And it irritated her that Krissy had suggested she'd sat around fantasizing about rock stars and living in California. She wanted to tell her to shut up. Just *shut up*. But that would hardly be a proper greeting. Warranted, maybe, but hardly proper.

As the one-sided conversation rambled on, Nikki just couldn't wrap her mind around the fact that Krissy's parents left. "Why didn't your mom and dad stay?" She took Krissy by the wrist just as her friend turned to pour coffee. She repeated a little louder, "Krissy, why didn't your parents stay?" She shook her arm.

"Ouch," Krissy yelled as hot coffee splashed onto both their hands.

"I— I'm sorry." Nikki sank her free hand into a goblet of ice water and grabbed a handful of cubes from the bottom. She pressed them to her friend's burn.

"The coffee got you too," Krissy said, pointing to the dark droplets on Nikki's other hand.

"Your hand's going to blister." Nikki moved the ice to a spot where bright-red skin began to pucker on Krissy's wrist.

"Not yours."

Nikki angled her hand. Where the coffee had splashed, there was nothing. Not even a tinge of discoloration. She didn't even remember feeling the hot liquid hit her skin.

Krissy shrugged. "No surprise. I've been in the sun for three days, so my skin is probably a little sensitive. And as far as my parents, Mr. Vessler thought it would make you sad because your parents are—"

"Dead," Nikki finished for her. "Because they were murdered."

Krissy's eyes widened. "So, well, he thought I should stay

and they should go. His assistant Betty is here with us as an adult chaperone and there's the, um, staff." Her smile returned in full force. "He's like the most *amazing* godfather."

"So it would seem," Nikki mumbled and split her alarm between Krissy's parents and her over-the-top godfather. A voice in her head whispered that cages came in all shapes and sizes.

The dark ocean churned beneath her balcony.

She and Krissy had spent the day catching up, since Nikki'd refused to see her in Missouri—a fact that mortified her now, but she reasoned she'd had to work through her parent's belongings. There'd only been time and energy for them, no one else. Except Damon. Strangely, Krissy hadn't complained or asked why; she just hugged Nikki over and over and told her she missed her. Now the two of them sat before the setting sun watching the waves cascade and roll onto the shore.

When he appeared, Nikki's breath caught. Without meaning to, she seized the railing and leaned toward where he stood like a Greek god highlighted against the glistening sea. Perhaps even Titus, emerging from the water to claim his bride. Fifty yards below, she felt his eyes on her. Mace looked so much like a wounded angel, her soul cried.

Restraining her emotions, Nikki turned to her friend. "What's he doing here?" She released her grip on the rail and took a few cautious steps back, crashing into the balcony door.

"I don't know, Nikki." Krissy said. "But I think it means Mace loves you."

"What do you know about it?" Nikki spat, and was instantly

troubled by her response. "I'm sorry. I don't know why I said that." Nikki searched her best friend's face for the unforgiving stare she was sure to find.

Instead, a wide smile enlivened her features. "It's okay, Nikki."

Come to me, Nikki.

The sound of his voice, though barely a whisper, crashed through all those barbed wire fences she'd been constructing. Bombarded with memories of him, her chest ached from the weight. Images danced through her mind like embers from a campfire, but each landed and burned. And that, *that right there*, was the problem. Burning holes in an already compromised nucleus, while she was courting more punctures to a damaged core. How stupid could she be? There was only a portion of her heart left. Did she really intend to ice-pick the rest into oblivion?

She started to turn toward her room.

No. Come to me. He must have sensed her intention. *Of course he did.*

He took a step toward her. *Don't run away, Nikki. You're too strong to run.*

Krissy grabbed her shoulders. "What's wrong with you?"

Nikki's eyes pleaded with her friend. How could she explain? With no ally, with no one to share her pain, her resolve started to crumble. If she hadn't left him at Viennesse, maybe things would be okay now. But *Mace* had been the one to walk away, not her. Maybe not physically, though hadn't he done just that when they argued in his room at the castle? She loved him. It barely mattered. "I can't be with him. Not the way my heart tells me to."

"But he cares for you. You need him right now, Nik."

The hard box that kept Nikki's fragmented heart safe began to shut. "It's easy for people to talk about *right now* when they have a future."

Krissy's innocent eyes clouded.

"You have a family, Krissy. People to love you. You have a *future!*" she screamed.

"Mr. Vessler is going to give you a great future. He told my mom and dad he'll see that you go to the best college. Have every opportunity. Work in whatever field you want."

At what cost? The certainty of more pain confronted her. Crossing her arms, she squeezed, hanging onto what warmth remained inside her body. Hanging on to her strength.

"Nikki, Mace *loves* you."

Everyone who loves me dies. She choked on the thought. It took her by surprise and, unguarded, slid into her being. She had to make Krissy understand. Nikki couldn't divulge the truth, so she opted for practicality. "But his family moves, Krissy. One day soon, they'll leave. And he'll have to go. One more thing I love will be stolen from me. How many losses can I survive? One more?" She dragged Krissy inside. "I can't take the chance." She threw one last look out the balcony's glass door, where Mace still stood waiting. "It would destroy both of us." Eyes still on his face—she could see it incredibly clearly, even from the distance—she locked the patio door.

I won't give up filtered to her through the glass.

Later, while she lay in bed, the voice returned. *I'm still here.*

She shoved the pillow onto her face and pressed. But the battle was over before it began. She'd go to him. She had to.

Once she'd known he'd arrived, he'd consumed her thoughts. And that realization only added to her confusion.

Rising from bed, she pulled a chenille robe around her body. Though dressed in sweats and a T-shirt, the robe offered an extra layer of cover. Cover she needed right now. She swung the doors open and stepped onto her private balcony overlooking the sparkling water.

The breeze tugged her hair, gently at first, then intensifying as she stepped out.

He wasn't at the water's edge. She panicked until she heard the rustle of feathers beside her. Nikki turned slowly, facing Mace just as he tucked his wings behind him. He'd touched down near the banister and waited.

She read no emotion on his face, which was good. For a moment, she just needed to take him in. No smiles, no frowns, no greetings. They understood each other that way. His face was smooth and the moon played in his eyes, sending sparks toward her. The muscle in his jaw tightened and his throat made a sound that was neither a cough nor a swallow but somehow both. Then she saw it—the tear in the corner of one of those beautiful cerulean eyes.

And it undid her. Nikki's emotions surged to meet his. Relief, sorrow, joy all crashed together. When he opened his arms, the feelings collided in a desperate release of all the tension and fear she'd harbored. She tumbled into his waiting embrace.

He kissed her hair, her cheeks, her jaw. His hands roamed across her back as if making sure she wasn't a figment of his imagination. Had his mind orchestrated this moment? Played it over and over so many times he couldn't trust if it was really happening or if it was just another of a thousand fantasies?

He pressed against her as if his forward momentum alone held the power to keep her forever. Step by step, he backed her to the balcony wall. Once there, he whispered, "Nikki," capturing her face. He paled as he searched her. She knew of the dark circles that hung beneath her eyes, making even her irises appear darker. And then he was confessing, words pouring forth in a rush of desperation. "I'm so sorry for what I put you through. I never should have talked to you like I did." Hands cradled her jaw. "You've been through so much, and I added to it with my stupid jealousy. I have a fallen nature, Nikki. One I'd like to forget, but it prods me sometimes, pushes me. Can you ever forgive me?"

She nodded, her cheeks rubbing against the smooth skin of his palms. "I didn't want to see you," she said, throat closing around each word. "I don't want to lose you. Isn't that horrible? Isn't that awful? Being with me would cost you eternity, and I'm worried about myself. Nothing makes sense anymore."

"This does." Cautiously, he tilted toward her lips.

She drowned in the Mediterranean-blue gaze she'd come to love. His eyes closed, dark lashes shadowing his cheeks. When his mouth lightly feathered against hers, she felt like her body could float away. He tasted sweet, like powdered sugar, her favorite ingredient when baking. Mace was her perfect ingredient, his mouth against hers conjuring warm thoughts of a home, a promise, a recipe for life.

But that was no more real than the hope of her ever having a normal life again. Desperation lit a fuse inside her. She broke the kiss. "Promise me something," she rasped.

"Anything." His fingers threaded into her hair, combing through methodically as if making up for the time they'd lost. When he reached the ends of the strands, his hands slipped to her temples and began the trek again, soothing her with each stroke.

Nikki sank into his touch. "Mace, I'm so perplexed about everything. Tonight, can we just *be*? Promise me we won't talk about tomorrow or what will happen to us." She squeezed her eyes shut. "I know it's wrong, but can we just forget all the horrible things we're involved in?" The words caught in a throat too hoarse to cry anymore.

"Nikki, I'll give you the moon if you ask. Tonight is yours. Where do you want to go? What do you want to see? I'll fly you to Europe so you can watch the sunrise, or we'll go to where it's setting. Whatever will make you happy, I'll make it happen."

To fly across the ocean on angel's wings. To watch the sunrise atop the Eiffel tower. "Anything? Anywhere?" she said.

"Anything you want."

She pressed into the rock-hard muscles of his chest. "I just want you, Mace."

And as the moon smiled down at the tumbling sea, Nikki and Mace held each other with the promise of right now the only dream they dared hope for. She felt like their emotions ignited the space around them, seeping into the wooden slats of the balcony, drifting on the ocean's constant rush, replacing the atmosphere of doubt with that of purest love. If she only lived another day, she'd die with the knowledge that she'd felt something this strong. Though every obstacle remained in their way, love had conquered. Sliding from his embrace, she slipped into her bedroom and emerged with her sketchbook and a charcoal pencil. "Do something for me?" she asked, words soft as a kitten's purr.

A slow smile spread across his face. "Yes?"

"Take off your shirt and show me your wings. You still owe me."

His brow arched, but he obeyed, drawing his shirt up and over his head to reveal the smooth muscled flesh beneath. With one great snap, his wings flew open, catching her by surprise.

White with tiny flecks of gray, they stretched out and into the air. Caught by the ocean wind, they danced, pushing against the current. Mace's body flexed to hold him on the balcony. The wind grabbed with persistence, causing the muscles in his chest and arms to strain and enlarge. He nodded to the sketchbook. "You sure that's safe?"

"Mm-hmm." Her cheeks were fire hot.

A grin toyed at his mouth.

"It's safe. Will taught me how to tell when I'm tapping into the other realm. As long as I work slowly and I'm careful, it'll be fine."

A rakish smile replaced the playful grin. "Work slowly, huh?"

"Yeah, you'll just have to stay like that for a while."

"An angel's work is never done."

"You'll survive."

Nikki forced her gaze to her sketchbook. Flipping past drawings, she stopped at a blank page. With warmth pooling in her stomach, she pulled a steadying breath and began to draw. He would be her masterpiece.

Chapter
21

"What's it like when Halflings fall in love?" Nikki asked, snuggled up against Mace on a deck chair. Once she'd finished her drawing, they'd settled onto a cushioned seat by the water. Waves rolled toward them, pushed along by the current just like the two of them had been pushed. Together, apart, then back again.

Mace really did stabilize her world. He truly was the one who made everything make sense. With Raven, she wanted to run away. But Mace forced her to face the hard, unforgiving truth head-on. And there was a strength in that she couldn't deny.

Mace maneuvered his head to look at her face.

She smiled. "It must be amazing."

He kissed her forehead. "Do you know much about eagles?"

She shook her head.

He leaned back against the cushion. "Eagles mate for life. But before they do, they go through this elaborate ritual where the female soars to these amazing heights."

"She's showing off for him?" Nikki asked.

"No, she wants to make sure he's worthy. She carries a stick high into the air and drops it." His fingertips traced her arm.

She quivered. "And?"

"He has to catch it."

"Sounds simple enough." She moved just enough to press the length of her leg against his.

"That's just the beginning. She chooses another stick and another." Mace angled and kissed the side of her head. "Until finally she picks a tree branch that weighs the same as her."

"And she drops it?" Nikki asked.

"Yes."

"Why?"

He pivoted to look at her. "Because every female should know that the mate she chooses can catch her if she falls." Then his arms were there, all around her, holding her, protecting her. That's what Mace did. Always. And she'd not made his job easy. Over and over she'd fallen, and over and over he'd been there.

As if he heard her thoughts, he whispered, "I'll catch you, Nikki."

She nuzzled deeper into him, drawing his scent into her nose. "You already did."

Some horrible, irritating thing was pulling at her arm. She moaned before realizing it was Mace, and that she must have dozed off. She squeezed her eyes shut when he tried to rouse her.

"Come on," he said. "I want to show you something."

"Can't it wait until … oh, say, next year?" she teased.

"We've been out here on the deck for two hours."

For all she cared, time could stop.

"And, no, it can't wait until next year." He rose and tugged her dead weight.

"Fine," she said in a breathy whisper. "Where are you taking me?"

"To watch the eagles."

Her interest piqued, she lumbered off the chair.

Once standing, Mace caught her in a firm hold. A sexy smile crossed his face. "Hang on," he said, and unfurled his wings and leapt. From above she could perceive the earth below, but as if through a veil. A golden hue tinted everything. Other times she'd flown, they'd been moving at such a phenomenal speed her eyes hadn't adjusted in time to see anything.

But now they watched it through a dazzling fog. Cities came into view and disappeared as they passed.

Sometimes Mace beat his powerful wings, body tensing with each push. But most of their time was spent soaring on the thermal drafts. She spotted a city below. Gatherings of lights illuminated various portions until it appeared to be made up of miners with their oil lamps huddled together. "What is that?" she asked, awed by the light so beautiful she wanted to stare at it forever.

"Prayers," he said.

"What?"

He nodded below. "The youth groups in that city are holding an all-night prayer vigil."

Upon closer inspection, she realized the gatherings of lights were concentrated within buildings, many of which sported crosses on the rooftops. The golden lights were visible *through* the buildings.

"What you're seeing are their prayers rising to the Throne."

"Wow. Does it … you know, make a difference?"

He scanned the area beneath them. "It can change a city. If caught, it can change a state, even a nation."

She started to ask him what he meant by *caught*, but she noticed he'd slowed as he angled toward a distant mountaintop.

She didn't know how long they'd flown. She didn't care; time seemed so inconsequential now. They touched down on a flattened rock with a natural seat carved into the stone.

He snapped his wings shut and gestured for her to sit. "Do you need me to build you a fire? I realize it's a little cooler here."

"Not if you sit by me. Keep me warm?"

He sank into the seat and pulled her close. "Look." He nodded toward another rock face.

Two majestic eagles soared and dipped in the sky as the sun began to peek over a mountaintop near them.

Awestruck, Nikki gasped when the first bird climbed higher and higher. When the eagle dropped a stick, the other sailed on the wind to capture it. The dance continued as sticks became branches. As Mace had said, the final limb was so heavy, the female seemed barely able to lift it. Once in flight, she carried it to an incredibly high point.

Mace whispered against her hair. "Look closer, Nikki."

She flashed a frown, but concentrated.

"Closer," he encouraged.

She focused her attention on the eagles as the female dropped the tree limb. "Halflings," she whispered almost reverently. Her eyes widened, blinked, then widened again. "They're actually Halflings."

The branch plummeted toward the earth. Mace pointed. "The male must wait until the last possible moment before capturing this one."

But Nikki could barely listen, and couldn't move. The limb rolled and tumbled closer to the ground. Just behind it, a male Halfling with wings tucked in rocketed like a bullet. He gathered speed until he was only a blur, gaining on the branch as he dropped.

Her hands shot up to cover most of her face. "Will he make it?"

But Mace wouldn't let her hide. He grabbed her hands and dragged them from her eyes. "Watch and see."

After excruciating moments, and just before the branch crashed into the rocky ground, the male's wings cracked open as he snagged the limb.

Nikki released the breath she'd been holding.

Meeting in the air, the two Halflings tumbled into one another's arms, drifting, climbing, falling. "It's beautiful," she said. *It's something I can never give you.* But she forced the thought from her mind. Tonight was perfect, tomorrow seemed forever away, even if the sun was rising near them.

"I've never seen anything like it."

"Me either."

She pushed back to look at his face.

"Just heard the stories." His eyes followed a trail to the Halflings. "I didn't realize it would be so …"

"Amazing," she finished for him.

"Yeah." But there was something there. Some irritating little worm boring into their perfect night. Nikki recognized it as reality and rejected it with fierce determination. Nothing would steal her perfect night. It might be the only one she got.

238

Mace touched down on her balcony and hugged her.

Nikki snagged her water from beside the lawn chair and chugged the whole thing. "So thirsty these days," she said.

Faking an English accent, he bowed. "Other than water, did the evening meet your expectations, my lady?"

She frowned. *My lady.* Damon's special nickname.

Damon. His name officially brought reality crashing down. What was she doing? What was she thinking? She'd reacted carelessly. Watching the Halflings only solidified the stupidity of her actions. She slid a hand through her hair. "Everything is so confusing right now." Nikki hugged the bottle like it was a lifeline.

Mace frowned.

The last month flashed like fireworks in her mind. She had a job to do. She had to find the man who killed her parents. Then, only then, could she move on to a life with ... What? With Mace? No, certainly not that. She couldn't give him what he needed. Damon was the only hope of a real life, one separate from boys with wings, and eagles ... and love.

Mace noticed the change in her. His eyes sharpened.

"I'm confused," she repeated, and placed her palm against her throbbing temple. "Everything is ... wrong."

Mace placed a hand on her arm, and she could feel the panic coursing through him. "No, Nikki. It's not. We'll find a way to be together."

Was it possible? She didn't see how. Maybe once she settled the score for her parents, but not now. She wouldn't ask Mace to trek that path with her. It would definitely destroy him. Wasn't it destroying her bit by bit, wearing away her conscience like a poison corroding her emotions? "This was a mistake," she said.

"A mistake? How can you say that?" His fingers tightened. "Everything is right when we're together."

"No," she pulled from his grasp. "The only time I feel all right is when I'm with Damon. He makes everything better."

"Nikki, *don't* trust Damon Vessler."

She felt her eyes harden. "Damon protected me."

"I'm telling you, he's an evil man. And I'm the one who can protect you."

Her chin jutted forward. "We're about to find out who killed my parents. Once we've avenged their deaths—" Damon told her she'd never be able to move on without closure. That the mystery of their deaths would cripple her. She *had* to find the killer.

"Nikki, do you hear yourself? The path of revenge only leads to death. Revenge harbors hatred, and hate destroys everything. You're only hurting yourself by continuing this. You can't bring your parents back."

Resolve overrode the pain in her eyes while vengeance wrapped around her. If she spoke the words rising to the surface, they would destroy any hope of a relationship with Mace. Ever. But if he kept talking, he might convince her the risk was worth it. Clenching her teeth, she barreled on. "And you didn't protect them."

His hands dropped. As if physically pushed, he stumbled back. "What?"

She let her fury gush forth. "You could have protected them if you'd wanted to."

So much hurt wafted from him, she had to step back for fear of being caught in its orbit. "No," he shook his head. "I didn't know."

She swallowed. She had to, because if she didn't, she'd

vomit. *He'll survive*, she assured herself. *Mace is a survivor.* So she continued, pushing him to the absolute brink. "I'll never forgive you for it. You didn't save them, Mace." Piece by piece, her heart was cracking. "And I don't need you to save me. For the first time I realize I have to face things on my own. When I return home, I'm moving out of Damon's mansion and back into my own house, but I don't want you there. I need you to stay away."

His tone became a plea. "Nikki, listen to me. We can't cross a human's will. If you say I can't come onto your property, I won't be able to. No matter what." Everything in him pleaded. His eyes, his body language. "Take it back, baby."

"Why? It's what I want." Her head tilted defiantly. "And if you remember, you promised earlier to give me whatever I want." She pulled from his touch and disappeared into the room.

When she was sure he'd gone, Nikki collapsed onto the bed, trying to erase the picture of him from her mind. Lying there, she understood what it meant to be heartless.

Two days later, she settled in at the home she'd grown up in, but Damon had bought new furniture for the space. Good thing, because she'd gotten rid of most of her parents' belongings. "You don't need anyone to raise you, since you're grown," Damon had told her. She agreed. He'd said she was free to choose between living at the mansion with him or at her own house with a full staff. She'd almost laughed. How much of a staff could one teenager in a three-bedroom ranch house need?

Despite her wishes, Mace appeared every few hours and

stood at the edge of her property. She could feel his presence. When he drew near, her chest ached. Every. Single. Time. And she hated him for that. Or maybe she hated herself. Though she couldn't help it. She felt strangely disconnected to her past, like it wasn't her own. Again, her memories seemed more like a long, sad movie than reality.

The following morning, Damon arrived with a bouquet of fresh flowers. He handed them to the housekeeper and barked for her to put them in water. He'd also brought a case of the imported water she'd grown so fond of. Crossing the living room, he took Nikki's hands in his. "Are you settling in, my lady?"

"I am." But his grasp sent a cold chill through her.

Making sure the housekeeper had disappeared into the kitchen, he grinned. "We found him."

"What?" The whoosh of anxiety took her by surprise.

"The man responsible. He had your father's wallet, your mother's credit cards, and the case of swords. He'd sold one for three hundred dollars, and was attempting to sell the others on eBay when we found him."

Anguish and disgust fueled her hostility. *My parents' lives reduced to a few hundred dollars and a classified on the Internet.* "There's no justice."

"Worse than that, a police officer who's a friend of mine says the evidence is circumstantial. If turned over to the authorities, he'll likely go free."

"No!"

"We have to make our own justice, Nikki. I can order a kill on him, but—"

"But what?" she insisted.

His black eyes cooled. "Nikki, you need to make this kill."

"What?" She grabbed his arm for support and detested her reaction; so filled with weakness. Hadn't she wanted that very thing? Hadn't she invested the last month into training to do exactly what Damon proposed? But now that the opportunity arose, she couldn't imagine taking a life, even one that didn't deserve to continue.

Damon's suggesting it himself also seemed wrong. She'd kept quiet about her desire for revenge, fearing Damon would try to talk her out of it. Instead, he *suggested* it. Shouldn't he want to protect her? Seriously, what kind of man urges a seventeen-year-old to kill someone? Maybe she'd misunderstood. He couldn't have said what she thought.

Then he repeated it. "You need to make this kill—to set you free. Then you can move on. It'll all be over."

On the outside her emotions were raw and bleeding and eager, but far deeper she knew she couldn't murder. It just wasn't in her. She shook her head. "No," she mumbled. "I don't think I can."

His once-gentle touch became painful. "You can! Think about them, Nikki. Your mom and dad, robbed of the chance to see you graduate. Imagine your wedding day, with no father to walk you down the aisle. This man has taken everything from you."

Her teeth clenched while visions of a familyless life played in her head. Everything she loved, stolen from her by someone who deserved to die.

Damon slid her hands into his. "Come outside with me, Nikki," he purred. "Show me what you can do."

His words pounded in her head, a drumbeat growing in intensity. Joining the anger she already felt, her emotions coalesced into a frenzied desire to destroy the monster who'd shattered her world. She allowed him to lead her outside. With each step, blackness hovered at the edges of her vision, darkening the boundaries, but the center was in sharp focus.

Once on the lawn, Damon caressed her hair. "You know my ability as an opponent?"

She nodded, trying to separate his words—so soft, so caring—from the fury burning in his eyes. "There is none better."

"Try to kill me. You won't succeed, but you have to let it turn. Forget about my life. Only see the killer. Do it for your parents, Nikki. Do it for yourself."

She blindly obeyed by raising her hands and sliding into a fighting stance. An image of her parents' attacker emerged in her mind. Nikki jumped and landed a front kick to his chest.

Damon reeled back, but his quick reflexes made it appear as if she'd never made contact. "Good girl."

Something deep within churned. Her reason dimmed like a streetlamp that had outlived its life span, flickering before finally going out. Once it had, a tarlike loathing inched through her, suffocating every desire to preserve life.

The killer stood before her now. His smile a sickening gloss of hate. His smug posture, tilted head, his coaching her like she was a first-year karate student. She tuned in to the fury driving her, and it was glorious. More vivid than the most beautiful of paintings, sweeter than the choicest of fruit. She faked a punch, spun, and connected a ridge hand to his head. His skin compressed as she felt bone, then sliced as her fingernail slit his cheek.

Seeing the bright crimson beginning to leak, she dropped her hands, and the shadowy veil fell from her eyes. *What am I doing?*

When she retreated, Damon struck and pain exploded

244

across her face, then down her neck as her head snapped back violently.

"You gotta do better than that," he scoffed, his tone condescending. "Poor little fatherless girl," he continued to taunt, shoving her to the ground. She landed with a thud. He hovered above her and screamed, "Come on, Nikki. Try to kill me. Pretend I'm him. Because I did it. I killed them."

Calm descended on her, like the quiet assurance she'd experienced whenever jumping off the high dive. *Water is below, and soon it will swallow me.*

"And you know what?" He leaned within a breath of her face. "I loved it. The way your father pleaded for your mother's life. The way she cried and called out your name. She was calling for you, Nikki. You could have saved them if you'd been there."

Her bent fingers flew out and grabbed his pompous, gelled hair. She entwined her digits and jerked his head down while using her legs to fling him over her head.

He landed flat on his back, air hissing from his lungs.

Nikki jumped up and had to suppress a feeling of giddiness rising in her throat. *Do you want to see what else I can do, Mr. Vessler?*

He gasped for air as she pressed her foot into his chest. The toes of her tennis shoes dug into his throat. "The thing about having the air knocked from you is that if enough pressure is then applied, it will collapse your lungs," she said with soft, controlled words. "Eventually your respiratory system will shut down." She pressed harder. "I bet you didn't know that."

His arms flailed as he attempted to suck gasps of oxygen, but she made sure his efforts were in vain. Vessler's face reddened.

She pressed a little harder.

His eyes bulged.

Nikki fisted her hand. She had no intention of waiting until *eventually*. One blow to the throat—that was all it would take to stop the pathetic sucking and wheezing sounds. She drew back, ready to finish him. And she would have if she hadn't heard the voice.

Chapter
22

"Nikki, no!" Mace yelled as he touched down at the edge of her yard. He started to step, but couldn't. She'd ordered him to stay off her property.

At least his interruption gave Vessler just enough time to squirm from under her grasp and lumber to his feet. As much as Mace hated to see the guy live, watching the girl he loved commit murder was far worse.

Nikki, tell me to come and save you, Mace pleaded.

She looked across the lawn to him but only shook her head. *I'm already dead.*

While her attention was on Mace, Vessler, who'd regained a bit of breath, seized the moment and punched her in the stomach.

She doubled over.

Nikki. Don't give in.

Vessler swept her leg, causing her to land on her knees.

Raven appeared beside Mace and started to step onto the

property. "No." Mace stopped him after a moment's shock. Raven must have seen him leave in a hurry and followed. "She's ordered us to stay back."

Raven's weight shifted from side to side. "You, maybe. She'll die." His foot moved onto the blades of grass.

Mace grabbed him and dragged him back. "If you cross her will, you'll disappear from this journey." He shook him. "Raven, you know that."

Turning their attention to the center of the bright-green lawn, they watched helplessly.

While Nikki was on her knees, Vessler grabbed a handful of hair along her hairline. As she started to writhe he punched her in the kidney then jerked her head back to examine her face.

Her eyes met Mace's across the lawn. He watched the gold in them darken, deepening almost to black. He staggered, grabbed Raven for support. *She can't be ... Will said it would be impossible to hide.*

Damon slowly fisted his hand.

Nearly black eyes shone on Nikki's face.

Raven stammered, "She's a ..."

"She's a Halfling."

Mace turned to Raven, and the expression on his face confirmed they were thinking the same thing. "That means she's not human, and we don't have to honor her free will." The Lost Boys charged onto the lawn.

Mace caught Nikki before she could hit the ground.

Leave it to Lover Boy to give me the dirty work. Raven dove on top of Vessler. Like an animal, he attacked him, sinking deep blows wherever he found an opening.

At one point it seemed Vessler may obtain the advantage. As Raven shifted in an attempt to regain the upper hand, he noticed Mace was laying Nikki softly in the grass and preparing to enter the fray.

One man should be no match for two Halflings. For that matter, one dozen men wouldn't be able to overcome *one* Halfling. Vessler's brute strength and fighting ability surprised them both. Still, he offered opposition only for a fleeting moment. Raven stood and took control once more, prompting Mace to return to Nikki and lift her into his arms. Not that she seemed to notice her pretty little boyfriend had trotted back: she was staring at the fight.

And that was all he needed to know. "You tried to turn her," Raven screamed, holding Vessler by the now-bloody lapels of his expensive Italian shirt.

Vessler's arms dangled lifelessly at his sides.

"What are you?" Spit flew from Raven's mouth as he shook the man. *How did one human almost take the advantage in a fight against me?*

Vessler's head bobbed forward, back, forward, back, but no words formed on his lips.

Raven searched his face for an answer.

Vessler licked his swollen, bloody mouth. "She belongs to me."

The choked words almost made Raven's vision go red. He grabbed the freak's throat and squeezed. "We belong to no one," he hissed.

"I …" he gasped. "I made her."

The human throat could only sustain a limited amount of pressure before collapsing. Raven's fingers dug into the tender flesh, enjoying the feel of muscle, tendons. Within Vessler's veins a ball of blood attempted to force its way beyond Raven's grip, but he denied it access.

"Wait," Vessler rasped, his eyes widened in fear. "I can offer you the world." His jittering gaze darted to Nikki, now in Mace's arms.

Reluctantly, Raven followed his trail for a moment.

"Please." Vessler's hand came to rest on Raven's, fingers trying to pry free, though his voice was getting weaker. "I can offer you ... her."

For an involuntary instant, Raven's fingers loosened.

Vessler's gaze softened. "That's all you really want, isn't it? Don't you deserve her? She loves you—she told me she did. I can make it so the two of you live a long life together."

Raven tried to keep his mind from traveling that road, but it wasn't a choice he could make. Him and Nikki. Together. Forever. But rather than loosen further, his grip tightened. He lifted Vessler off the ground. "Are you also offering thirty pieces of silver?" Straightening his arm, he flung the demented freak down. As he was ready to drive Vessler six feet under with one final blow, a hand landed on his shoulder.

Mace's grip was firm. Loving. "Come on, Brother."

Raven shook his head. One more blow, one more hit, and Nikki would never have to worry about Vessler again.

"Brother," Mace repeated, letting a dazed Nikki slide from his arms. "If you murder a human, your fate is sealed. Do not expect me to walk eternity without my brother at my side."

Raven's heart hammered.

Mace placed a protective arm around Nikki when she swayed. The other he placed around Raven.

Unwinding his fists, Raven attempted a smile and nodded toward Nikki.

She scratched her head, eyes clearing slowly.

Raven reached to her cheek and dragged his finger along the side of her face. He swallowed hard and gestured to Mace. "Carry her," he ordered. "She needs you."

Mace nodded, understanding. He swung Nikki into his arms.

As the three walked off the lawn, her eyes began to focus on Mace. She shook her head. "Damon's not what I thought he was."

Mace and Raven both laughed.

Mace kissed her forehead. "Neither are you, baby. Neither are you."

"You're telling us Nikki's a Halfling?" Will asked while sitting in the living room beside Zero and Vegan, who'd arrived a few minutes earlier. Feeling the rumblings of intrigue and munching on Sweet Tarts, Vine meandered down the stairs to join them and see what was up.

Zero nodded. "As best I can tell."

Vegan scooted closer to him, but he shot her a warning look.

When Vine realized the statement wasn't a joke, he nearly choked on the candy. *Nikki? A Halfling?*

"We're worried about her." Vegan dropped her hands to her lap and threaded them together. "Damon Vessler is capable of anything. He's literally orchestrated her entire life."

"But why?" Will asked.

"Isn't it obvious?" Zero stood. "Look, Vessler wants to build Halflings that are loyal to him. If he had a female specimen, fully under his control, he could use her DNA to create an entire race."

Will's face paled. "But female Halflings can only have one child."

"You're the one who told us there had been anomalies, remember?" Zero said. "Which may be why it's taken him so long to accomplish this."

"So Vessler's main interest is in genetics?"

"Electromagnetic studies are a cash cow for Vessler. I uncovered files from around the globe where his projects bring in billions. He must use it to fund the genetic research."

"Nikki's a Halfling and he planned to turn her?" Will said, repeating everything they already knew. But Vine saw the shock had yet to be erased from their guardian's face or voice. "Then use her to create an army …"

Zero threw his hands into the air. "When a Halfling is fully given over to evil, the DNA changes. There's no good left within—only hate, pure darkness. And there's no going back. Maybe Vessler's tried to turn Halflings in the past without success. So he constructed one."

"Constructed?" Vine interrupted, sinking onto the couch.

"Yeah, I'm not sure if Nikki's an in vitro baby or a clone of some kind, but make no mistake, she was birthed in a laboratory. And she's important because she has the ability to birth more than one offspring."

"And how did you discover that?" Will said.

"When I found the report with her name and the word *surgery*, I did a search on every file we've obtained from Omega."

"Omega Corporation, aka Damon Vessler," Will said.

Zero shot him a *duh* look. "Anyway, they intend to stick her under the knife and remove some of her eggs."

"That's why you think she may have been an in vitro baby herself?" Will said. "A common practice these days, but cutting-edge seventeen years ago when Nikki would have been born. Besides, even if they removed hundreds of eggs, that's not an army and it would take the offspring twenty years to be battle ready."

Zero leaned forward. "It's the *beginning* of an army. They have the theoretical capability to use the DNA to clone the eggs, but some will surely die in the process. I'm pretty sure they are working with hormones and a cold-process to induce rapid aging."

Vegan nodded. "Hundreds would become thousands, and thousands can become millions. And that *is* an army. If he can do in five years what normally takes twenty ..."

"So why hasn't Vessler done it? Why hasn't he extracted the eggs from Nikki?" Will asked. Then he answered his own question. "She had to turn first, and I would assume she would need to tap into her angelic power as well. If she's fully given over to her fallen impulses, her DNA would ensure a race of dark Halflings. Otherwise, he could be birthing an army that could fight against him rather than for him. No wonder she was being chased and tormented, but never killed. It was all an attempt to turn her. Vessler wants her filled with hatred."

"Yeah, and that also gives a reason for all the titanium shipments. His work is unprecedented, so he'd want plenty of wingcuffs on the off chance that his plan failed and the dark Halflings turned against him," Zero said.

Vine grabbed a handful of candy and chewed anxiously.

Zero leveled his cold stare at Will. "Plus, he'd want plenty to trap the Halflings fighting on his enemy's side."

"And it all depends on Nikki." Will rubbed his hand over his face.

"She has to tap in *and* turn. Nikki's a Halfling, but since she hadn't unearthed her angelic side, none of us saw it. Even you, Will."

Will nodded. "Halflings who are untapped seem pretty much like everyone else."

Vegan shrugged. "She could tap in any day. And if Vessler's played it right, she'll become dark the instant she finds those powers. The entirety of Vessler's plan—whatever it encompasses—rests on her shoulders."

Vine set the rest of the package of Sweet Tarts on the table. They didn't really sound good anymore. "What about her parents?"

Zero shot a look to Vegan. A tiny smile and nod coaxed him onward. "We think Mary and Dale Youngblood were scientists."

Will slumped onto the couch.

Vine chewed his cheek as he thought about Zero's theory. *Poor Nikki.* "Do you think her *dog* was a real *dog*?" he blurted before he could stop himself. But it just seemed so unfair. So ... awful.

Zero's head dropped a degree. "Nothing would shock me now. But Dale and Mary aren't her real parents. Who knows if she even *has* parents? The point is, as Halflings we know who and what we are from the time we're born. It's what keeps us on the side of good. Imagine being a human, hitting the age of accountability, and suddenly having supernatural powers. And—"

"And having everything you love stripped from you." Will pressed his hands together in a prayer posture. "She was to be the queen after all," he mumbled.

Zero shared a confused glance with Vegan. "What?" he asked Will.

"Checkmate."

Another glance. Zero shrugged.

"I don't want Nikki hit with all this information," Will said. "Not yet. She needs time to absorb her unique origin and who she is. Understood?"

Three Halflings nodded. Vine still couldn't get over it. *Nikki a Halfling ...*

A question burst from Vine's mouth. "Where's Nikki now? It's not safe for her to be with Vessler."

Will looked weary as he answered. "Mace and Raven went to her house to talk with her."

"To Vessler's mansion?"

"No. Vessler let her move into her parents' home. She should be there now."

Zero pressed thin lips together, then spoke. "There's more."

Will's lightning-blue eyes met Zero's silver ones. A warning rested there—Vine figured Will had heard enough for one day. But that didn't stop Zero, who presented a plan so destructive, Vine's stomach churned. He stared down at the coffee table and wondered if Sweet Tarts would ever sound good again. *Maybe in a few years.*

After several minutes, Will interrupted. "What you're suggesting could alter the entire existence of humans in as little as a generation."

"It could alter it," Zero repeated. "Or worse."

"Worse?" Will asked.

"It could end it."

"It was a dangerous game, sir," the short, thin scientist said while sliding the needle through Vessler's skin. *If I wasn't in so much pain, he'd pay for that comment. But there's always later.*

Vessler gripped the edges of the examination table while the scientist tied the last knot. "She couldn't kill me."

"She's quite capable, Mr. Vessler."

"No. I am the world to her. She just has to be reminded of that."

"Well, it may have to wait. Your cargo arrives in a few days, and I'm certain you'll want to make decisions on where the shipment will go from here. With the last one lost ..."

Vessler's eyes closed, a slow burn working through his system. Details. He didn't have time for details when the star of his plan had escaped. Not escaped—kidnapped. Nikki wouldn't leave. Not on her own, at least. She may stray a bit, like that ridiculous stunt to Europe, but he was her universe. He was her life.

He was her god.

All he had to do was find her. Especially now that she'd ... What did they call it? Tapped in. He'd seen her eyes go dark, and that would only happen once she was in possession of her powers. Satisfaction took the place of frustrating disappointment. It had worked. All his difficult labor, everything he'd sacrificed to bring her to fruition, had not been in vain.

"I'm sorry for the pain," Dr. Shindler said.

Damon realized his eyes had become misty—the doctor must have thought he'd actually hurt him. Did this throwaway in a lab coat have any idea what he'd suffered to get to this point? Of course not. When he'd lost Project J, it nearly destroyed him. With the others, there hadn't been time to bond. But J ... Well, Nikki had done well to take the place of the dead specimen. She'd been his last hope. And she'd excelled as she grew.

"I fear she may be gone for good, Mr. Vessler."

"No, she'll be back." He smiled. "And sooner than you think."

The white-haired man shook his head. "Turning her in the confines of a fight, you're lucky you escaped with your life."

He grabbed the scientist's wrist. "This *is* my life," he gritted. "*She's* my life. Everything rests on her."

The scientist's eyes fanned to the edge of Vessler's mouth, where Damon's stitches strained beneath his anger.

Vessler shoved the man's hand away.

"We've shown promise in Nashville," Shindler said hopefully. "Especially with the group of new scientists working around the clock."

"No. She's the one. Only her."

"But, sir, without the DNA change completed, there's no promise that the ... offspring ... would be Darklings."

"Even if it's not by her choice, I'll find another way to complete the change." Vessler rested his head against the cool table. No more Halflings. Just darkness. Just hate. A beautiful army of his Darklings. Light, golden skin and eyes as dark as the coldest night.

And all in allegiance to him. Their father. Their creator.

Will was huddled over her when she woke. Nikki sat up, her side screaming in protest. She put a hand over her right kidney and applied gentle pressure. About a million sets of eyes were on her when Will stepped back, unblocking the rest of the room. She was on the couch and *they* were all around her.

Mace and Raven were about a foot away, a little blood

splattered here and there on their T-shirts and jeans. Vine stayed in the corner, sitting on the floor with his legs crossed, and straight across from her, the females and Zero stared down, looking anything but confident.

Vegan spoke first. "Nikki, we're so glad you're okay."

The last time she'd heard Vegan's voice was when the females were bashing her and wishing her gone. When she should have heard Vegan, *her friend*, rally in her defense. But she hadn't. Now, she was suddenly glad Nikki was okay? *Really?*

"What were you thinking, running away from us in Europe and going to stay with—" Zero stopped midstream when Vegan elbowed him in the stomach so hard it disturbed his white hair.

She turned from Zero and happened on Mace. He studied her with the intensity one gives a freshly polished gemstone. She knew what he was thinking, that maybe Vessler pushed her beyond the point of no return. Could she ever come back to him out of that strange blackness she'd sunk into?

She ached for him, but it hadn't been her choice to leave Viennesse in the first place. He'd—they'd—*all* pushed her away. Even Will, the only one she thought she could count on to be objective. Her gaze narrowed slightly, and she was sure Mace noticed the change. He always reacted when she showed some sign of strength. She took a careful breath and tried to ignore the poker in her side. "Wow, you all seem so worried." She hadn't meant for her tone to be sardonic, but hearing her voice caused a spike of pride.

"Of course we were worried," Winter said. "We didn't know what Vessler would do to you. Nikki, there's something we need to tell you."

She froze for a moment, trying desperately to remember what had just happened beyond "something horrible." She and Damon were fighting. On the lawn. Mace and Raven were there. Her eyes fanned to the two of them for a moment—both still fresh from the fight—but neither offering any clue. What had happened? Her head was aching, make that pounding, out rhythmic blasts to her brain. She pressed her hands to her temples and squeezed her eyes shut.

"Nikki, I know this must be difficult, but—"

Movement around her. Tension in the air. Mace's voice. "That's enough." Then he was there, hovering and reaching around her to lift her into his arms like she was some broken china doll. "No more talk until she rests."

She didn't want to go with Mace. She'd pushed him away at the beach house, though now she couldn't remember why she'd been so angry. Everything was blurry, and she wondered if she'd been drugged.

A stiff voice, filled with irritation, ended her thought. "We need to know what happened. This can't wait, Mace. We need answers." *Well, whatever happened, it has Zero all worked up.*

"No!" Mace's words so abrupt, she squeezed her eyes tighter. "Not. Another. Word. Until. She. Rests."

And he swept her from the room and up the stairs. *Rescued. Again.*

Chapter
23

"Welcome back," Mace said as Nikki turned and stretched. He looked like he'd been sitting in the chair by a window for some time. "How's your side?"

She yawned and looked down at the covers. "Okay, I guess. Not as bad."

"Going to be sore for a few days if your kidney is bruised."

She nodded and noticed the movement of her hair against the pillow. She chanced a quick peek to the right and to the left. Hair fanned around her. Had he done that as she slept? She remembered being angry with all of them—including Mace—but now she just felt relieved to be here. Safe.

He rose and stood with his back against the door. Her sentry, her guard. And she doubted any being—regardless of its origin—would be able to penetrate the wall of Mace. She watched his hands fist. Not angrily; this was a motion she'd seen many times. He'd contract, then flex his fingers, and then they were usually touching her somewhere. As if the digits had a will of their own and wouldn't resist, no matter what his mind said. She realized she was anticipating his touch. But Mace just smiled down at her and clamped his hands behind his back.

She hoped her disappointment wasn't too easy to read. But of course, it was. Mace seemed to have an instant translator where she was concerned. "Looks like I need a babysitter after all."

"Is that what you think of me?"

"You tend to order me around a lot." Where had that come from? Then again, she couldn't deny it.

He sank onto the bed. "Remember on the boat when I told you my judgment is all messed up where you're concerned?"

She nodded. "I do, but I don't want to be locked in a cage."

"Nikki, your life is more important than we ever imagined. From the beginning I've felt the urgency to protect you. But I don't want to lock you up in any way. If anything, I want to help you fly. But you're like a bull ..." He ran his hands through his hair.

"A bull?"

"Yeah. I'm sorry, but you're constantly taking on risks, trying to test the boundaries."

"That's who I am, Mace. And it's not going to change."

"I don't want it to change. That's what I love about you. But you're also called to be a leader. And a leader doesn't always get to do what he wants."

She was called to be a leader? Seriously? With pounding surety, his words rang true and scared her. "That's why it feels like you're constantly pushing me but at the same time holding me back?"

He shrugged. "I guess. I've never thought of it that way. Leading isn't easy. You have to make the hard choices. It's seldom the thing you want."

A new respect for Mace sifted into her system. With all his infuriating stop signs, he was really trying to prepare her to move forward.

She needed to change the subject. "You saved me, didn't you?"

The lines of his face contorted for a moment, then the tension smoothed. "You were doing all right on your own."

"I don't know what happened. There was this blind rage that just overtook me. Damon, he … he …" Her voice cracked and her throat closed.

With a sigh, Mace reached toward her and allowed his index finger to trail along her hairline, coercing stray strands from her face.

Instinctively, she knew he intended to discuss the obvious: her, Damon, what happened. She'd have to somehow guide the conversation into a different direction, because she needed to sort the vivid things she'd dreamed while he stood guard at her door.

She forced out the words. "Raven is downstairs. Is he staying here? Are things back to normal?"

The index finger slid to her chin and moved silently back and forth beneath her bottom lip. She really wished he'd stop that. It made it difficult to continue.

"He spends a lot of time with Dr. Richmond and at the lab these days."

"The lab?"

"Yeah, he's been watching Vess— He's watching Omega. Things are as back to normal with Raven as they can be. Before today we'd been taking turns sitting outside the gate of Vessler's mansion."

"For me," she said, voice so soft it could have been an echo.

"What kind of guardian would I be if I didn't?"

Nikki stared at the door for a long time. "You rescued me twice today."

The perfect face flashed a frown. "Twice?"

She nodded. "Downstairs."

His jaw tightened. "Yeah, about that—"

Nikki lifted her fingertips to his lips to stop his words. It worked. Mace was almost always leveled by her touch. The tightening of his lips beneath her fingers, the quickening of his breath as he exhaled puffs that landed on the back of her hand, the look in his brilliant-blue eyes …

With great force, Nikki pushed all that aside. Everything had changed. *Everything.* The weight of that pressed against her shoulders like the safety harness of a roller coaster that spun and tossed you from side to side then left you inverted.

His breathing slowed and remained steady—Mace was always steady—but somehow comfortable now, as if he'd eased into a warm pool. When her gaze touched his, she saw it—relief and awe and joy all rolled into one package. He tried hard to contain his emotions, but she'd studied him as much as he had her. The cadence of his voice, the soft sound of his breathing, the firm feel of his battle-toughened hands that could turn to silk against her skin. He was pulling her into that place of quiet safety that she only knew with Mace.

She looked away.

But that moment of eye contact told her everything she feared. Nothing stood in their way now.

What Mace couldn't understand was that at the same time a new wall stood in their path. One that rose higher than ever before. He couldn't know, and she couldn't blame him for that. But, oh, she wanted to. It would make this so much easier.

"We need to talk about ... you." His lips brushed against her fingertips as he spoke.

Nikki's eyes drifted shut in an attempt to capture and seal the emotion he was giving off. What would it be like to simply *feel*? To be allowed a sensation separate from all the pain attached to it? She didn't know. And unfortunately, she was about to give up her one chance of learning, as she knew what Mace was talking about. They needed to discuss who and what she was. The day's adventure was a blur, but tiny portions flickered with crystal clarity in her mind. Nikki wasn't human. She'd heard Mace and Raven say it. And if her suspicion was correct, it was the worst kind of trick. Because it meant her actions in the next few days would ensure her ticket to hell.

"How is she?" Vegan asked as she handed a cup of coffee to Mace.

"Resting again."

Vegan motioned with a dip of her head to Zero, who widened his eyes in question. She dipped her head again, a little more forcefully.

"Sorry, dude, for pushing her earlier," he conceded on an exhale.

"It's all good, Zero." Mace stared into the depths of the coffee mug. *Things should be good. Should be better on every level, and yet ...*

"What's wrong, Mace?" Winter asked. A blanket of her long, dark hair framed her face, and when combined with the way she sat arrow-straight on the couch she looked like a portrait from a different time. No, not just seemed; Winter belonged in a different time. Her perfect posture, her manners, the frequent glints of wisdom in her golden eyes. How long had she lived? What had she endured?

Mace hadn't given much thought to the hundreds of years that stretched before him. That now stretched before him and Nikki.

Nikki was raised by humans. And the confines of human life rested within a hundred or so years. But that limit became meaningless when he watched her eyes change. Why wouldn't she talk about the fact that she was a Halfling? She'd deliberately shut him down, even though he'd seen in her eyes she knew.

When Winter repeated the question, he stared at her a moment before answering. "It's Nikki. She wouldn't talk about what happened on the lawn with Vessler."

Heads nodded. But they didn't understand. This went beyond a need to adjust. There was a fierce determination in Nikki's eyes, a resolution in the set of her jaw, and the hint of a departure in her touch. Nothing had been spoken. Words wouldn't have been as loud.

But one thing Mace knew for certain: he was no closer to claiming the female that was his match than he had been on the day they met.

"She just needs time, Mace," Winter said.

"Well, time's the one thing she's got plenty of now." He couldn't help the bitterness that crept into his voice. He should be laughing; instead, he felt like the girl he loved had been dealt one mammoth of an unfair hand. And to make matters worse, she was about to bluff the dealer.

Glimmer stood. "Let's go home. We girls have to at least keep up the illusion normal people live in that apartment downtown." She tilted her head toward the stairs. "Nikki will probably sleep the rest of the night, but we should be here for her in the morning … You know, for support."

Several sets of eyes turned to Glimmer and widened.

"What?" she barked. "She's one of us now."

"Let's do something nice for her," Vegan added. "Maybe a party."

Zero mumbled something about girls and rolled his eyes.

"Yeah," Glimmer agreed. "We'll think of something on the way home."

But Mace wasn't in a mood to enjoy any sort of get-together. Everything he'd dreamed of and never thought he could have was slipping away, before he even got a chance to enjoy it.

By the following morning, Nikki was rested and full of questions. She had to be careful though. She wanted answers, but only answers to the right inquiries. Maybe if she was careful that no one uttered what she was, it would sort of make a loophole big enough to slip her eternity through. Because of all the things she was uncertain of, one thing remained clear: she had to find—no, she had to hunt—the man responsible for killing her mom and dad. If her parents were alive today, they could explain this mess to her. Were they the same as she was? Could they have hidden their true identity for her entire life?

Nikki seized the railing and slipped down the stairs to find Will waiting for her in the living room. A sweet scent wafted from beneath the kitchen's swinging door, and male and female voices mingled together as well. It sounded as if they were arguing.

Will put down his paper. "Did you sleep?"

"Some," she said, rubbing her hands on her thighs. "Thanks for letting me crash here."

"Of course."

She dropped onto the couch beside the giant teddy bear of a man ... er, angel. "How could I not know?" she asked, careful to avoid the word, and hoping Will would pick up on that little fact. "How could *you* not know?"

"Male Halflings reach the age of accountability in their teen years. For each it's different. Raven was barely seventeen when he tapped in. Mace was seventeen as well. Vine, my early bloomer, was fifteen. Halfling females tend to reach the age of accountability around eighteen, sometimes nineteen or even twenty."

"Vegan, Glimmer, and Winter. Do they live with a heavenly angel like the Lost Boys?"

"Females are raised to the age of accountability by Xians— do you know what a Xian is?"

She nodded. "Yes, Mace explained it to me once. They're humans who are tuned in to the supernatural realm, right?"

"Yes. Since females tap in later, they are raised by Xians with a heavenly angel overseeing their lives. They are usually grown—college-aged—when they tap in. So they live together, but a heavenly angel doesn't need to be there as well. Winter, Vegan, and Glimmer have their own apartment downtown. But there's still an overseeing angel."

"Why haven't I seen their angel?"

"The girls were placed in my care. I'm the overseeing angel now."

"Oh."

He studied her for a long time before launching deeper into

the discussion. "In your case, Vessler kept an eye on you, and when you began to show the signs, he threw his plan into high gear."

Vessler. She knew him as her godfather, her protector. *Some protector. He tried to kill me on my own front lawn.* "Show what signs?"

"First, it was fortunate for him that you'd become a Seer. It made tapping into the supernatural realm easy. He'd simply drop something before your eyes that would cause you to draw. You'd sketch what your mind saw, not realizing it was actually *in* the other realm."

"That's why the hell hounds showed up in the woods the first day I met Mace, Raven, and Vine?" It seemed like it had happened to another Nikki.

"Exactly. Hounds can kill you or torment you to the point of—"

She held up a hand to stop him. "Yes, I know." Mace had explained their capabilities on the night she first met Zero in his secret underground hideout. "So all that time Vessler was making me into a monster like him."

"Yes, with fear as his wingman. But you're not like him, Nikki. Not physically, emotionally, or genetically."

Not like him. Oh, but she was about to be. She forced her thoughts away. There was time, lots of time, to put her plan into motion. "What *am* I, Will?" It was not a question to be answered; Nikki made that clear by the tone of her voice. Her gaze drifted to the window, where the sun's rays warmed the yard beyond. But a bleak indifference closed around her. The same one she felt over and over at Vessler's house, like a dark veil shading her world. She actually detested the heat the sun offered. Even the green grass and gently swaying trees repulsed her. They were liars, acting as if the world was a beautiful place, when all the while they'd sat back and watched its ugliness time and again. This morning she hated the sun for shining. "I just don't understand how I couldn't know."

"You've told me time and again lately that you don't feel like yourself. Remember, on the boat? Mace and Raven said the same thing. You've been sensing something, something evil."

She laughed without humor. "Yeah, I didn't expect it to be me."

"You are not evil, Nikki. You have fallen blood streaming through your veins, yes. But it is your choices that determine what your soul reaps."

That fallen blood drained from her face and right to her feet.

Will must have sensed it was too much for her to take in, so he shifted the conversation. "Mace and Raven both shared instances where you said you could *feel* their emotions. You killed a hell hound with your bare hands. That's hardly human."

"That was a long time ago. And right before that, I got burned in the laboratory fire and Mace didn't," she argued. "So how could he and I be of the same species?"

"Having angelic abilities and being able to utilize them are two different things. A Halfling must tap into her angelic power."

She leaned forward. This could help her execute her plan.

"First, abilities arrive a little at a time. If you were to be burned now—"

She gasped softly. "I did get burned while at Damon's beach house. Except I didn't. Krissy's hand blistered instantly. Mine didn't even turn red."

"And I would venture to say your eyesight has improved drastically."

Nikki grabbed a throw pillow and hugged it. She thought of the clarity of Mace's face when he stood at the water's edge and she on the balcony. Every detail was in sharp focus. "It has." But even farther back, her eyesight had been strong. "When we first went to visit Zero in the underground, Mace said, 'I bet you need a light,' but my eyes had adjusted."

Will smiled. "No, they didn't."

She frowned. "They did. I could see everything. All I needed was that little bit of light."

"There was no light to adjust to. You were seeing in the dark. Once the door to the surface is closed, it's pitch-black in the tunnel."

So many disjointed things connected together, it made her dizzy. "That's why Zero examined my eyes. He first thought I was a Halfling female. And even after Mace assured him I wasn't, I could tell Zero didn't believe him. Wow." She sank back. "What about seeing things in slow motion?" *Oops, just broke my own rule about admitting what I am.* But her dark veil had lifted, and she couldn't help being drawn into the awe of what she was.

"What about it?" Will shrugged.

"Well, Raven said that the realm of the supernatural moves so fast humans are hardly ever aware of it. But in instances like car wrecks, sometimes everything slows down. For a brief moment of time, humans see what it's like in the other realm. But for Halflings, it's as if everything is always moving more slowly."

"Yes." Will reached to the coffee table behind him, picked up a coaster, and lobbed it at her.

Excruciatingly slow, it flipped end over end, rising first, then falling to shoulder height as it tumbled in her direction.

On one side of the coaster she read the words, 'My house shall be a house of prayer.' The phrase disappeared as it flipped, replaced by the cork-covered side of the coaster. Lifting her hand, she caught the disk with no effort. As soon as it landed in her grasp, she dropped it to the ground. "How'd I do that?"

"You've probably been doing a lot of that without realizing it." He leaned toward her. "Nikki, you are a Halfling. Half-angel. It's second nature to you. A child who's a prodigy doesn't realize he's anything special. He simply does what he knows to do. As you embrace who you are, you'll grow more and more at ease with your ability. And more aware of when you're utilizing it."

Unsure eyes scanned his face.

"Nikki, you *are* a Halfling." Will stretched back, placing a large hand to his forehead. "I can't believe I didn't see it. I should have known the moment the females first arrived. Standing by them, you could be their sister." He leaned toward her for emphasis. "You *are* their sister."

But she was no longer listening. She settled her mind comfortably around the words *you'll grow more and more at ease with your ability. And more aware of when you're utilizing it.* That, she could use.

Nikki blinked, and confusion fluttered around her. Her conscience and her thoughts were unequally divided, weighing far more heavily on the side of revenge. But the still, small voice that had become an almost constant companion beckoned, and before she could silence it, a question slipped quietly from her lips. "Will, what's going to happen to me?"

He placed a reassuring hand on her shoulder. "Heaven will tell us. But you're not safe on your own. Vessler won't give up so easily. He's going to hunt you, Nikki. He'll use humans and hell hounds and wraiths. Make no mistake, he will try to get to you."

Fingers tickled along her spine. "Will, I'm afraid."

"Don't be. We're on the winning team." He stood and pulled her to her feet. "Until we hear differently, you'll remain with me. We'll continue to protect you. And I will train you in the proper use of your angelic ability."

As if life hasn't been crazy enough in the last months, as if I'm not already enough of a freak, let's add more training and some wings.

Wings. Her blood pressure dropped, leaving a sluggish *whoosh, whoosh, whoosh* in her ears.

"Are you okay?" Will asked.

"Uh, do I have … I mean—" She pivoted to show Will her back and looked over her own shoulder. "Are there … you know …"

"Wings?" he finished for her.

"Yeah."

He grabbed her shoulders and spun her around. "Nope. Not that I can see." His fingertips roamed her shoulder blades before turning her to face him. His eyes twinkled. "Can you feel them?"

She concentrated. "Um." She shook her shoulders. "No, I don't feel anything."

"Well, I wouldn't worry. They'll be along soon enough."

His condescending tone irritated her. *They'll be along soon enough? What in the world did that mean?* It's not like they were talking about a litter of puppies here. But rather than argue, she answered, "Okay." She rolled her eyes. "This is so weird. Are yours heavy?"

He seemed to bite back a smile. "No. They're as much a part of me as my shadow."

Voices in the kitchen rose. She turned toward the door. "Is everything all right in there?"

"Probably not. Vegan, Glimmer, Zero, and Winter arrived an hour ago with the ingredients to bake you a birthday cake."

Her eyes rounded. "Really?"

Will placed his hands on his hips. "Yes, and Raven, Mace, and Vine are certain they're doing it wrong. They've been battling the better part of the hour. Though I don't know what they're fighting about now. The cake is in the oven."

"I can smell it. It's for me?"

"We're your family now, Nikki. We all want you to feel like you belong."

"But I don't, do I?" She pulled her bottom lip into her mouth and bit down. Something flashed in his eyes. Secrets, that's all she could think to call them. And it angered her that he wasn't telling her. "What are you hiding, Will? I have a right to know." Her hardened voice seemed to take the giant by surprise.

"I have no argument. In time, I promise you will know. But right now, you have enough to absorb. And you have a birthday cake to eat."

She conceded, for now. Besides, she'd actually won that battle, whether the angel knew it or not. "Birthday cake for breakfast." She paused at the kitchen door. "Oh, what kind is it?"

"Angel food, of course."

As he led her into the kitchen, seven Halflings yelled, "Surprise!"

273

Chapter 24

That night Nikki lay on her belly on the cool earth, staring through the French doors that opened to Vessler's office. He'd just left the room with another man trailing his steps. A friend? A late-night business meeting? Her godfather kept conspicuous hours.

A spider crawled onto her arm from a blade of grass and she flicked it away.

At that moment, she almost backed out. Was she nuts? No, not nuts, *desperate*. Although he hadn't come right out and told her, Vessler had information on her parents' deaths. She needed that information, and his office was the best place to start looking. She'd ceased to think of him as Damon, the man who "loved" her, the man who gave her a hundred-thousand-dollar concept bike and promised her the world. The man who'd bought her a dog as a child then sent the very hell hound that stole its life. No, she'd never call him Damon again, unless, of course, it was to gain the advantage. Because annihilating an opponent was all about having the advantage. *Vessler* had taught her that.

Now he was the enemy, the man with a plot to destroy her by turning her into a dark creature. But darkness had become shades of gray, and Nikki prepared to sink to a depth Vessler wouldn't believe her capable. When she was done, gray would be a welcomed if not unattainable gift. For where she intended to go, there was no color at all.

Learn your opponent's weakness, he'd taught her. Who knew him better than her, the person he'd trained? No one. If he had a weakness, she'd find it. Then she'd use it to annihilate him.

Because she was finally free to make her own choices.

The chilly earth made a comforting bed. Silent, still, she rested her cheek against the grass and closed her eyes. Something inside begged caution, and her eyes snapped open as if denying the sound, the conscience, the warning. Dark surrounded her, but she had no trouble seeing through it. She was a Halfling, after all.

Along the driveway, two black sedans sat at the ready, cars Vessler kept in the adjacent garage. Her eyes scanned the oversized building. Inside, her concept bike waited patiently. When she was done in Vessler's office, she'd go get her motorcycle. Even if she only drove it out of the garage and into the nearest lake on her way back to the room under Will's roof, she'd take one more ride on the awesome machine.

Because this trip was just a quick investigation, something her Halfling "siblings" could know nothing about. She couldn't afford to tip them off before her real mission began.

Yet her gaze trailed the walls of the garage. Something in her core pulled her toward the place, dimly lit by a security light and scrunched by a row of trees butted against its backside like chairs shoved against a table.

A half moon hung over the building, but something about it was off. Her eyes fanned the treetops. Yes, that was it. In the very center, a division in the trees on either side split the woods like a curving river. It was subtle, and if she shifted her body a few feet to the left or to the right, she'd not even notice the breach in the foliage. But there was no doubt it signaled a path that led into the woods from the back of the garage. As if looking at something for the very first time, Nikki tilted onto her elbows. She'd passed the garage a million times, parked inside it on numerous occasions. How could she have missed the trail?

Vessler's office held little interest for her now. The garage waited, ready to divulge its secrets, and Nikki was eager to listen.

She slipped along the back wall of the structure. Through a thicket of shrubs and overgrowth, she tried to keep her movement silent, though there was no one to hear but the bugs and spiders. She stepped onto the path leading from the back of the oversized building and inspected the wall, her hand running against the wood. No, not wood—metal. The framing, the blades of grass trampled and caught beneath the ground-level section—it all told her what she'd expected. This wasn't a wall, but another garage door. But there seemed to be no way to get in. She looked down the trail, newly scarred by car tires. The winding dirt road must lead to the main street beyond.

Counting off each step, Nikki returned to the front of the garage then tucked inside. From the door she started counting again, suspicions confirmed. The garage was much deeper than the inside wall suggested. With her knuckles she rapped on the structure and listened as the echo floated and disappeared. Hollow.

Within minutes she found tiny scrapings of paint on the floor beside a large tool closet. Point of entry? If there was a hidden garage behind the known one, maybe there was a way to get inside separate from the outside door.

Nikki shoved the tool closet, but it wouldn't budge. She went to the other side and inspected the scrapes. It definitely slid this way. *Think like Vessler.* She paced for a few minutes, avoiding the three sports cars and her Ducati. *What tricks would he use?* Nikki spun and returned to the side of the closet, but opened its door before pushing. The entire closet slid easily out of her way.

She entered a cavern of a room where a large vehicle took up much of the space. Should she risk leaving the door open? Someone could come in and catch her. Judging stealth was best, she reached through and closed the entryway, hoping there was a trigger from her side as well. Along a wall was another closet like the one she'd moved. She pulled it open and found a flashlight resting among three shelves of various handguns. *All Vessler's guns aren't locked in the gun room inside the house. Interesting.*

Vessler had taught her to shoot at his private firing range, offering her a mix of guns to practice with. When she spotted her favorite, she reached for it: a Smith and Wesson .357 Magnum, with a corresponding box of hollow-point ammo. Her hand had paused over the Ruger Blackhawk, but no, too heavy. Then the Colt 1911. She loved its accuracy, but the Smith and Wesson felt more comfortable in her hand. She'd spent more time practicing with it than the others. And since the shot she may need to make was an important one, comfort factored in.

Nikki turned her attention to the vehicle, and as she looked at it her blood began a slow drain from her head to her feet. Nikki hugged her upper arms, handgun dangling beneath an elbow.

A yellow Hummer.

Mace had told her a yellow Hummer had been parked nearby the night the lab was on fire, and the man beside it had shot and killed the scientist she'd just resuscitated, missing her by mere inches.

This was the car of a murderer. *And it sat in her godfather's garage.*

She should leave. Instead, she reached to the door handle and pulled open the driver's side. She smirked at the discovery the keys were dangling from the ignition. *Always so confident, so sure of yourself, aren't you, Vessler?* Had her godfather pulled the trigger on the scientist? She figured not. He had thugs to do his dirty work.

She slid into the driver's seat and closed her eyes.

She could smell the guy, could taste in the blend of sweat and precision that this man was a professional. Deodorant barely masked the scent of stale flesh and old coffee that lingered. Nikki glanced down to the cup holder splattered with the brown evidence of an uncareful drinker.

She got out and climbed into the backseat. Nothing unusual. Her hand trailed along the edge of the seat, but still felt nothing out of the ordinary. Then she saw it, a darkened stain in the puckered corner where fabric met fabric. She had to press with her fingers to see it, but in the bright dash light, it was unmistakable. Dried blood.

Why should she be surprised? She'd already established this as a murderer's car. But something about the blood cried out to her.

Nikki closed her eyes and pressed her fingers into the crease of the seat. *Talk to me,* she urged. All was still and quiet. When her father's face flashed in her mind, she jolted. Nikki's eyes flew open and she jerked her hand from the spot. The silence of the room closed in with fresh horror.

Pulse racing, she slowly reached toward the fabric again, hoping—*praying*—she'd imagined it. Her fingertips trembled as they approaching the stain. And again she saw her father's face.

Her fingers closed into a fist, trying to capture the life that was no more. "No," she whispered to the hollow room. It was a plea and a cry and a resolution. So this was it, proof they were truly gone. Dead. At the hands of the man who'd killed the scientist and who was parked in *Damon Vessler's* garage. Sorrow turned to rage, its slow transformation burning away any innocence that remained.

She didn't need to be told her eyes were darkening. She felt it. She was turning. Killing the killer would complete the change, she was sure, but she gave it little thought. If she'd been uncertain about what she'd do, now it was evident and the only thing she *could* do. Nikki would kill the man who'd killed her parents. Then she'd deal with Vessler.

She checked the gun's safety and tucked it into the back of her jeans, gangster-movie style, but that felt completely uncomfortable, so she returned to the gun closet and searched. On the bottom shelf were a variety of holsters. Vessler had taught her how to shoot, how to handle a gun, but how to use a holster? No. She pulled a smaller one out and gripped the largest section upside down so the straps dangled below and offered a clue how it worked. Then she flipped it over and slid the shoulder harness into place. The gun fit nicely and she adjusted the straps for comfort. She pulled the gun from the holster and held it in her hand.

Nikki settled in to wait.

She heard movement outside and slid into the back of the car to hide beneath a wadded-up tarp. She couldn't kill him here on Vessler's property—too obvious—so she'd tag along and discover where murderers go late at night.

The man's smell intensified as he got into the driver's seat. Movement of keys, the motor's rumbling, and soon they were bouncing along the hidden path. She wished she'd found something else to hide beneath or nothing at all. The tarp seemed to screech and moan every time she moved. Her leg and shoulder ached, but she didn't dare readjust. Her side was screaming in protest of every pothole until the driver finally pulled onto the smooth street.

When Nikki heard his voice, she nearly screamed, until she realized he must have called someone. "Almost to the park."

Then another voice filled the air. A familiar voice, muffled through the tarp and a phone speaker, but undoubtedly Vessler's.

"Leave it in the bin in the center."

"You sure you want me to follow through with this? This is a lot of cash. It'd be easy to just finish them."

"No, I may need them later." Vessler's tone was clipped.

"A lot of good that will do if they flee the country," the driver said.

"The money is marked. I'll know everywhere they go."

"So this is just insurance?"

"Exactly."

"Why now?"

"Because the bird has left the nest. Obviously, they've been watching." Vessler did nothing to disguise his frustration.

"But you weren't worried at all when they disappeared, so you must have expected this."

"What could they do without me? I'm their life."

"Will you need me tomorrow to start the search for her?" The driver was reaching for something, Nikki could tell by the change in his voice. "Hold on a sec, gotta plug in my cell."

Vessler released an aggravated sigh. "Tomorrow morning my shipment comes in at eight. I'll call you after."

"You need me to go along?"

"No. There's no threat."

"Okay. I just reached the park."

Nikki felt the motor slow to an idle as the car rolled to a stop. If only she could breathe more silently. She prayed he wouldn't shut the motor off completely, and someone up there must have been listening because the Hummer continued to rumble. Not that it was enough to allow her movement. Her left leg was asleep and stabbing her with tiny little needles. It masked the pain in her side. A glorious—albeit painful—reprieve.

"You're sure you need them alive? I've got a great vantage point above the trash bin. It'd be like shooting fish in a barrel."

"No."

"I've got a new scope too. Need to try it out."

She could feel the tension on the other end of the line as Vessler said, "No."

The man rustled something on the seat beside him. It sounded like a trash bag.

When he got out and she heard his footsteps become faint,

she felt relief. Now to get out of the car. Nikki peeked over the seats and carefully transferred the tarp to one side. He was almost halfway to the trash can and carrying a lumpy bag. She had to move fast and wasn't sure how loud opening the rear door might be, so instead she clambered over the seats and slipped out of the driver's door and into a patch of woods about fifty feet from the vehicle.

They hadn't driven far. Once she did what she had to do, she'd walk back to the house on Pine Boulevard. She wouldn't drive his car. You don't kill a man then drive away in his vehicle.

Nikki took her station in a row of trees near the Hummer. She was a good shot, but not a perfect one, so she stayed close. Probably too close, but what did it matter? There was no going back. With the gun in her hand and the safety off, she sat patiently.

Once he'd dropped the bag into the bin below, he started back up the incline to the Hummer, which was still running, lights shimmering on a row of trees across the park.

As he approached her position, he slowed his pace and stopped to face the trees, and her. Keen eyes, one with a teardrop tattooed beneath, scanned the ground around her. Nikki closed one eye and took aim, hand shaking.

But the man did something unexpected. He reached to the ground and lifted a butterfly into his hands. Palm flat, he studied the insect. With a fingertip he nudged it to the edge of his hand until the butterfly tumbled downward. He caught it; this time its wings spread to show the injury that kept it from flight.

Nikki squeezed her eye shut, willing the man into motion. *Smash it*, her mind screamed. *Smear it on your pant leg or grind it into the dirt, anything to make me able to do this!*

But he didn't. Her eye opened when he carried the butterfly toward her and sat the wounded creature in the crook of a tree.

It was such a *human* thing to do, and it turned her inside out.

Her teeth clenched. She hated herself for not being able to get vengeance on the man who took her world. A stupid, *stupid* wounded butterfly was all that kept her from pulling the trigger. And not pulling the trigger was all that kept her from hell.

As the man got in his Hummer and drove away, Nikki sat down in the grass and cried until nerves that had been taut with adrenaline and fear melted into emptiness.

Several minutes passed, but she remained there with the sounds of the forest blanketing her. Strange that she felt no fear now that the man was gone. But the whine of a far-off engine triggered her attention, and she brushed the tears from her face as if an approaching vehicle meant she'd be caught in her moment of frailty.

The small white car approached slowly. She craned her neck and watched it entering the park from a different road. The vehicle doused its lights, and she had to chuckle. Like anyone wouldn't see the glowing white car on a surprisingly bright half-moon night. It slowed to a crawl, so excruciating she wanted to scream at the driver, *It's all clear, he's gone.*

This was no expert bad guy.

After an eternity, the man stopped the car and eased the door open. Dressed in a long coat and a misshapen hat, he approached the trash can like it would explode if he moved too suddenly.

He looked of average build. And something about his gait seemed familiar to her.

He dug in the bin like a hobo, then came up fast, eyes darting in all directions. Halfway back to the car he broke into a run, and the added momentum coupled with a bit of wind stripped the hat from him. His hand clamped onto his head, trying to grasp what had already escaped. The man spun around, ran a few steps toward the hat, then stopped, his feet doing a confused little dance as he turned and headed to the car again.

But Nikki felt as if her platelets congealed, stopping her systems and shutting them down. No oxygen entered her lungs, and she didn't feel strong enough to encourage any. Because from fifty yards above, Nikki stared down into the eyes—not the face, not the body, but certainly the eyes—of her father.

Chapter 25

It took several breaths before she could process what she'd seen. It *wasn't* her dad. Her dad was dead. And the man's body size and facial structure were all wrong. But he had her dad's eyes. Bile rose in her throat as her mind concocted gruesome scenarios inside Omega's laboratory, and all the horrific things that must go on there.

But this wasn't like that. The guy looked like a ... relative ... of her father's. A brother or a cousin, maybe. Which was impossible, because her parents didn't have any relatives. Or did they? Vessler knew her parents well enough to know every detail of her life. And he was tied to the man in the yellow Hummer, and the man in the Hummer killed the scientist as well as shot her mom and dad. Vessler had manipulated her life. And in doing so, maybe he'd forced her parents to deny her the rest of her family.

Every trail led back to Vessler. Nikki's hatred stirred. Seeing the man run to the trash bin like a mouse hoping for a few morsels of food made her despise Vessler even more. She hadn't been able to kill the man in the Hummer. But she was certain of one thing. It would be her pleasure to pull the trigger on Vessler. As soon as possible.

Nikki waited until the car was gone before she stood. She stretched, ignoring the pain in her body, and reached down to pick up the gun before starting the long walk back to town. When she took the first step, her eyes focused on something in the dirt. At the edge of her shoe, the butterfly lay dead.

She walked a lonely stretch of road with only the moon to guide her. A small green sign assured she'd gone in the right direction. Halfway back to Vessler's house, a pick-up pulled over.

A door opened and a young man stepped out. "Hey, are you all right?"

Nikki kept moving forward, closing the distance.

"Are you okay? Did you have an accident or something?" She watched him look beyond her, searching for a car. "Did you break down?"

Purposeful steps carried her onward, ignoring the tension in his tone.

"Nikki, is that you?" His words loosened with more than a little relief.

She recognized the voice from somewhere far away. Red taillights shined in her eyes, making his figure appear tall and broad, cartoonish. She didn't answer, but kept moving toward him. Her steps neither slowed nor sped.

He stopped a few yards away. "It's Michael, from school." He lifted his hands and dropped them. "What are you doing out here?"

She continued her approach and didn't stop until they were face-to-face. She searched his eyes, the curious bend of his mouth. Had Vessler sent him? Her gaze narrowed.

No. He'd approached weaponless, yet she had a handgun strapped to her shoulder. Besides, Vessler didn't know he was being hunted.

His eyes trailed to the holster. "Are you … okay?"

Fear and concern laced his voice. Concern for her, or for himself now that he knew she was armed. Her hand covered the weapon. He'd asked a question. What was it?

"Nikki, are you okay?"

His gaze was split between her face and her hand, now petting the gun in the holster. The metal felt cool to her fingertips.

"Your car break down?" he asked.

Her mouth started to form the word no, but her voice had slipped away in the night. She shook her head.

He offered a nervous smile. "That thing loaded?"

Her eyes fanned down to it. Was it loaded? She couldn't remember loading it, but it was ready for Vessler's lackey, so it must have been. Then she remembered clicking the button to red. "Safety's on," she mumbled.

This seemed to satisfy him. He offered a hand. "Come on, I'll take you wherever you're headed."

She climbed into the cab of his pick-up.

"I was camping down on Bull Shoals," Michael said.

She glanced over her shoulder to the back of his truck: camping gear, a cooler, lanterns, and a stack of firewood. "That's good," she said.

He gave her a long look with brow raised. "Uh, yeah. It was good. Where to?"

"Damon Vessler's mansion at the edge of town."

"So, the girl *can* string an entire sentence together. I was starting to wonder." He'd relaxed. Heart rate slowed, breathing normal, scent of fear and confusion leaving him. *I really am a freak.*

"It wasn't a sentence."

"Huh?"

"No verb. It was a fragment."

Michael nodded.

"And stop looking at me like I'm crazy."

"Sorry, Nikki." He nodded toward the gun. "You just don't find a lot of hot teenage girls walking alone late at night with a handgun." He laughed. "Well, there was that dream I had once, but uh, I'm pretty sure stuff like that doesn't happen."

It settled into her bones how far she'd sunk, the depths of melancholy she'd disappeared into. After tonight, there was no going back to so many things. Least of all school and friends. Yes, she'd graduated early, but that didn't exempt her from football games, bowling nights, pizza and movies. Why hadn't she appreciated those opportunities when she possessed them? Nikki dropped her head to the dashboard. Why was she always so busy telling Krissy no, like all that stuff was beneath her, when right now she'd trade her Ducati for a night with friends and laughter and fun. And really, wasn't she trading much more for much less? Revenge wouldn't fill the hole in her heart. At best, it was a rotten patch filled with too many faults to be useful for long.

She was doing exactly what Vessler had taught her.

The truck seat squeaked as Michael reached over and patted her shoulder. She felt the closeness of his hand as it hovered above her back. But he didn't touch her again, must have decided against it.

As instructed, he dropped her off a block from Vessler's house. "Do you have any blankets in the back?" she asked as Michael opened the door for her.

"Sure. A sleeping bag and a quilt."

Without asking why, he fumbled around the bed of the truck and held them out to her.

She took the sleeping bag. "I can pay you for it."

He placed his hand over hers. "Don't worry about it." He grabbed a small pillow from the bed and rested it on top of the sleeping bag in her hands. The motion brought him close, and her eyes locked with his. "Nikki, I've always admired you. Wow, that sounded cheesy, didn't it?"

Admired her?

He nervously brushed a hand through his hair. "If you need some help …"

Her feet carried her a step back, head shaking, steamrolled by his words and the honest offer in them. She'd prefer to deny it, but there it was. Undeniable humanity in all its glory. She skittered farther away.

"Okay, okay." Michael held his hands out in surrender. "Just … Well, if you need anything, give me a call. Maybe my dad could do something to help."

Nikki's heart sank. His dad. The sheriff. She'd just had the sheriff's son drive her to her crime scene. "I don't need any help," she said, but her hands had tightened on the sleeping bag and pillow.

He nodded, studied her with sheriff's son's eyes, and finally gave a tiny smile. "Well, if you need me to do anything for you, my number's on the tag on the sleeping bag." He turned to walk around the truck.

"Michael, wait." Such a pathetically weak little voice.

He stopped and rested a hand on the bed liner.

"Promise me you'll do one thing."

"Okay."

"Tomorrow morning after ten o'clock, tell your dad you gave me a ride here and I took your sleeping bag, okay?"

He stared up the hill at Vessler's house for a long time. "Anything else?"

No. But she heard herself saying, "Then go to the Victorian house on Pine Boulevard and let them know ..." *Let them know what?* "Tell them everything is going to be okay. Tell Mace ..." But no more words came. Her throat squeezed and pinched them off. Besides, there were no words that could express what she felt, and nothing that could excuse her actions. She shook her head. "Scratch that last part."

"All right, Nikki."

"Promise you'll wait until morning, *late* morning."

He crossed his arms.

"Promise!"

"I promise." He headed to the driver's door. "Don't get into any trouble, Nikki."

Into trouble? Oh, she couldn't possibly get into more than she was already. She painted on a cheery smile. "I won't." As an afterthought. "I promise." And the lie didn't even taste bad on her lips.

She slept curled up in a corner of the garage, with the scent of tires and grease keeping her company. She wouldn't dare try to do anything to Vessler at his house. Too many bodyguards and servants, too much could go wrong. She'd have to follow him.

And this morning—with a shipment of whatever coming in—was the perfect opportunity. After all, he'd told the Hummer driver there was no threat.

She wouldn't be able to hide in his vehicle, because he had three different cars he could choose depending on his mood. She'd follow on her Ducati. Good thing she'd tossed that whole "drive it into a lake" thought. What had changed her course of action? Oh yes, finding the man who killed her parents while visiting her so-called godfather.

Vessler appeared in the garage, and her heart started kicking against her ribs. She was hidden from sight, and he seemed to be alone. He chose the red Porsche, and it was all she could do not to plug him right there.

She followed from a safe distance until they reached a small airfield about thirty miles from town. The shipment must have come in by plane. Near a white metal hanger, a tractor trailer rig sat at the ready. A dark cargo plane—looking like something that belonged to the army—sat at the base of a landing strip as if it were ready to take off again. Vessler was alone. No one had come with him, and from what she could tell, no one was meeting him.

He traversed the landing strip, but just before climbing aboard the aircraft through an open cargo door he turned and stared at the tree line where she watched. Her breath caught when she realized he looked right at her. Everything in her wanted to move, to shrink farther into the trees, but she held her ground. There was no way he could see her. Impossible.

But when a slow smile spread across his face, she had to wonder.

Chapter 26

I'm going after her, Will." Mace brushed past Vine and headed to the door, with Raven right behind him.

"Me too," Raven said.

Upon waking, they'd discovered Nikki missing. It wasn't until the females arrived a few minutes later and checked her room that they realized she'd been gone all night.

"We don't even know where she is," Glimmer said.

"All I know is that she's in trouble. We need to find her now." Mace's mind ran through scenarios, especially those where Vessler had somehow gotten to her, kidnapped her. Or maybe she'd gone back to him. Her behavior following the party yesterday had certainly been strange.

Will nodded. "Let's spread out. Glimmer and Winter, go to the lab. See if she's there."

The girls nodded and leapt from the living room.

"Vegan and Zero, check her parents' house. Vine, the Omega warehouse."

"I'll go with you two," Will said to Mace and Raven. "We'll go to Vessler's front door."

"What if they won't let us in?" Mace asked.

"Then we'll let ourselves in." Will's apprehension was evident. "She's at too vulnerable a place to be with Vessler. Even for a short time."

When the pick-up truck pulled into the driveway, Mace, Raven, and Will ran toward it. It had to carry news of Nikki. Maybe she was fine, and had only gone to Krissy's house or something. But as the guy stepped out—someone Mace remembered from Waterside High—his worst fear was confirmed. Nikki was in trouble.

Nikki peeked inside the open plane door, but couldn't see Vessler. Voices floated out to her. From the conversation, he must be talking to the pilot who'd landed the plane. Words like *fuel* and *landing gear* drifted from the discussion.

Off to the left, another truck rumbled down the gravel road headed toward the airfield. She had to move now. Nikki stepped onboard the plane and pulled the gun from the holster. She felt queasy instantly and hoped she had the nerve to finish the job.

He was facing the pilot and hadn't seen her yet. Vessler's crisp white shirt was tucked into designer jeans. His gold bracelet glinted where his hand was clasped around the pilot's chair. Nikki's heart had stopped hammering and settled into a sluggish rhythm, making her legs and arms weaker by the second.

She'd prefer to be alone with Vessler, but this was the best she could expect. Everything was right. She tucked behind a stack of large wooden boxes, a large number of which filled the cargo space. Nikki raised a hand and swept sweat from her brow. The night's restless sleep was playing against her. Her legs were jelly.

As if hearing her thoughts, Vessler answered, "It's titanium, my lady."

Nikki's eyes widened in horror, seeing the boxes for the first time as what they really were: stacks and rows of titanium. Which used to mean nothing to her personally. But now that she was a Halfling, it was her kryptonite.

Again he answered her thoughts. "You walked right into your weakness, my dear." Then he turned to face her and motioned for her to step out. "Come on, Nikki. You don't hide behind boxes. You're a warrior."

She swallowed and stepped out. "Yes, I am. You saw to that, didn't you?"

He sighed heavily, and she wanted to smack that condescending grin from his face. It made her feel small, like a disobedient child. "Training you has been my life's crowning achievement."

Nikki leveled the gun at him.

Vessler only smiled. "Really, dear? A handgun? That's the best, most creative thing you could come up with?"

"I'm not trying to be creative, Vessler, I'm trying to get a job done."

He angled a look over his shoulder at the pilot. "Take off," he barked.

Nikki panicked. *Take off? Was he kidding?* What would happen if she fired the gun while in the air and missed? But it was too late to wonder, because before she could protest, the plane was bounding along the runway. And she felt weaker with every leaden movement. She had to think. She'd had the advantage; now it was gone.

Think like Vessler.

Nikki braced herself against one of the boxes. "Toss me your gun."

Vessler always kept a small handgun in an ankle holster.

When he refused to comply, she screamed it at him, but he swatted the air like one swats a fly and shrugged. "Fine. We'll play your game. For a while. Though I warn you, Nikki, I make up my own rules."

He propped a foot on a box and removed the Robar nine-millimeter, then slid it halfway to her. It wasn't as far away from him as she'd like, but it would have to do.

"Do you really think you're going to shoot me?" he asked.

"No. I *know* I'm going to shoot you."

"Then what are you waiting for?" He took a step closer, tightening the twenty-some-foot gap between them.

Think like Vessler. Right now, they were pretty evenly matched. She had a gun, but he had a plane in the air. What happened if she missed? Would a bullet through the plane's fuselage cause it to crash?

"Drop altitude," he told the pilot. "Then rise high as she'll take us."

The engine noise changed, and Nikki felt her body being propelled toward Vessler. Instead of fighting the momentum, she threw herself forward and crashed into his chest. He hadn't braced for that. A desperate gasp of air left his lungs as he landed on the floor. She tumbled on top of him.

Putting the gun in his face, she pressed her free hand against his throat as she felt the plane begin to incline.

The rumble of a laugh surprised her. But not as much as the snap of a handgun to her right, cocked and ready. Vessler raised the Robar—which must have slid to him in the dive—inches from her nose.

"Here we are again, Nikki. Check." Vessler's training in the weeks spent at the mansion came back to her. *Never allow yourself to be in a fight that's evenly matched. Find the advantage. An opponent always has a weakness. Use it against him.*

Why didn't she pull the trigger? She wanted to, she just couldn't.

"You can't kill me, Nikki."

Tears stung her eyes and her gun trembled. "And you can't kill me. So we're at an impasse."

"You're wrong." He pressed the gun against her cheek. "I could pull this trigger easily." And in the depths of his eyes, she knew he could. But she also sensed he *wouldn't*. There was a lie hiding in his words.

"Then do it," she bluffed. "If I'm dead, so is your plan."

He snatched the barrel from her face. "Sadly, you're right. I suppose you think that gives you the advantage."

"Not really. What gives me the advantage is knowing that when I pull this trigger you die and your plan dies with you."

Vessler laughed. "Oh, Nikki. Sometimes you think too small. You can only destroy my flesh. You can't kill my soul or the essence of who and what I really am. It will live on to see all my dreams reach fruition. Killing me only solidifies your transformation into what you were born to be, what you've been trying so hard to deny."

Cold washed over her. "Killing me will complete you, Nikki. I win either way."

Panic crept at the edge of her conscience. She knew he was right. And when he raised the gun to her again, she almost hoped he'd pull the trigger.

The shot rang through the airplane, and Nikki felt the engine's drastic change. Her eyes followed Vessler's hand and the weapon. He'd shot the pilot through the back.

"What did you do?" Nikki jumped off Vessler and pressed her back to the wall of the plane that was holding steady, regardless of the loss of pilot.

"Taking the advantage, of course. You see, Nikki, you have two choices: Leap and take me with you, and we continue our chess match on the ground, or leap alone and leave me to die in the airplane that's headed straight for downtown St. Louis … and all those innocent people."

Nikki's mind raced. Leap? She couldn't leap; she didn't have wings. A thought struck her. "A Halfling can't leap with this much titanium."

His face flashed shock but he quickly recovered. "No problem." Vessler moved to the side door, unlocked its safety bar, and slid the door open. "We can jump. Your wings can open once you're away from the titanium."

Wings open. Ha. They were going to die. Both of them. And no matter what happened, the plane would crash into downtown St. Louis and kill hundreds of others. Hate built inside her.

Vessler, who'd snaked to the opposite side of the plane, had noticed her emotional shift, if his smug look was any indication. But what she couldn't understand was why he was so willing to give up his life.

"You're such an evil man."

"Oh, I'm not evil. You are, Nikki—bouncing from one side of the war to the other. You're the worst kind of evil, because you justify playing on both teams and never really choose a side. You know what that means? The rest of us have a purpose; we all serve a greater power. But you, selfish little spoiled Nikki, you only serve yourself. You're already on the way to being the general who will lead my dark army, and the best part is you don't even realize it because you're too busy manipulating people into doing what you want."

Out the front window, she could see land, the first signal that the plane was slowly going down.

Nikki's knees buckled and she dropped to sit on the floor. "If I'm so evil and destined to serve you, maybe it's best we both die. Right here, right now."

Shock replaced the calm on his face. Vessler leapt toward her, but Nikki raised the gun and fired. His hands clamped his leg as he crumbled.

"God, please forgive me," she cried, throat closing on the words.

Vessler jerked a cabinet open and dragged supplies from inside. He found a bungee cord and tied it around his wound to stop the bleeding. *Why would he do that? We'll both be dead in another five minutes.*

"Nikki, please. Leave me here, but you can jump."

She chanced a spiteful look at him.

"Go, Nikki. You deserve to live."

"A moment ago I deserved to die."

"Live, Nikki."

"With the fact that this plane will kill innocent people? No, Damon."

He didn't want to die. She could see it in his face, the way he struggled to stop the blood flow. But she wouldn't be bluffed this time.

Again, they were at a stalemate. *Think like Vessler.*

Vessler loved his life. Yes, if she jumped alone, it would ensure her turning into a dark creature, but he'd be dead, at least physically. No, there's no way he'd give up his life that easily. Nikki's eyes drifted to the pilot, now slumped over a board of controls with blood seeping from the wound to his back. Then her eyes found Vessler's.

"You want me to jump because you can fly the plane."

He tried to cover his reaction, but his nostrils flared. She'd found him out. "I'll survive, you'll land the plane, but my willingness to let you go down will be my ruin? That's what you're gambling on."

Fire burned in the depths of his inklike eyes.

But, being Vessler, his loss of composure was only temporary. "If you don't jump, we'll crash. And all those deaths will be your fault."

"It won't matter. I'll be dead too."

"No, you won't. You're a Halfling, Nikki. You'd be amazed at what you can survive."

Was he right? She couldn't be sure. Could she live with the deaths of innocent people, with innocent blood on her hands? With renewed vigor, she lifted the gun so it was aimed at his chest. "Land the plane." She had to find his weakness.

"That's an empty threat, my lady. If you shoot me, I can't land the plane."

She cocked the gun. "Land the plane, Vessler." Then she saw it. Hurt in his eyes when she called him Vessler. Nikki saw her opportunity and softened her voice. *She* was his weakness. "Land the plane, Damon. Please. Don't you want to watch me fulfill my destiny? Don't you want to be there? To be able to smell the scent of fresh kill on my flesh and taste the vengeance you've worked for?"

He was like a deer caught in the beam she was casting. It was working.

She angled a step closer and chanced a glance through the front window. The earth was moving closer, green blobs becoming individual trees. She had only another couple of minutes at the most. "Please, Damon."

But a fierce flash of resistance overtook him. "No. You're not as strong as I thought you were."

She frowned.

"You couldn't even shoot me—at least not to kill."

The flash of the gun surprised her, and she stared at her hand as if it belonged to someone else. She'd pulled the trigger. Her aim had dipped to his opposite leg, and now Vessler crumpled over to grab the new injury, his gun flying from his hand and landing behind a box.

She hadn't meant to shoot. Had she?

When his face came up to meet hers it was red with anger, and sweat poured from him like the blood pouring from his new wound. Hands slick with both, he reached for a strap to tie around his newly wounded leg.

"Land the plane, Damon." It was an order. A cold, solid order given by one in charge. His eyes trailed from her to the wound, still shocked, still uncertain.

Yes, she'd taken the advantage.

He hauled himself up and stumbled toward the cockpit, but stopped. "No!" he screamed in defiance.

Nikki angled the weapon toward his arm. Her eyes flashed back to his. "I'll take you apart one piece at a time if I have to, but you are going to land the plane."

He shook his head and braced for the shot.

But her adrenaline had seeped out through every pore, leaving her weak. She couldn't pull the trigger again. Nikki sank to the floor. It was over.

Vessler would bleed to death, and she'd go down in a cargo plane filled with titanium and kill a mass of innocent people.

She imagined the plane hitting a park. Children, families, all dying together in one giant fireball. Nikki pulled her thighs to her chest and, still holding the gun, wrapped her arms around her legs. Across from her, Damon worked to tighten the tourniquet around the fresher wound. His breathing was unsteady, and it seemed that all the blood in his face was escaping through the bullet holes in his legs.

"Checkmate," she mumbled, and put her head down. She pressed her eyes into her knees so hard, it hurt. She thought of her dog, Bo, her parents, the karate tournament where she won a national title. She wouldn't allow herself to think of Mace. That was too painful and it might be enough to change her mind.

Suddenly, his presence was there all around her. Warm hands closed gently on her shoulders and he uttered her name.

Chapter 27

Mace?

When Nikki looked up, he was standing between her and Vessler. *Have we crashed? Am I dead?*

Mace slid the gun from her hands. "Come on, Nikki. It's time to go home."

Confused, she let herself be lifted from the floor. *If this is death, it's quite nice.* But the smell of blood, the scream of the plane engine, and the wind from the open door proved she was still part of the world. She focused on Mace: he was life, he was hope, and she was safe. Her relief turned to fear as she scanned his arms, bloody and scraped.

"It's time to go," he said, and placed a steadying arm around her.

"How'd you get in here?" She looked from side to side, confirming they were still inside the plane.

"I wasn't able to get in until you opened the door. I'd tried to leap inside and kept hitting the side of the plane and bouncing off." He moved her gently toward the open door.

"The plane's filled with titanium," she said.

"I figured that out. We need to hurry. Raven can't hold the plane up, only slow its decent. The titanium is taking its toll."

The wounds on Mace's body were from trying unsuccessfully to leap inside the plane?

He tightened his grip on her. "We'll have to jump, and it'll be a bit bumpy until my wings can open."

Nikki grabbed the side of the door. "Wait." Her gaze traveled to the front window. "Mace, if Vessler doesn't land the plane, it will strike downtown St. Louis. People will die."

Mace gave a long, surrendering sigh. He released her reluctantly and moved to Vessler. Grabbing him by the shirt, he lifted and dragged him to the cockpit. After removing the dead pilot, he dropped Damon before the controls. Mace leaned down, leveling his face with Vessler's. "It's the people she's saving, not you," he growled.

Vessler grinned through a sweat-smeared face. "Keep telling yourself that, boy."

"And don't even think you'll get to keep the titanium." Mace returned to Nikki and together, they jumped.

They stayed in the air until the plane touched down in a field inside the busy St. Louis metro area. She'd expected Raven to follow them, but he hadn't.

"With any luck, Vessler will bleed to death," Mace said.

"Well, my luck hasn't been dependable lately." Nor her instincts. She was going to kill Vessler. It seemed impossible, but she'd actually planned to murder him. Nikki put a hand to her temple where a headache pounded.

To Mace, nothing stood in their way now. But Nikki wasn't who she used to be. When they touched down and he reached to steady her, she pushed gently from him.

"What's wrong, Nikki?"

"Everything, Mace. You don't know what I was going to do."

"Michael told us he'd met you last night."

When he moved to get closer to her, she stepped back. "I was going to kill Vessler. It's sort of a blur now."

"I know you've had a huge internal monster to fight, but Nikki, I think Vessler was poisoning you." Mace shook his head. "Or drugging you."

She frowned.

"Raven told me that Omega can inject a serum that will cause a violent creature to be docile. Maybe it would work in reverse too."

"And I'm the creature."

"I'm just saying. You were pretty obsessed with that designer water Vessler gave you. Could he have been dumping something into them?"

"Could he? Sure." But her actions couldn't be completely blamed on some unknown drug. She'd wanted revenge. Had been desperate for it. So much so it made her crazy inside. No, she couldn't simply blame drugs. She had to be responsible for her actions. Actions that almost included taking a life.

"You're alive, Nikki. You're okay now, and you're a Halfling. It changes everything." Mace looked so full of hope, it made her want to cry. Mace always believed the best. Especially of her. But once again, she would set him up to fail, because she wasn't who she once was, and she saw no way to go back. Vessler's promise haunted her. "This isn't over."

Mace used his thumb to rub away the worry lines on her forehead. "It never is."

"If Vessler lives, he'll continue his quest."

"But you know what you are now. He can't have you."

"I'm spoken for?" If it were only that simple. She'd changed forever in the last few weeks. Who knew if Mace would even be interested in the new, damaged Nikki she'd become?

"Exactly."

"Well, don't think you're going to get the blessing of my legal guardian."

"How about if I'm your guardian?"

"No."

He flashed a frown.

Her headache lessened enough to allow the tiniest smile. "You're way too bossy."

"Is that right?"

She nodded. "And you're always trying to protect me instead of teaching me how to defend myself."

He raised his hands in surrender. "I promise to help you learn to defend yourself. Although what I just saw in the airplane would suggest you need little instruction."

"I need a partner, Mace. Not a boss."

"Okay, okay. I get it. If I was over the top, it's just because I love you."

Oh.

"You were saying?" He gestured with an upturned hand for her to continue.

"No more damsel-in-distress heroics?"

"No more. You've been called to be a leader, Nikki. I owe it to you to help prepare you."

"Still, I don't think of you as my guardian."

"No?"

"You're my angel."

He led her to a river's edge. For a long time they listened to the cadence of water against rock. "Think we can rest now?"

she asked, but she knew she wouldn't. She needed to discover who this new Nikki was. Maybe Mace could still love her. But she doubted it because …

Because she was too much like Raven.

A week after Zero reported Nikki was safe and back with the other Halflings, Raven stretched back, resting his hands on his stomach. The sky looked different from his ruins. Closer somehow, and more like an ally than a distant onlooker. The North Star winked at him. He thought of Debra the horse and Adam Cordelle. Huh. His list of friends had been reduced to a pathetic guard and a mutant mare. *Wow, the depths one can sink to over a female.*

Female. Nikki. A Halfling. Could life be any more ironic? *I fall for a human, ready to give up everything for her, only to discover the human's been a Halfling all along. To top it off, now that loving Nikki won't lead to my damnation, I get to watch her spend eternity happily ever after with Mace.*

The rocks at his back bit into his flesh like tiny piranha chewing away at his strength, mocking his stupidity. It was easier when she was a human and the real threat was heaven or hell. He could have beaten Mace at that game.

But now everything had shifted. For Mace, Nikki had represented the one weakness that could send him to the pit. For Raven, she'd represented something to live for. He'd sink into darkness, of that he was certain. His eyes had been dimming into the blackness of the forever damned for years. Until Nikki. For all his unrestrained life, he'd allowed himself little time to ponder the hideous consequences of his actions. And he wouldn't now, either. Because this, this empty hole of an existence, was horrid in its trappings.

What could possibly be worse? The shrieking moans from those on the other side shot into his mind. And even now their tenor leeched the blood from his veins. No, there were things worse than a broken heart.

Maybe tonight would be the night. Maybe he'd awaken with the Dark Prince whispering a soothing lullaby of revenge into his ear. Maybe *he'd* be the one to hunt the Halflings ...

Raven clamped his arms around his head and shut his eyes tight, interlacing his fingers and squeezing out the demonic influence. With solid intention, he threw his eyes open and stared up. The North Star again, once a symbol of a promise, was now a small-but-guiding drop of radiance. "Help me," he whispered.

He'd prayed on many occasions. Hey, he served the Throne. When you're packing fully automatic weapons, you don't reach for the hunting knife. But Raven had never prayed for himself. It felt weak, somehow, to petition the One who'd commissioned him. A lack of faith in the omniscience of the Great Stabilizer.

A fisted hand fell to his heart; the physical pain, dull but constant, surprised him. Could he talk about Nikki to the quiet sky? Would his voice hold or shatter like ice under too much pressure?

She'd be at Viennesse by now. Will had moved the group there once again, opting to keep them in Europe until the dust cleared around Vessler. Another week, maybe two, then they would probably head back to Missouri. Raven hadn't gone with them, but he'd felt her leave; a strange sensation, one he could only liken to having a section of skin ripped from his body.

And so he'd followed. But he stayed at the castle ruins rather than go home.

"Look, I try not to bother you too much."

Silence.

"I, uh ..." He was surprised at how hollow his voice sounded, how spent. "I just need to know that she's going to be okay."

Nothing.

His lungs filled and emptied. Filled and emptied. "So, is Nikki going to be okay?"

A dazzling light whirred before his eyes, and for a moment Raven thought someone must have snuck up and whacked his head, though he felt no pain. He leapt to his feet, hoping the blood would move with him.

In the center of the light, a being took shape. It was clothed in layers of glory, and he knew it had been at the Throne.

For once, Raven's voice was gone.

The angel was the size of Will, but smelled like the place where life particles danced until the One called each to an individual purpose. He'd only dreamed of such a location, but knew of its magnificence and power somehow inherently. For Halflings, the midplane was the closest they'd ever get to heaven. For most, it was enough.

The angel stood toe-to-toe with him, eyes alight with the fire of the One he served. He was ... waiting for something.

"Uh," Raven uttered. "Why are you here?"

"To answer your question." There was little emotion or inflection in the being's voice, just pure, smooth, and resonant words.

A question? What had he asked? What was he even thinking about? *Nikki.* "Is Nikki Youngblood going to be okay?"

The angel's answer sparked and ignited a fire of fear throughout Raven's being. "No."

Raven's mouth dried instantly, as if all moisture had been drawn from his body with the single word. He needed more information, but the angel was turning away like he intended to go.

Raven leapt forward and seized him, arms closing on the angel's waist. But the magnificent being flicked him off. This was not an evenly matched confrontation. *New plan.* "Why not? Why won't she be okay?"

"Because a Seeker has been released from the pit."

Raven's knees buckled and crashed against the rock-strewn ground. Fear and urgency pinched his lungs into crumples, making him unable to pull even the smallest of breath.

A Seeker.

Released to hunt Nikki.

Suddenly, the angel was offering the same hand that moments ago brushed Raven from his garment. Powerful golden fingers drew him to his feet.

Still, Raven was too stunned to speak. The angel turned once more, this time slowly, as if awaiting another ambush.

"Wait," Raven finally mustered, throwing his remaining oxygen into the plea. "Why did you tell me?"

Was that a slash of a smile that appeared? "Because you asked."

And then the angel was gone.

Raven was left with one hammering thought. He had to get to Nikki before it was too late.

Discussion Guide for *Guardian*

1. Near the beginning of the story Nikki makes the following statement: "I've never had faith in anything except what is tangible. I doubt I ever will." Describe Nikki's journey of faith throughout the book. How do you think the Nikki who emerges at the end of the book would describe her views on faith?

2. Raven gives Nikki the nickname "Freedom" (pg. 59). Do you think the nickname suits her? In what ways does she represent freedom to Raven?

3. In trying to make a case for why Nikki should choose himself over Mace, Raven refers to Mace's "firm foundation" as a "cage" for Nikki (pg 185). Do you agree with Raven's line of thinking? Do you think Mace's sense of purpose and single-mindedness of mission will somehow thwart Nikki? If so, how?

4. Mace and Raven seem to be polar opposites, with each of them bringing out different character traits in Nikki. Who is Nikki when she is with Raven? Who is she when she's with Mace?

5. In addition to the spiritual battle that is being waged, we see an emotional battle being waged inside of Nikki when it comes to her affections for Raven and Mace. Which one of the two do you think is the better match for Nikki? Why?

6. It is clear that Damon Vessler is dangerously controlling and manipulative, but the book is vague as to his origins. Who or what do you think Damon Vessler is?

7. At one point Nikki seems absolutely determined to avenge the loss of her parents by killing Damon Vessler's thug (the man who drives the yellow Hummer) as well as Damon Vessler himself. What do you think keeps her from actually following through with murdering them?

8. We are left wondering exactly what has become of Nikki's parents. What do you think happened to them? Do you think they're really dead? Do you have any thoughts about the identity of the man who seemed to have Nikki's dad's eyes (pg. 285)?

9. There are several references to prayer in this book. Nikki first experiences its power when she prays at the scene of the train crash (pg. 120). Later, she can visibly see the prayers of humans rising to the Throne as she and Mace are flying over a city (pg. 236). In the final chapter of the book, a tortured Raven turns to prayer for deliverance from the demonic forces around him, in what we learn is the first time he's ever prayed for himself (pg. 307). Why do you think it took him so long to finally draw upon the powerful resource of prayer? Do you think his willingness to pray for himself is evidence of a change within him? What kind of transformation might be at work in Raven?

10. Although Nikki now knows she is a Halfling, she seems more lost and confused than ever. What do you think she will discover? Who will she become as she seeks to make sense of her new identity?

Heather Burch

A Halflings Novel

Avenger

*Sometimes facing your destiny
means risking everything.*

Chapter
1

The blur lasted only a second before Nikki Youngblood's face exploded in blinding pain. *And I thought karate tournaments were ruthless.* Even the gentlest blow of this Halfling put her past competitors to shame; half human, half angels were lethal. Her lips throbbed with the beating of her heart, and for a few horrible seconds she wanted to call time out and collapse onto the ground.

But she wasn't a quitter, and the pain rumbling through her was only more incentive to pummel the Frenchman into the ground.

Even if it wasn't the smartest choice she'd ever made.

Nikki advanced, ignoring the cheers and gasps around her. A smattering of Halflings now dotted the courtyard surrounding the Cinderella-style castle, similar to the one where Nikki had been living like royalty since she and the others arrived. Though to her knowledge, Cinderella never kicked any butt, so any fairy-tale similarities between her and the blonde princess ended there.

Her lips were numb, a thankful reprieve from the pain of them smashing against her teeth as the Frenchman, Deux, made contact with a powerful fist. She didn't taste blood yet, but she could feel her mouth swelling. For all she knew, there was blood seeping from her lips — she was simply too adrenaline-driven to care.

If she was in a competition, officials would call the fight at the first sign of a cut. But this was no tournament. There were no senseis, judges, or black belts hoping to showcase their abilities as masters and students. And no called fouls when things got rough.

Nikki stood in a cat stance, trying to form some type of strategy, and used her newfound powers to take in her surroundings. It struck her that the French countryside was quite picturesque, and would be like a storybook — Beauty and the Beast, maybe, since Cinderella didn't fit — if not for the guy beating her to a pulp.

Pulp. That's what her mouth felt like.

She saw the fist coming and caught it in midair. When Deux tried to pull away, she held firm, stopping him and letting this new power — this new strength she'd begun to tap into — course though her, but carefully. Nikki knew what she was capable of. A night of stalking her demented godfather, Damon Vessler, had taught her that.

Her fingers squeezed until she heard Deux's bones begin to pop. His clear blue eyes clouded with a mix of surprise and dread.

"Oooooh" and "ewwwww" echoed from the crowd of spectators. *No disapproving groans. Mace must still be in the house; otherwise he'd be breaking things up.* One thing her boyfriend couldn't abide was Nikki fighting for no reason. Boyfriend — that sounded strange to her ears, but accurate. She and Mace were a couple. Mostly.

She released her grip marginally. After all, she didn't want to break Deux's hand, just disprove his theory that female Halflings were the weaker part of the species.

Nikki shoved his fist back, knocking him off balance.

Off to the right, someone said in a thick French accent, "I think you have misjudged her power, my friend. Or perhaps you have misjudged your own."

Snickers from the onlookers on both sides of the earlier argument. She tossed a glance behind her to the tall glass doors.

No Mace. She could continue the fight.

Deux was shaking his hand, massaging it, trying to encourage fresh blood flow. "You are waiting for Mace to return and rescue you, no?"

Nikki set her jaw and punched Deux in the face. His head jolted back, causing his carefully layered hair to whip.

"That hurt." A red welt materialized on his cheek and jaw, but a smile sliced through the darkened flesh. He wiggled his brows. "I think I am in love."

Maybe it was the fact that love had gotten her into more trouble than any person — human or Halfling — deserved, or maybe it was the cocky, condescending way he looked at her, but his words unleashed her fury. And her fury always meant real pain. Nikki sailed into a combination of kicks and punches that a fifth-degree black belt would envy. Each made contact, but not with the intended target. Over and over Deux cupped his hands and caught every punch. Kicks were absorbed by arm blocks. Even the low kick to his knee was halted by a shin block.

"You are good, Cherie. In a few years, you might even be a real opponent." He yawned.

A few chuckles from the crowd, along with some calls cheering her on and some telling Deux his skills were still amazing.

Even when outmatched, there's always a way to win. Find the hole in the machine. Then throw a wrench in it.

So Deux was a better fighter. It didn't matter. One thing this journey, this new life, had taught her was that things could change in an instant. Her whole world had. One second she was a semi-normal teenage girl, the next she was a Halfling. But her transformation of sorts gave her one serious advantage: the awareness brute strength — even Halfling strength — wasn't the only way to win a fight.

Nikki smiled and blinked a few times, ignoring the pain now flooding her lips. She lowered her hands and loosened her body posture. When she dropped a shoulder and cocked her hip flirtatiously — a move she'd learned by watching Glimmer — Deux's hands fell to his sides.

His gaze drifted down over her while she pretended not to notice. And to add to her attractive assault, Nikki pulled the two pencils out of her hair — her makeshift hair clasps — and tossed them to the ground. Her long hair cascaded around her shoulders, and when the wind grabbed it she shook her head, letting the breeze have its way. Deux was helplessly pinned — a boy attracted to a girl, one who suddenly seemed interested.

"I could learn a lot from you." Nikki's voice dropped to a purr. "Like those blocks. Could you teach me?" *Being this bad shouldn't come so easy.* But she didn't want to linger on that truth.

"I would enjoy teaching you many things, Cherie." He took a few steps toward her, one brow arched seductively.

Except it wasn't seductive at all. It made her want to snicker. She bit her cheeks to keep from laughing, because he was playing right into her plan. He mistook her reaction for more flirtation and winked.

For a while, she listened as he instructed her on the blocking

316

technique. She took it all in and waited for the right moment to strike. When Deux rocked back on his heels and crossed his arms over his chest, the opportunity arrived. He was no more ready for an attack than a duckling in a pond was ready for the alligator lurking just below the surface.

Snapping with her signature jumping front kick, she planted her foot against Deux's stomach. Rock-hard abs softened and his body flew back as if yanked by a string. He landed on his behind with a roar of laughter rising around him.

From his seated position, feet straight out in front of him, he shook his head. "I can no longer consider dating you, Nikki. I'm sorry, but trust is paramount in a relationship."

She giggled — just couldn't stop herself — and reached out a hand to help him up. "You can trust me."

"It is not you I'm concerned about. I cannot possibly trust myself with such a wild animal. You are driving me crazy." Before she could pull away, he tightened his grip on her hand. His foot slid against hers. After a powerful tug, she landed on top of him.

She tried to roll off, but Deux's arms were suddenly every-where. As she tumbled, so did he. She squirmed, but he wouldn't let go. With each passing second, she struggled harder to break the hold. No luck. The crowd was chanting, for her, for him, for both of them.

When she had the upper hand and was almost free, they cheered for Deux. But when he clamped his powerful arms on her, they cheered for Nikki, shouting ideas on how to break his hold. *Fickle crowd.*

Grunting and now face-to-face on the fresh grass, Nikki reached behind her back, curled her fingers around his thumb, and pulled.

Deux arched his back and let out a yell so loud that Nikki felt terrible. But she was free at least. She sprang to her feet, turned, and hit a brick wall.

Mace.

He glowered at her from eyes filled with a curious blend of concern, anger, and maybe a tinge of disappointment. Her wrist was in a stranglehold. *Drat, trapped again.* This time in Mace's iron grip as he dragged her from the courtyard and into the house.

"Can I not leave you alone for two seconds without you getting into trouble?" Mace tried to slow his racing heart, but when he stepped outside and saw Nikki and Deux fighting, rolling on the ground, his pulse had gone into overdrive and wasn't likely to slow down anytime soon.

"He was helping me."

Fresh fire coursed down his body. "He was helping himself to you."

Her eyes — now darkened to melted gold — narrowed on him. "You said yourself that Deux is one of the best fighters there is."

"So?" *Brilliant argument there.* He just kept imagining Nikki and Deux rolling on the ground, and something, some horrible monster inside him, wanted to grab Deux by the throat and ...

Oh. That's what this is about.

He watched Nikki blink, those feather-soft lashes hooding her eyes for a few seconds. She pulled in a deep breath and let it out slowly. Her cheek was smudged with a bit of dirt, and the corner of her mouth had a drop of dried blood on it. It too was caked with dirt.

He lifted his hand to her cheek. Fingertips touched the soft skin and she pressed into him. "Did he hurt you?" Mace whispered, praying Deux hadn't, because he'd hate to accept the Frenchman's hospitality then kill him in his own courtyard.

"Only my pride," Nikki said, nuzzling into the press of Mace's hand.

His thumb drifted over her bottom lip. "You're bleeding."

"A sucker punch. I shouldn't have fallen for it." Her eyes snapped open. "What should I have done differently?"

"Stayed out of the fight."

She leveled him with a look.

"Okay, okay." He stared at the ornate ceiling and worked the muscle in his jaw. He hated to see Nikki fight, but fighting was a certainty in her life. She was a Halfling. And even though she'd only just learned the truth about her angelic power, she was already enmeshed in the epic battle against darkness.

Since discovering what Nikki truly was, Mace had learned Halfling females tap into their power later than the males, around age eighteen or nineteen; at seventeen, Nikki was a bit of an early bloomer — like Vine, his "brother," who'd earned the Over-Achiever award for tapping in at fifteen. Mace was still amazed Nikki had adjusted so quickly — before her angelic side had begun to emerge, even their fully angel guardian, Will, had thought she was human. "Everything changes when we tap in."

"For me more than anyone."

That much was true. Nikki's life had been orchestrated by her godfather, Damon Vessler, who'd planned on turning her into a dark Halfling once she tapped into her power, and then using her to create an army at his command.

319

Since Mace first met her, in a field where she was being chased by hell hounds, he'd tried to protect her from … well, from all of it. But that wasn't fair, and in doing so, he'd almost lost her. He'd have to help her take on the evils herself, no matter how hard that was for him. "When I came out you were already on the ground. How'd you get there?"

"He pulled me down when I reached to help him up."

Mace chuckled. "And you said *his* move was a sucker punch? Seriously, Nikki, you fell for that?"

Her mouth cocked in a sheepish grin. "I should have known."

"Yeah." Mace ran a hand through his hair. He'd rather be running his fingers through hers, smoothing the messed-up strands, but that would only distract him. Though he itched to remove the blade of grass stuck in her hairline. "As soon as you felt him pull, you should have dove, caught him off guard. He wouldn't expect it, and it may have given you a few seconds to get away. At the least it would have — "

"Given me the upper hand," she said. Her brows dipped.

Thinking. Ah, he loved her when she was thinking. Beyond the glass door, another fight ensued. Deux and Vine this time. From what Mace could tell, the two looked pretty evenly matched. *Go, Vine.*

"Watch how Vine fights, always thinking ahead — always." He laced his arm around her waist and pulled her close while she studied the two combatants.

She smiled. "Thanks for helping me. I think your judgment may finally be clearing."

What was that supposed to mean?

"Don't be offended, Mace. It's just that your opinions haven't been the most sound where I'm concerned."

"You mean trying to leap into an airplane filled with titanium, and then letting Vessler get away?"

"You were with me when the airplane landed. You couldn't have known Vessler would make it out."

The whole scene entered his mind like it did every night when he fell asleep. He could hear gunshots, knew Nikki was in the plane, but the titanium zapped his strength, making him unable to leap inside. The kryptonite-like metal had caused his wings to feel like giant anchors; the closer he got, the worse it was. Finally, he'd moved to the other side of the plane and spotted the open cargo door. He got Nikki to safety while Raven — his rival and brother-in-arms — followed the plane. Will had contacted the other Halflings, who'd met the plane when it landed outside of St. Louis. *Sorry, Vessler, no titanium wingcuffs for you.*

Nikki's voice drew him out of the memory. "I really didn't think I'd make it out alive. Vessler actually told me to leap to safety at one point. Like I have wings."

"You'll have wings, Nikki. You've tapped into your angelic power, so it's just a matter of time now."

He could see she didn't believe it. "At least the titanium was intercepted. And thanks to you, Vessler was so wounded he'll be out of commission for a while."

When her body posture changed, he knew she'd gone back there in her mind as well. Tiny frowns appeared and disappeared on her face, each attached to a fact she'd not yet been able to accept. She'd shot Damon Vessler. Twice.

"You could have died, Nikki."

"I don't know what I was thinking, going after Vessler alone." Ever since getting her back, Mace had watched closely, trying unsuccessfully to understand her actions. Her darker side had been shocking, and the confusion over what she'd briefly become was taking a toll on Nikki as well.

He tilted back to look at her. "I know I asked you this before, but do you think Vessler may have been putting something in your drinks?"

She stiffened. "Mace, I know you want to believe that. And I do too — more than you can imagine. But I'd been away from Vessler and his influence — potentially spiked beverages included — when I decided to go after him."

"But Nikki — " Her fingers rose and rested against his lips.

She leaned in and placed her head against his heart. "I remember wondering if there might be something wrong with the water. He'd always fill my bottles for me. And once when I was finishing a cup of coffee, there was this little bubble of something in the bottom. I figured it had been dirty, but when I handed it to the housekeeper, she got really nervous."

Against his chest, he felt Nikki squeeze her eyes shut. "I don't know what he was doing to me. What I do know is, I have to be responsible for my actions. And I almost murdered Damon without a second thought."

"It wasn't you, Nikki. It had to be a product of whatever he was giving you. Your mood would change almost instantly. Remember when I found you at the beach house?"

She nodded, but he felt an unsettling distance between them, an invisible wall she raised whenever this subject came up. But that wouldn't stop him this time.

"It was like a veil came over you. Like you weren't in control anymore. And I think that's why you went after Vessler."

"And *I* think that's what you need to believe." She laced her fingers together at his back and held on to him, but he pushed from her.

"What are you saying?"

The gold in her eyes lost its shimmer. "Exactly what I said. You need to believe I was just a robot under someone else's control. If you don't, you have to consider the possibility that I have become the monster Vessler worked so hard to create."

"Nikki, that's crazy. You're not a monster."

"Aren't I? I shot him — twice — and I wanted to do a lot more." She shook her head. "I'm sorry. I'm not who I used to be. And I'll never be that carefree, innocent girl again."

Mace chose to hold her close rather than argue, despite the cold feeling that swept through him. Fact was, Nikki had changed. They'd all changed. And he wasn't sure how to navigate that new mountain before them.

He looked over her head to the door facing the courtyard. "Based on how Vine's fight is going, I don't know if we'll be welcome here much longer. We can only beat up our host so many times." Nikki gave a small laugh. "Come on, let's get the others and head back to Viennesse." Their ancestral home in Germany and across the Rhine Valley from Deux's compound. These days, Viennesse felt like the only safe place. And even that surety was slipping.

It was a short trip from the ruins to Viennesse, but Raven couldn't get there fast enough. Nikki was in more danger than he'd ever imagined, and if he hadn't questioned the heavenly angel who'd appeared as he'd petitioned the Throne, maybe it would already be too late to save her.

After Nikki's standoff with Vessler, and after she'd left with Mace, he'd prayed for some assurance that she would be okay. Instead, he discovered the exact opposite. The cold reality of what awaited her now fueled his speed. Night had fallen, but he could see perfectly as he sailed through a puff of low clouds and descended on the Viennesse castle. Built on a mountaintop, it has been chosen as a formidable foe for all human invaders, though what was coming after Nikki was neither human nor demon. And it had come for one reason: to destroy Nikki , the woman Raven loved and would never have.

But one thing he could do was protect her. Right? Why else would the angel have warned him about what was coming after Nikki? He'd find her, then he'd make a plan. Until he had visual confirmation she was still alive, his only focus would be getting to her side. True, he knew next to nothing about the evil being sent to destroy Nikki, and he honestly had no clue how to defeat it. But he did know that if Nikki could be saved, he was the one to do it.

Raven began running the moment he touched down and headed for the front door, shoving both doors open and rushing inside as his wings — sore from the long flight — tucked behind him.

Winter and Nikki sat in the library just off the main hall. He should have known where to find her. Nikki had a weakness for quiet spots.

They both stood when he barged inside. Normally, he was confident and self-possessed, almost cool in his demeanor. Doing the hair toss thing and planting his thumbs in his pockets as if to impart information only he possessed. But not this time.

Both females noticed.

"What's going on? Where have you been?" Winter took a cautious step toward him.

"Where are the others?" He shot a glance out the side door that led to a private patio.

Nikki is safe. For the moment.

Winter shook her head, a blanket of silky, dark hair falling from her shoulders. "Scattered throughout the castle. Raven, what's happening?"

He stopped only long enough to meet her gaze. "A seeker's been released from the pit."

Winter dropped into a nearby chair, the blood in her face draining, leaving her even paler than usual.

Nikki split her glances between the two of them. "Wha — what's a seeker?" He tried to hide the fear, and pain, from his eyes as he watched her. He soon had no choice but to look away.

Winter's eyes slowly drifted up to meet Raven's. "Sent here?"

There was no denying the terror in her voice. If Raven had thought meeting up with the other Halflings would somehow reassure him, he'd been dead wrong.

"Why? And how do you know?" Winter said.

"He's hunting Nikki."

Mace came in, sailing around the doorjamb, his narrowed gaze landing on Raven. "I thought I saw you." As soon as the words left his mouth, he dropped to silence, sparing a moment to take in the looks on everyone's faces. "What's going on?"

Raven nodded toward the door. "We have to get Nikki out of here. A seeker's coming."

"What?" Mace crossed the room and pulled Nikki to his side. "What are you talking about, Raven? Will hasn't sensed anything — "

"Will doesn't know everything. The thing's on the way. And he's after Nikki."

And, while you have her in your arms, I'm the only one who can protect her.

Mace's grip tightened, and though Nikki had no idea what a seeker could be, it was something terrible enough to strike fear in Winter, Mace, and even Raven. Four hours ago, she was sparring with a Frenchman in a mock fight. Was she really about to have to run for her life … again? Nausea wove through her and Nikki placed a hand on her stomach as if mere touch could keep the contents settled. She was supposed to be safe here. Vessler and his horrible plan for her were a half a world away. Like that mattered: Mace had once told her the enemy, the *real* enemy, wanted her.

Mace shook his head. "If a seeker had been released, Will would know."

"Well, you can go on telling yourself that, but you might be wasting the last minutes we have to get Nikki out of danger. I got my information directly from the source."

Mace fisted his hands and took a step toward Raven, leaving Nikki behind. "If a seeker is coming, there isn't anywhere safe to go."

Raven threw his hands in the air. "So go find him. Ask All-Mighty Will what we need to do."

Mace reached back and grasped her hand. "Come on, Nikki."

Her palm was sweaty; she hadn't realized until he gripped it. "I don't feel well."

Winter stood and dragged her chair a few feet to where Nikki stood, and along with Mace lowered her into the seat. "I'll stay here with her. Go find Will."

Mace dropped a kiss on her forehead. "I'll be right back. Don't worry, because everything will be fine."

Fine? She wanted to scream, but her mind couldn't get the sound to travel to her mouth.

Raven dropped onto his haunches at her feet, the midnight blue of his eyes so intense it jolted sanity back into her system. "Listen to me, Nikki." He closed his warm hands over hers, so softly she felt her breath catch. "We have to go. We have to run. It's the only way."

Thoughts, jumbled thoughts, bounced around in her head. "Safe, here," she managed.

"I know it's hard to understand, but a seeker's like a tsunami. He'll rush through this castle and destroy everything. And he'll take you when he's done, even if I and every Halfling here tries to stop him. As long as you're here, no one is safe."

Her eyes trailed up to Winter.

"I don't know, Nikki. Seeker's are ..." But her words dropped and she looked at Raven. "Maybe you're right."

Raven squeezed Nikki's hands just enough to pull her from the chair. "We can be a thousand miles away from here in two hours. But we can't waste any more time."

Winter dropped a hand on Raven's shoulder. "You may be right, but perhaps she *should* stay. Will is here, and at least ten Halflings. What can you do on your own that we cannot do here?"

Raven traced the lines of Nikki's face as if she held the answer. His only concern seemed to be keeping her safe, and his promise to protect her was imprinted in every inch of his being. She thought he might concede, decide it was best to be here at Viennesse. *How many times have the Halflings bragged about how fortified the castle is?* Raven opened his mouth. He was going to agree.

That's when they heard the scream.